W9-AUX-174

ENCYCLOPEDIA OF
CONTAINER
GARDENING

ENCYCLOPEDIA OF
CONTAINER
GARDENING

FOG CITY PRESS

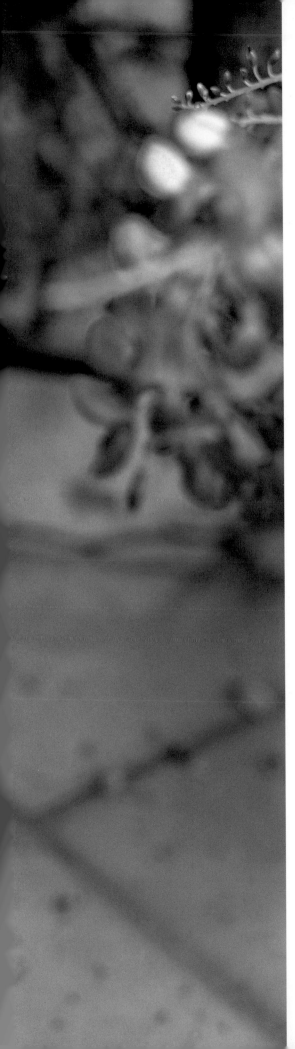

Published by Fog City Press
814 Montgomery Street
San Francisco, CA 94133 USA

Copyright © 2002 Weldon Owen Pty Ltd

Chief Executive Officer: John Owen
President: Terry Newell
Publisher: Lynn Humphries
Managing Editor: Janine Flew
Art Director: Kylie Mulquin
Editorial Coordinator: Tracey Gibson
Picture Research and Editorial Assistant: Marney Richardson
Production Manager: Martha Malic-Chavez
Business Manager: Emily Jahn
Vice President International Sales: Stuart Laurence

Project Editor: Ariana Klepac
Designer: Kylie Mulquin
Consultant: Geoffrey Burnie

All rights reserved. Unauthorized reproduction,
in any manner, is prohibited.
A catalog record for this book is available from
the Library of Congress, Washington, D.C.

ISBN 1 876778 61 X

Color reproduction by Bright Arts Graphics (S) Pte Ltd
Manufactured by Kyodo Printing Co. (S'pore) Pte Ltd
Printed in Singapore

A Weldon Owen Production

Contents

How to Use This Book

The Encyclopedia of Container Gardening is designed to help, encourage, and inspire gardeners, both novice and experienced. It is packed with information about growing and living with houseplants, and planting and maintaining outdoor container plants. The book is easy to read and each page has colorful photographs showing how beautiful your container garden can be. Sections Eight and Nine of the book provide an encyclopedia of houseplants and container plants to help you choose and identify them.

Each section is color-coded for easy reference.

General information about growing, propagating, and caring for your houseplants and container garden to achieve optimum results.

The beginning of a new chapter within one of the nine major sections in the book. The line above is the section heading.

Colorful photographs give you guidance and inspiration in planning and planting your containers.

Clear and simple step-by-step illustrations and photographs, in this case show you how to create a dish garden.

Helpful illustrations feature throughout the book.

---

64 SUCCESS WITH HOUSEPLANTS
Creative Houseplant Displ

There is no need to be limited in your choice of houseplants by the conventional. There are some amazing plants that can adapt to growing in your home—and a host of wonderful ways in which you can display them.

Terrariums, Dish, and Bottle Gardens
To get even more enjoyment out of your houseplant collection, you can create decorative groupings of colorful or unusual plants in terrariums, dish, or bottle gardens. These simple projects are fun, and they provide great, movable accents for any part of your home.

Try a Terrarium or Bottle Garden
Terrariums or bottle gardens are simply clear, glass containers in which you grow a group of plants. They work especially well for plants that require high humidity, such as ferns and insect-eating bog plants, such as Venus fly-traps. The moisture emitted by the leaves in...

Maki
Dish gardens are an excellent way to display a collection... landscape with these plants in a wide, shallow dish. Di...

---

108 CARING FOR CONTAINER GARDENS
Container Garden Primer

When planting groups of flowers in a container, ensure their light requirements are compatible.

In many ways, caring for container gardens is the same as for houseplants. They all need good soil, periodic fertilizing, and regular watering. However, the main difference is that outdoor containers are exposed to more light and more wind, so they'll need more water and more fertilizer to stay in top shape. And since they can't spread their roots to search out water and nutrients, container plantings are completely at your mercy for their needs.

To keep your container plants healthy, you'll have to pay attention to them at least every other day—maybe every day in midsummer. But if you set everything up carefully at the beginning, your plant care chores won't amount to more than a few minutes a day. There are a few techniques you can use to make your container plantings as low maintenance as possible.

Starting with large containers and using a rich, moisture-retentive potting mix are the two key steps to success. You'll find that large containers will look better than smaller pots, and they won't need to be watered as often. Plastic pots tend to lose water more slowly than clay pots, so they're a good choice for reducing your watering chores. (You'll find everything you need to know about containers in "Choosing Containers" on page 18.)

Rich, organic soil is the foundation of any good garden. It is important to choose a commercial container mix that will provide good rooting conditions for your container plants. You can also learn how to blend your own potting mixes to create a growing medium that's perfectly suited to your plants and less expensive as well. (For more information, see "Selecting Container Mixes" on page 22.)

Once your container gardens are established, routine grooming, fertilizing, and watering will keep them growing strong. "Container Care," below, offers pointers on planting, pinching, and preventing pest problems to keep your container gardens in peak condition.

Container Care
You've got the pot, and you've got the soil—now it's time to get your container garden started! Planting containers is easy, and it's a fun chance to try out new flower and foliage

Use small stakes to keep weak-stemmed plants from sprawling.

combinations to create pleasing groupings. Once you have your potted plants settled in, you'll want to groom them occasionally to keep them looking their best through the season. You'll also want to keep an eye out for pest and disease problems so you can catch them before they get out of hand.

Planting
There's no special trick to planting containers; simply do it just as you would garden beds, spacing transplants according to the instructions on the seed packets or the transplant labels. You can space them a little closer in containers if you want, but don't overdo it and try to put too many plants into one container. Remember, the container won't look full and lush immediately, but the little transplants will grow up quickly. It's more likely that you'll need to trim them back than worry about them looking too sparse.

Grooming
Through the season, a little regular pruning will keep all of your container plants looking first-rate. Just grab a bucket and your garden shears and visit each of your container plantings. Snipping back long shoot tips on annuals and removing spent flowers on perennials will stimulate bushy growth and more flowering. Removing any damaged or dead leaves or branches will keep the plants looking fresh and healthy. Collect the clippings in the bucket for later composting. If you've included taller plants in your containers, you may need to stake them to support their upright growth. You can buy bamboo stakes in various heights, or just use small branches pruned from shrubs in your yard. (If you save a little

pile of branches when you prune in late winter, you'll have a perfect source of free material for staking. And the branches actually work better than the bamboo stakes because all of the side twigs help to support the plants better.)

Coping with Container Problems
Keeping your container gardens well watered and fertilized will go a long way toward keeping the plants healthy and vigorous. Insects tend to attack plants that are weak or stressed, so if you prevent the stress, you protect the plants.

Occasionally, though, conditions may be right for insects or diseases to attack even healthy-looking plants. Once a week or so, take a few minutes to really look at your plants and see if you notice any problems developing. Turn over a few leaves, and check the shoot tips for any indications of pests.

If bugs do show up, the same sprays that protect your houseplants will also work well outside. Spraying plants thoroughly with water will keep aphids and spider mite levels down. Insecticidal soap is generally recommended primarily to control soft-bodied insects (such as aphids), although it also works against tough customers like Japanese beetles. Just be sure you spray plants thoroughly, hitting both the tops and bottoms of leaves. Soap sprays must hit the insects directly to be effective. Handpicking or flicking pests into a tub of soapy water also works well for larger insects, such as caterpillars. But be sure you know what you're killing—some very nasty-looking bugs are actually beneficial insects that prey on plant-eating pests.

If you have trouble with slug or snail damage (the usual symptoms are large holes in the leaves), sprinkle some finely crushed eggshells over the surface of the container mix in the pots. The snails and slugs will be deterred since they won't want to

CONTAINER GARDEN PRIMER 109

Snails cannot reach hanging baskets, but are a problem for pots on the ground, wall baskets, and window boxes.

crawl over the rough edges of the eggshells. (As a bonus, the empty eggshells will provide a slow-release source of calcium, an important plant nutrient.)

Diseases are seldom a problem on container plants. As long as there are holes in the bottom of the container, root rots due to poor drainage aren't too common. If you let the plants dry out often, the leaf tips may turn brown—prevent further damage. Pinch off and discard plant parts that show fuzzy, white or gray patches—signs of powdery mildew—or off-color spots. Brown or white scorched spots on indoor plants that you've recently moved outside for the summer indicate sunburn. Plants generally will be somewhat weakened for a while. To avoid this problem, follow the guidelines covered in "Inside Out and Outside In" on page 61.

Japanese beetles feed on a wide range of edible plants and herbs, as well as ornamentals.

LEFT: When planning container plantings, consider how they'll look through the whole season. Bulbs are great for spring, but you'll need to replace them with annuals for later color.

CREATIVE HOUSEPLANT DISPLAYS 65

Plants with patterned or variegated leaves, such as peperomias, look great in bottle gardens.

particularly well, as do brandy snifters and recycled, clear glass wine jugs.

Next, decide what type of plants you want to grow. Tropical plants that like warm temperatures and high humidity, such as miniature gloxinias (*Sinningia* hybrids), polka dot plant (*Hypoestes phyllostachya*), ferns, and mosses, are generally a good choice. If you have a cool room, you could select a group of temperate woodland plants that like shade, humidity, and cool temperatures. Just be sure all the plants you choose like reasonably similar conditions. And unless you're using a large container, choose plants that won't grow very big.

Once you've chosen your container and selected your plants, place 1 inch (2.5 cm) of coarse sand or gravel in the bottom. Then add several inches of container mix and set in your plants. If you're planting in a bottle with a small opening, you may need to use special long-handled tools to slide plants into the container. Water the plants to settle them into the mix.

Give the finished terrarium whatever light level the plants you selected require. However, be aware that the clear glass sides of the container will trap considerable heat, so keep the terrarium out of direct sunlight. And don't over-water—there are no drainage holes, and the container traps and recycles most of the moisture that evaporates from the soil and leaves. You may have to water only once a month, especially while the plants are small.

Dish Gardens

A dish garden is any open container in which you grow several different plants to create a miniature garden. This technique works especially well for smaller kinds of cacti and succulents, which grow well in a wide, shallow dish. As with the terrarium, you should choose relatively small plants, with shallow root systems, that all share similar requirements.

If you plant a dish garden of cacti or succulents, use a special cactus container mix, or make your own by mixing equal parts of standard container mix and sand. For other plants, standard, all-purpose container mix should work fine.

You can also decorate your dish garden with stone chippings, gravel, or even colored glass or tiny seashells. Many nurseries and garden centers stock these materials. Aquarium dealers also have a good selection of colored pebbles.

Training Houseplant Topiaries

Topiary is the art of training plants to a particular shape. It's actually quite easy, and there are many houseplants that adapt well to topiary training. There is a vast array of suitable shapes, so you can continually experiment with new topiaries to add to your houseplant collection.

Setting Up Standards

The simplest topiaries are known as "standards." To create a standard, you train a single-stemmed plant up a long stake, then trim the tip of the plant to form a round ball on top of the stem. One of the best houseplants to train as a standard is myrtle (*Myrtus communis*). It grows slowly in medium light, so you can enjoy the plant for many years. Plus, the leaves have a sweet fragrance when cut or crushed.

Training Plants to Topiary Forms

You can also make topiary by training an ivy, jasmine, or other vining plant onto a special wire form. Circles and heart shapes are common, but you can find them in a practically unlimited range of other shapes, too. To train a plant to a form, simply insert the form in the pot, then fasten the stems to whatever part of the form you

ABOVE: You can train vines around various frames made from wire, bamboo, plastic, or rattan. Here jasmine is trained around a hoop-shaped wire. LEFT: A stunning effect can be created by topiaries. Small-leaved, evergreen plants are most suitable for topiary training.

Top Picks for Topiaries

Many plants can adapt to life as a topiary, but some tend to be better-suited than others. You want a plant that will grow fast enough to give you results fairly quickly, but not so fast that it will outgrow its shape without weekly trimming. Here's a sampling of some of the best choices for indoor topiary projects.

English ivy (*Hedera helix*)
Lantana (*Lantana camara* or *L. montevidensis*)
Lavender (*Lavandula* spp.)
Myrtle (*Myrtus communis*)
Rosemary (*Rosmarinus officinalis*)
Scented geraniums (*Pelargonium* spp.)

Ivy

... Garden

...ing cacti or succulents. You can create a miniature desert ...k great displayed in the center of a coffee table.

2. While the plants are still in their original pots, place them in the dish and move them around to experiment with the design, until you are happy with the arrangement.

4. Place the plants in the dish in your desired arrangement. Fill the dish with container mix by pouring the mix gently around the plants' roots.

Chapter heading indicates the subject being discussed within the section.

Feature boxes highlight additional information and suggestions.

Photograph of individual plants, showing what they look like when grown in the right conditions.

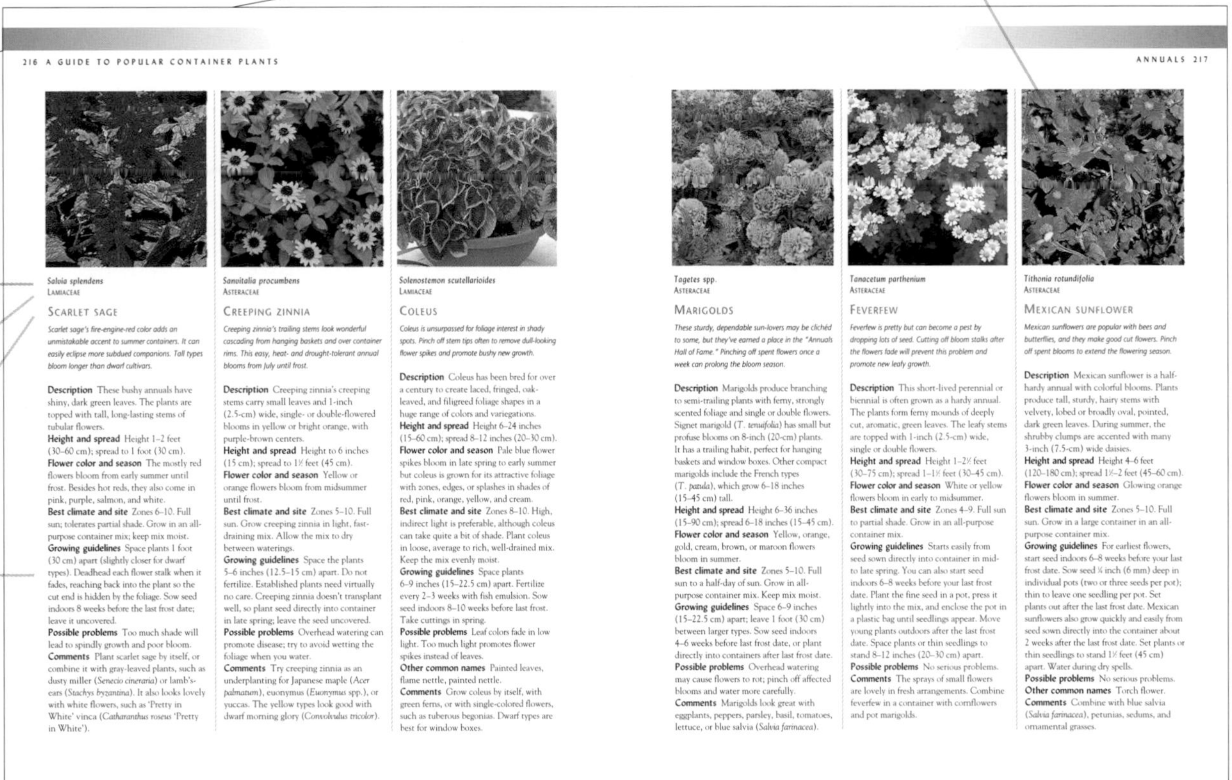
216 A GUIDE TO POPULAR CONTAINER PLANTS

ANNUALS 217

Salvia splendens
LAMIACEAE

SCARLET SAGE

Scarlet sage's fire-engine-red color adds an unmistakable accent to summer containers. It can easily eclipse more subdued companions. Tall types bloom longer than dwarf cultivars.

Description These bushy annuals have shiny, dark green leaves. The plants are topped with tall, long-lasting stems of tubular flowers.
Height and spread Height 1–2 feet (30–60 cm); spread to 1 foot (30 cm).
Flower color and season The mostly red flowers bloom from early summer until frost. Besides hot reds, they also come in pink, purple, salmon, and white.
Best climate and site Zones 6–10. Full sun; tolerates partial shade. Grow in an all-purpose container mix; keep mix moist.
Growing guidelines Space plants 1 foot (30 cm) apart (slightly closer for dwarf types). Deadhead each flower stalk when it fades, reaching back into the plant so the cut end is hidden by the foliage. Sow seed indoors 8 weeks before the last frost date; leave it uncovered.
Possible problems Too much shade will lead to spindly growth and poor bloom.
Comments Plant scarlet sage by itself, or combine it with gray-leaved plants, such as dusty miller (*Senecio cineraria*) or lamb's-ears (*Stachys byzantina*). It also looks lovely with white flowers, such as 'Pretty in White' vinca (*Catharanthus roseus* 'Pretty in White').

Sanvitalia procumbens
ASTERACEAE

CREEPING ZINNIA

Creeping zinnia's trailing stems look wonderful cascading from hanging baskets and over container rims. This easy, heat- and drought-tolerant annual blooms from July until frost.

Description Creeping zinnia's creeping stems carry small leaves and 1-inch (2.5-cm) wide, single- or double-flowered blooms in yellow or bright orange, with purple-brown centers.
Height and spread Height to 6 inches (15 cm); spread to 1½ feet (45 cm).
Flower color and season Yellow or orange flowers bloom from midsummer until frost.
Best climate and site Zones 5–10. Full sun. Grow creeping zinnia in light, fast-draining mix. Allow the mix to dry between waterings.
Growing guidelines Space the plants 5–6 inches (12.5–15 cm) apart. Do not fertilize. Established plants need virtually no care. Creeping zinnia doesn't transplant well, so plant seed directly into container in late spring; leave the seed uncovered.
Possible problems Overhead watering can promote disease; try to avoid wetting the foliage when you water.
Comments Try creeping zinnia as an underplanting for Japanese maple (*Acer palmatum*), euonymus (*Euonymus* spp.), or yuccas. The yellow types look good with dwarf morning glory (*Convolvulus tricolor*).

Solenostemon scutellarioides
LAMIACEAE

COLEUS

Coleus is unsurpassed for foliage interest in shady spots. Pinch off stem tips often to remove dull-looking flower spikes and promote bushy new growth.

Description Coleus has been bred for over a century to create laced, fringed, oak-leaved, and filigreed foliage shapes in a huge range of colors and variegations.
Height and spread Height 6–24 inches (15–60 cm); spread 8–12 inches (20–30 cm).
Flower color and season Pale blue flower spikes bloom in late spring to early summer but coleus is grown for its attractive foliage with zones, edges, or splashes in shades of red, pink, orange, yellow, and cream.
Best climate and site Zones 8–10. High, indirect light is preferable, although coleus can take quite a bit of shade. Plant coleus in loose, average to rich, well-drained mix. Keep the mix evenly moist.
Growing guidelines Space plants 6–9 inches (15–22.5 cm) apart. Fertilize every 2–3 weeks with fish emulsion. Sow seed indoors 8–10 weeks before last frost. Take cuttings in spring.
Possible problems Leaf colors fade in low light. Too much light promotes flower spikes instead of leaves.
Other common names Painted leaves, flame nettle, painted nettle.
Comments Grow coleus by itself, with green ferns, or with single-colored flowers, such as tuberous begonias. Dwarf types are best for window boxes.

Tagetes spp.
ASTERACEAE

MARIGOLDS

These sturdy, dependable sun-lovers may be clichéd to some, but they've earned a place in the "Annuals Hall of Fame." Pinching off spent flowers once a week can prolong the bloom season.

Description Marigolds produce branching to semi-trailing plants with ferny, strongly scented foliage and single or double flowers. Signet marigold (*T. tenuifolia*) has small but profuse blooms on 8-inch (20-cm) plants. It has a trailing habit, perfect for hanging baskets and window boxes. Other compact marigolds include the French types (*T. patula*), which grow 6–18 inches (15–45 cm) tall.
Height and spread Height 6–36 inches (15–90 cm); spread 6–18 inches (15–45 cm).
Flower color and season Yellow, orange, gold, cream, brown, or maroon flowers bloom in summer.
Best climate and site Zones 5–10. Full sun to a half-day of sun. Grow in all-purpose container mix. Keep mix moist.
Growing guidelines Space 6–9 inches (15–22.5 cm) apart; leave 1 foot (30 cm) between larger types. Sow seed indoors 4–6 weeks before last frost date, or plant directly into containers after last frost date.
Possible problems Overhead watering may cause flowers to rot; pinch off affected blooms and water more carefully.
Comments Marigolds look great with eggplants, peppers, parsley, basil, tomatoes, lettuce, or blue salvia (*Salvia farinacea*).

Tanacetum parthenium
ASTERACEAE

FEVERFEW

Feverfew is pretty but can become a pest by dropping lots of seed. Cutting off bloom stalks after the flowers fade will prevent this problem and promote new leafy growth.

Description This short-lived perennial or biennial is often grown as a hardy annual. The plants form ferny mounds of deeply cut, aromatic, green leaves. The leafy stems are topped with 1-inch (2.5-cm) wide, single or double flowers.
Height and spread Height 1–2½ feet (30–75 cm); spread 1–1½ feet (30–45 cm).
Flower color and season White or yellow flowers bloom in early to midsummer.
Best climate and site Zones 4–9. Full sun to partial shade. Grow in an all-purpose container mix.
Growing guidelines Starts easily from seed sown directly into container in mid- to late spring. You can also start seed indoors 6–8 weeks before your last frost date. Plant the fine seed in a pot, press it lightly into the mix, and enclose the pot in a plastic bag until seedlings appear. Move young plants outdoors after the last frost date. Space plants or thin seedlings to stand 8–12 inches (20–30 cm) apart.
Possible problems No serious problems.
Comments The sprays of small flowers are lovely in fresh arrangements. Combine feverfew in a container with cornflowers and pot marigolds.

Tithonia rotundifolia
ASTERACEAE

MEXICAN SUNFLOWER

Mexican sunflowers are popular with bees and butterflies, and they make good cut flowers. Pinch off spent blooms to extend the flowering season.

Description Mexican sunflower is a half-hardy annual with colorful blooms. Plants produce tall, sturdy, hairy stems with velvety, lobed or broadly oval, pointed, dark green leaves. During summer, the shrubby clumps are accented with many 3-inch (7.5-cm) wide daisies.
Height and spread Height 4–6 feet (120–180 cm); spread 1½–2 feet (45–60 cm).
Flower color and season Glowing orange flowers bloom in summer.
Best climate and site Zones 5–10. Full sun. Grow in a large container in an all-purpose container mix.
Growing guidelines For earliest flowers, start seed indoors 6–8 weeks before your last frost date. Sow seed ¼ inch (6 mm) deep in individual pots (two or three seeds per pot); thin to leave one seedling per pot. Set plants out after the last frost date. Mexican sunflowers also grow quickly and easily from seed sown directly into the container about 2 weeks after the last frost date. Set plants or thin seedlings to stand 1½ feet (45 cm) apart. Water during dry spells.
Possible problems No serious problems.
Other common names Torch flower.
Comments Combine with blue salvia (*Salvia farinacea*), petunias, sedums, and ornamental grasses.

Botanical name

Family name

Common name

Information about plant

Container Gardening Basics

Growing plants in pots offers all the enjoyment of in-the-ground gardening, plus so much more! Indoors and out, containers give you the freedom to move plants around, creating a constantly changing display of foliage and flowers. As with regular gardening, it is important to understand plants and how they grow, in order to provide the best possible conditions, and to keep your plants looking their best. In addition, choosing the right container, with adequate space and drainage, and selecting a suitable container mix, will give you the best headstart to container gardening success.

Gardening in Containers

People have been growing plants in containers for thousands of years. Ancient Egyptians created temple gardens out of bare rock and transformed these terraces with container-grown trees and other plants. Similar, though less grand, gardening traditions developed in ancient Greece, Rome, China, and the Americas.

Although pots were common in the gardens of the Middle Ages, it was not until the Italian Renaissance that they became essential to horticulture. In the late seventeenth century, Italian, Dutch, and French container styles made a big impact on the development of English gardens. Ornate containers, tubs, pots, and vases became features of great gardens and modest cottages alike.

Modern gardeners share many of the opportunities and the challenges faced by these historic gardeners. Like them, we can grow plants in containers that under normal circumstances would never grow naturally where we live—including inside our home. With a little effort, you can create an artificial environment that will fit the needs of virtually any plant you might want to grow—camellias, azaleas, and rhododendrons won't mind if you have very alkaline garden soil, if they are planted in containers in an acidic potting mix that suits them perfectly.

However, container-grown plants are much more dependent than plants in the open garden, whose roots can stretch out and search for nutrients and moisture in the soil. We have to take care of most—if not all—of their needs.

The Versatility of Containers

Growing plants in containers gives you great flexibility. If something does not grow or look good in one place, you can move the plant to another position—either inside your

The stunning flowers of cyclamen can be planted indoors, and brighten up the home on dull winter days.

home, on a deck or balcony, or in the open garden. You can also rearrange your plants to show off those that are at their best at the time, throughout the year, or bring plants inside your home when they are in bloom and place them outside again when the flowers fade. Tender plants can be moved to more sheltered positions, or even indoors, as the weather cools in fall and winter. You can temporarily park plants in containers while you make space for them and prepare their final positions in the open garden. You can use containers to multiply your favorite plants by sowing

Flowers bloom in pots built into the walls of the formal gardens, at the Italian Renaissance-style Villa Vizcaya in Coconut Grove, Florida.

seed or growing cuttings. And, if you are having trouble deciding just what sort of garden design you want, and where each plant will finally go, you can keep moving plants in containers around, to try various effects, until you are happy with the result.

Space Saving

Containers allow you to garden even where you have little space—and even no soil, if you want to experiment with hydroponics. If you live in an apartment or condo, or if you want to create a garden on your balcony or deck, around a mobile home, or in a tiny yard, containers offer you all kinds of gardening possibilities.

The Mobile Garden

If you are renting or move home quite often, with containers you can take your plants with you, too. However, remember that large plants in containers can become very heavy. The ultimate size of large plants may need to be restricted, or you will not be able to move the container easily, or even at all. Some fast-growing plants can rapidly become too big for their location and surroundings.

Terraces and Balconies

You can grow plants in containers on terraces and balconies, which provide shelter from prevailing winds, or protective shade in the hottest time of the year. Pots and tubs should be substantial enough so that taller plants and small trees are not blown over by wind.

Types of Container

Anything that can hold soil securely can be used as a garden container. It is a good idea for it to have watertight sides and a fairly stable base so that the container won't easily be knocked over. A good container should also resist rot and corrosion. Unless you intend growing

aquatic plants, the container should also have one or more drainage holes. You can poke holes in softer materials with a nail or use a drill (but beware of drilling metal and ceramic containers).

From classic terracotta pots and tubs to colorful ceramic pots and much more, the range of containers now available means that your selection of container shape, material, and color is greater than ever. Plastic pots are easy to clean and very light to handle. They are also much more durable, and need less frequent watering, than terracotta pots. Tubs may be constructed of wood, metal, plastic, or fiberglass. Redwood, cedar, and cypress make the most durable wooden tubs—but they are also usually the most expensive varieties.

Make sure that any wood for use as plant containers has not been treated with any wood preservatives that are toxic to plants. If you need to use a wood preservative, use a copper napthenate product or use salt-treated lumber.

A mass of scented geraniums (*Pelargonium* spp.) tumble out of a window box, creating a stunning effect against the stone wall.

Stone troughs are popular containers as they can almost look as if they are part of the landscape. They can be heavy to lift, though.

More specialized container types include hanging baskets, which can be made of plastic, with drainage saucers or, less obtrusively, of a wire or plastic frame lined with wet sphagnum, bark, peat moss, or synthetic basket liners. Remember, though, hanging baskets with well-grown plants can become heavy, especially when they have been fully watered, so take care that the weight will be adequately supported.

Window boxes are popular but they must also be well secured. They can be made of wood, metal, terracotta, fiberglass, or plastic. Such boxes should ideally be lightweight, durable, and easily handled. Window boxes can be planted directly, or potted plants can be arranged in the box and replaced as necessary.

There's no need to limit yourself to commercially produced containers. As long as the container provides enough drainage, markets and garage sales can offer antique, quaint, or just plain crazy containers that you can adapt to a new life holding your favorite

Impatiens

plants—kettles, basins, barrows, or even old boots are just a few examples.

Remember, too, that you can conceal plants in utilitarian plastic pots by hiding them inside much more creative, larger outer containers. For more detailed information about containers, see "Considering Containers" on page 18.

Getting Started

Many people get started with container gardening when they happen to receive a plant or houseplant as a gift. This is a great way to get to know the basic needs of plants—soil, light, fertilizer, water, humidity, and temperature.

Choosing Plants for Containers

When you are starting your container garden, you should select plants that are reasonably easy to grow and that will perform well over a long period of time. Because containers confine gardening to a limited space, each plant you select is important. Of course, you will choose plants that you enjoy, but you also need to ensure that they combine well with other plants in the same container or in nearby containers. Or, if your container plants are part of a conventional garden, how will they relate to their neighbors growing in the open soil and how will they contribute to the overall appearance and performance of your garden?

In addition to the basic needs of each plant, it is important to pay attention to the plant color, shape, texture, and scent. Disappointment can be the result of concentrating on the individual plant while forgetting the part it plays in the container setting, or garden as a whole.

Available Conditions

Be realistic about the available conditions, and whether plants are to grow inside your home, outside, or somewhere in between.

ABOVE RIGHT: You can grow a whole garden of bulbs on the deck or patio in a large, flat container.
BELOW RIGHT: In a large trough, combine ornamentals with your productive container garden.

Will the plant be in full sun or shade, sheltered or in a windy, exposed position? How much maintenance will be needed by the particular plants you have in mind? How much time, effort, and money can you spare to look after it? It would be silly, for instance, to attempt to grow exotic orchids where there are hard frost winters unless you are prepared to devote considerable resources to the task.

Houseplants

Building a collection of healthy houseplants can be a very rewarding hobby that can be enjoyed by everyone. It need not be difficult. If you give the plants what they need, they

will flourish. Give houseplants a little less than they ideally need and the plants will usually still survive anyway.

Any failure is generally the result of too many plant needs being ignored. However, a plant failure is something from which we can learn, and it happens even in the best-run, most experienced commercial garden centers.

Know Your Plants

It is worthwhile taking the time to learn the needs of each plant you want to grow before you actually buy it. Cultural notes on plants sold in supermarkets may not be entirely accurate and may not match the real needs of your new plant in your home or in your climate zone. Impulse buys can

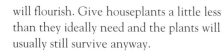

Flowering houseplants generally need lots of light, so make sure you have a bright spot for them.

turn out well, but may not—your luck in raising plants can be closely related to your knowledge of your new plant.

You can check "A Guide to Popular Houseplants," starting on page 132, and "A Guide to Popular Container Plants," starting on page 164, to find out about a wide range of plants suitable for containers.

Types of Container Garden

As your container gardening skills develop, you will see more opportunities to use plants in containers inside your home, on decks, patios, and balconies as well as outdoors in the open garden.

Edible Container Gardens

You can grow vegetables and other edibles in containers. You can even grow some kinds indoors if you have a room that gets lots of light. The containers you use should be generous in size (especially for root vegetables) and have very good drainage. Vegetables suitable for growing in containers include lettuce, spinach, radishes, dwarf carrots, beets, turnips, and patio tomatoes.

Container Herb Gardens

Herbs are an even easier choice for many container gardeners since they are often less demanding than vegetables, and cooks love to be able to snip fresh herbs whenever they need them. Chives, parsley, thyme, basil, and many other herbs can even grow well indoors if given the right conditions. Suitable containers include window boxes, flower pots, recycled styrofoam coolers, packing boxes, or half barrels.

Basil and parsley

Scented Container Gardens

You might like to grow a scented container garden with fragrant plants placed in an outdoor area where you can sit and relax at the end of a long day, or place the plants outside French doors or under windows, where breezes can waft the perfumes into the home.

Special Container Gardens

Plants grown in containers are so versatile that there can sometimes be unexpected benefits from their use. Containers can also make it easier for elderly or disabled gardeners to pursue their hobby by simply making it easier to reach and handle plants. Container gardens are ideal for gardeners who have to work from their wheelchair.

Container Plant Care

There are some important considerations when you garden in containers. In hot weather your container plants will have to be watered and fertilized more often than plants growing in the open ground. However, new gardeners frequently overcompensate—more plants die from overwatering than from any other cause.

BELOW: Nasturtiums are rampant plants and will probably grow to completely cover the hanging basket.

You can create a Southwest-theme container garden, with potted cacti and succulents.

Balcony, deck, and roof container gardens may need special considerations. Is the surface watertight? Can the flooring support the considerable weight that can build up in a substantial container garden?

Large collections of container-grown plants can consume a considerable amount of water—will the water supply be adequate during dry periods? Is the sunlight sufficient, too little, or too much?

However, apart from these special considerations, there has never been a greater number of people gardening in containers, and there are more products and services available than ever before to assist the home container gardener. In addition, more and more types of plant can be grown successfully in a pot and, as the quality of container mixes, fertilizers, and containers improve, many gardeners who have struggled with poor soils and other meager resources are now choosing to grow their favorite plants in containers, rather than in the garden bed.

Understanding Plants

You don't need a degree in botany to be a successful gardener, but understanding a little about how plants are named, plant groups, the lifecycles of plants, and what their basic needs are, can help you to keep your container plants happy.

Plant Names

At first, the scientific names of plants can seem daunting and confusing. New gardeners can sometimes feel a touch of panic when faced with doses of botanical Latin. However, using precise plant names can be very useful.

Becoming familiar with the scientific names of the plants you want to grow helps you buy exactly what you need. Botanical names tell us, first, the genus the plant belongs to. The genus name ("Acer" in *Acer palmatum*), often honors the person who discovered or first scientifically described a member of that genus.

The second element, the species name ("palmatum" in *Acer palmatum*), can tell us more about that particular plant. As you become more familiar with botanical names, you will notice some names used for different plants that share particular characteristics—"alba" signifies white flowers, "caerulea" indicates blue flowers, "contorta" means twisted or contorted, and "rugosa" denotes wrinkled.

Cultivars are distinct horticultural types that are selected or produced by breeding under cultivation. Cultivar names

can be spotted by the single quotation marks that surround them (for example, *Carex elata* 'Bowles Golden').

Sometimes plants from different species or genera will cross-pollinate, producing offspring that share the characteristics of both parents. These "new" plants are called hybrids. An "x" in a plant's name (as in *Astilbe* x *arendsii*), usually indicates that the plant is a hybrid.

Plant Groups

There are three main groups of plants—ferns, conifers, and flowering plants. Ferns do not produce flowers, so any plant that has flowers cannot be a fern. Most fern

RIGHT: Perennials live for more than two growing seasons.
BELOW: Annuals, like nemesia, have just one goal—to reproduce themselves.

Bulbs store energy and water below ground in an enlarged root stem. This storage area allows the plant to grow and flower in favorable conditions.

leaves grow directly from a rhizome just below the surface of the soil.

Conifers, such as pines, firs, spruces, and junipers, have needle-like or scaly leaves and do not produce flowers. Their fruits are either cones or berry-like cones.

The flowering plants include plants with obvious flowers such as roses and daisies, as well as plants like the grasses, which bloom more inconspicuously.

Flowering plants are further classified by other characteristics, including life cycle, growth habit, methods of reproduction, and seasonal growth.

Life Cycles

Life cycle basically means the number of growing seasons that a single plant lives. The usual definition of an annual is a plant that germinates from seed, flowers, sets seed, and dies all in one growing season. Gardeners grow many plants for one season, although they may not be true annuals. Plants that may be perennials in their native environment, may be

better treated as annuals in cultivation, especially in much cooler climates.

Biennials live for two years. Growth in the first year is usually a cluster of leaves at ground level and, in the second year of growth, a flowering stalk appears.

Perennials live for many years. Many perennial plants do not flower or produce seed until they are several years old. The structure of true perennials is either woody (brown, gray, or hard) or herbaceous (green, sappy, or soft). Perennials grow for the long term and usually have more extensive root systems than annual or biennial plants.

Some half-hardy perennials, such as dahlias, geraniums, and tuberous begonias, are often treated as annuals.

Some Common Botanical Names

Alba: white flowers
Alpina: alpine
Aurea: chartreuse to yellow leaves
Caerulea: blue flowers
Chrysantha: yellow flowers
Contorta: twisted, contorted
Edulis: edible
Grandiflora: large flowers
Grandifolia: large leaves
Japonica: from Japan
Lutea: yellow flowers
Macrophylla: big leaves
Maculata: spotted
Maritima: of the sea
Montana: of the mountains
Nana: dwarf
Nigra: dark
Occidentalis: from the West
Odorata: scented flowers
Orientalis: from the East, Asia
Palustris: swampy, marshy
Paniculata: flowers in panicles
Pendula: hanging
Pubescens: hairy
Pumila: dwarf
Purpurea: purple
Racemosa: flowers in racemes
Repens, reptans: creeping
Ruber: red
Rugosa: wrinkled
Sanguinea: bloody, red
Scandens: climbing
Sempervirens: evergreen
Spicata: flowers on spikes
Stricta: upright
Sylvestris: of the woods, forests
Tomentosa: woolly, downy

Growth Habit

Growth habit describes the size of a plant, whether it is woody, whether it is grass-like or broad-leaved. Trees are woody plants, usually more than 15 feet (4.6 m) tall at maturity. Trees usually have one main stem with radiating branches on the upper portion of the plant. Shrubs are woody plants, usually less than 15 feet (4.6 m) tall, with several more-or-less equal main stems.

Plant Needs

All plants need light to photosynthesize, the process by which light, chlorophyll, energy, carbon dioxide, and water act together within the plant to produce the sugar and starches it needs to survive.

Light requirements vary from plant to plant but, generally speaking, the lower the light, the slower the plant grows and, when there isn't enough light to photosynthesize, the plant dies. It is important to know whether your plant has low, medium, or high light requirements so that when you select the position, you have the right plant for the right light conditions.

In situations where you can't supply sufficient light for the plant, you can artificially produce light using fluorescent lights or other types of lights.

Plants also need water. However, more plants die from overwatering than any other cause. If overwatered, the plant will drown—its roots will sit in

Purple coneflower

Shrubs are woody plants that range in size from just a few inches to several feet in height.

water and all air spaces in the soil will be filled. Underwatering can also be a problem. The main symptom is wilting, beginning with the youngest leaves at the tips of the stems. Older leaves may not show any effect for a few days or more, but soon their edges will turn brown.

It is not easy to gauge the right amount of water. A plant will use water based on its location, temperature, humidity of the room (if indoors), the size of the pot, light conditions, and the time of the year. In general, plants fall into three categories of moisture needs—water-loving plants, moderately dry plants, and dry soil plants.

Most container-grown plants will also require fertilization, particularly since, unlike garden plants, their roots cannot search through the soil for nutrients. Keep in mind that plant food will cause a plant to grow more rapidly. Nitrogen helps promote leaf growth, phosphorus helps promote sturdy cell growth, and potassium promotes balance of the plant systems.

Considering Containers

Nearly everyone can have a window box or two, even if they live high above the ground.

flowering annuals and perennials, pots that hold about 2 to 4 gallons (9 to 18 l) of growing medium will work best. Small trees or shrubs can start out in 2- to 4-gallon (9- to 18-l) pots, but you'll probably need to move them to larger containers after their first season. Large vegetable plants, such as tomatoes and peppers, will be more productive if you give them plenty of room. Five-gallon (23-l) containers are a good size for peppers; full-sized tomatoes should have at least 10-gallon (45-l) pots.

If there's one general rule to follow when deciding what size pot to use, it's bigger is usually better. Small pots can really look out of scale and get lost when

While all pots will hold plants, some are more effective than others, some more attractive, some better value, and some more appropriate to their mundane duties. Picking the right container can go a long way toward creating a good-looking, easy-care container garden.

Generally, plants can be grown in anything that will hold soil and allow proper drainage. Traditional containers include terracotta or clay pots, plastic pots, hanging baskets, wire baskets lined with sphagnum moss or fibrous liners, concrete planters, planter boxes, barrels, tubs, metal and enamelled containers, and bushel baskets. Some of these containers are much more durable than others. But there is no need to limit yourself to the purely traditional. Containers can be wooden wine crates, garbage bags filled with growing medium ("sausage gardens"), or even an old, broken coffee pot.

Containers can be either utilitarian or decorative, or a mixture of the two. When choosing a container you will need to consider whether the container will be in a highly visible location, or buried in a window box. And if it is to be visible, remember to coordinate the container color with the colors of the plants you

select. While containers can be painted to create a totally different look or a less heat-absorbing surface, these may be unnecessary chores.

When you're shopping for a new pot or planter, it is important to consider the size of the container, the material the container is made from, as well as the container's drainage capabilities.

Select the Right Size

The container size that's right for your needs mostly depends on what plants you want to grow. Containers should be large enough to hold the minimum amount of container mix needed by your plants to grow in until they are mature or you repot them. For herbs, small to medium-sized vegetables, and

Terracotta (clay) pots

What to Look for in a Container

How much space do you have and how do you want it to look over time? For small spaces, use smaller containers and avoid bigger plants with overly large leaves, flowers, and other features which can make the whole thing seem cramped.

Make sure there are enough drainage holes in the container or that it is made of a material that you could drill into or cut holes in.

Will your container mix be able to breathe? In most conditions porosity in a container is a plus, unless you live in a very dry climate where the container might dry out.

In colder climates, a container that retains heat and protects root systems against temperature extremes will prolong the life of your plants in the fall and allow you to plant earlier in the spring.

Extremes of temperature are bad news since they can cause pots to break open and spill out the plants and container mix. In very cold conditions, plastic can become brittle and terracotta pots can freeze and crack.

Your container is going to be full of wet mud. Will it be too heavy for your deck, balcony or roof? Will the cumulative weight of your containers be crushing? Will it be too heavy for you to move?

you set them down in the great outdoors. The bigger the pot, the better it will look in your overall garden design. Plus, the larger pots don't dry out nearly as fast as little ones, so you won't have to water them as often. However, one factor to bear in mind is weight—mature, well-watered plants in suitable containers can be very heavy. You may want to use lighter materials if you are going to rearrange your plants often or if you move home regularly. Use large pots sparingly if you're gardening on a balcony or rooftop. (In fact, you may want to have a structural engineer check out the stability of these areas before you set up any containers.)

Consider the Materials

The material that a container is made from can be just as important as its size. Each kind of material has advantages and disadvantages, depending on what you're growing and where you're growing it.

Clay and Terracotta

Containers made from clay or terracotta look very attractive, and they have the advantage of providing extra bottom weight so that taller plants won't blow over in the wind. However, containers made of terracotta and other porous materials can absorb water that may be needed by your plants, so they may need extra watering. If temperatures dip below freezing where you live, you will need to take extra care of terracotta containers. (There are now terracotta pots that are promoted as frost-resistant, so choose these if you can.)

When the growing season slows in the fall, you will need to empty, clean, and sterilize your terracotta pots, and store them where they won't be subject to freezing. If left filled through the winter, moisture can get into the soil, which will expand as it freezes and can crack the pot. If you do not relish these extra tasks, don't choose terracotta. Concrete is generally more durable for year-round growing than terracotta. Large clay and concrete containers can also be quite heavy to move.

Plastic and Fiberglass

For plants that you need to move inside in winter and outside in summer, a plastic or fiberglass container will be

ABOVE LEFT: Bulbs in wickerwork baskets.
ABOVE RIGHT: The natural beauty of terracotta lends itself to effective window boxes and pots.

The spiky and dramatic agave contrasts well with the tall, graceful lines of the mosaic pot.

Tubs and barrels are ideal for planting trees and shrubs, or simply for large plantings.

Metal

From lead to cast-iron (plain, painted, or slightly rusted) to galvanized tin or wirework, metallic plant containers can look stunning. However, in hot climates, metal containers can really heat up, and make plants dry out very quickly.

Container Color

Whatever kind of container material you choose, look for pots and planters that are light-colored, especially if you live in a hot climate. Light-colored pots help to reflect the heat and keep the roots cool. Black pots are the worst choice in hot climates, since they can absorb enough heat to damage tender roots.

Drainage

The other important factor to consider when choosing a container is to make sure it has adequate drainage holes. Many gardeners place coarse rocks or broken pot shards in the bottom of pots to improve the drainage. This helps a little, but adequate drainage holes are the critical thing for healthy root growth and top-growth. Most commercially available pots and planters already have drainage holes in them. However, if you are creating your own containers from wood or recycled plastic buckets, make the drainage holes at least ½ inch (12 mm) in diameter. Drill at least six holes in medium-sized containers and more in larger ones.

What if you have a great-looking container that doesn't have drainage holes? You can still use it for outdoor growing if you're willing to give it a little extra attention. First, put a few blocks of wood in the base. Next, set in an already-potted plant so that it is resting on the wood blocks. The blocks will keep the plant roots from sitting in the water that collects in the base of the outer pot. Over time—and especially after heavy rains—however, the water level may rise to the level of the inner pot. During very wet weather, lift out the inner pot every day or two, and dump out any water that has collected in the pot; otherwise, your plants may suffer or even die.

much lighter than clay, concrete, or wood. Plastic containers also won't dry out as fast as those made of clay, and plastic is usually much less expensive. If you need to buy several large pots, this could be a major factor. The main disadvantage of plastic and fiberglass pots is that they are more likely to blow over in windy areas.

Wood

Wood falls in between plastic and clay in weight and porosity. It has the advantage of insulating the roots from overheating when the summer sun strikes the planter. However, wood can be a problem, since water has a rather unfortunate effect on many timbers. Cedar or redwood can be used without painting and are rot-resistant, but many chemically treated timbers should be avoided. You'll probably need to replace wooden planters every few years. If you like the look and insulating value of wooden planters but want to help them last longer, you could use plastic liners or set already-potted plants inside them.

You can make a container out of anything that will hold soil, including an old bathtub. However, don't forget to add drainage holes at the bottom.

Things to Avoid in a Container

One of the great things about container gardening is that you can put a plant in just about anything and call it a container. However, there are some types of container that it's best to avoid and some important points to note:

• Avoid containers that have a small opening at the top. This will limit air circulation in the container and make it very difficult for you to water the plant adequately.

• Containers with narrow bases have a tendency to tip over. Containers with wide, stable bases are best, especially for larger plants that can become top-heavy as they become full-grown.

• Do not use containers that have too few or no drainage holes.

• Terracotta pots dry out rapidly.

• Very shallow containers tend to dry out more quickly.

• Cheap plastic pots can deteriorate in ultraviolet sunlight.

• Glazed ceramic pots can be excellent choices, but make sure they have several drainage holes.

• In warm weather or in full sunlight, dark-colored pots can dry out the soil and overheat your plant.

• Avoid containers that claim to be biodegradable—they may degrade to the point that they spill out your plants and soil at an inconvenient moment.

• Avoid any container that has been used to store chemicals or any caustic materials.

• Beware of containers that are made from concrete or cement. Possible leaching of chemicals from the container might make the container mix extremely alkaline and might harm acid soil-loving plants such as camellias, azaleas, and rhododendrons.

A special, large planter, such as a carved stone urn, can become a focal point for the whole garden.

Selecting Container Mixes

Once you've picked the perfect container, it's time to fill it with the best possible growing medium. While soil is just fine in the garden, it is a bad choice for plants in pots when used alone. The frequent watering demanded by container plants will cause most real soil to compact into a tight, brick-like mass (or if your garden soil is very sandy, it will dry out much too quickly in a container). The answer is to use a soil mix that is specially blended for plants in containers.

Since container plants have less soil for roots to grow in and to extract nutrients from, the soil must be carefully prepared. The container mix should be sterile (free from weeds and disease), be light enough to provide for air space (as well as allowing the container to be moved easily), and meet the needs of the individual plant to be grown.

Picking the Right Container Mix

Like "ideal" garden soil, a container mix should hold enough water for good root growth but allow excess water to drain out. It should also contain a balance of nutrients to steadily nourish a wide variety of plants for normal, healthy growth.

You can buy a variety of container mixes at your local garden center. Those that contain some amount of real soil are called soil-based mixes. These tend to feel heavy, and they generally hold more water. Soil-less mixes usually contain peat moss and/or vermiculite to hold moisture. These mixes usually feel very light and can dry out more quickly.

When you are faced with a row of different products at the garden center, it can be hard to choose which one to buy. If you grow a lot of one kind of plant (cacti or African violets, for instance), you may want to try a mix formulated especially for that type of plant.

Hyacinths

In most cases, though, an all-purpose container mix is fine. Buy a small bag and see how your plants grow in it.

Some gardeners get good results by purchasing a heavier mix and adding perlite or vermiculite to improve drainage, or adding peat to improve water retention. "Making Your Own Container Mixes" below offers recipes for blending your own customized container growing medium.

Using Commercial Container Mixes

For annuals, which will only live in their pots for one growing season, you can use any well-drained, commercial container mix. Most such mixes don't have any compost or soil in them—they are primarily composed of peat and usually some vermiculite (to absorb and hold water) and perlite (to improve drainage). If you use these soil-less mixes straight from the bag, you'll need to fertilize regularly.

To improve a commercial soil-less mix for growing perennials, shrubs, and trees, you can add up to 20 percent compost or a combination of

Good drainage is important for healthy container plants, so look for a container mix that contains some perlite or bark.

10 percent compost and 10 percent garden soil. Both the compost and the soil provide slow-release nutrients and generally improve the ability of the mix to hold moisture and nutrients. And there's another big bonus when you add compost to your container mix— microorganisms in the compost will help prevent diseases and keep your plants healthy! Composted bark chips are also an excellent addition to keep the mix loose for good root growth.

If you need to keep your container mix as light as possible—for a large window box, for example—add the 20 percent compost but no soil. Instead, add some extra perlite (about 10 percent). Or, if you need the mix to be heavier to help prevent a taller shrub from blowing over in the wind, add some extra soil or sand to the container mix.

Making Your Own Container Mixes

Blending your own container mix from scratch is also a possibility for creating the perfect mix. It allows you to custom blend a variety of different ingredients to match the needs of your particular plants. Your main goal is to combine ingredients that have a variety of particle sizes so the mix is not too fine. You'll also always need to add some compost to provide slow-release nutrition and to help prevent diseases.

Making good container mix is an art, not a science. There are many different recipes that will give great results. The recipes given here are just guidelines, and your plants will still grow well if you need to use more or less of any ingredients.

Basic Container Mix

This simple blend will work well for a wide variety of container plantings.

4 parts peat moss (mixed thoroughly with ½ ounce [15 g] dolomitic limestone per gallon of peat)

Fork   Trowel

1 part compost (or ½ part compost and ½ part garden soil)

1 part perlite or vermiculite

Pile all of these materials in a large tub and use your hands or a shovel to mix them thoroughly. These materials can be very dusty, so it's a good idea to wear a dust mask during the mixing process.

Deluxe Container Mix

This blend is especially good for long-term plantings (including trees, shrubs, and perennials) in larger containers.

4 parts sphagnum peat

2 parts compost (or 1 part compost and 1 part garden soil)

1 part small bark chips (composted)

1 part perlite

Combine materials as you would for the basic mix. To each cubic foot (or 7½ gallons [34 l]) of mix, add the following slow-release organic fertilizers:

To get top performance from large containers, add compost and organic fertilizers to the mix.

4 ounces (110 g) of dolomitic limestone

4 ounces (110 g) of bonemeal (or 1 pound [500 g] of rock phosphate or colloidal phosphate)

1 pound (500 g) of greensand

2 ounces (55 g) of bloodmeal

2 ounces (55 g) of kelp meal

With this deluxe container mix, your plants will have plenty of nutrients to get off to a great start, and you shouldn't need to begin supplemental fertilizing until at least a month after you plant.

Fertilizing Potted Plants

Even the best mix can't provide all the nutrients that your container plants and houseplants will need. For a nutrient supplement, use a liquid fertilizer poured onto the container mix. You can use fish emulsion, seaweed extract, or a combination of the two. Or you could make a nutrient tea out of compost, as explained in "Successful Containers Start with Compost" on page 113.

For best growth, you should feed your outdoor container plants each week. Houseplants vary in their appetites. Some people feed houseplants with very diluted fertilizers each time they water, some use regular strength with every other watering, and some feed monthly. Whichever routine you choose, remember to cut back or stop fertilizing during the winter, when low light slows growth.

Overfertilizing can be as harmful as underfertilizing. An overfertilized plant produces weak, lanky growth that's susceptible to diseases and insects. And overfertilizing can make salts accumulate in the soil, creating conditions few roots like. The sure sign of salt buildup is a white crust on the soil surface or on the surface of clay pots. To get rid of it, pour water through the soil continuously (until water runs out the drain holes for a few minutes) to wash out the salt. For severe problems, move the plant to a new pot, or scrub the old pot to remove the salt crust; wash the pot and repot the plant in fresh soil.

How Much Do You Need?

If you need to fill more than a few small pots, it can be hard to decide how much mix to buy or blend. You need to do a little calculating, but that's a whole lot easier than lugging home more mix than you need or having to go back to the store for more.

Some containers are labeled by volume, usually given in gallons (liters). In this case, most of your work is done, especially if your mix is measured in gallons. (If the mix is measured in cubic feet, divide the number of cubic feet by 7.5 to get the number of gallons of mix.)

To find the volume of a square or rectangular pot, simply multiply the length and width by the height. Divide the number of cubic inches by 1,728 to get the number of cubic feet of soil you need. If your mix is measured in gallons, multiply the number of gallons by 7.5 to find the number of cubic feet.

To find the volume of a round pot, you first need to figure out the area of the top circle of the pot. Lay a ruler across the top of the pot to measure the diameter (how far it is from side to side). Now, divide that number by 2, multiply it by itself, and then multiply it by 3.14. Take that answer and multiply it by the height of the pot to find the number of cubic inches of mix the pot can hold. Divide the number of cubic inches by 1,728 to get the number of cubic feet of mix you need. If your container mix is measured in gallons, multiply the number of gallons by 7.5 to find out the number of cubic feet.

Plant Style

*Container gardening gives you the freedom to create beautiful
and innovative combinations of plants in attractive containers
that can be moved around, like furniture, to brighten up areas
of the house and garden. Plants have a huge range of growing habits,
as well as a seemingly endless variety of leaf and flower sizes,
shapes, colors, and textures. For the most stunning displays,
it is helpful to study the decorative qualities of plants so you
can create the most harmonious and eyecatching blends of plants
and containers, and achieve a planting theme that enhances
the particular style of your home and garden.*

The Basic Shapes of Plants

Plants all have individual shapes that gardeners have been making use of for centuries. Today, with our busy modern lifestyles we haven't the time to clip and train plants into desired shapes, so we must rely on the natural growing qualities of plants—and you'll find there's a green shape to suit every decorating style.

When you shop for plants, you'll often buy on impulse and then come home to find that the plant is not quite right for the desired position. However, many container plants have a long life, so let's look at the various shapes and how you can use them to best advantage to get the maximum benefit for your dollar.

Choosing the Right Shape

First, it is important to consider where you want to position the plant. In a tight corner that people often walk past, a good choice is an upright, slim plant such as a camellia (*Camellia japonica*) or a clipped box (*Buxus sempervirens*). Or you could select a trailing or climbing plant such as a Chilean jasmine (*Mandevilla laxa*) or stephanotis (*Stephanotis floribunda*), and then train it on a totem pole indoors, or on a lattice screen attached to an outside wall. This will allow for unhindered traffic, as well as prevent the foliage being bruised by everyone who passes by.

Architectural Plants

Larger plants with tall, arresting shapes, such as yuccas or false aralia (*Dizygotheca elegantissima*), are sometimes called "architectural plants" because of their dramatic outline. These can be more expensive yet, with care, you will have them for a long time, so they are worth the cost. Place one as a single focal point in a plain courtyard or against an inside wall, rather than lessening its impact by grouping other plants around it. You'll need to take care, though, since placing plants with spiky foliage in confined spaces can be a problem if people often brush past, or children play in the area.

Arching and Weeping Plants

In areas of your home or garden with more space, you could introduce a plant with an arching habit such as a Boston fern (*Nephrolepis exaltata*), or a ponytail palm (*Nolina recurvata*). These plants, often with long stems, look good standing alone or, if space permits, grouped with other shapes at their base. Often, though, plants such as ferns include species with very long, arching stems which weep below the level of the base of the container. These look best when placed on a pedestal of their own, or in a hanging basket, where their graceful, weeping outline can be fully appreciated. And don't overlook the re-curving, mounded shapes of some of

Cacti and succulents add a different range of textures and shapes to your collection of houseplants.

the ornamental grasses, such as the *Pennisetum alopecuroides* hybrids that look so good in contemporary courtyard settings.

Rosette-shaped Plants

On a coffee table, where you would look down on a plant, a low-growing African violet (*Saintpaulia* hybrid) would be ideal. Other plants that grow in rosette shapes— that is, with the leaves radiating out from a central growing point—like many of the bromeliads, are also best positioned below eye level for the maximum impact. Other low-level plants include the smaller-growing bulbs with tufty leaves, such as grape hyacinths (*Muscari armeniacum*), which look marvelous grouped in a decorative container even when they're not in bloom. In summer, try a bowl overflowing with some cascading, annual petunias in a sunny outdoor area. Also,

LEFT: Architectural, or upright, plants, such as aloe vera, have a distinctive growth habit.
RIGHT: Elegant Boston ferns have swordlike, arching fronds that hang down over the sides of a container or hanging basket.

ABOVE: Nasturtiums (*Tropaeolum majus*) are vigorous annuals that grow either as a bushy mound, or as a trailing vine. Some cultivars can climb or trail up to 6 feet (180 cm) or more.

don't overlook the many species of cacti. You can gather a collection either in a large, shallow bowl or grow them in a group, in matching individual pots, on a shelf or window sill. You'll find that there are so many shapes to mix and match with these fascinating plants.

Bushy Plants

Bushy plants are perhaps the most popular of all. Due to their adaptability, they also make ideal house gifts, since among this group there are plants that suit all light levels, as well as those glorious flowering orbs of chrysanthemums and tuberous begonias that delight for so many weeks. Within this range of plant shapes there is also a myriad of foliage, rather than flower interest, that you can choose to form the mainstay of your plant display. Consider the interest that a well-grown schefflera (*Brassaia actinophylla*) or aralia (*Fatsia japonica*), with their distinctive leaves, will contribute to your display. These bushy plants can fill an empty corner and remain in place for years. On a smaller scale, popular lady's-mantle (*Alchemilla mollis*) can form a dense mound of low-growing foliage that fits beautifully into a hanging basket or bowl and looks great when placed on a table on the patio.

Trailing Plants

If you like to tinker with your plants, include trailing plants in your collection. You will get hours of pleasure training an English ivy (*Hedera helix*) over a wire frame into a dense, bushy tripod, ball, or animal shape, rather than letting it run riot. However, trailing plants such as grape ivy (*Cissus* spp.), Swedish ivy (*Plectranthus australis*), or syngonium (*Syngonium podophyllum*) have some valuable uses indoors and many are particularly hardy, having learnt to survive in dense, dimly lit, tropical forests. If floor space is limited you can use them to form spheres of overhead foliage, and they make great hanging basket specimens in bathrooms, since they relish the steamy atmosphere. You can easily nip off trailing stems as they dangle toward the floor to create a more compact plant.

Poinsettia

Climbing Plants

Don't be discouraged from growing true climbing plants indoors because, while they can ramble unfettered outdoors in the garden, you can contain them indoors

The trailing strawberry plant looks lovely cascading over the sides of a hanging basket.

by twisting their supple stems around a totem or through a wire support to the height you require, nipping off any wayward shoots to encourage more bushy growth.

Creeping Plants

In a small container you'll be able to grow low-growing, creeping plants. Plants such as baby's tears (*Soleirolia soleirolii*), with its fine foliage, are often used in terrariums or grown as a living mulch to give interest to a container of taller plants.

Whatever shape you choose for your plant, a container needs to be found to complement it. If it's a case of finding a plant to suit your favorite container, take the container along to the garden center to be sure of a perfect match.

Place climbing wax vine (*Hoya carnosa*) in a container next to a trellis that it can cling to.

All About Leaves

When browsing through the plant display at your local garden center, you can't fail to notice a wonderful collection of foliaged plants. It can be quite overwhelming when it comes to making a selection. First, you'll notice that the plant display people have cleverly arranged their stock so that the leaves of plants complement one another, making it almost impossible for you to choose just one plant to take home.

There is such a huge variety of leaf size, shape, and texture—let alone the color variations. The leaves with the really interesting shapes are more likely to be found in the indoor plant section because foliage plants can flourish in lower light conditions. But don't let that faze you, for many of these beauties can be used on shaded patios in warmer climates. And there are plenty of outdoor plants with exquisite and decorative leaves.

Leaf Size

The size of individual leaves varies from the tiny green dots of baby's tears (*Soleirolia soleirolii*) to the outsized leaves of fiddle-leaf fig (*Ficus lyrata*). Use the plants alone and they look good, but when you combine the baby's tears as a groundcover below the fig you'll notice how these opposing-sized leaves complement each other and double the impact. Don't

limit yourself, though. Think even bigger. If space permits, think of the drama you can introduce with arching fern fronds, which cast some marvelous shadows when backlit by the early morning sun, or a well-placed spotlight. Although large in overall size, these graceful fronds, holding a series of filigreed leaflets, don't overwhelm,

Succulent leaves come in a vast array of shapes, and are fleshy so they can store water.

whereas a dense leaf surface of a similar size might be too dominant for your space.

You'll notice, too, that the larger leaves tend to be more eye-catching than a pot plant full of small green leaves on its own, so don't be shy in using these flamboyant leaves as part of an exuberant scheme, regardless of whether you are decorating an indoor room or an outdoor area.

Leaf Shape

But it's not only size that counts— there are many variations in shape that add zing to a display. If you want a single container plant to dominate, try using a plant with large, unusually shaped, eyecatching leaves. Or, if you want plants to blend into the background of a room or patio, look for smaller sized, inconspicuous leaves. You'll be amazed

Bracken fern

Leaves offer year-round interest and, indoors where light levels are low for flowers, foliage plants are the best choice.

Variegated holly

Aucuba

how you can alter your visual space by just using this simple know-how.

Consider deep green, strappy leaves, such as those of clivia (*Clivia miniata*), or the slender leaves of irises, when you want to give height to a display. The diverse shapes of herb leaves can create a decorative, as well as practical, display near the kitchen door, or on a sunny windowsill indoors.

Botanists have scientific names for all leaf shapes to help them identify plants. But you'll get by just fine if you choose a plant because you like its leaves, whether they have saw-toothed edges, are perforated, fan-shaped, or fernlike.

Leaf Color

Another thing you'll notice about leaves is the huge range of color variations. There are many shades of green, from deep, dark, and glossy greens, to bright and cheerful emeralds—not to mention the blue-gray colorings of plants that revel in the outdoor sun. Also let's not forget all the dazzling multi-colored hues.

Who needs flowers when you can have the exquisite combinations of leaf colors of coleus (*Solenostemon scutellarioides*), the yellows and reds of the tropical crotons (*Codiaeum variegatum* var. *pictum*), or the spectacular fall display of the maples (*Acer palmatum*)? You'll find the variegations of creamy yellow and green leaves a great help in brightening up dark areas. Japanese aucuba (*Aucuba japonica*), creeping lilyturf (*Liriope spicata*), and some hosta hybrids can be used to great effect, since the splashes of pale colorings on their leaves help to reflect light and therefore lighten up a shady, dark area of the garden.

A note of caution, though, in using these colorful plants—one or two mottled, spotted, veined, or otherwise variegated leaves in a display of container plants is usually sufficient. If you use too many, you will lose the surprise effect.

Maple leaf

ABOVE: When planning color theme plantings, don't forget to consider the colorful leaves of plants like coleus.

Leaf Texture

If you are building up a collection of plants with interesting foliage, try to include some with unusual textures. If you garden indoors, scout around and find peperomias (*Peperomia* spp.), which have a variety of textures from flat and smooth to puckered and wrinkled. For outdoors there is the wonderful lamb's-ears (*Stachys byzantina*), with its silvery coating of tiny hairs which gives the leaves a velvety feel.

Scented Foliage

One of the joys of a potted garden is that you can have your favorite scented-leaved plants in positions where their perfume can be appreciated during the heat of the day or as you brush past them. Try some rosemary (*Rosmarinus officinalis*),

RIGHT: Bold, variegated leaf patterns are a delightful foil for brightly colored spring bulbs, such as daffodils.

lavender (*Lavandula angustifolia*), or scented geraniums (*Pelargonium* spp.), if your containers are in full sun, otherwise mints will give you pleasure as you nip their tips to use in cooking.

Caring for Foliage

Most container plants, regardless of whether they are houseplants or outdoor plants, retain their leaves for a long period, so the larger the leaf surface, the more evident any disfiguration will be. You'll need to keep a sharp eye out for pests. And remember, if you've placed an indoor plant on the balcony overnight to catch a shower of rain, bring it back inside, otherwise you may come home the following evening to find that its beautiful leaves have been scorched by the sun. A better practice is to wipe the large leaves of an indoor plant over with a dampened paper towel once or twice a week, and just leave them safely indoors whatever the weather.

RIGHT: The aromatic leaves of mint are popular for their strong, fresh fragrance.

The Beauty of Flowers

Pansies (*Viola* x *wittrockiana*) have heart-shaped flowers with layers of soft, lobed petals.

There are no two ways about it—plants with flowers are always way ahead in the beauty stakes, no matter what their size, color, or shape may be. These are the plants you'll want to place in and around your home to brighten up a winter's day or to surround you when you are sitting outdoors in the courtyard or on the balcony during the summer months. By choosing a flowering plant, rather than simply arranging a vase of flowers, you'll get many more weeks of color for your dollar, with many plants giving another show same time next year!

Experiment with Color

Color is the first thing you'll notice about a flowering plant, especially in those colorful pots that catch your eye when you visit the garden center. These beauties—annuals such as pansies (*Viola* x *wittrockiana*), petunias (*Petunia* x *hybrida*), or begonias (*Begonia* Semperflorens-Cultorum hybrids)—give you weeks of instant color. But don't limit your choice. Grow more permanent plants, such as shrubs or trees, that produce flowers each season. Or select perennials or bulbs that you can mix and match as they come into seasonal flower.

Color know-how makes container gardening fun. It's simple to create a color scheme with pots. You can experiment with warm colors like oranges, reds, and hot pinks during winter; in summer, try mixing various shades of blue flowers to create a cool atmosphere. You'll also want to include white flowers in your palette, since these seem to glow and brighten up shady areas.

By choosing flowers that will bloom at different times you'll never be without color in your life. And when you buy a pot of instant color, don't forget to select one that has many buds.

Consider Flower Shape

Flowers come in all sorts of shapes and sizes. Plant breeders are constantly enhancing the shape of flowers to give us more ruffles and more petals—as well as larger-sized blooms. And this feast isn't only available in the indoor plant range— you'll find your favorite annuals, bulbs, and perennials (even roses) have all been touched by the same wand. You can't fail to notice the bold and brassy amaryllis (*Hippeastrum* hybrids), with their outsized, colorful trumpets sitting on top of a single stem, or the increasingly decorative shapes of the newer kinds of tulips.

But there are many flowers that have evolved naturally—to catch the eye of particular insects, birds, or moths. Some of these are showy performers; others have to be viewed up close to reveal their magic. Take for instance the lovely mountain laurel (*Kalmia latifolia*), whose flattened bells are held in bunches. It is really only when you can look closely at each single blossom and bud that you fully realize its delicate beauty. Or you can grow a pot of lavender cotton (*Santolina chamaecyparissus*), with its tight, yellow balls seemingly floating atop the gray foliage during summer. Other plants form star-shaped flowers or pea-like flowers, or magnificent urn shapes (such as the magnolias), while daisies have a ring of petals radiating from the

Shasta daisy

LEFT: The tall colorful, flower spikes of plants such as lupins (shown) or delphiniums, always stand out in a garden display or container.

center to entice their pollinators to land. There is a diverse range of shapes that we can use for our container gardens.

Apart from the individual flower shapes, there are plants with profusions of tiny, perfectly formed flowers, such as baby's breath (*Gyposphila paniculata*), which can act as a background foil for their bolder cousins. There are also plants that produce arching canes or long spikes that display a myriad of blooms to complement their green leaves. These long-stemmed specimens—among them the Cymbidium orchids, delphiniums, and lobelia (*Lobelia cardinalis*)—can add a new dimension to your container collection. This is not so important when only one

Fuchsia flowers are pendant, single or double blooms, often in two or more colors.

The unusual flowers of ladies' purse, or slipper flower, (*Calceolaria* spp.) have a bulbous lower lip.

plant is being selected, but you'll end up with a more interesting display if you keep this in mind when grouping plants. Mix and match is the name of the game.

The Bonus of Perfume

Scented flowers are ideal for container gardening. You can place the container in a position where you can appreciate the perfume. For the best of both worlds— beauty and scent—you'll be hard pressed to go past roses (*Rosa* spp.). Luckily, roses are now sold all year round—not just when they are dormant—so you will be able to smell them when you buy. Roses like lots of sunshine, though, so if you don't have a sunny garden, look instead for a daphne (*Daphne cneorum*), gardenia (*Gardenia jasminoides*), or a fragrant climber, such as a sweet pea (*Lathyrus odoratus*), stephanotis (*Stephanotis floribunda*), or star jasmine (*Trachelospermum jasminoides*).

Flower Care

By picking off dead or fading flowers (a process known as deadheading), you can prolong the flowering of many plants and lengthen your garden display. This is particularly good for annuals, since these plants have one aim in life and that is to set seed before the cold weather arrives. Many perennials with individual flowers that grow along

long stems can have the older, fading flowers at the lower section pinched off. And we all know that picking a rose for the house encourages the bush to produce more sumptuous blooms.

Edible Flowers

There is a bonus with some flowering plants. Nasturtiums (*Tropaeolum majus*) and daylilies (*Hemerocallis* spp.), among others, have edible flowers. You can cut the surplus blooms and use them to decorate a salad.

Sweet pea

Gardenia

Tulip

When selecting flowers for containers, you can't go wrong with old favorites such as tulips, gardenias, sweet peas, and roses.

Rose

The Basics of Healthy Houseplants

Indoor plants depend on us to meet all their needs—adequate light, a suitable temperature range and level of humidity, and the right amount of water and nutrients. However, you can easily achieve good results if you select your plants wisely and take a little time to understand their basic requirements, as well as ensure you establish a routine to provide the necessary care and conditions.

Discovering Houseplants

Most common houseplants are truly easy to grow if you understand their basic needs for light, water, and fertilizer. Even the blackest thumb can grow a drought-tolerant jade plant or ponytail palm. But why settle for just the most common, easiest plants when there is a wonderful world of colorful flowers, sparkling variegated leaves, dramatic cacti, and exotic orchids waiting for you to explore? Whatever time and skills you have and whatever the conditions in your home, there are dozens of beautiful houseplants that you can grow!

You need to start off by learning how to choose the right plants to suit the conditions in your home, as explained in "Buying the Best Plants" below. Once you bring your plants home, giving them the right amount of light is probably the single biggest key to keeping them healthy and happy. "Provide the Right Light" on page 36 will help you to understand how to estimate how much light each location receives, so you can pick the ideal location for each plant.

Many houseplants can grow just fine in the temperatures and humidity levels found in the average home, but some need special treatment. If you choose a fern that needs high humidity, for example, there are special techniques you can use to give it a more humid environment. "Humidity and Temperature" on page 38 will tell you what you need to know about these important factors.

Buying the Best Plants

Let's face it. If you're out shopping, you see a houseplant you like, and the price is right, you're probably going to bring it home. It may not be the best way to get the perfect plant to match the conditions in your home, but most of the time it works out just fine. Check the plant tag, or look up the plant in "A Guide to Popular Houseplants," starting on page 132; then find a site in your home that can provide the right growing conditions.

If, on the other hand, you want a plant that will thrive in a particular location, you need to be more careful to choose just the right one. A little advance planning is especially helpful if you intend to buy a large (and therefore more expensive) plant.

Estimate the Light

Your first step in buying the right plant is to consider how much light is available in the location you've chosen. Unless you're planning to place the plant directly in front of a large south, east, or west window, you should avoid buying

Plant-shopping Guidelines

When you're looking for just the right plant for a particular spot, remember to keep these key points in mind:

- Decide where you want the new plant to grow and estimate the light level available in that location.
- Browse through the entries in "A Guide to Popular Houseplants," starting on page 132, and make a list of plants you like that have light requirements that match the conditions you can provide. (Or you can check the tags on the plants as you shop to see if the ones you like can take the conditions you can offer.)
- Shop around for the best color and size selection and prices.
- Choose a well-shaped plant. When buying a flowering houseplant, also look for one that has plenty of buds, with just a few flowers beginning to open.
- Be sure there are no signs of insect or disease problems before you buy. You don't want to take home any problems that could spread to your other plants!

Flowering maple

houseplants that need bright light or direct sun. Instead, stick with those that only need medium light. Flowering plants require more light than plants grown only for their attractive foliage, so if you're expecting flowers, it's especially important to be sure the plant gets enough light. If you have to place a plant well away

LEFT: When shopping for plants it is important to select plants that suit the conditions in your home. BELOW: It helps to combine houseplants that have similar light and watering requirements.

from the windows, try to select a plant that can tolerate low light levels. (For details on estimating light levels, see "Provide the Right Light" on page 36.)

Do a Little Research

Once you've estimated the light levels available in the location you've chosen, turn to "The Right Houseplant for the Right Place" on page 68, and make a list of plants suitable for your chosen location. Look up each of the plants listed in "A Guide to Popular Houseplants,"

starting on page 132, and use the color photographs to help you decide which plants you like best. Jot down the names of your favorites.

Now that you know what you're looking for, you can shop around a little. Prices can vary a lot, especially for large plants, so it's worth investigating several sources; check out the garden centers, florists, and grocery stores in your area. Talk to the employees and find someone who can help you make a good plant selection.

When you've decided exactly which kind of plant you're going to buy and where you're going to buy it, look over all the plants of that type that the seller offers. Some plants will have a nicer overall shape than others; look for those that you find most appealing. Once you decide which plant you want, inspect it closely for any signs of insect or disease problems before you take it home. (For specific tips on identifying common problems, see "Handling Pests and Diseases" on page 48.)

Consider Flowering Habits

If you're buying a flowering plant, there are some factors to consider. First of all, be aware that many flowering houseplants are grown under special controlled conditions in commercial greenhouses and are not likely to rebloom for you next year unless you have a greenhouse or can give them special care. Some, such as Persian violet (*Exacum affine*), are actually annuals that won't live more than a year or so, even with the best care.

Even though they can be relatively short-lived, flowering plants are still a good choice for brightening up indoor spaces. Live flowering plants will last at least two to three times longer than cut flowers, and some—including florist's cyclamen (*Cyclamen persicum*), orchids, and African violets (*Saintpaulia* hybrids)—will bloom nonstop for many months. So go ahead and feel confident to bring flowering plants home to enjoy; just don't feel like it's your fault if they don't bloom again next year.

When you are choosing a flowering houseplant, always try to pick one that has lots of buds, with just a few already open. That way you'll get the maximum bloom time as the unopened buds bloom over the next several weeks.

Provide the Right Light

When you're growing plants indoors, light is the factor you need to consider most carefully. Indoor light—whether it comes from sunlight coming in through the windows or from artificial electric lights—is nowhere near as bright as the sunlight that plants receive when they're growing outdoors. The light in a room may seem almost as bright as sunlight, but in reality it's usually only about one-tenth as bright. (The brightness seems similar to us because the pupils in our eyes open wider to make the dim light appear brighter.)

Healthy Plant Checklist

In the fun and frenzy of spring plant shopping, it's easy to overlook quality in the quest for getting the "perfect" plant. But as you choose, keep in mind that bringing home a stressed, diseased, or pest-infested plant is a recipe for disappointing results. Before you pay for your purchases, take a minute to check them over carefully—following the points here—to make sure you're getting the best plants possible.

1. **Peruse the plant.** It should be similar in size and color to other plants of the same type. Avoid plants that seem stunted or off-color.
2. **Look at the leaves.** Avoid plants that have yellowed leaves or brown tips (signs of improper watering). Carefully turn over a few leaves and check the undersides for signs of pest infestation. Avoid plants with tiny white insects that fly up when you move the leaves (whiteflies); clusters of small, pear-shaped insects (aphids); or yellow-stippled leaves with tiny webs underneath (caused by spider mites).
3. **Check the stems.** The stems should be stocky and evenly colored, with no visible cuts, bruises, or pests.
4. **Inspect the roots.** It's okay if a few roots are coming out of the drainage holes at the bottom of the container. However, masses of tangled roots indicate that the plant is long overdue for transplanting. Overgrown plants can be saved if you loosen or remove some of the matted roots at transplanting time, but it's better to start off with younger plants if you have a choice.

Entrance halls look welcoming if decorated with plants. However, they are often low in light. Plan your displays using the most tolerant houseplants.

low-light plants. To identify plants suitable for the varying light intensities in your home, see "The Right Houseplant for the Right Place" on page 68.

There are several things besides direction that affect the amount of light coming in through a window. A very large east-facing window might actually be brighter than a small, south-facing one. Shade from trees may make a west-facing window more like a northern one. Fortunately, most houseplants are very adaptable. Your plants should do fine, as long as you do your best to match the right plant to the right window.

If you're the type of person who feels more comfortable with a little more precision, you can buy an inexpensive light meter, which will measure the actual amount of light at any given spot. These meters usually measure light in units known as "foot-candles" and come with a chart that tells you how many foot-candles various plants require.

Place Plants Properly

Matching your plants to the best available windows is important, but placing each plant so it's right up near the glass is probably even more important than having the right window.

The intensity of light drops off very rapidly as it enters the room, so a plant even a few feet from the window will get only half as much light as it would if you kept it right next to the window.

If your windowsills are too narrow to hold plants, consider adding a shelf to make the sill wider, or place a table in front of the window so you can set plants on it. Keep the windows clean and remove any sheer curtains that might cut down the light intensity.

ABOVE LEFT: Sunrooms are not only attractive places for humans to relax, but they also provide the ideal conditions for a wide range of plants, being warm, light, and airy.
LEFT: Flower production takes lots of energy, so blooming plants generally need all the light that they can get. A sunny window is an ideal spot.

Most common houseplants have become popular precisely because they can tolerate the lower light conditions found inside our homes. As long as you know whether a plant prefers low, medium, or high light, you'll do just fine in providing the right conditions.

Find the Right Spot

South-facing windows let in the most light, and most houseplants will flourish there. Although east and west exposures don't provide as many hours of bright light as south windows, many bright-light lovers (and all plants that need medium light) will grow well in most east- or west-facing windows. Save north-facing windows for

Move Plants to Manage Light Levels

There may be times when you want to position a plant in a spot that you know doesn't provide enough light for it. For example, say you buy a spectacular flowering azalea and you really want to keep it on the dining-room table where everyone can enjoy it. You can usually get away with this for a week or so; then you will need to move the plant back into the brighter light next to a window. Most plants won't suffer much from such a procedure. Obviously, the lower the plant's light needs, the longer it can tolerate a dim location.

Another way to keep plants thriving in low light locations is to rotate two plants between the dark location and a bright window every few weeks or so. That way you get to enjoy a plant right where you want it all the time, and the two plants will get enough light to thrive. This is how shopping malls and offices keep their plants looking so good: The plants are moved back to a greenhouse periodically to recuperate, then they go back to the mall or office.

By the way, placing a plant close to an incandescent light bulb doesn't help much, but there are other types of lights that work very well for growing houseplants if your window space is limited. For more information, see "Gardening under Lights" on page 56.

Humidity and Temperature

Although humidity levels and temperature levels are not as critical for good growth as light intensity or proper watering, they can have an effect on the health and vigor of your plants.

Handling Humidity

Almost all houseplants will grow better if you can give them higher humidity levels than those found in the average home. Indoor air is usually much drier than outdoor air, especially during the

Is Your Plant Getting the Right Light?

If your plant isn't getting the right light, it may show symptoms that tell you it needs a new location. Sometimes, you may notice that plants growing in bright windows develop a yellowy tinge or white or brown patches on the leaves that get the most sun. This may mean the plant is getting too much light. This doesn't happen often with houseplants, but it could be a problem if you put a low-light plant like a Chinese evergreen (*Aglaeonema* spp.) directly in a south-facing window. If these symptoms occur, move the plant away from the window.

The opposite problem—plants not getting enough light—is far more common. A plant trying to grow where there's not enough light will gradually become leggy and spindly, and its lower leaves may turn yellow and drop off. Or the plant may just sit, not putting out any new growth at all.

If you notice that a plant is not growing, or if there's new growth but it looks weak and spindly, try moving the plant to a brighter location in your home.

Some plants, such as weeping fig (*Ficus benjamina*), may drop a lot of their leaves when you first bring them home. This is because they were probably grown outside in very bright light. When you move them to the much dimmer interior of your home, they simply don't need as many leaves because there isn't as much light, so they drop them. Don't be alarmed at this. Keep the plant in the brightest location you have, water it moderately, and wait for it to adjust. It should stop dropping leaves after a few weeks. If a plant continues to drop leaves or grow poorly, consider moving it to a brighter spot. Too often when houseplants grow poorly, people give them more water or fertilizer thinking that will solve the problem. Some plants do drop leaves when their soil is dry. But if the real cause is low light, extra water or fertilizer is the last thing they need.

Aglaeonema 'Silver Queen'

Weeping fig

winter when heating systems drive away moisture. Summer air-conditioning also creates dry indoor air.

In general, plants with thin, delicate leaves tend to be more sensitive to low humidity, while plants such as Chinese evergreens (*Aglaeonema* spp.), with their thick, waxy leaves, can tolerate typical home humidity levels. There are some plants on the market, such as bird's nest fern (*Asplenium nidus*), that look great at

the store (because they just came from a greenhouse) but usually grow poorly in most homes unless you provide extra humidity. Always check the label and avoid buying a plant that needs extra humidity, unless you just like it so much that you want to give it that extra care.

You can buy an inexpensive humidity gauge (at hardware stores) to monitor the water vapor in the air. Most plants thrive in humidity levels similar to those humans

A pebble tray—a shallow tray filled with pebbles and some water—is a great way to provide a more humid atmosphere for your indoor plants.

To provide extra humidity for indoor herbs, place a layer of pebbles in a bowl, add enough water to cover the pebbles, and set the pot on top.

Humidifiers If you happen to have a room humidifier or an automatic humidifier installed in your heating or air-conditioning system, you'll be able to raise the humidity in the whole growing area of your home. Both you and your plants will be very comfortable year-round.

The Right Temperature

Most common houseplants prefer typical home temperatures of around 65°F (18°C) during the day and 55° to 60°F (12° to 15°C) at night. However, some need cooler temperatures during part of the year. Certain flowering plants, such as azaleas and camellias (*Camellia japonica*), won't bloom well unless you give them a period of cooler temperatures. Check "A Guide to Popular Houseplants," starting on page 132, to find out the temperature preferences of each kind of plant.

like—around 40 to 60 percent humidity. It's more likely, however, that the humidity in your house is below this. In winter, in fact, it may be as low as only 10 or 20 percent (which is as dry as a desert!).

Symptoms of low humidity include brown leaf tips and edges and leaf curling. If you notice these signs, consider the following techniques for increasing humidity levels for your plants.

Grouping Plants One way to increase humidity is to cluster your houseplants together. This happens naturally when you place plants in groups near windows. As the leaves release water vapor, the extra moisture creates a more humid microclimate for the plants. Using clay pots instead of plastic also helps a little

because water vapor evaporates from the sides of the clay pots.

Misting Some people like to mist their plants directly to increase humidity, and this does help a little. However, as soon as the mist evaporates, the humidity level will drop. Misting plants so heavily that water stands on the leaves is not good, either, since that can lead to disease problems. If you decide to mist, do it during daytime hours and do it lightly.

Pebble Trays A better choice than misting is to grow houseplants on trays containing pebbles and water. You can use any kind of saucers or shallow trays to hold the water—plastic cafeteria-type trays work well; even baking sheets are fine. Set the plants on a 1- to 2-inch (2.5- to 5- cm) layer of pebbles or gravel. Add enough water to bring the water level just below the top of the pebbles. (You don't want the bottom of the pots to be sitting in water.) Moisture will evaporate steadily from the trays and rise to increase humidity around the plants' leaves. This is a very effective way to raise humidity levels, and humidity-loving plants like ferns will definitely benefit if you grow them over these water-filled trays.

Grouping plants helps to keep the humidity levels adequate.

Defining Light Levels

What exactly do "high light," "medium light," and "low light" mean? Check the descriptions below to see which apply best to your available conditions.

- **High Light** Areas directly in front of most south-facing windows and large, unobstructed east or west windows. These locations will usually provide between 4 and 6 hours of direct sun per day.
- **Medium Light** Areas directly in front of unobstructed small or medium-sized east or west windows. Plants will also get medium light from partly shaded, large south, east, or west windows.
- **Low Light** North windows and other windows shaded by large trees, porches, buildings, or awnings. Low light also applies to all locations more than a few feet away from windows.

Caring for Houseplants

Well-designed containers can give you a garden's worth of beauty in a relatively small space.

All the elements of a houseplant's environment must be in balance to ensure continuing health and growth. An understanding of how the plant grows and how light, watering, and fertilizing affect plants will help you to determine which plants are right for your home.

Some people have trouble knowing how much to water their plants, and too much or too little water can spell trouble. But with the tips and techniques covered in "Watering Wisely" below, you'll know exactly when to water and when to wait.

The foundation of organic gardening is nutrient-rich, disease-preventing compost. You'll want to combine compost with slow-release organic fertilizers to feed your houseplants. In "Fertilizing for Healthy Growth" on page 42, you'll find out how to mix your own fertilizers using household wastes such as coffee grounds and wood ashes, along with products such as bonemeal and bloodmeal.

As your houseplants thrive, they will eventually outgrow their containers. "Potting and Repotting" on page 43 will tell you how to know when repotting is in order and exactly how to do it.

Another aspect of keeping your houseplants in peak condition is covered in "Grooming and Pruning" on page 44.

This section covers basic plant pruning techniques that you can use to keep plants vigorous but still compact and well shaped.

When you find out how much fun and how rewarding it is to grow gorgeous, vigorous houseplants, you'll probably want to expand your collection. In "Making More Plants" on page 45, you'll learn all the basics of propagating your existing stock to fill every part of your home with lush and lovely houseplants.

Light

Light is as important as water to plants. Although a plant may not die through lack of light, it will not develop in the expected way. Windows facing north give an even light without direct sun throughout the year, while windows facing south give direct sunlight in winter, but less in summer. But during summer these windows are

A sunny south window is the perfect spot for cacti and succulents. A sunny east or west window could also be suitable.

too hot for all plants except cacti. Plants should be placed at least 3 feet (90 cm) from the window to prevent heat damage.

Windows facing west and east give the most direct sun on a year-round basis. East-facing windows can become as hot in summer as south-facing windows. How much light a plant receives also determines how much care is needed. A houseplant receiving high light during summer needs to be watered and fed more regularly than during winter when the light is less intense and photosynthesis slows.

Watering Wisely

Next to getting the light levels right, watering is probably the most important aspect of houseplant care. You can't just water this plant once a week and that one twice a week; there are too many different factors that will affect how much water a plant needs. If you understand what those factors are and how they increase or decrease your plants' water requirements, then you'll know what to expect and be

better able to give each plant the right amount of water.

The major factors that will affect how much water a certain plant needs include:

The plant's particular moisture preference. The entries in "A Guide to Popular Houseplants," starting on page 132, tell you if a plant needs dry conditions (as succulents and cacti do) or if it needs constantly moist soil (as many ferns prefer). Most houseplants fall in the middle and need a steady supply of moisture with the soil surface drying out between waterings.

The container the plant is growing in. Plants in terracotta or clay pots will dry out faster than those in plastic pots. Large plants growing in small pots will also need water more frequently. (That's one of the reasons plants need to be repotted into larger pots as they grow.)

The container mix the plant is growing in. Container mixes containing ample compost or peat moss will absorb and hold more moisture than mixes containing lots of sand.

The amount of light the plant gets. Plants growing in bright light need more water than those placed in dimmer areas.

The weather conditions. Plants will use much more water during bright, warm, summer periods when they are actively growing than in the winter, when the temperatures are cooler and the daylight hours are much shorter. They will also require very little water during sustained periods of cloudy weather.

Considering all these varying factors, it's easy to see why it's so important to check each plant's soil before you water.

When to Water

Your first clue about when to water should be the soil surface, which usually turns a lighter color when it's dry. If it's dark colored and damp, do not water.

If the surface is dry, you can use your finger to check the soil an inch or two

Reticulated irises

(2.5 to 5 cm) below the surface. If you still feel moisture, wait a day or two and test again. When that top layer feels dry, it's the right time to water.

Another way to check soil moisture is to lift the pot. You can tell immediately if the plant feels really light and thus needs water or if it feels relatively heavy, in which case you should wait a few more days before you water. This technique works especially well for small to medium-sized plants in lightweight plastic pots.

Some pots are just too big to lift, and the soil near the surface may dry out while there's still plenty of moisture deeper in the soil. Always check for moisture several inches deep in large pots; if you go only by whether the soil surface is dry, you could easily overwater. When in doubt, always underwater rather than risk giving too much water and thereby destroying the roots.

How to Water

Once you're sure a plant needs watering, water it thoroughly so a little water runs out into the saucer under it. When you apply more water than the soil can absorb, the excess flows out the bottom into the saucer. This flow of water through the soil, similar to what happens in the garden when it rains, serves an important function in container plants. As the water runs through the mix, it pushes out used air and allows fresh air to move into the spaces between the soil particles. (Plant roots need both water and air to thrive. That's why it's so important to have a loose, well-drained container mix and to always water thoroughly.)

Always use pots with drainage holes, and always put saucers under them. Without drainage holes, it's too easy to overwater and make the soil soggy. (The excess water trapped in a pot without

Signs of Overwatering and Underwatering

Overwatering is just as bad for your plants as underwatering—maybe even worse. When plants are too dry, their leaves will droop, so at least you have a clue that they need to be watered (although it's best to water just before leaves start to droop).

When plants are kept too wet, you may see the same symptom—drooping leaves—but it will be because the roots are rotted and the plant can no longer obtain the food and water it needs from the container mix. If this happens, your plant may or may not recover; your only hope is to reduce watering and cross your fingers.

Underwatered, wilted plants

drainage holes could cause the roots to rot and the plant to die.) And if you don't have a saucer under the plant, you'll be tempted to underwater to avoid having water run out the bottom and make a mess.

Occasionally when you water, you may notice that the water seems to be running rapidly through the soil and out the bottom without being absorbed by the soil. When this happens, you've let the soil get too dry. When container mix dries out, it shrinks away from the sides of the pot, leaving space where water can run right through. To water a dried-out pot, you need to set the entire pot in a bowl or sink full of water up to the pot's rim and let the soil slowly absorb the water. After the soil is thoroughly rewetted, let the pot drain, then return it to its saucer.

Water-quality Considerations

Not all water is suitable for houseplants. The chlorine in our drinking water doesn't seem to harm plants, although some gardeners like to let tap water sit overnight so the chlorine evaporates. Fluorine, on the other hand, has been shown to cause slight damage to some plants. If you use city water that has fluorine added, then you might want to collect rainwater and use it. Home water softeners add salts to the water, so avoid using soft water; otherwise, the salts can build up to toxic levels in the soil.

If you have water that is naturally hard or alkaline, it may eventually cause the pH of the container mix to become too high. (pH is a measure of how acid or alkaline the soil is. A pH below 7.0 is acid; a pH above 7.0 is alkaline. Most plants grow best when the soil pH stays around neutral, between pH 6.0 to 7.5.) You can offset the effects of hard water by using compost in your container mix and adding vinegar to your watering solution once a month. (Use 1 tablespoon of vinegar per gallon [4.5 l] of water, and water as usual.) The pH level is more important for some plants than others; check the entries in "A Guide to Popular Houseplants," starting on page 132, to find out if the plant you're growing has specific pH preferences for healthy growth.

Watering for Vacations

If you'll be away for more than a few days, there are several techniques you can use to get extra water to your plants. If you're only going to miss one of your usual watering days, you can water the plants thoroughly and add some extra water to the saucers. (While you shouldn't make a habit of leaving water standing in the saucers, it's okay to do it occasionally.)

If you're going to be gone for more than just a few days, you can set your plants up to be wick-watered. To do this, use a strip of nylon pantyhose, a rolled-up paper towel, or some other absorbent material for the wick. Insert one end of the wick into the bottom of the pot, making sure it makes good contact with the container mix, then run the other end into a container of water. Recycled margarine tubs with lids work well for small plants; just cut a hole in the lid, fill the tub with water, run the wick down through the hole, and set the plant on top of the reservoir. Capillary action will draw water up along the wick and into the container. (This method also works well year-round for plants that need constant moisture, such as gardenias and ferns.)

Fertilizing for Healthy Growth

If you want your houseplants to thrive, you have to give them food as well as water. The best organic fertilizers for houseplants are the same ones that work well outside—bloodmeal, bonemeal, and fish and seaweed products.

A wick-watering setup is a handy way to water plants if you're going on a long vacation.

A drip irrigation system is an easy and effective way to water your indoor container plants.

You can also use household "wastes" such as wood ashes and coffee grounds. But the first item on your fertilizer list should always be compost, which is the organic gardener's secret for success.

Compost is especially good for pot plants because it releases nutrients slowly over time, just the way plants growing in the wild receive their nutrients. Compost will never burn roots or cause major salt buildup like synthetic chemical fertilizers. Plus, compost doesn't just feed your plants—it prevents disease and improves the structure of the soil, so air and water can reach the roots better. Ample compost also helps the soil retain moisture, so you won't have to water as often. Compost also contains the major plant nutrients nitrogen, phosphorus, and potassium, plus minor nutrients and trace elements not provided by chemical fertilizers.

If you aren't already making your own compost, consider starting. It's easy. And if you can't make your own compost, check with your local government—many communities are now composting yard wastes and offering the compost free to anyone who wants it.

A Simple Program for Feeding Houseplants

Use compost whenever you pot up a new plant or re-pot an old one, adding up to 1 part compost for every 3 or 4 parts container mix. Each spring thereafter, take your plants to a sink or bathtub and water them heavily with warm water until water runs steadily out the bottom for a few minutes. This leaches out any harmful salts, which can build up over time. It's a good idea to do this once a year, but you should also do it anytime you notice a crusty deposit in the saucers or around the pot rims. Rinse the leaves thoroughly, too.

After you've completed the spring leaching treatment, add a ½- to 1-inch (12- to 25-mm) layer of fresh compost to all of the pots. (If there's not room in the pot, just wash away some of the soil with a hose.) Mix a small amount of a balanced organic fertilizer into the compost before you apply it to the pots. That should feed

If you notice a white crust or buildup, run water through the soil to leach out the harmful salts.

most plants well into midsummer. (Check the fertilizer packages for guidelines.)

Most houseplants will be getting much more light during the summer than in the winter, so a couple of months after the spring compost/fertilizer treatment, begin feeding them about once a month with a half-strength liquid fish fertilizer. The fish fertilizer contains plenty of nitrogen, the nutrient most likely to be in short supply. It also contains the other major plant nutrients—phosphorus and potassium—and important trace elements. Keep feeding the plants until growth slows in

fall. Remember that too much fertilizer can be just as bad as too little. Go easy when you fertilize plants in dim locations, and don't fertilize at all during the short days of winter unless you have a plant that continues to grow actively then.

Potting and Repotting

Your houseplants will eventually need to be repotted, either because they grow too big for their pots or because they need to be moved into fresh container mix.

Generally, you should repot your plants about once every year or two in the spring or summer, when plants are actively growing. If they get too big for their pot, they can become "root-bound," which means they have grown so many roots that there's not enough container mix left to support further growth. Most (but not all) plants shouldn't be allowed to become root-bound. You can check to see how crowded the roots are becoming by lifting the plant and tapping the pot until it slips loose. Lift out the plant to examine the rootball. If you see lots of soil with some roots, all is well. But if you see mostly roots and little soil, it's time to repot.

How to Repot a Houseplant

You have a choice when you repot—you can move the plant to a larger pot size, or you can keep the plant in the same pot. If

Understanding Organic Fertilizers

The three major nutrients plants need most are nitrogen (N), phosphorus (P), and potassium (K). Fertilizer labels carry these "N-P-K" numbers, which tell you the percent of each nutrient. Bonemeal, for example, typically has a ratio of 1-11-0, meaning it contains 1 percent nitrogen, 11 percent phosphorus, and no potassium.

To keep plants happy, you want a balance of all three. It doesn't have to be exactly 5-5-5 or 2-2-2, but try to get the numbers as similar as possible. For flowering plants, switch to a formula with more of the middle number (phosphorus) when it's time for the plant to set flower buds, since this will stimulate flowering. Foliage houseplants generally prefer a high-nitrogen formula, such as 5-3-3.

You can buy balanced organic fertilizers, or you can mix your own. Listed here are some common organic fertilizer materials. To determine the N-P-K ratio, add up the percent of each nutrient in the ingredients, and divide by the total number of parts to get the N-P-K ratio of the mixture. Say you combine 2 parts bloodmeal (2 x 11-1-1 = 22-2-2) with 1 part bonemeal (1-11-0) and 2 parts wood ashes (2 x 0-2-8 = 0-4-16). Add up each part of the ratios, and you get 23-17-18. Divide each part of the ratio by 5 (since you're using 5 equal parts of fertilizer), and you'll see that the resulting mix has an N-P-K ratio of 4.6-3.4-3.6, a good balance.

Bloodmeal: 11-1-1
Bonemeal: 1-11-0
Coffee grounds: 2-0.3-0.2
Compost: 0.5-0.5-0.5 to 2-2-2
Cottonseed meal: 6-2-1
Fish emulsion: 4-1-1
Granite dust: 0-0-4
Greensand: 0-2-7
Kelp meal: 1-0.5-2
Manures: 1-1-1 (typically)
Phosphate rock: 0-3-0
Tea leaves: 4-0.5-0.5
Wood ashes: 0-2-8

Feeding with liquid fertilizer

you want the plant to grow bigger and don't mind going to a larger container, choose a new pot that's 1 to 2 inches (2.5 to 5 cm) in diameter larger for small to medium-sized plants, or 4 to 6 inches (10 to 15 cm) larger for bigger plants. (If you move a small plant into a very big pot, you run a risk that the excess soil around the plant's roots will stay too wet and cause the roots to rot.)

When you're moving a plant to a larger pot, add some container mix to the bottom—enough so that the soil level will be an inch or two (2.5 to 5 cm) below the pot rim when you set in the plant to allow room for watering. Then remove the plant from the pot it's growing in. Holding the base of the pot in one hand, lift the plant slightly and tap around the rim with your other hand to loosen the pot. Carefully lift the plant out and set it on the soil in the new pot. Then add container mix around the edges, using a trowel or stick to gently settle the soil around the root ball. That's it—it's as easy as one, two, three.

If you'd prefer to keep the same pot, remove the plant and shake away as much of the old soil from the roots as you can. If the plant's root ball is so dense and tangled

that the soil won't shake loose, use a large knife to slice away an inch or two (2.5 to 5 cm) of the root ball on all sides and the bottom. Add fresh container mix to the bottom of the pot, then set the trimmed plant back in and add fresh soil in the space you created around the sides. This root pruning allows you to keep the plant to a manageable size. If the plant itself can be pruned, trim it back a bit to bring the top into better balance with the reduced

If you see roots circling the outside of the root ball when you remove the plant from the container, it's time to do some repotting.

roots. (See "Grooming and Pruning" below for details on pruning.)

If you're repotting a very large plant, you may want to ask someone to help you. Removing the plant will be easier if you lay the container on its side, then carefully pull out the plant.

Container Mixes

You can use any commercial container mix for most houseplants, but your plants will grow much better if you add some compost and slow-release organic fertilizers before you plant. If you want to blend your own growing mix, see "Selecting Container Mixes" on page 22 for some recipes. There are a few plants that prefer special container mixes. Cacti and succulents, for instance, appreciate extra sand for drainage, while African violets (*Saintpaulia* spp.) thrive with extra peat moss for acidity and moisture retention. The entries in "A Guide to Popular Houseplants," starting on page 132, indicate if a plant has a preference.

Grooming and Pruning

It's natural for houseplants to lose some of their older leaves as they grow. Shrubby plants such as weeping fig (*Ficus benjamina*) may also shed leaves when they're moved to a new location, sometimes leaving a tangle of bare twigs in the center of the plant. If you spend a few minutes now and then trimming off these yellowing leaves or dead twigs, your houseplants will look much better.

Many houseplants don't require pruning beyond this grooming. If all of the leaves grow out from a single center or crown of the plant and there are no stems or branches (as on African violets

African violet

Repotting a Houseplant

Young, healthy plants grow quickly, and can soon fill their pots with roots. Once the roots have filled the pot, they can go through the drainage holes or over the surface of the soil. This makes the container mix dry out quickly. It's time to repot.

1. Choose a new pot that is slightly larger than the old one. Add a layer of container mix.

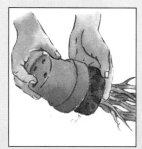

2. Carefully turn plant over onto one hand, and use the other to pull off the old pot.

3. Settle the plant at the same level in the new pot, and fill in around the sides with mix.

[*Saintpaulia* hybrids] and florist's cyclamen [*Cyclamen persicum*]), then you can't (and don't need to) prune the plant.

Trailing or vining plants (such as passionflowers [*Passiflora* spp.] or wandering Jew [*Zebrina pendula*]), on the other hand, benefit from pruning. Simply pinch or snip off unwanted leaves and stems with your fingers or scissors; use pruning shears to remove woodier stems cleanly.

There are three basic reasons to prune your houseplants, as follows:

Pruning for Shape Regular trimming improves a houseplant's appearance by eliminating any long, awkward stems or branches that grow out of proportion to the rest of the plant. Don't hesitate about this—cutting back gangly branches will help, not harm, the plant.

Pruning to Promote New Growth Pruning is also helpful to trailing plants, such as Swedish ivy (*Plectranthus australis*). Cutting back the growing tips causes the plant to put out more shoots and become bushier. You should always make your pruning cuts right above a side branch or leaf node (the spot where a leaf joins the stem). In many cases, the plant will produce two new stems from the cut point, leading to bushier, more attractive growth.

Pruning for Size Control Pruning is also helpful in keeping plants a manageable size. If a bushy plant, such as a citrus, has become larger than you want, you can prune it back hard, cutting off as much as a third of the leaves. In this way, you keep the top in balance with the roots without having to move the plant to a larger pot.

To find out about special pruning needs, refer to "A Guide to Popular Houseplants," starting on page 132.

Making More Plants

With just a few simple materials, you can propagate a wide variety of wonderful houseplants. Once you learn how to take cuttings, prepare

air layers, divide plants, and propagate from runners, you'll have dozens of new plants to expand your collection or give away.

Some plants can be reproduced several different ways; others propagate best with one particular technique. To find out what's recommended for your houseplant, check the entries in "A Guide to Popular Houseplants," starting on page 132.

Taking Stem Cuttings

It is possible to propagate most types of houseplants from stem cuttings. Remember to use very sharp secateurs, knives, or razor blades when making the cuts, since bruised or split stems may rot. It is a good idea to water the plant about 2 hours before taking cuttings, as this will ensure that the stems and leaves are moist. If you are taking cuttings from a flowering stem, gently pinch off the flowers first. Using hormone rooting powder on the cut end will speed up the process.

1. Select healthy, green growth and make a cut just above a leaf axil or node.

2. Trim the cutting just below the lowest leaf node and remove the lower leaves.

3. Make a hole with a stick in the container mix and plant the cutting in the new pot.

Taking Cuttings

Cuttings are pieces of stem (or sometimes just a single leaf) that can produce roots and grow into new plants. This is a fairly easy way to reproduce bushy or vining plants, such as ivies (*Hedera* spp.) and passionflowers (*Passiflora* spp.). Here's how:

1. Cut short pieces from the shoot tips of the plant, so there are about two nodes (those joints where the leaves come off the stem) below the three or four leaves on the shoot tip.
2. Remove the leaves from the two bottom nodes on the shoot.
3. Insert the base of the cutting in water or moist sand or vermiculite, so the two exposed nodes are covered. (You might want to try a few cuttings in each of these materials; different plants root better in some conditions than others.)
4. Slide a clear plastic bag over the pot of cuttings to keep the humidity high until the stems root.

Miniature roses bloom on new wood, so the plants will require regular trimming in order to promote fresh, new flowering growth.

Taking Leaf Cuttings

It is possible to propagate some plants by leaf cuttings. A whole leaf, together with some of the leaf stalk, is cut and then transplanted into slightly moist container mix. The new roots and shoots will develop from the cut end of the leaf stalk.

1. Remove a leaf and trim the leaf stalk to a length of about 1½ inches (3 cm).

2. Plant the leaf in the new pot, placing it in the soil at about a 45° angle.

3. Rest the leaf stalk against the side of the container to support the cutting.

5. It is best to place the cuttings in a warm, bright spot out of direct sunlight. Some cuttings root very quickly; others will take weeks. You can tell when roots have formed because the plant will begin to send out new growth. When this happens, replant the rooted cuttings into regular container mix and fertilize them.

Leaf Cuttings for Even More Plants

It's hard to believe that a single leaf—or even just a small piece of a leaf—can turn into a new plant, but it's true. Succulents such as jade plant (*Crassula argentea*) and burro's tail (*Sedum morganianum*) will readily sprout new plants from single leaves that fall from the main plant, if you know what to do. Just stick the fat, fleshy leaves halfway into sandy container mix and water them as usual. Soon you'll have a handsome crop of new succulents.

Other plants are not quite as simple to grow from leaf cuttings, but cape primrose (*Streptocarpus* hybrids) and rex begonia (*Begonia rex*) leaves can be pinned onto moist container mix after you make small cuts through the larger veins on the leaf. Keep the leaf moist by covering the pot loosely with plastic wrap, and tiny plants will eventually form at the cuts.

African violet (*Saintpaulia* hybrids) plants can be propagated from the leaf and a little of the stem, or from the leaf alone. The new plant can form either at the base of the stem or from the midrib of the leaf blade. To propagate African violets, make a diagonal cut at the base of the leaf and place the cutting in a growing medium containing half peat and half sand.

Air Layering

With air layering you create a root system on a stem or branch as it grows in the air. It is best to begin air layers in spring or early summer that are detached in fall when growth is dormant.

Air layering is also good for preventing some plants from getting out of control. Dracaenas (*Dracaena* spp.), dumbcane (*Dieffenbachia amoena*), rubber tree (*Ficus elastica*), and some other plants gradually grow taller until they reach the ceiling. You can prune these plants by simply cutting them back, but here's how to return this type of plant to a manageable height while also gaining some new houseplants for your collection:

1. First, get some fibrous sphagnum moss. The stuff you want is coarse, stringy, and light-colored. Moisten the moss well.

2. Make a shallow cut across the trunk where you want new roots to form—about a third of the way through, at an angle.

3. Press a little moss into the cut, then take a large handful of the damp moss and wad it around the trunk at the cut point.

4. Wrap the moss tightly with plastic wrap so it's held firmly in a ball all around the trunk. Secure the plastic-wrapped ball of moss with tape or twine.

5. Check the moss every few weeks to be sure it's still moist (open wrapping and add water if it isn't), and watch for roots. Eventually they'll become visible through the plastic. Depending on the plant, it can take 8 to 12 weeks for the roots to form.

6. When they seem well formed, cut off the plant just below the new roots, and pot up your new shorter plant. Keep in a cool shaded position for a couple of weeks until the plant has had time to adjust to its new environment.

The now topless trunk will reshoot or, if you'd like even more plants, you can cut pieces off the trunk, lay them sideways in a fresh container of container mix, and just barely cover them with more mix. The pieces will sprout new shoots and turn into new plants. Keep the remaining trunk base in the pot, and water it lightly; it too will sprout new leaves.

It is a good idea to cover a container of cuttings with a plastic bag to provide extra humidity.

Dividing

Division is one of the easiest ways of propagating. Plants with multiple stems that arise from the base of the plant are usually propagated this way. Division of indoor foliage plants should be carried out during early spring.

Some houseplants grow from a center point but produce additional offshoots as they grow, expanding into larger and larger clumps. The popular aloe plant (*Aloe vera*) grows this way; so do asparagus fern (*Asparagus densiflorus*) and moses-in-a-boat (*Rhoeo spathacea*).

How to propagate by division:
• Remove the plant from its container.
• Carefully shake some of the soil away so that the roots can be easily seen.
• The rootball can now be divided by using a sharp knife or simply by pulling it apart with your hands. However, be careful not to damage the roots.
• Repot the divisions immediately into a good-quality container mix.
• Place the divisions in a shaded position for at least two weeks until the plant has had time to recover. Water when the soil surface appears dry.

Plantlets or Runners

A runner is a specialized stem that develops from the axil of the leaf at the crown of a plant, grows horizontally along the ground, and forms a new plant at one of the nodes—spider plants (*Chlorophytum comosum*) and piggyback plants (*Tolmiea menziesii*), along with strawberries, are the most commonly known examples of this type of plant. These are easily propagated by placing a small pot, containing a good-quality container mix, next to the parent plant. Without severing the runner, lay the plantlet on the container mix in the new pot and hold it in place with a bobby pin. Sever it from the parent plant when new growth appears.

Another approach is to remove the plantlet from the parent plant and place it in a good container mix. Enclose the pot in a plastic bag to provide humidity until the roots have formed.

Rooting Medium

The correct rooting medium will influence both the quantity of the cuttings that will root and the quality of the root system formed. A mixture of sand and peat moss

You can place plantlets from stem ends of the spider plant (*Chlorophytum comosum*) and set the base of the plantlet in a container of water. When new roots begin to form, move the plantlet to a new container.

is the most common combination. River sand only should be used and the best type is the sand used by plasterers in the building trade. The sand should be fine enough to hold some moisture but coarse enough to allow water to drain through.

Peat moss is actually the remains of aquatic, marsh, swamp, or bog vegetation that has been preserved underwater in a partially decomposing state. Peat moss is used in conjunction with sand to increase the water-holding capacity. When using peat moss you should take care not to overwater the plant, as this can cause the new roots to deteriorate.

A medium consisting of 2 parts sand to 1 part peat moss is the most effective for rooting plants. Half sand and half peat can be used, but take care not to overwater.

Plant Hormones

Plant hormones are helpful in propagation by cuttings. When applied to cuttings, plant hormones encourage the production of plant roots and produce a greater number of evenly distributed roots. Plant hormones also shorten the time taken by the plant to root. Rooting hormones are widely available and come in a powder form. The end of the cutting is dipped into the powder before it is placed in the propagating medium.

Aloe (*Aloe vera*) plants produce additional offshoots as they grow. You can remove and replant these offsets at any time.

Troubleshooting Houseplants

The best defense against pests and diseases is strong, healthy plants. And that's what you'll get using the techniques explained in this book. If pest or disease problems do show up on your plants, you'll find safe, nontoxic solutions below.

Handling Pests and Diseases

Outdoors, organic gardeners keep plants healthy by protecting and encouraging the natural balance between bad bugs and good bugs (the ones that prey on the bad guys). But plants growing indoors don't have any good bugs around to keep the pests in check, so sometimes the pests may multiply and cause problems. Indoor plants also face a few disease problems.

The most important thing you can do to prevent insect or disease outbreaks is to keep your plants healthy and vigorous: Give them sufficient light and fertilizer and the correct amount of water and humidity. For reasons scientists don't yet fully understand, pest insects are actually attracted to plants that are weak or stressed. Strong, organically grown plants are far less likely to have pest problems than plants that are weak and unhealthy.

The second important pest-prevention technique is to learn the symptoms of common houseplant problems and inspect

Whiteflies are easy to identify because they will fly up into the air whenever you disturb the plant. Whiteflies multiply rapidly, so you'll have to spray them quickly, before they get out of control.

your plants regularly. Most pests don't cause serious damage until they've been around awhile; if you spot an outbreak early, you can nip it in the bud (so to speak!).

Common Houseplant Pests

The trick to handling pests is identifying them correctly, so you can choose the most effective control measure. Below you'll find descriptions of the pests you're most likely to encounter, along with suggested controls.

Aphids Aphids are small insects about 1/16 inch (2 mm) long. They may be white, green, black, brown, or orange in color, and may or may not have wings. They are often found in clusters on tip growth and flower buds. Rub off aphids by hand or prune out infested leaf tips. For serious infestations, take plants outside and blast them weekly with a strong spray of water, or use soap spray.

Fungus Gnats These are small, slow-moving, dark-colored insects that you may notice running across the soil or flying up into the air when you water. Controls usually aren't necessary. If you have many flies, you can drench the soil with Gnatrol, a microbial pesticide containing a bacteria that kills the larvae.

Mealybugs These look like tiny tufts of white cotton. They are usually found clustered in sheltered areas of stems or on the undersides of leaves. Apply rubbing alcohol to individual mealybugs using a cotton swab. Be persistent in inspecting plants and repeating treatment as needed.

Mites These bugs are about the size of a grain of salt. Leaves attacked by mites are stippled or mottled; flowers may be deformed. If you look closely, you can usually see fine webbing over the damaged areas. Webs don't necessarily mean the plant has mites; they may just be webs from small spiders. Leave those spiders to

The best way to prevent pests and diseases from destroying your houseplants, is to keep your plants strong and healthy.

Sprayer

help you control the pests. Wash mites off with a strong spray of water. Insecticidal soap or oil sprays also control these pests.

Scales These insects live underneath a shell about 1/8 inch (3 mm) in diameter. Sticky specks appear on leaves. Check the leaves and stems above the sticky area for little bumps that can be rubbed off. Young scales are flat and semitransparent; they get darker and larger as they get older. Rub off scales by hand or spray with horticultural oil. Move plants outside in warm weather to allow natural enemies to control the scales.

Whiteflies These are tiny, white bugs about 1/16 inch (2 mm) in length. If you notice white specks flying up when you brush against a plant, you'll need to spray promptly. Use yellow sticky traps to capture adult flies. Spray with insecticidal soap or oil to control immature, wingless nymphs (which are usually found on the undersides of leaves).

Controlling Houseplant Pests

You can treat houseplant pests with just a few simple, nontoxic materials.

Sticky Traps Sticky traps are basically just pieces of cardboard or plastic (usually yellow and about the size of an index card) that are covered with an adhesive material. When flying pests, such as aphids and whiteflies, land on the trap, they get stuck. Hang a few traps around your houseplants, or attach them to the ends of stakes and insert the stakes into the plant pots.

Water Sprays A spray of plain old water is often enough to knock pests off your plants. You need a spray that's forceful enough to remove the pests but not strong enough to damage the plant. Wash the plant off in the shower, or take it outside and spray it thoroughly with your garden hose.

Insecticidal Soap Insecticidal soap is specifically formulated to kill pests such as aphids and mites without harming you or your plants. It's widely available in garden centers in both ready-to-use spray bottles or in a liquid concentrate that you mix with water. (The concentrate is much better value than the ready-mixed sprays.) If you have "hard" tap water, mix the soap with distilled water, or it won't work well. (You'll know you have hard water if soap makes a scummy ring in your bathtub.)

Horticultural Oil Horticultural oil works by smothering insects and eggs. It is also effective in helping prevent certain diseases, especially when combined with baking soda. The oil now comes in several grades, so be sure you buy the superior grade oil that is labeled for use directly on plant leaves. (Until recently, horticultural oil was less refined and could only be used on outdoor plants that were dormant and leafless during the winter, such as fruit trees.) Mix and apply oil sprays according to package directions.

Dealing with Diseases

Most popular houseplants aren't likely to have diseases—that's one of the reasons they're widely grown. Keeping plants healthy by providing good air circulation and adequate light, water, and fertilizer is your best defense against disease.

One common disease that may show up is powdery mildew. It causes distinctive, white powdery spots on the leaves of begonias and other susceptible plants. If you notice mildew or other suspicious spots on leaves, remove the infected leaves and spray the plant with either a sulfur solution or a homemade spray of baking soda and oil (follow the recipe in "Homemade Sprays for Pests and Diseases" below).

Keep in mind that these sprays only work to prevent the spread of disease, not to cure infected leaves. Always try to spray at the first sign of disease, and remove all infected leaves first. If a plant becomes severely damaged by disease, it may be best to discard it altogether.

Dumbcane

Diseases can also attack plant roots, where they are difficult to detect or treat. Sudden wilting or poor growth for no apparent reason are the main symptoms. Be sure you aren't over-watering, as this can promote root disease. Try letting the plant dry out between waterings; it may recover. If it doesn't, throw it out and be careful not to overwater in the future.

Homemade Sprays for Pests and Diseases

Commercial organic pest and disease sprays are convenient, but it's also easy to mix your own. You'll find two easy recipes here.

Whenever you spray, always cover the top and bottom surfaces of every leaf. If the plant can be pruned, do it before you spray. Repeat the spraying a week or so after the first spray to catch any bugs you missed or to prevent any remaining disease spores from attacking. To avoid marking walls, floors, and furniture, always move plants to some place where you can clean up easily—perhaps your shower, kitchen sink, or laundry tub, or outdoors if the weather's warm—before you spray.

Soap-and-oil Pest Spray

For a homemade insecticidal soap spray, mix 1 cup of vegetable oil and 1 tablespoon of dish soap. When you need to spray, mix 1 to 2 teaspoons of this oil/soap stock with 1 cup of water. Homemade soap-and-oil sprays may have a slightly greater risk of burning leaves than a commercial spray; test them on a few leaves, then wait a few days to make sure no damage appears before spraying a whole plant.

Homemade Fungicide

Mix together 1 tablespoon of baking soda, 1 tablespoon of horticultural oil or vegetable oil, and a few drops of dish soap with 1 gallon (4.5 l) of water. Try to use this fungicide spray solution on your plants before the disease symptoms develop, or as soon as you notice a problem.

It's easy to overlook scales until plants are infested. Check leaves and stems frequently for tiny bumps.

For an aphid infestation, rub the aphids off with your fingers, or spray with water or soapy water.

Houseplant Troubleshooting Chart

Symptoms	Possible Problem	Suggested Treatments
Dying plants or seedlings	Too much fertilizer	Water thoroughly to flush excess fertilizer. Halt or severely reduce feeding program.
	Water-logged plants	Improve drainage. Halt or severely reduce watering. Repot.
Weak-looking, stunted, pale plants	Insect attack	Isolate plant. Try to identify insects. Remove insects; wash with soapy water. See "Common Houseplant Pests" on page 48.
	Water-logged plants	Improve drainage. Halt or severely reduce watering. Repot.
	Under-nourished plants	Feed regularly with complete fertilizer or specialized plant food.
Weak-looking, straggly plants	Not enough light	Move gradually into a position with better light. Provide artificial lighting if necessary.
	Overcrowded	Divide plants. Repot.
	Too much nitrogen	Reduce or halt feeding. Use a low- or no-nitrogen fertilizer.
	Water-logged plants	Improve drainage. Halt or severely reduce watering. Repot.
Fading, wilting plants	Not enough warmth	Check recommended temperature range for plant.
	Not enough moisture	Water, if badly wilted. Immerse in water for quick recovery. Check for causes of excessive drying such as heaters, air-conditioning vents, or drafts.
	Too much moisture	Improve drainage. Halt or severely reduce watering.
Slow plant growth	Not enough light	Move gradually into a position with better light. Provide artificial lighting if necessary.
	Too little water	Check plant's watering needs. Follow correct watering procedure.
	Too little fertilizer	Add liquid fertilizer every 2 to 3 weeks.
	Roots pot-bound	Repot.
	Natural dormancy in winter	Be patient. Wait for spring.
White crust on soil	Build-up of fertilizer salts	Remove crust, leaching salts by flushing with pure water.
Lower leaves turn yellow, but remain on plant	Too little fertilizer, particularly nitrogen	Add high-nitrogen fertilizer.
Base of stem is soft or mushy	Too much water, particularly in cold weather	Let soil surface dry out between waterings. Improve drainage. Repot if necessary. Add coarse sand to container mix to improve drainage.
	Fungal attack in damp, cold conditions	Isolate plant. Move to warmer situation. Allow it to dry. Repot if necessary.
Collapse of plant	Extreme heat or cold	Check for cause of change, such as window left open. Move to position with more moderate temperature.
	Gas fumes	Check for source of fumes. Remove carefully.
Brown-edged leaves	Too hot, too dry	Check recommended temperature range for plant. Immerse in a bucket of water and place out of direct sunlight.
	Container mix saturated with chemical salts	Water repeatedly to flush excess salts from container mix.
	Leaves have been splashed with strong chemicals or fertilizer	Rinse leaves with water. Take care that leaves are not splashed with unwanted chemicals.

Symptoms	Possible Problem	Suggested Treatments
Brown patches on stems and leaves	Die-back, fungal disease or other infection	Isolate plant. Remove affected leaves and stems and destroy. Check for other symptoms to diagnose infection.
Powdery mold on leaf surface	Powdery mildew	Remove affected parts and destroy. Move plant to airier position. For severe infestations, use a systemic insecticide.
Reddish-brown, powdery marks on leaf surfaces	Rust	Isolate plant, cut off affected areas and destroy. For severe infestations, use a systemic insecticide.
Speckled leaves	Virus infection	Destroy infected plants
Sudden loss of leaves	Rapid temperature or light change	Check recommended temperature range for the plant. If necessary, restore previous temperature or light conditions.
Bronzed or abnormally reddened leaves	Not enough heat	Check recommended temperature range for the plant. If necessary, move to a warmer, more sheltered position.
	Not enough phosphorus or potassium	Use higher phosphorus or potassium fertilizer.
Dry and brittle leaves	Too little water or low humidity	Follow the proper procedure for watering houseplants. Increase humidity.
Leaf drop	Too much sun	Move to a location with less light.
	Too much fertilizer	Halt fertilizer for 3 to 4 weeks.
	Too much water	Follow the proper procedure for watering your houseplants.
	Too little water	Follow the proper procedure for watering your houseplants.
	Exposure to cold or draft	Check the temperature. Control cold source.
Brown or yellow leaves	Occasional yellowing of lower, older leaves is natural	No treatment necessary.
Yellow or white ring and spots on leaves	Splashing cold water on foliage while watering	Water more carefully. Do not splash foliage.
Swellings on leaves, corky ridges, water-soaked spots that turn red or brown	Too much moisture absorbed from warm, moist soil and cool, moist air	Increase warmth. Lower humidity. Place pot where soil will not get warmer than surrounding air.
Yellowing between veins of young leaves, older leaves less severely affected	Too little iron or magnesium	Boost with trace element fertilizer.
Healthy leaves but no blooms	Not enough light	Move to a position with more light.
	Not enough warmth	Check recommended temperature range for plant. If necessary, move to a warmer position.
	Too much nitrogen	Reduce or halt feeding. Use a low- or no-nitrogen fertilizer.
	Plant is too young or a late-flowering variety	Some plants take years to flower and some varieties bloom much later than others. Be patient.
Bud drop	Too much heat or cold	Check for cause of change such as window left open. Move to position with more moderate temperature.
	Shock from moving from greenhouse to home	Check plant's growing requirements. Adjust growing conditions to restore previous conditions, if possible.
	Poor humidity	Increase humidity.
	Draft shock	Control source of draft, or move plant to another location.

Success with Houseplants

There is a skill to matching plants to the right place in your home. Each area or room in your home has its own mini-climate, best suited to particular types of plants. Even if your living space has no bright windows, you can still grow a variety of plants with the help of artificial lights. You can also create your own mini-climates by planting miniature gardens in terrariums or bottles, which provide the optimum conditions for humidity-loving specimens, or by experimenting with water gardens, or hydroculture.

Living with Houseplants

Houseplants can be so much more than just a spot of greenery on a windowsill. Use them to fill your home with sweet fragrances, such as those of orange blossoms and jasmine. Brighten up the dull days of winter with the brilliant flowers of amaryllis and long-lasting, exotic orchids. Grow lush tropical plants to decorate the living room, and raise tasty herbs for the kitchen.

However, it is important to learn how to select the right plants for your available space. Different areas around your home will be suitable for different kinds of plants. See "Microclimates in Your Home", below.

Even if your home doesn't have big, sunny windows, you can still enjoy growing houseplants by using electric lights to create a garden even in the darkest corner of your home. See "Gardening under Lights" on page 56, for more information.

Whatever ways you choose to bring plants into your home, they will bring you much pleasure. They are a source of living and changing beauty, providing color, form, and fragrance throughout the year.

Microclimates in Your Home

Just as in the open garden, there is no single climate that covers every area in your home. Critical plant requirements—light, heat, moisture, and humidity—vary from room to room, and in different sections of each room, so it is worth the effort to find out where specific plants will grow best. However, remember that microclimates are not static—conditions vary with the season and with the ways in which you use your home.

Windows

When you are choosing a window for a particular plant, you have to consider more than the direction the window faces. A south-facing window opening onto a large, open area is going to provide your plants with a lot more light than it would if tall buildings, a shade tree or, worse, a mature evergreen were growing just outside.

Light intensity also varies with the season, from a maximum in summer,

ABOVE: The two large windows in this room provide enough light for a variety of plants.

declining in fall to a minimum in winter, and then gradually increasing again in spring. Watch your plants for signs of light deficiency—pale, spindly growth and feeble looking leaves—during fall or early winter. If your plants are affected, gradually shift them to brighter windows.

Be careful, though. Moving a houseplant from a north-facing window directly to a sunny south-facing window can result in scorching. If a plant must be moved from low light to bright sunlight, place the plant to the side of the sunny

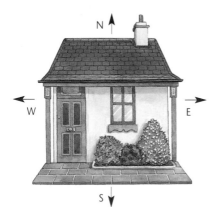

When placing houseplants, you need to consider the exposure of each window in your home, as well as features outside that may block the light.

window. After several weeks, move the plant into the direct sunlight.

Temperature

Temperature is a very important consideration, especially in those areas where air-conditioning and central heating are necessities in most homes. Most houseplants do not like rapid indoor temperature fluctuations and these often occur without us realizing it, especially in fall as cold fronts blow in.

A window above a heat vent or radiator may provide perfect light exposure but the temperature and humidity levels may be catastrophic for plants that like humid conditions and warm, but not hot, temperatures.

If you place a houseplant near a heater, when the heater kicks in, the temperature around that plant can increase very quickly and the warm air movement can rapidly dry out the foliage due to the warm air movement. *Ficus* trees can suddenly, and dramatically, shed their leaves when this happens.

Cyclamen

Winter holds another potential problem for houseplants—drafts. Plants that are kept inside during the winter months enjoy a warm environment. If a plant is located close to a frequently opened door or a cracked window, then temperatures can rapidly fluctuate every time the door opens. Such positioning may or may not be detrimental to plant health depending on the species.

Windowsills pose another problem due to heat buildup on sunny days and cold pockets on cold winter days. Monitor the temperature and choose hardy plants that tolerate these changing conditions.

Another problem area can be electrical appliances—especially televisions, VCRs, and stereos, which are likely to have plants placed nearby or even on them. These appliances produce heat and can rapidly heat up the air around your plants.

Humidity

Humidity is directly related to temperature. As temperature increases, the air is able to hold more water. Consequently, cool air tends to be dry. Most tropical plants come from the warm regions of the world and prefer high humidity. People, however, like to live in climate-controlled buildings with air-conditioning that actually reduces humidity. To combat this problem—especially with sensitive plants like ferns, orchids, and bromeliads—you can increase humidity by adding water to the air with humidifiers, and using other methods (see "Humidity and Temperature" on page 38).

RIGHT: Maidenhair ferns (*Adiantum* spp.), like most ferns, are tropical plants and like fairly high humidity. It is a good idea to provide extra moisture to the air in the room with a humidifier.

ABOVE: Flower production takes lots of energy, so blooming houseplants generally need all the light they can get.

LEFT: A mixture of flowers and foliage adds a welcoming touch to a sunny entranceway.

"medium," or "high." Hold a hand between the source of light and the spot where a plant is to be set. The amount of shadow gives a rough measure of available light. If there is no shadow, or if it is very hard to see, low light exists. If the shadow is somewhat blurred, but definitely there, medium light exists. A sharp and distinct shadow indicates high light conditions.

A plant sitting in a sunny window receives less light than it would in a greenhouse or garden. A plant growing in a window gets most of its light from just one side and may grow in a lop-sided fashion toward the light. Turning the plant keeps it straight but it doesn't cure the lack of adequate light exposure.

Light duration greatly influences plants, as flowering and rest periods are triggered by particular daylengths. Actually it is the length of the dark period, or night, that controls the response. For instance, poinsettia blooms when given long nights. Blooming is prevented by a few minutes of light, given during the dark period. Some plants enter rest periods during the fall and winter in response to shortening days.

Fluorescent Lights

Fluorescent lights obviously aren't nearly as bright as sunlight, but they'll work fine to grow relatively short plants that only

LEFT: A mixture of flowers and foliage adds a welcoming touch to a sunny entranceway.

Plants that require high humidity are best grown in terrariums or closed containers where it is possible to regulate the humidity (see "Creative Houseplant Displays" on page 64).

Bathrooms and kitchens, if they are sunny, often have a higher humidity than other areas of the home, and may be more suitable for humidity-loving houseplants.

Gardening under Lights

Even if your window space is limited, you can still have a colorful collection of houseplants—just set up your indoor garden under artificial lights. Besides allowing you to grow more plants, a well-designed light garden can really brighten up dark corners in the living room, kitchen, or other areas. There are two main kinds of lights to choose from—standard fluorescents (like those used in stores and offices) or special high-intensity discharge lights.

The light requirements for plants are often given as "low,"

A light setup can expand your houseplant options if your windows aren't bright enough for good growth.

LEFT: A sunny south-facing window is the perfect position for a collection of cacti and succulents.
RIGHT: Most bromeliads thrive in sunny windows, but they can also adapt to bright north windows or fluorescent lights.

require low to medium light levels. Just be sure to keep your houseplants as close as possible to the lights for best growth.

The best size fixture of fluorescent light is one that holds two or four 48-inch (1.2-m) long bulbs. You can find "shop light" fluorescent fixtures and tubes at most hardware and home-supply stores. A two-tube, 4-foot (1.2-m) long setup complete with bulbs is quite affordable.

At your local garden center, you may also find more expensive fluorescent bulbs which are sold as "plant growth lights." Manufacturers claim that these lights are best for plant growth, but most research has concluded that these bulbs are really no better than the standard, and more inexpensive "warm white" or "cool white" bulbs that are widely available at most hardware stores.

High-intensity Discharge Lights

If you want to grow houseplants that are larger than about 1 foot (30 cm) tall under artificial light, you should consider using a high-intensity discharge (HID) light instead. HID lights use special sodium or metal halide bulbs, and they come in very bright-wattage ranges from 175 to 1,000 watts.

The 1,000-watt units are probably too intense for use anywhere except in a greenhouse or basement—you just wouldn't want to have such a bright light on in your living areas. But the 400-watt type is perfect for a spare corner in your living room or bedroom. It will provide an ample amount of light for a growing area about 6 feet (180 cm) square. HID lights are bright enough to grow virtually any plants you want—even large,

What about Light Bulbs?

Regular incandescent light bulbs don't work well for growing houseplants. Part of the reason for this is that the glow the bulbs give off doesn't provide the right wavelengths of light for good plant growth. The other reason is that they are very inefficient, releasing a lot of their energy as heat.

There are special "grow light" incandescent bulbs on the market, and these may help a little if you use them on a large plant in a dim corner. In general, though, you'll be spending a lot of money (for electricity and replacement bulbs) for little benefit. For best results, stick with fluorescent or high-intensity discharge (HID) lights.

sun-loving vegetables such as peppers and tomatoes. The lights aren't as bright as outdoor sunlight, but you can make up for some of the difference by leaving the lights on for up to 16 hours per day.

HID lights are generally available from specialty suppliers (such as those that sell equipment for greenhouse or hydroponic gardening). To find a source, look for ads in gardening magazines, or check your local phone book for greenhouse suppliers.

Special Growing Guidelines

If you grow plants under electric lights (especially the brighter HID types), you'll need to fertilize regularly to keep up with the plants' growth. (Unlike outdoor or window plants, which slow down during cloudy weather, plants under lights keep growing steadily.)

To provide the right amount of light every day, you may want to buy a timer to automatically turn the lights on and off. Timers are available at hardware stores. Most experts suggest that you leave the lights on for 14 to 16 hours per day, unless you're growing day-length-sensitive flowering plants, such as Christmas cactus (*Schlumbergera bridgesii*) and poinsettia, which need short (12-hour) days to trigger flowering.

Poinsettia

Growing Plants Indoors

Whatever ways you choose to bring plants into your home, they will give you much pleasure. They are a source of living and changing beauty, providing color, form, and fragrance throughout the year. If flowers are your favorite, check out "Flowering Houseplants" below. "Growing Bulbs Indoors" on page 59 also has ideas on adding beautiful blooms to your home with amaryllis, paperwhite narcissus, and other easy-to-grow bulbs.

To keep your houseplants happy and healthy, consider giving them a summer vacation outdoors. When you bring them inside again in fall, you can also pot up garden plants such as rosemary, geraniums, and other tender herbs and flowers to enjoy indoors over winter and then move out again next spring. You'll find all the details on shifting plants around safely in "Inside Out and Outside In" on page 62.

Flowering Houseplants

Foliage houseplants are attractive and dependable, but it's really the brilliant colors and the fantastic fragrances of flowering plants that grab and hold the interest of houseplant-lovers of all levels. Flowering plants tend to demand a little extra care, but it's all worthwhile when you get to enjoy the beautiful blooms.

To get an idea of the wonderful plants you can pick from, stroll around any local greenhouse, or flip through "A Guide to Popular Houseplants," starting on page 132. When you find a plant you simply must have, use the guidelines here to help keep it happy and vigorous.

Choose the Right Site

To grow flowering plants successfully, you must consider the available light levels carefully. If you put a foliage plant in a location where it gets less light than it would really like, it may still grow reasonably well. But without the necessary amount of light, a flowering plant will bloom poorly or may refuse to flower at all. Most flowering plants, such as hibiscus (*Hibiscus rosa-sinensis*), require high light—at least 4 hours of direct sun in a south window, for example. A few, such as the popular African violet (*Saintpaulia* hybrids), will flower in medium light levels, but almost none will bloom well in low light.

Generally, you should always give flowering plants your brightest windows. And if you can, move the plants outdoors for the summer. In many cases, a few months of brighter outdoor light will be

The best place for most houseplants is in a sunny window but, for flowering houseplants, a high light position is usually mandatory.

Try Moth Orchids for Months of Bloom

One of the best-kept secrets of indoor flower growing is the lovely moth orchid (*Phalaenopsis* hybrids). Orchids have a reputation of being difficult to grow, but these elegant hybrids will thrive easily on a bright windowsill in your home.

The most amazing thing about colorful, winter-blooming moth orchids is that their graceful, arching flower sprays can last for many weeks. For the price of a bouquet of cut flowers (which only lasts a week or two), you can enjoy the beautiful blooms for up to several months at a time. Just water and fertilize them regularly, and give them a few weeks of cooler nighttime temperatures in the fall to set new flower buds. For more details on succeeding with orchids as houseplants, see the Orchids entry on page 141.

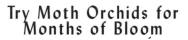

enough for the plant to grow strong and set flower buds, even if you can only give it medium light during the rest of the year indoors. (Be sure to read "Inside Out and Outside In" on page 62 for information on how to safely move houseplants outside.)

Fertilize for Flowers

Besides giving them plenty of light, you'll also need to fertilize flowering houseplants carefully for the best blooms. To flower healthily, plants must have plenty of phosphorus, which is the middle number in the N-P-K rating you'll see on any bag or bottle of fertilizer. (If you're not clear on how the N-P-K ratings work, turn back to "Understanding Organic Fertilizers" on page 43 for a review.)

If you buy a plant that's already in flower, you don't need to worry about fertilizing it while it's blooming. But when

Most cultivars of spring crocus respond well to forcing. You can pack many bulbs into one pot.

it finishes flowering, and if it's a kind that's likely to flower again for you (check the individual plant entries in "A Guide to Popular Houseplants," starting on page 132, for that information), then you should begin feeding it. Give the plant a regular "balanced" fertilizer (one with roughly equal amounts of N, P, and K) as long as it's actively growing. Shortly before it's time for the plant to flower again, you should change to a fertilizer that contains extra phosphorus (such as a 5-7-4 fertilizer) to stimulate flowering.

Don't Expect Miracles

Despite your best care, there are some flowering houseplants that just simply refuse to bloom again the following year after you bring them home. Some plants may need special greenhouse conditions; others demand carefully maintained periods of light and darkness each day to repeat their colorful show.

Poinsettia (*Euphorbia pulcherrima*), Reiger begonia, and florist's cyclamen (*Cyclamen persicum*) are a few examples of houseplants that are difficult or nearly impossible to get to rebloom without a lot

of fussing. (If you're not sure whether your plant will reflower, check the entry in "A Guide to Popular Houseplants," starting on page 132.) If you really like looking at the leaves, you can keep these as foliage plants when they are done blooming; otherwise, discard them after flowering and buy replacements.

Growing Bulbs Indoors

Indoor bulbs are a terrific way to enjoy brilliant flowers and fragrance, especially during the winter months. You can even "force" some spring bulbs to flower early in order to enjoy their blooms ahead of time. Even though the process is called forcing, there's not much force involved. You simply provide a condensed version of the winter the bulbs would otherwise get when growing in the ground outdoors. All you have to do is pot them in the fall with pointed ends up and just the tips showing. Store them in a cool, dark place for several weeks (15 weeks for crocuses, 15 to 17 weeks for daffodils, 11 to 14 weeks for hyacinths, and 14 to 20 weeks for tulips), and keep them watered as needed. Then bring them inside to a bright windowsill. In a few weeks, you'll have beautiful bulbs blooming indoors even if there's still snow on the ground outdoors.

Bulbs for Forcing

Most spring bulbs can be forced, but some perform better in pots than others. Spring-blooming crocus, Siberian squill (*Scilla sibirica*), and reticulated iris (*Iris reticulata*) are very easy to chill and bring into bloom. A few

tulips that perform especially well in containers include pale orange 'Apricot Beauty', plum purple 'Atilla', and some of the small, rock garden species (such as the lovely yellow-and-white *Tulipa tarda* and the yellow or bronze-pink *Tulipa batalinii*).

Tulips

Daffodils are also gratifyingly easy to force. Although the large, yellow, trumpet daffodils are traditional favorites, many gardeners also enjoy smaller, free-flowering cultivars such as 'Pipit', 'Hawera', and 'Tete-a-tete'. Hyacinths, too, usually perform well in pots; a few that are especially good include pale pink 'Lady Derby', darker pink 'Pink Pearl', deep

Easy Amaryllis

Amaryllis bulbs are easy to grow, and bloom year after year. Set potted amaryllis in a bright window and water lightly until they start growing—it takes just a few weeks for the flowers to open. Turn the plant regularly so the stalk won't become lopsided. Use a bamboo stake and a rubber band to hold the stalk once the giant flowers begin to open.

While amaryllis is flowering, you can move it to a table where everyone can enjoy it. When the flowers fade, cut off the stalk and return the plant to a bright window. During summer, put the potted plant outside in light shade. Water and fertilize, and let it grow to replenish the bulb. (You can continue growing it inside if you prefer.)

Before frost in the fall, bring the plant back inside and gradually reduce watering. As the leaves begin to die back, place the plant in a cool, dark area. The leaves will die down, and the bulb will go dormant. Don't water the plant during this period.

After a month or two, top-dress the pot with 1 inch (2.5 cm) of fresh mix and a teaspoon of bonemeal. Bring the plant back into a warm spot, water lightly until new growth begins, and then return it to a bright window and watch those wonderful flowers appear again!

When forcing bulbs, plant your bulbs in pots with the tips of the bulbs just visible over the soil.

Set pots of forced bulbs in a cool, dark place until the shoots start to appear; then give them light.

Paperwhite Narcissus

Another great candidate for easy indoor bulb growing is paperwhite narcissus. Paperwhites are not hardy outdoors in most regions; they are sold specifically for indoor growing.

Just pot the plants up in container mix or coarse gravel, with the tips of the bulbs showing. You can even grow them with their roots in water, using a special vase designed for bulbs. Once the bulbs have some moisture and begin to grow, the flower stalk will quickly become visible among the leaves, and you'll have flowers in just a few weeks!

Paperwhite flowers last for several weeks, especially if you keep the plant in a cool, bright location. Staking plants with small bamboo stakes and string helps as the leaves and flowers grow. To have flowers in bloom all winter long, buy a couple of dozen bulbs in fall and store them in your refrigerator; then pot up a few every 3 to 4 weeks.

Unfortunately, you can't really expect the bulbs to bloom again another year, so it's best just to discard the plants when the flowering is done.

For a spectacular show of mixed bulbs, plant different varieties of bulbs in several layers in a large container, and wait for the show!

blue 'Blue Jacket', and salmon-pink 'Gypsy Queen'. Their sweet fragrance is ideal for curing a case of the winter blues!

For more ideas of bulbs to choose, check catalogs or garden-center bulb displays for the phrase "good for forcing." The individual plant entries in "A Guide to Popular Container Plants," starting on page 164, also call out those that are particularly well suited for forcing.

Preparing Bulbs for Forcing

The best time to plant bulbs for forcing is in late fall and early winter. Set the bulbs shoulder to shoulder in clay or plastic containers in ordinary, well-drained container mix. The "nose" of the bulb should just peek above the soil surface. Label the pot with the name of the bulb and the date, water it thoroughly, and stash it in its winter quarters for chilling.

Giving Bulbs a Chance to Chill

Bulbs need a cool, dark place while they're producing roots. The ideal temperatures for forcing bulbs are between 33° and 45°F (1° and 7°C). You can use an unheated garage or basement, or a crawl space, potting shed, or cold frame. You may need to protect bulbs with a heavy layer of straw, newspapers, or old blankets to keep them from getting too cold.

Refrigerators can work well for chilling if you only have a few pots. They're especially useful if you live in a mild climate where outdoor winter temperatures don't get cold enough for proper chilling. An old-fashioned, round-top refrigerator (which does not have a frost-free feature) is the perfect place for storing potted bulbs. Modern refrigerators tend to be rather dry, so you should enclose potted bulbs in plastic bags (punch a few holes for air) to keep them from drying out too much.

If you don't have another place to chill your bulbs, you can try the mound technique. Simply set the bulb containers on the ground outdoors (perhaps in a corner of the vegetable garden), cover them with several inches of perlite or container mix, and then top the whole thing with a thick insulating layer of straw or wood chips. Keep in mind, though, that this pile will provide an inviting home for local mice, which may move in and snack on your bulbs. It's also a messy job to dig your bulbs out of a snow-covered pile in the middle of winter.

Bringing Bulbs into Bloom

No matter where you chill your bulbs, check on them every few weeks to see if they need more water. At the same time, look for signs of growth. Your bulbs will signal they're ready to grow in two ways: tiny white roots will be visible in the drainage holes of the pot, and new shoots will appear at the tops of the bulbs. Crocus and reticulated iris may be ready in as little as 8 weeks, while larger bulbs can take 12 weeks or longer.

When the shoots are an inch or two (2.5 to 5 cm) tall, bring them inside to a cool, bright window. Fertilize lightly each time you water, and turn the pots regularly to keep the shoots from stretching unevenly toward the light. Keep the pots away from radiators, hot-air registers, and other heat sources; bulbs like it cool.

Keep watering and fertilizing the bulbs until the foliage begins to wither. Then transplant the bulbs to your garden at that

Grow herbs on a sunny windowsill in the kitchen so they'll be within easy reach for cooking.

time, or wait until fall. If you've cared for the bulbs well, they will likely settle in and bloom again in a few years.

Growing Herbs Indoors

Some herbs adjust well to being grown indoors. For many gardeners, indoor cultivation is a convenient approach, particularly in areas which have cold, frosty winters. Growing indoors means you can have tender herbs all year round.

Glassed-in sunrooms and balconies are ideal for indoor herb cultivation because they create a hothouse environment. Window ledges are also suitable places for growing a wide selection of herbs. If you remember that many herbs require plenty of sun and frequent watering and feeding, success will be yours.

Herbs require good drainage and rich container mix, and should ideally be grown in terracotta herb pots or specially designed plastic herb trays. Only small quantities need to be grown at a time, so a wide variety of herbs can be grown in a relatively small area.

Start with the Right Soil

As we have already mentioned, the container mix for herb cultivation needs to be rich, but it should also be light and

Herbs for Indoor Containers

You can grow the following herbs indoors in sunny positions:

Basil Basil is a low-growing annual with a slightly peppery flavor when used fresh, while the dried herb tastes more like curry. Basil likes a rich container mix with good drainage. Pick the stems when the plant reaches 7 inches (18 cm) in height, before the flowers appear.

Basil

Caraway A very attractive herb with fern-like leaves and white flowers. Grow in well-drained, moderately rich container mix. Only the seeds are used, so the flower heads should be picked as the fruit is ripening.

Chervil A delicate annual herb with a slightly aniseed flavor. Plant in a large pot in a well-drained, moderately rich container mix enriched with compost. Chervil likes semi-shade in summer and full sun during winter. In summer chervil goes to seed quickly. You can delay this process by pinching back to stop the flowering.

Chives A delicious herb with grassy foliage and mauve flowerheads. Grow chives in a sunny position indoors in a rich and well-drained container mix. Cut back to the base with scissors as needed. Frequent harvesting promotes growth. Chives may be propagated either from seed or by division.

Chervil

Dill A delightful herb with delicate, aromatic leaves and pale yellow flowers. Both the leaves and the seeds of the plant can be used. Plant in a fairly large pot in well-drained container mix. Harvest seeds by collecting the ripening flower heads in late summer and placing them in a dry place until the seeds can be easily rubbed off. Propagate from seed.

Marjoram Marjoram has a low growing habit and small, white flowers. Grow in rich, well-drained container mix with plenty of watering during summer. Can be picked and used fresh or dried and stored in an airtight container. Propagate from seed or from cuttings taken in spring.

Dill

Mint Garden mint is ideal for growing in a pot because of its tendency to spread and take over in a garden bed. Grow in full sun or partial shade in a rich container mix with added peat. Water well in summer. Pick leaves as required and use fresh, or dry by hanging bunches in a cool, dry spot.

Parsley Parsley has brilliant green foliage and a thick, bushy habit. Plant parsley in full sun or partial shade in a medium-sized pot. Use a rich container mix that has either animal or poultry manure (well rotted) added. Propagate from seed.

Sage Sage is a bushy, low-growing perennial herb with grayish green leaves and pale blue or lilac flowers which appear in midsummer. Grow in a well-drained container mix. Fresh sage can be picked as required. Collect the leaves in fall for drying before the flower stalks become too large. Hang the leaves in bunches in a dry, shady place. Propagate from seed or cuttings.

Thyme There are many varieties of thyme, all of which are edible. Garden thyme is a low growing perennial evergreen. The entire bush is fragrant with small leaves and pale mauve flowers. Grow thyme in full sun or partial shade in a light, well-drained mix. Don't use artificial fertilizers as they can kill the plant. Thyme can be picked fresh or dried. When drying, pick the leaves prior to flowering, tie the stems together and hang in a dry, shady position. Propagation is by division.

Thyme

Pots dry out more quickly outdoors, so ensure you check them frequently to prevent wilting.

Before moving plants outside, wait until the weather is warm and settled. Introduce indoor plants to outside sunlight gradually. If you don't, their leaves can show brown or white scorched spots.

To give your houseplants time to adjust, always place them in full shade when you first move them outside. After a few weeks in the shade, you can move the kinds that enjoy brighter light out from the shade to partial or full-sun locations.

Plants growing in the brighter, airier conditions of the great outdoors grow much faster than they do indoors, so they'll need more water and fertilizer than normal. Pay special attention to make sure they don't dry out; they may need daily watering when temperatures peak in summer. Check the entries in "A Guide to Popular Houseplants," starting on page 132, to see if your particular plants have any special needs when they are living outdoors.

Bringing Outdoor Plants In

Many plants typically grown outside can also be enjoyed inside. Plants classified as "tender perennials" will keep on growing

To avoid sunburning your plants' leaves, always put indoor plants in a shaded spot for a while when you first move them outside.

friable. Add well-rotted animal or poultry manure or compost to the container mix. If the soil is to be light it should contain a percentage of sand to assist the drainage and prevent the soil from becoming hard-packed. The base of the container should be filled with a shallow layer of drainage material such as gravel or crushed rocks before the soil is added.

Inside Out and Outside In

Just like people, many houseplants appreciate a vacation. Moving your houseplants outdoors for the summer months is a great way to keep them healthy and happy. When you bring them back in for the winter, you can also dig and pot up rosemary, geraniums, and

other flowers and herbs for indoor enjoyment. To help your plants through these transitions, try the tips below.

Moving Indoor Plants Outside

Many indoor plants benefit from spending a summer outside. Flowering plants, which require bright light, will especially appreciate some time outdoors. If your plants have aphids, scales, or other pests, moving them outdoors can give beneficial insects a chance to attack the unwanted insects, solving your pest problems. If you have a large number of indoor plants, you may want to move the bright-light lovers outside for the summer and shift some medium-light plants to the brighter spots vacated by the high-light lovers.

Wax begonia

if you protect them from freezing temperatures by moving them indoors for the winter months.

Geraniums (*Pelargonium* spp.) are a perfect example. You can enjoy their colorful flowers or pleasant scents in the garden all summer, then bring them indoors in fall and keep them in a bright window. Other great plants for indoor growing include rosemary (*Rosmarinus officinalis*), wax begonias (*Begonia* Semperflorens-Cultorum hybrids), and coleus, just to name a few. You can even bring hot pepper plants inside to hold them over for the next year.

To move plants indoors, you can dig them up and set them in a pot. Usually you'll want to trim them back pretty hard to bring the top growth into balance with the now much smaller root ball. After they're potted up and trimmed, keep them well watered, and let them stay outside for a few weeks in part shade. This transition period will help them recover from the shock of being transplanted, so they can grow back nice and bushy. Be sure to bring any cold-tender plants inside as soon as frost is predicted.

If you'd rather have smaller plants (which fit better on windowsills), you can easily take root cuttings from many garden plants in summer or early fall. Cut off 3 or 4 inch (7.5 to 10 cm) long shoot tips, and remove all but two or three of the top leaves. Insert the bottom 2 to 3 inches (5 to 7.5 cm) of each cutting into a small pot of moist sand, vermiculite, or container mix, and cover the cuttings with a clear plastic bag to keep the humidity high. Place them in a warm, medium-bright location until they root and begin growing, then remove the plastic and move them to your brightest south windows for the winter. You can move the plants back out

RIGHT: Geraniums make both excellent indoor and outdoor container plants.

to the garden in spring, after all danger of frost has passed.

When you bring any outdoor plants inside, there's always a chance you may bring in some pest problems as well. Once those pests are inside they can spread to your other plants quickly, since there are no natural enemies to keep them in balance. To minimize the chance of problems, inspect your plants carefully before you bring them in; refer back to "Common Houseplant Pests" on page 48 to remind yourself of what to look for and how to control any problems you find.

Certain garden plants are very susceptible to aphids when grown indoors. Hot peppers are a good example. If you find that aphids keep coming back even when you have sprayed the plant several times, it may be best just to enjoy that particular plant outdoors each summer

and not try to keep it indoors. Or, if it's a plant you really love, you can order specific beneficial insects from mail-order suppliers and release them to munch on the aphids or other troublemakers.

Bring coleus plants indoors during winter to brighten up the house with the colorful foliage.

Creative Houseplant Displays

There is no need to be limited in your choice of houseplants by the conventional. There are some amazing plants that can adapt to growing in your home—and a host of wonderful ways in which you can display them.

Terrariums, Dish, and Bottle Gardens

To get even more enjoyment out of your houseplant collection, you can create decorative groupings of colorful or unusual plants in terrariums, dish, or bottle gardens. These simple projects are fun, and they provide great, movable accents for any part of your home.

Try a Terrarium or Bottle Garden

Terrariums or bottle gardens are simply clear, glass containers in which you grow a group of plants. They work especially well for plants that require high humidity, such as ferns and insect-eating bog plants, such as Venus fly-traps. The moisture emitted

by the leaves inside the glass container condenses and runs back into the soil.

You can purchase beautiful, leaded-glass terrariums that resemble miniature conservatories, or you can use a container of virtually any shape. Old aquariums work

Plants with patterned or variegated leaves, such as peperomias, look great in bottle gardens.

particularly well, as do brandy snifters and recycled, clear glass wine jugs.

Next, decide what type of plants you want to grow. Tropical plants that like warm temperatures and high humidity, such as miniature gloxinias (*Sinningia* hybrids), polka dot plant (*Hypoestes phyllostachya*), ferns, and mosses, are generally a good choice. If you have a cool room, you could select a group of temperate woodland plants that like shade, humidity, and cool temperatures. Just be sure all the plants you choose like reasonably similar conditions. And unless you're using a large container, choose plants that won't grow very big.

Once you've chosen your container and selected your plants, place 1 inch (2.5 cm) of coarse sand or gravel in the bottom. Then add several inches of container mix and set in your plants. If you're planting

Making a Dish Garden

Dish gardens are an excellent way to display a collection of low-growing cacti or succulents. You can create a miniature desert landscape with these plants in a wide, shallow dish. Dish gardens look great displayed in the center of a coffee table.

1. Take a wide, shallow container and line it with about 1 inch (2.5 cm) of gravel. Cover the gravel with a 1-inch (2.5-cm) layer made up of half sand and half soil-based container mix.

2. While the plants are still in their original pots, place them in the dish and move them around to experiment with the design, until you are happy with the arrangement.

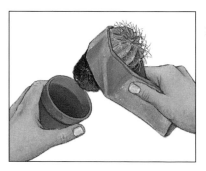

3. A good way to remove cacti from their original pots, without getting pricked by the spines, is to fold a piece of paper around the cactus and use this as a "handle" to lift the plant out.

4. Place the plants in the dish in your desired arrangement. Fill the dish with container mix by pouring the mix gently around the plants' roots.

array of suitable shapes, so you can continually experiment with new topiaries to add to your houseplant collection.

Setting Up Standards

The simplest topiaries are known as "standards." To create a standard, you train a single-stemmed plant up a long stake, then trim the tip of the plant to form a round ball on top of the stem. One of the best houseplants to train as a standard is myrtle (*Myrtus communis*). It grows slowly in medium light, so you can enjoy the plant for many years. Plus, the leaves have a sweet fragrance when cut or crushed.

ABOVE: You can train vines around various frames made from wire, bamboo, plastic, or rattan. Here jasmine is trained around a hoop-shaped wire.

LEFT: A stunning effect can be created by topiaries. Small-leaved, evergreen plants are most suitable for topiary training.

Training Plants to Topiary Forms

You can also make topiary by training an ivy, jasmine, or other vining plant onto a special wire form. Circles and heart shapes are common, but you can find them in a practically unlimited range of other shapes, too. To train a plant to a form, simply insert the form in the pot, then fasten the stems to whatever part of the form you

in a bottle with a small opening, you may need to use special long-handled tools to slide plants into the container. Water the plants to settle them into the mix.

Give the finished terrarium whatever light level the plants you selected require. However, be aware that the clear glass sides of the container will trap considerable heat, so keep the terrarium out of direct sunlight. And don't over-water—there are no drainage holes, and the container traps and recycles most of the moisture that evaporates from the soil and leaves. You may have to water only once a month, especially while the plants are small.

Dish Gardens

A dish garden is any open container in which you grow several different plants to create a miniature garden. This technique works especially well for smaller kinds of cacti and succulents, which grow well in a wide, shallow dish. As with the terrarium, you should choose relatively small plants, with shallow root systems, that all share similar requirements.

If you plant a dish garden of cacti or succulents, use a special cactus container mix, or make your own by mixing equal parts of standard container mix and sand. For other plants, standard, all-purpose container mix should work fine.

You can also decorate your dish garden with stone chippings, gravel, or even colored glass or tiny seashells. Many nurseries and garden centers stock these materials. Aquarium dealers also have a good selection of colored pebbles.

Training Houseplant Topiaries

Topiary is the art of training plants to a particular shape. It's actually quite easy, and there are many houseplants that adapt well to topiary training. There is a vast

Top Picks for Topiaries

Many plants can adapt to life as a topiary, but some tend to be better-suited than others. You want a plant that will grow fast enough to give you results fairly quickly, but not so fast that it will outgrow its shape without weekly trimming. Here's a sampling of some of the best choices for indoor topiary projects.

English ivy (*Hedera helix*)
Lantana (*Lantana camara* or *L. montevidensis*)
Lavender (*Lavandula* spp.)
Myrtle (*Myrtus communis*)
Rosemary (*Rosmarinus officinalis*)
Scented geraniums (*Pelargonium* spp.)   Ivy

want to cover. Use coated wire or soft string ties to secure the plant's stems to the form as they grow.

Maintaining a Topiary

Care for topiaries the same way you would regular plants of the same kind. The only extra thing you need to do is trim the plant regularly to maintain the shape. Fast-growing plants may need trimming every few weeks to keep their shape; slower-growing species may only need clipping once or twice a year.

Hydroponics at Home

Hydroponics is the art of growing plants in water or another medium rather than soil. Some gardeners experiment with hydroponics inadvertently when cuttings of certain plants start growing roots after they have been a while in a vase or jar of water. More elaborate hydroponics systems are either active or passive.

Active hydroponics systems work by actively passing a nutrient solution over your plant's roots. The engine required to pump nutrient solution to your plants need be nothing more complex than a small aquarium water pump.

Passive hydroponics systems provide plants with nutrients through a capillary

Many types of palm are slow-growing, and can take several years to reach their maximum height.

You can grow bulbs in hyacinth glasses. Place the bulb in the top of the glass and fill it with water until it just touches the bulb.

or wick system. Working like an oil lamp, the wick draws nutrient solution from the reservoir to the growing medium and roots.

Hydroponic gardening is so different to conventional forms of gardening that it can take a bit of experimentation until you feel comfortable but, once you have started, you may find it a flexible system for growing virtually any kind of plant.

Hydroponics kits are now available at many nurseries and garden centers and there are specialist hydroponics stores where you can get advice and support.

Exotic Plants

Are you looking for houseplants that fit the style of your home, or plants that explore some of the more unusual areas of houseplant gardening? You can add a special touch to your home with exotics such as palms, orchids, cacti and succulents, and other unusual plants.

Palms

Palms add a wonderful, tropical feeling to the indoor garden. They are bold houseplants that command attention. Palms suited to indoor cultivation are slow-growing while young, or have a small mature size. Some of the best palms for growing indoors include parlor palm (*Chamaedorea elegans*), a small palm, never taller than 3 feet (90 cm); bamboo palm (*Chamaedorea erumpens*), taller, forming clumps of smooth, slender stems; miniature date palm (*Phoenix roebelinii*), an elegant palm with dark green, glossy fronds and a textured trunk; and kentia palm (*Howea forsterana*) which has a slender trunk and a crown of

RIGHT: Showy cattleya orchids are among the most recognizable types. They can adapt to intermediate temperatures and medium light.

dark-green, drooping, feather-shaped fronds. For more information about palms see the entry in "A Guide to Popular Houseplants," starting on page 132.

Orchids

Orchids are extremely popular and, with more than 35,000 kinds available, they are the largest family of flowering plants on earth—wild orchids grow everywhere except the Arctic and Antarctic. The popularity of orchids is no doubt due to the huge variety of flower colors and shapes. Orchids can be white, red, orange, yellow, green, purple, brown and even blue.

While some orchids can be expensive and difficult to cultivate, there are many others that are well within the average budget and no more difficult to grow than any other flowering plant.

Two easy orchids for the beginner are Dendrobium hybrids and Phalaenopsis

hybrids. Both of these orchids come in a wide variety of colors, but you will be most likely to find purple, pink, lavender, and white. Phalaenopsis orchids (sometimes called "moth orchids" because of the shape) are striped or spotted as well.

As you become more experienced at growing orchids, and learn how to meet their needs in your home, you may want to branch out into named varieties and rare species types. This is part of the fun of orchid culture and judicious selection will guarantee that something is in bloom all year long. Serious growers buy their plants from professional orchid breeders. For further information about orchids, see "A Guide to Popular Houseplants," starting on page 132.

Carnivorous Plants

Carnivorous plants can be fun to grow and are of special interest to children, who find these specimens fascinating.

Pitcher plants (*Sarracenia* spp.) are flowering plants that use their leaves, shaped like pitchers, to trap insects. The pitchers produce nectar on the top of the plant to attract insects. The insides of the pitchers are lined with downward-pointing hairs that are used to prevent the insect from escaping once it is in the pitcher. The juices that are contained in the bottom of the leaf eventually digest the insect.

Venus fly-traps (*Dionaea muscipula*) supplement their nutrient intake by catching insects. They are low-growing, rosette-shaped plants with leafy stalks topped with two rounded, hinged blades. The leaves are touch-sensitive, so when an insect touches the leaves, the hinges snap shut and trap the insect.

Sensitive Plants

There are some plants that are sensitive to touch. If you simply touch them with a finger, the fern-like leaves will close up and droop on contact, reopening after several minutes. Sensitive plant, or touch-me-not (*Mimosa pudica*), is one of the most popular and widely

Venus fly-traps are moisture-loving plants, and are ideal for terrarium or bottle garden culture.

available varieties. It has attractive balls of pink flowers, as well as the sensitive leaflets. It is easy to raise from seed if you can't find plants at your garden center.

Cacti and Succulents

There are so many varieties of cacti and succulents that at first the range can seem bewildering. Cacti and succulents have adapted to growing in the arid and semi-arid regions of the world. Their leaves have become smaller and their stems larger in order to store water and, in almost all cacti, the leaves have completely disappeared so that only the thickened green stems remain. Where they have not disappeared, the leaves may be thickened or insulated with coverings of hair, wax, or fleshy scales.

Cacti and succulents can be excellent houseplants for they are both adaptable and tough. They are suited to wide variations in temperature and can survive a certain amount of neglect. They need plenty of light; a bright, warm, south window is satisfactory for many. A window greenhouse is ideal and can accommodate many plants.

Because cacti and succulents can survive in relatively small amounts of soil, they can live in small pots. You can even combine an interesting collection of several types in one container. Large pot size can make moisture control difficult and may actually harm your plants.

There are many varieties of cacti and succulents and, as the plants differ in family, they also differ in physical characteristics in an enormous variety of form and color. Some unusual cacti include the bishop's cap (*Astrophytum myriostigma*), the old man cactus (*Cephalocereus senilis*), and the feather cactus (*Mammillaria plumosa*). The wax vine (*Hoya carnosa*) has clusters of waxy, delicately fragrant flowers. Many cacti and succulents will flower in a spectacular fashion when the growing conditions are ideal. For more information about cacti see "A Guide to Popular Houseplants," starting on page 132.

An indoor succulent and cacti garden can be easy to maintain, as the plants tolerate a fair amount of drought.

The Right Houseplant for the Right Place

The key to growing houseplants successfully is matching your plants to the growing conditions they prefer. To help you make the best choices for the conditions you have, the following chart summarizes the specific needs of over 75 houseplants. You can see at a glance exactly which plants grow in low light, which need bright light, and which prefer cooler temperatures or need extra humidity to thrive. (If you're not clear on the definitions of low, medium, and high light conditions, see "Defining Light Levels" on page 39 for an explanation.) Pick the plants that will thrive in the growing conditions your home has to offer.

Flowering Houseplant	Light Needs	Water Needs	Comments
Flowering maples (*Abutilon* hybrids)	High	Moist; drier in winter	Keep at 50°–60°F (10°–16 °C) at night. Pinch shoot tips and fertilize for bushy growth and best flowering.
Chenille plant (*Acalypha hispida*)	Medium to high	Evenly moist	Needs warmth and high humidity.
Lipstick vine (*Aeschynanthus* hybrids)	Medium	Moist; drier in winter	Good for hanging baskets.
Flamingo flowers (*Anthurium* spp.)	Medium	Constantly moist	Must have warmth and high humidity.
Flowering begonias (*Begonia* spp.)	Medium	Allow to dry slightly between waterings	Discard Reiger types after flowering, as they will not usually rebloom next season.
Bougainvilleas (*Bougainvillea* spp.)	High	Allow to dry between waterings; water less after flowering	Needs warmth indoors; grow outdoors in summer.
Ornamental pepper (*Capsicum annuum*)	High	Evenly moist	Grow plants in the garden in summer and move them inside to a warm spot for the winter.
Chrysanthemums (*Chrysanthemum* spp.)	High	Moist	Prefer cool temperatures. Discard or plant outside after bloom.
Citrus (*Citrus* spp.)	High	Allow to dry slightly between waterings	Outstanding winter fragrance and fruit if you keep the plants outside for the summer.
Clivia (*Clivia miniata*)	Medium to high	Moist in summer, drier in winter	Keep cool (40°F [4°C]) in fall. Long-lived, reliable bloomer.
Coffee plant (*Coffea arabica*)	High	Constantly moist and high humidity	Needs a warm spot. Seldom produces flowers or beans when grown indoors.
Cigar plant (*Cuphea ignea*)	High	Allow to dry between waterings	Blooms readily.
Florist's cyclamen (*Cyclamen persicum*)	Medium to high	Evenly moist	Prefers cool nights. Blooms over a long period, but may not rebloom.
Crown of thorns (*Euphorbia milii*)	High	Allow to dry between waterings	Easy to grow.
Poinsettia (*Euphorbia pulcherrima*)	High	Allow to dry slightly between waterings	Prefers cool nights. May not rebloom.
Gardenia (*Gardenia jasminoides*)	High	Evenly moist with high humidity	Keep plants warm. 'Prostata' blooms more readily than standard types.
Hibiscus (*Hibiscus rosa-sinensis*)	High	Evenly moist	Keep plants warm. Hibiscus may grow to 6 feet (180 cm) tall.

None of the plants in this chart is difficult to grow if you provide the right conditions. If you're just getting started, though, you might want to try some of the plants that have a leaf symbol (🌿) after their name. These are some of the easiest houseplants you can grow. They can tolerate some neglect, they're not fussy about how they're watered, and they're not particularly susceptible to pests or diseases. These plants are also easy to find: You'll find them at almost any garden center or grocery store. Once you've gained confidence, you can start looking for more challenging kinds in specialty catalogs and greenhouses.

Flowering Houseplant	Light Needs	Water Needs	Comments
Amaryllis (*Hippeastrum* hybrids) 🌿	Medium; high when flowering	Moist while in active growth	Keep bulbs warm to start new growth after the rest period. Amaryllis will rebloom every year with minimal care. Keep the plant cool while in bloom, so flowers last longer.
Wax vine (*Hoya carnosa*) 🌿	Medium to high	Allow to dry between waterings	Very durable vining plant.
Jasmines (*Jasminum* spp.)	High	Evenly moist	Jasmines generally prefer warmth, but some need a cool period in fall to flower. Superb fragrance. Prune after bloom season.
Kalanchoe (*Kalanchoe blossfeldiana*)	High	Allow to dry between waterings	Thrives in average to cool temperatures. May not rebloom.
Orange jasmine (*Murraya paniculata*) 🌿	Medium to high	Evenly moist	Easy to grow, with superb fragrance.
Orchids	Ranges from low to high	High humidity; allow to dry between waterings	Moth orchids have very long-lasting flowers.
Sweet olive (*Osmanthus fragrans*)	High	Allow to dry slightly between waterings	Plants prefer cool conditions. The small flowers have superb fragrance.
Oxalis (*Oxalis* spp.)	High	Evenly moist	Some types require a dormant (rest) period after flowering.
Passionflowers (*Passiflora* spp.)	Very high	Keep moist while growing	Plants need warmth. Many types are fragrant; robust vines will require a trellis.
Geraniums (*Pelargonium* spp.)	High	Allow to dry between waterings	Geraniums can take average to cool temperatures. Grow them outside in summer. There are many types of geranium with scented or patterned leaves.
African violets (*Saintpaulia* hybrids)	Medium	Allow to dry slightly between waterings	Keep African violets warm. They make excellent long-blooming houseplants.
Christmas cactus (*Schlumbergera bridgesii*) 🌿	Medium to high	Moist while blooming; then drier	Requires long, dark nights and cool temperatures in fall to set flower buds.
Gloxinias (*Sinningia* hybrids)	Medium to high	Keep moist and provide high humidity	Gloxinias prefer warmth, but they appreciate a cool rest period after flowering.
Jerusalem cherry (*Solanum pseudocapsicum*)	High	Keep moist	Keep plants cool. May grow to 4 feet (120 cm) tall.
Stephanotis (*Stephanotis floribunda*)	High	Keep moist	Vining plants produce clusters of fragrant star-like flowers.
Cape primrose (*Streptocarpus* hybrids)	Medium	Keep moist	Cape primrose offers a long period of colorful bloom.

Foliage Houseplant	Light Needs	Water Needs	Comments
Century plants (*Agave* spp.)	High	Allow to dry between waterings	Dependable slow-growing plant.
Chinese evergreens (*Aglaeonema* spp.)	Low	Evenly moist	Prefers warm temperatures; otherwise, very easy.
Medicine plants (*Aloe* spp.)	Medium to high	Allow to dry between waterings	Juice from the leaves will relieve pain from burns.
Zebra plant (*Aphelandra squarossa*)	High	Keep moist and provide high humidity	Keep plants warm. Cut the stems back hard after flowering to promote new growth.
Norfolk Island pine (*Araucaria heterophylla*)	Medium to high	Evenly moist	Excellent houseplant; can grow to 10 feet (3 m) tall in containers.
Asparagus fern (*Asparagus densiflorus*)	Medium to high	Just moist	Plants prefer average to cool temperatures. Divide and repot when roots fill the container.
Cast-iron plant (*Aspidistra elatior*)	Low	Evenly moist	Very sturdy houseplant.
Foliage begonias (*Begonia* spp.)	Medium to high	Allow to dry between waterings; give extra humidity and warmth	Some types need a dormant (rest) period for part of the year.
Schefflera (*Brassaia actinophylla*)	High	Allow to dry between waterings	Prefers warm temperatures. Very tough plant. May grow to 8 feet (2.4 m) tall.
Bromeliads	High	Water in leaf cup	Prefer extra humidity and warmth.
Cacti	Medium to high	Allow to dry well between waterings; no water in winter	Many different types and sizes are available.
Spider plant (*Chlorophytum comosum*)	Medium	Allow to dry between waterings	Easy to grow; excellent in hanging baskets.
Grape ivy (*Cissus* spp.)	Medium or high	Evenly moist	These plants look good in hanging baskets.
Croton (*Codiaeum variegatum* var. *pictum*)	High	Keep moist and give extra humidity	Fast-growing. Must have warmth and high light for best colors.
Jade plant (*Crassula argentea*)	Medium or high	Allow to dry well between waterings	Excellent, sturdy houseplant.
Dumbcane (*Dieffenbachia seguine*)	Low to high	Allow to dry between waterings	Very easy to grow. May reach 6 feet (180 cm) tall.
False aralia (*Dizygotheca elegantissima*)	Low to medium	Allow to dry between waterings	May be short-lived.
Dracaenas (*Dracaena* spp.)	Low to high	Moist	Prefer warm temperatures; otherwise very sturdy and adaptable.
Aralia (*Fatsia japonica*)	High	Just moist	Prefers cool temperatures. Fast-growing; prune in spring.
Ferns	Medium to high	Moist	Very graceful; many different types and sizes.
Figs (*Ficus* spp.)	Medium to high	Allow to dry between waterings	Many types are excellent houseplants.
Fittonia (*Fittonia verschaffeltii*)	Low	Must have high humidity; keep moist	Beautiful leaves but may be difficult to grow; needs warmth.

Foliage Houseplant	Light Needs	Water Needs	Comments
Haworthia (*Haworthia* spp.)	Medium	Allow to dry between waterings	Very tough houseplants.
English ivy (*Hedera helix*)	Low to high	Allow to dry between waterings	Plants prefer average to cool temperatures. Many cultivars have attractively patterned leaves.
Polka dot plant (*Hypoestes phyllostachya*)	High	Allow to dry between waterings	Needs lots of light to keep its spots.
Prayer plant (*Maranta leuconeura*)	Medium	Keep moist; likes high humidity	Beautifully marked leaves.
Split-leaved philodendron (*Monstera deliciosa*)	Medium to high	Barely moist	Prefers warm temperatures. This vining plant needs a trellis to grow upward.
Ponytail palm (*Nolina recurvata*)	Medium to high	Allow to dry between waterings	Sturdy and slow-growing.
Palms	Medium	Allow to dry between waterings	Parlor palm (*Chamaedorea elegans*) needs only low light.
Peperomias (*Peperomia* spp.)	Low to high	Keep moist; water less in winter.	Be careful not to overwater.
Philodendrons (*Philodendron* spp.)	Medium to high	Barely moist	Plants prefer warm temperatures. Cuttings root easily in water.
Pileas (*Pilea* spp.)	Medium to high	Just moist; extra humidity	Prefer warm temperatures. Best to take cuttings and start new plants annually.
Swedish ivy (*Plectranthus australis*)	Medium to high	Moist	Grow in hanging pots and pinch back regularly.
Pothos (*Raphidophora aureum*)	Low to high	Allow to dry between waterings	Very easy to grow.
Moses-in-a-boat (*Rhoeo spathacea*)	Medium to high	Allow to dry between waterings	Easy to grow.
Snake plant (*Sansevieria trifasciata*)	Low to high	Allow to dry between waterings	Sturdy and slow-growing.
Strawberry begonia (*Saxifraga stolonifera*)	Medium	Keep moist; drier in winter	Prefers cool temperatures. When plants start to look ragged, repot plantlets and discard old plants.
Burro's tail (*Sedum morganianum*)	Medium to high	Moderately moist in spring and summer	Grow in hanging baskets.
Baby's tears (*Soleirolia soleirolii*)	Medium	Needs lots of water and extra humidity	Best grown in terrariums.
Peace lily (*Spathiphyllum* hybrids)	Low to medium	Moist	Peace lily adapts to average to warm temperatures. An excellent plant for low-light areas.
Syngonium (*Syngonium podophyllum*)	Medium	Evenly moist	Prune frequently; very easy to grow.
Piggyback plant (*Tolmiea menziesii*)	Low to medium	Keep moist and humid in spring and fall, slightly drier in winter	Prefers average to cool temperatures. Grow in hanging baskets.
Wandering Jew (*Zebrina pendula*)	Medium to high	Allow to dry between waterings	Likes cool nights. Pinch back to maintain full shape.

Gardening in Containers

*Container gardening allows you to grow many
kinds of plants—including flowers, trees, shrubs, vines,
vegetables, fruit, and herbs—even if you don't have any land
to have a regular garden. You can enjoy flower-filled planters on
your patio or perhaps a little window box salad garden outside
your kitchen window. And you can be as imaginative as you
like with your containers, creating exciting combinations
to add visual impact to your garden.*

Getting Started with Container Gardening

The great thing about gardening in containers is the flexibility you get. Since the plants aren't rooted in the ground, you can place them exactly where you want them. You can create a miniature landscape filled with your favorite plants right around your deck or patio, where you get to relax and really enjoy their beauty and fragrance. If you live in a high-rise apartment building or condo where you have no ground for a garden, you can create a lush green oasis on a tiny balcony or outdoor stairway. City dwellers can grow large gardens entirely in containers on building rooftops. Even if you have nothing but a wall and windows to call your own, you can fill hanging baskets with trailing plants and pack window boxes full of flowers, herbs, and vegetables. In this chapter, you'll learn creative and exciting ways to use container plants to liven up your living spaces.

With plants in containers, you can rearrange and replace each pot as needed, maintaining a garden that always looks picture-perfect. While the plants are flowering, you can place the container where you'll see it best and enjoy it most. Then, as the blooms fade, you can retire

Grouping together many small pots of annuals and bulbs creates a colorful and stunning display.

Flowering shrubs such as camellias and roses are a great choice, since they bloom every year.

the pot to the basement or garage until next year. Or, if your season permits, you can redo it with fresh plants and enjoy it all over again. For more ideas on displaying containers creatively, see "Planning Your Container Garden" below, and "Creating Great Plant Combinations" on page 76.

In Northern areas, container growing has another big advantage—it allows you to grow all sorts of perennial plants that are not cold-hardy enough to live outdoors year-round. Camellias, for instance, are hardy outside only to Zone 8, where winter minimum temperatures average 10° to 20°F (–12° to –7°C). As container plants, however, you can grow them anywhere by

moving them outside in the summer and indoors to a bright, cool sunroom or breezeway in winter. (Plus, they can bloom from November to April—a time when their splendid flowers will be especially welcome.) Fragrant orange and lemon trees are other tender plants Northerners can enjoy if grown in containers.

The fact is, you can grow practically any plant you want in a container—all kinds of flowers, bulbs, vegetables, and even small trees and shrubs. "Flowers for Pots and Planters" on page 78 is full of tips on choosing annuals, perennials, and bulbs for colorful containers all season long. If you have room for a large pot, you may want to try adding a few trees or shrubs to give height and year-round interest to your collection; see "Trees, Shrubs, and Vines for Containers" on page 84 for details. Fragrant and culinary herbs such as lavender, lemon verbena, and basil adapt well to life in containers; so do many compact cultivars of peppers, zucchini, tomatoes, and other favorite fruits and vegetables. For more information on choosing productive crops, see "Edibles and Herbs for Containers" on page 88.

Planning Your Container Garden

A container planting can be as simple as a single pot of flowers, or a larger pot with a combination of plants as lush and full as any garden border. You'll get the most enjoyment from your container plants when you choose and group them to fit in with the setting in your home or garden.

Choose the Right Size

Plants in single, small containers can look out of place all alone on a deck or patio. To get the best effect, you want your container plants to be in proper scale with the great outdoors. Whenever possible, opt for larger containers, at least 10 inches (25 cm) in diameter; generally the bigger, the better. (Large planters get very heavy, so be sure to place them where you want them before you fill them with container mix.) Using larger containers will cost a

Don't Forget Foliage

It is important to consider foliage as well as flowers when planning a container garden. If your courtyard, balcony, or patio receives sun or part sun, you can choose from a range of plants featuring colors from green to gold, yellow, gray, silver, copper, pink, and purple. While the choice for shady areas is more limited, there are still many interesting combinations of leaf shape and texture.

Leaves come in a surprising array of different greens, from the blue-green of California poppy (*Eschscholzia californica*) to the yellow-green of 'Bowles Golden' sedge (*Carex elata* 'Bowles Golden') or the deep green of geraniums. Silver-leaved plants such as dusty miller look great in almost any kind of garden. Yellowish leaves, such as those of golden feverfew or some coleus, can be pleasing with pinks and blues. As you select annuals for your container garden, try to include a few with interesting foliage to add extra color and season-long interest.

LEFT: Fortunately, nearly all greens—from blue-green to yellow-green—are agreeable colors that go well together and set off most flowers.

little more up front, but the plants will definitely grow better, you'll have to water less often, and the overall effect of the container garden will be better.

If you prefer to grow plants in smaller containers, group them together to create an eye-catching effect. It also makes the regular watering and maintenance much easier, since all the plants are in the same place. For extra interest, it's a good idea to vary the heights of plants in a group of pots. You can use short plants in smaller pots for the front and taller plants in the back. Or use bricks, plastic milk crates, or upside-down pots to vary the height of individual pots in a grouping.

Consider the Colors

To get the most enjoyment out of your container garden, don't forget to think about color combinations when you're buying the plants. Groupings usually look best when one or two colors dominate. For example, a yellow accent (maybe dwarf marigolds) works well with a group of blue flowers, such as ageratum. White is also a good accent color—it looks good with

A silver and white garden looks crisp and clean during the day, and the colors stand out at night.

every color. Sweet alyssum (*Lobularia maritima*) is an excellent, white, trailing plant that always looks nice as it spills loosely over the sides of the pots. (It also has an outstanding sweet fragrance.)

A mixture of many different colors can look too "busy," but you can create an attractive grouping with several shades of the same color. You might, for instance, try red pansies with pink primroses or try light-blue petunias with deep-blue lobelia (*Lobelia erinus*). Plants with attractive silvery or green foliage, such as dusty miller (*Senecio cineraria*) or parsley, make great accents for these kinds of plantings.

Creating Great Plant Combinations

Great-looking gardens are basically a series of many individual plant combinations. The combinations available to you will, of course, depend on the space you have, the climate, and the amount of sun your garden receives. The best combinations aren't just based on flower color and season of bloom; they consider the quality, color, and texture of the leaves, too. Good combinations also feature different plant heights and forms: short, medium, or tall; mat-like, spiky, or rounded. Equally important is overall texture—whether a plant is fine and delicate looking, like baby's-breath (*Gypsophila* spp.), or coarse and dramatic, like peonies and hostas.

If you're looking for can't-miss color, an orange and red combination might be the perfect accent for your courtyard or patio.

Contrasts and Complements

Well-planned gardens balance contrast and similarity. Contrasting colors, sizes, or other design elements are bold and stimulating. Use contrast to draw attention to a particular location and to add a lively feel. Overusing contrast— too many different textures or strong colors—can create a jumbled, chaotic look.

Similarity—the absence of contrasts—increases the sense of harmony. Use subtle variations of closely related colors and gradual height transitions to create soothing designs. Too much similarity risks being uninteresting, so add a touch of contrast—a few containers with plants of different height, color, or texture.

Repetition acts as a bridge between similarity and contrast. Repeating similar elements will unify even the boldest of designs. Exact, evenly spaced repetitions of particular plants or combinations create a formal look. You can use containers of the same size containing the same plants

Annuals for an All-blue Container Garden

Blue theme container gardens have a cool, restrained look, but they're tricky to pull off successfully. Blue and green are such similar colors that blue flowers tend to blend into the background sea of green leaves.

Varying the different kinds of blue—from soft lavender-blue to bright sky-blue and deep cobalt-blue—is one way to add extra interest to a cool-color planting. Companion plants with silver or chartreuse leaves, such as dusty miller (*Senecio cineraria*) or golden feverfew (*Tanacetum parthenium* 'Aureum'), are also excellent additions.

The following list contains a few blue-flowered annuals you might want to include in your cool-color garden. For more information, see the entries in "A Guide to Popular Container Plants" starting on page 164.

Ageratum (*Ageratum houstonianum*)
Browallia (*Browallia speciosa*)
Cornflower (*Centaurea cyanus*)
Rocket larkspur (*Consolida ambigua*)
Edging lobelia (*Lobelia erinus*)
Forget-me-not (*Myosotis sylvatica*)
Baby-blue-eyes (*Nemophila menziesii*)
Love-in-a-mist (*Nigella damascena*)
Mealy-cup sage (*Salvia farinacea*)
Wishbone flower (*Torenia fournieri*)
Pansy (*Viola* x *wittrockiana*)

Baby-blue-eyes

to create a "bed" of plants. Combine different plants with similar flower colors or leaf shapes to give an informal garden a cohesive but casual look.

Color Combinations

Different colors have different personalities. Warm colors—those related to red, orange, or yellow—are bold. They are stimulating and appear closer to the viewer. Cool colors—those related to violet, blue, or green—are more tranquil and appear to recede from the viewer. Mixing warm and cool colors together will add depth and interest to your container plantings.

Combining colors in gardens is as easy as combining colors in clothes—possibly even easier! The green of foliage can be used to harmonize strong colors—such as reds and oranges—that you probably wouldn't think to combine in an outfit. Pastel colors like soft pinks, blues, and yellows may look washed out against a light-colored shirt, but they never get lost against dark-green leaves.

Color combinations are very personal creations. While certain types and combinations of colors tend to create specific effects, only you can decide whether you like that particular effect. Some gardeners enjoy the lively result of mixing orange and yellow with purple or blue; others prefer the crisp look of whites or the restful feel of pale yellows, soft pinks, and silvers. Color combinations in container gardens are not limited to plants, as you can create bold contrasts by placing massed white flowers in a black container.

Combining similar flower colors creates a harmonious effect. Try grouping reds with oranges and yellows, yellows with greens and blues, or blues with purples and reds. Colors sharing the same degree of lightness or darkness often look good

Blues and purples look best in a position where you can see them up close. From a distance, they'll blend into the background.

together; for instance, several different pastels—like pale blues, yellows, and pinks—blend more harmoniously than several pure hues.

If contrast and excitement are what you're after, choose complementary hues like yellow and violet, red and green, or blue and orange. Or place a light tint next to a very bright or dark shade of the same hue (try pale blue with intense blue, dark blue, or pale pink next to fuchsia or burgundy).

White and gray aren't part of the color wheel, but they play an important role in garden schemes. White has a split personality—it can be exciting or soothing. Bright white is surprisingly bold; it stands out among bright and dark colors, even in a group of soft pastels. A dash of pure white in a combination of harmonious colors is as dramatic as a dash of a bright complementary color. Cream and similar

A particularly striking combination can be created with two containers of all-white and all-black tulips.

muted whites are softer and they blend well with everything.

Gray is the great unifier. Silver or gray foliage works even better than green to soften the transition between two complementary or bold colors. Gray adds a drama of its own by contrasting with green foliage.

Always consider the color and texture of your container material when you are designing a container garden. Terracotta, plastic, timber, and concrete create very different effects.

Stocks and browallia

Texture and Form

Two other plant characteristics—texture and form—are as important as color in creating interesting combinations. Masses of even-textured foliage can tone down bold colors, while dramatic leaf shapes can add extra zip to a pastel planting. Here are some other tips you can try when designing effective plantings:

• Balance rounded clump-formers, such as shasta daisies (*Leucanthemum* x *superbum*) and coreopsis, with spiky plants such as mulleins (*Verbascum* spp.), globe thistle (*Echinops ritro*), and spike gayfeather (*Liatris spicata*).

• Contrast shiny leaves—such as those of heart-leaved bergenia (*Bergenia cordifolia*) and Italian arum (*Arum italicum*)—with velvety or fuzzy leaves, such as those of lamb's-ears (*Stachys byzantina*) or lungworts (*Pulmonaria* spp.).

• Contrast fine foliage, such as lacy fern fronds, with the smooth, broad leaves of hostas and similar plants.

• Include spiky leaves, like those of irises and yucca (*Yucca filamentosa*); they'll stand out from mat-like or mounded plants long after their flowers fade.

Flowers for Pots and Planters

Nothing says summer like pots and planters filled to overflowing with lush foliage and beautiful blooms. Create your own colorful container gardens with a bounty of easy annuals and bulbs and dependable, long-blooming perennials.

Choosing a Container

Container possibilities are endless. You can buy commercially made plastic or clay containers or make your own out of old barrels, washtubs, or even buckets. Be creative; almost anything you can put drainage holes in—from clay drainage tiles to old leather work boots—can be pressed into service.

Solid-sided containers, such as plastic pots, hold water longer than porous clay. Plastics are great if your summers tend to be hot and dry, since you'll have to water less often. But if you live in a wet climate, or if you tend to overwater, porous pots are probably best. Plastic pots are lighter, making them easier to move, but they are more prone to blowing over. Clay pots are heavy and less likely to blow over, but they often crack when they do tip.

In windy areas or for tall plants, place rocks in the bottom of any pot to increase stability. Dark pots heat up in bright sun

A combination of tall tulips and low-growing English daisies, both in pale pink tones, is an eyecatching combination.

and dry out quickly; avoid black plastic pots for container gardens that are growing in full sun. For more information about types of containers, see "Considering Containers" on page 18.

Caring for Annuals and Perennials in Containers

Container plants share closer quarters than garden plants, so they need special care to stay lush and lovely. Large pots tend to provide the best conditions for growth, since they hold more soil, nutrients, and water, but they are also quite heavy if you need to move them. Pots or baskets that are about 8 inches (20 cm) deep can usually hold enough soil for good growth without getting too heavy. If you don't plan to move the planter, it can be as big as you want; containers as large as half-barrels will give you ample planting space for a wide variety of flowers.

Best Bets for Butterflies

Here are some beautiful perennials that are especially popular with butterflies. You can learn more about the plants listed below by looking up their individual entries in "A Guide to Popular Container Plants," starting on page 164.

Asclepias tuberosa (butterfly weed)
Aster novae-angliae (New England aster)
Astilbe x *arendsii* (astilbe)
Baptisia australis (blue false indigo)
Centranthus ruber (red valerian)
Dianthus gratiopolitanus (cheddar pinks)
Echinacea purpurea (purple coneflower)
Erigeron speciosus (daisy fleabane)
Gaillardia x *grandiflora* (blanket flowers)
Helenium autumnale (common sneezeweed)
Leucanthemum x *superbum* (shasta daisy)
Phlox paniculata (garden phlox)
Rudbeckia fulgida (orange coneflower)
Sedum spectabile (showy stonecrop)

Common sulfur butterfly and New England aster

Planting Your Annuals and Perennials

You should fill your container with an all-purpose container mix purchased from your local nursery or garden center. You need to choose a growing medium that will hold some water but not too much. Straight garden soil isn't a good choice, but you can improve it by mixing 2 parts soil with 1 part finished compost (or peat moss) and 1 part perlite. Commercial container mixes are easy to use, and they can support a variety of different plants. Or you can use sterilized, premixed "soil-less" container mixes. These are free of soilborne diseases and they weigh much less than regular container mixes—an important consideration for rooftop gardeners and for plantings in large pots. Set your plants into the container mix, firm them in, and then water well.

Watering

Keeping the right water balance is a key part of successful container gardening. Some containers may need watering every day, others only once a week. A general rule is to wait until the top 1 inch (2.5 cm) of container mix is dry; then water well, until some comes out of the bottom. If the water seems to run right through the pot, put a tray or saucer underneath; empty any water that remains the next day. Very small pots, small and medium-sized clay containers, and hanging baskets dry out especially quickly; you may have to water these as often as twice a day.

If a pot or basket dries out completely, you still may be able to save the plants. Set the pot or basket in a larger container filled with water, let it sit there for an hour or two, and then set the pot or basket in a shady spot for a few hours until the plants perk up again. Then move the pot or basket back to its original spot, but be extra careful to keep the plants well watered from then on.

Fertilizing

Besides regular watering, the other key to lush-looking annuals and perennials is regular fertilizing. Since their rooting space is limited, annuals and perennials in containers need fertilizer much more often than plants growing in the ground. Give them a boost by watering them with diluted fish emulsion, liquid seaweed, or a balanced organic fertilizer; follow the instructions on the package to find out how often and how much fertilizer you should apply. You can also water the plants with compost tea (made by soaking a shovelful of finished compost in a bucket of water for about a week, then straining out the soaked compost).

Start in late spring by feeding once every 2 weeks, then check the containers in midsummer. If annuals and perennials look lush but aren't flowering well, change

The orange-yellow of the marigolds and calendulas is a great complement to the purple-leaved ornamental cabbages and kale.

to fertilizing once every 3 weeks. If the plants begin to look somewhat spindly, start fertilizing every week. If the plants seem to be growing and flowering well, stick with the 2-week schedule.

Solving Challenges with Containers

With a little creativity, you'll find many different ways to use containers filled with annuals and perennials. If you can't kneel, or if you garden from a wheelchair, you can grow plants at a convenient height in raised planters. If your soil is too hard or rocky to dig, you can grow flowers in half-barrel planters instead of in the ground.

If you've got a shady spot that's just crying out for color, you can use potted annuals or perennials to create a rotating display: As flowers fade, move the shady pot to a sunnier spot and replace with a container that's robust from sunshine. Or tuck a few pots into a dull planting to add quick color. If space is really limited, you could create your own garden paradise on a rooftop or porch, or in a window box.

Containers can also make great garden accents. Choose bold, sculptural perennials such as yucca (*Yucca filamentosa*) for formal designs; mix different colors and cascading plants for a cottage look.

Annuals

Annuals make perfect container plants. They grow quickly, flower profusely, and provide a long season of good looks. Some also offer distinctive foliage, while others perfume the air with their sweet scents.

Groups of small and medium-sized containers create charming spots of movable color; large planters can showcase a stunning mix of colorful annuals in a relatively small space. Window boxes and hanging baskets are other options for displaying a wide range of flowering and foliage annuals.

You can insert small, individual pots of flowers, such as primulas, inside window boxes, for an instant display.

Choosing Annuals for Containers

While most annuals do extremely well in containers, the many compact cultivars of marigolds, petunias, impatiens, begonias, and ageratum are especially good. These annuals begin blooming early and put on a non-stop show of color all season long.

As with any kind of garden, the first step to planning successful container plantings is choosing plants that have similar growth needs, such as their light requirements. The amount of sun or shade your container garden receives is a major consideration for your choice of plants.

Most flowering annuals prefer plenty of sun. Sunny spots can support a wider range of colorful annuals, including treasure flower (*Gazania rigens*), mealy-cup sage (*Salvia farinacea*), and narrow-leaved zinnia (*Zinnia angustifolia*). Be sure you don't plant sun-lovers, such as marigolds, in the same container with shade-loving annuals, like coleus.

If you're planting a container for a shady spot, take care to select plants that thrive in shade. If you're looking for plants for a shady location, some of the best choices include flowering tobacco (*Nicotiana* spp.), bergenia (*Bergenia cordifolia*), wishbone flower (*Torenia fournieri*), impatiens (*Impatiens* spp.), wax begonias (*Begonia* Semperflorens-Cultorum hybrids), and monkey flower (*Mimulus* x *hybridus*).

Each cell pack or seed packet will come with a label that tells you if the plants prefer sun or part shade. However, be skeptical of those sun/shade ratings; labels sometimes say a particular plant can take part shade when it really requires full sun to grow well. To confirm plants' light needs, check their individual entries in "A Guide to Popular Container Plants," starting on page 164.

When planning a container garden—whether it is a pot, hanging basket, window box, or planter—you also need to consider the ultimate height of the annuals you select. As a general guideline, try to choose annuals that are the same height or smaller than the height of the container; otherwise, the planting may look top-heavy.

When to Buy and What to Plant

Spring is when garden centers have the largest selection of annual flowers (and again in the fall for those of you in milder climates), and that's when you will probably want to fill most of your containers. Most annuals aren't frost-tolerant, so you should put them out after the danger of frost has passed. One major exception to this rule is the pansy. Pansies (and their cousins, Johnny-jump-ups [*Viola tricolor*]) are very fond of cool spring (and fall) weather; plant them outside just as soon as the garden centers get them in.

If you didn't get around to setting up your containers in spring, or if your pansy plantings are looking tired by midsummer, don't assume you're stuck with no flowers for the rest of the season. Grocery and discount stores often sell annuals only in the spring, but you can usually find some nice annuals at local garden centers later in the season.

Single-annual containers can be pleasing, but mixed plantings of three or four different annuals are even more exciting. While the plants you pick are up to you, there are some basic guidelines you can follow to create a successful container planting. First, select a "star" plant. Base your container planting around one centerpiece plant—perhaps a tall cleome, a tuberous begonia, or a bold love-lies-bleeding (*Amaranthus caudatus*). Then choose a "supporting cast" to complement the star plant and fill out the

Start Your Own Annuals

For an "instant" effect, you can buy and plant annuals that are already blooming. If you're not in a hurry, though, you can start your own; many kinds are easy to grow from seed. Growing your own annuals is also a good way to save money.

Some kinds of annuals, such as marigolds, mature quickly, so you can sow them directly into outdoor pots. Other annuals that are easy to grow from direct-sown seed include sweet alyssum (*Lobularia maritima*), nasturtiums (*Tropaeolum majus*), morning glories (*Ipomoea* spp.), and zinnias. Sweet alyssum is cold-tolerant, so you can plant the seed in early spring; for the rest, wait until after frost has passed.

Other annuals have very tiny seeds or might take a little longer before they start flowering, so they are best started indoors under lights. Check the instructions on the seed packets, and start the seeds the recommended number of weeks before your last spring frost so they'll start flowering shortly after you move them outside. If you live in an area with a long growing season, start another batch of plants in early summer; use these to replace tired container plantings in late summer or early fall in order to have an all-season display of flowers.

Nasturtiums

You can train lantana (*Lantana camara*) to grow upright into a stunning lollipop-shaped standard, or tree, form.

container. Try one or two with bold leaves or an upright habit—such as impatiens or snapdragons—and one or two that sprawl or trail—such as edging lobelia (*Lobelia erinus*) or creeping zinnia (*Sanvitalia procumbens*).

Growing Perennials in Containers

No matter what size or style of garden you have, growing perennials in pots can greatly expand your planting options. You will also discover how practical and versatile these movable gardens can be. Perennials work well in pots as long as you give them the growing conditions and routine care that they need. Plant several perennials in one pot or group several in individual containers. Top choices include those with a long season of bloom, such as the compact, golden orange 'Stella d'Oro' daylily. Other perennials that look especially good in containers are those with interesting foliage, such as hostas, ornamental grasses, lady's-mantle (*Alchemilla mollis*), heart-leaved bergenia (*Bergenia cordifolia*), and spotted lamium (*Lamium maculatum*). Try using some of these plants in large containers, mixed with annuals to provide constant color. Hardy bulbs also add spring color to containers.

Perennials need a little more care than annuals, as you don't just pull them out at the end of the season. Because they are growing in containers, they are much more susceptible to winter damage than plants growing in the ground. In Northern areas, you'll want to move container perennials to an unheated garage or cold basement to protect them from the alternate freezing and thawing cycles, which can damage or kill them. You'll need to water the pots lightly during winter.

Bulbs for Container Gardens

As you plan your container plantings, don't stop with common favorites like geraniums and petunias; liven them up with some colorful bulbs! Bulbs make excellent companions for annuals in pots, since the annuals usually root

Dependable, Easy-care Perennials

Here's a list of some of the most trouble-free perennials you can grow. All of the plants below thrive in sun and all-purpose container mix with little fuss.

Achillea tomentosa (woolly yarrow)
Alchemilla mollis (lady's-mantle)
Anemone tomentosa 'Robustissima' (Japanese anemone)
Armeria maritima (common thrift)
Asclepias tuberosa (butterfly weed)
Aster novae-angliae (New England aster)
Baptisia australis (blue false indigo)
Boltonia asteroides (boltonia)
Centranthus ruber (red valerian)
Coreopsis spp. (coreopsis)
Echinacea purpurea (purple coneflower)
Echinops ritro (globe thistle)
Gaillardia x *grandiflora* (blanket flower)
Geranium sanguineum (blood-red cranesbill)
Hemerocallis hybrids (daylilies)
Iris sibirica (Siberian iris)
Leucanthemum x *superbum* (shasta daisy)
Liatris spicata (spike gayfeather)
Lilium hybrids (lilies)
Narcissus hybrids (daffodils)
Nepeta mussinii (catmint)
Paeonia lactiflora (common garden peony, single-flowered cultivars)
Platycodon grandiflorus (balloon flower)
Rudbeckia fulgida (orange coneflower)
Salvia x *superba* (violet sage)
Veronica spicata (spike speedwell)
Yucca filamentosa (yucca)

Asters and bellflowers

Broad, shallow containers work well for displaying daffodils and other spring bulbs.

in the top soil layer while the bulbs are planted much deeper. The bulbs also benefit from the covering of annuals, which shade the soil and pot to some extent, keeping the bulbs cool. Some bulbs provide beautiful blooms; others provide eye-catching foliage. And there are bulbs for almost every exposure, from bright sunshine to dappled shade.

Container Bulbs through the Season

Pots of traditional spring-blooming bulbs—including hyacinths, tulips, and daffodils—are especially welcome early in the growing season. To coax them into bloom in pots, you need to give them a chilling period, as explained in "Growing Bulbs Indoors" on page 59. These spring bloomers combine beautifully with cool-season annuals, such as pansies, common stock (*Matthiola incana*), and English daisy (*Bellis perennis*).

When warm weather sets in, summer bulbs come into their glory. Asiatic lilies make a lovely show in early summer and look especially good with a cascade of annual blooms beneath them. Other great summer bulbs for pots include gladioli, crocosmia and Siberian iris (*Iris sibirica*).

For partially shady spots, tuberous begonias are among the most wonderful of potted bulbs. They bloom over a long period, in a wide range of colors and flower forms. Cascading types can look

charming tumbling out of hanging baskets or over the sides of large containers. For extra excitement, grow tuberous begonias with shade-loving annual companions, such as coleus, fibrous begonias, browallia (*Browallia speciosa*), and wishbone flower (*Torenia fournieri*).

Blooming Bulbs through the Year

With some planning, you can have bulbs blooming in your container garden from spring through fall. Below is an approximate bloom schedule for gardens in Zone 6. Zone 3 gardens are usually a good 2 weeks later; gardens in Zone 8 and warmer parts of Zone 7 are about 1 week earlier. (If you're not sure which zone you live in, see the USDA Plant Hardiness Zone Map on page 276.)

Species crocus (including *Crocus tommasinianus*): early March
Snowdrops (*Galanthus* spp.): early March
Reticulated iris (*Iris reticulata*): early March
Dutch crocus (*Crocus vernus* hybrids): late March
Early daffodils: late March to early April
Species tulips: April
Grape hyacinths (*Muscari* spp.): mid-April
Siberian squill (*Scilla sibirica*): mid-April
Daffodils and narcissus: late April
Hyacinths: late April
Crown imperial (*Fritillaria imperalis*): late April
Hybrid tulips: late April to May
Giant onion (*Allium giganteum*): early summer
Lilies: early to late summer
Autumn crocuses (*Colchicum* and *Crocus* spp.): early fall to midfall
Hardy cyclamen (*Cyclamen* spp.): fall or early spring

Containers for Bulbs

For best results, choose a large pot that can hold an ample amount of container mix. Large pots will provide ample rooting room for your bulbs, and they tend to dry out less quickly than small pots. For lilies, choose a pot at least 10 inches (25 cm) wide and deep. Smaller bulbs can grow in slightly smaller pots, but they'll also do well in large containers. Big plants such as cannas need plenty of room; try them in large planters or half-barrels.

Fill the bottom of the container with a well-drained commercial container mix. Adjust the thickness of this layer to match the needs of the bulbs you're planting. Lily bulbs should sit deep enough to have 5 to 6 inches (12.5 to 15 cm) of container mix over their tops; set smaller bulbs so they're covered with 3 to 4 inches (7.5 to 10 cm) of mix. Fill the container with container mix to within an inch or two (2.5 to 5 cm) of the rim. You can also plant young annual plants into the pot as you normally would, firming them in well and then watering thoroughly.

A container packed full of variegated tulips adds a touch of spring to any part of the garden.

If you're growing pots of warmth-loving summer bulbs—like dahlias and liliums—you can get a head start on the season by starting them indoors. Plant them inside in 6- to 8-inch (15- to 20- cm) pots, 6 to 8 weeks before nighttime temperatures hit 50°F (10°C). Grow them under lights, in a greenhouse, or on a sunny porch or windowsill while you wait for the weather to warm up. When you're ready to set them out in their outdoor containers, remove the bulbs from their pot and plant them at the same depth they were growing. Then plant annuals around the sides, being careful not to damage the bulb shoots.

Caring for Container Bulbs

Throughout the season, keep a close eye on your containers to make sure the container mix doesn't dry out completely. In hot, dry weather, you may need to water every day, especially for small containers. Fertilize several times during the summer months to keep the plants growing vigorously. For more information on basic container maintenance, see "Caring for Annuals and Perennials in Containers" on page 78.

At the end of the season, dig out the bulbs or tubers of tender bulbs for winter storage. Shake off the soil and let the bulbs air dry for several days. Store them in labeled paper or mesh bags, or bury them in wood shavings, styrofoam packing material, or peat moss to prevent the bulbs from drying out too much. Check the bulbs monthly and sprinkle them lightly with water if they look shriveled. Or simply leave the bulbs in their pot and bring the whole pot indoors for winter storage in a cool basement.

Grasses for Containers

Many small and medium-sized grasses are attractive in pots, urns, and planters. Northern gardeners can enjoy spectacular grasses that are hardy only in Zones 8 and 9 by growing them outdoors in pots during the summer, then moving them to a cellar or cool greenhouse for the winter.

In very hot weather, check plants daily and water as needed to keep the container mix evenly moist. Since frequent watering leaches nutrients out of the mix, give container-grown grasses a topdressing of compost or organic fertilizer during the hotter summer months.

In mild climates, you can leave the containers outdoors all winter as long as you never let the soil dry completely. In colder regions, either store the containers indoors or tip them on their sides, so water can't collect and drown the roots. Then bury them beneath a pile of leaves, evergreen boughs, or similar materials.

When rescuing buried plants from outdoor storage in the spring, wait until all frosts are over before uncovering them. If the plants have started to grow, put them in a sheltered, shaded spot for a few days until the foliage has hardened enough for them to withstand sunlight.

Ornamental grasses make exciting container plants. However, you may need to bring pots of cold-tender types indoors for the winter months.

Container Water Gardens

A small water garden adds a special sparkle to any collection of container plants. As a bonus, the open water will attract birds and even frogs and toads. You can use any large container—an old bathtub, half-whiskey barrel, or a special plastic tub sold complete with a filter and small fountain. Set the container on your patio or deck, or sink it into the ground for a natural pool effect.

A filter usually isn't necessary for a small water garden if you make sure you include a few oxygenating plants—such as *Elodea canadensis*—to help keep the water clear. Specialty nurseries sell these oxygenators, along with pygmy (dwarf)

water lilies and other water plants suitable for a tub garden. Grow the plants in individual containers set down into the tub, so that you can replace them as needed or dismantle the garden for the winter in the North.

Always include a few fish in the container to control mosquito larvae. Goldfish are a great choice, and they're easy to overwinter indoors in a goldfish bowl or small aquarium.

Trees, Shrubs, and Vines for Containers

Trees and shrubs are great choices for containers if you need a large plant for a certain spot. If you select a potted tree or shrub that's evergreen or has attractive bark even when its leaves are gone, you'll get year-round enjoyment. Container vines are good as they have the plus of providing quick shade or privacy for an exposed porch or patio.

Trees

The only limit to the size of a potted tree is your ability to lift the container. You'll find it rather difficult to carry a large specimen up many flights of stairs onto a narrow balcony, whereas a grouping of smaller shrubs and vines will be easier for you to manage. What's more, in a windy position, large, top-heavy specimens can be easily blown over, so your first step is to select a large container that will help to anchor the plant. In many situations, though, one large tree in a container is all you need to add a spectacular focal point to your courtyard. These large trees are not cheap to buy, so when visiting your garden center keep clearly in mind what you are trying to achieve.

Your garden or balcony might be overlooked by a neighboring window at a particular height, so you will need to select an evergreen for year-round privacy. Then, if your ground space is limited, you could consider a standard tree on a long trunk, so that the foliage can spread out in a canopy above a seating area, with the added bonus of giving you shade while affording privacy. If you're faced with a blank wall, though, you'll want to cover it, and what could be smarter than a series of troughs filled with quick-growing sasanqua camellias (*Camellia sasanqua*) to provide a deep-green, evergreen camouflage which pays dividends every fall with a wall of flowers. Some of the conifers, such as *Chamaecyparis*, *Juniperus*, and *Picea* species, could also be used in this situation, but you'll forgo a floral bonus with these more structured beauties.

Making Light Work of Moving Large Containers

Large trees need large containers, but if you've ever tried to move one you'll realize how difficult it can be—that is, unless you place the container on a movable base, before filling it with compost and the plant. These wheeled wonders, which come in a variety of styles and finishes, make moving a plant child's play! You'll find them really handy to move a plant as the seasons change, whether it be to protect a plant from winter chill or to move the pot to a more sheltered position, away from the fierce sun in the height of summer.

Shrubs

Maybe you just want a garden at eye level to enjoy with no particular need for privacy considerations, so here you can indulge to your heart's delight as there are shrubs ideally suited to container gardening no matter what your climate zone and weather conditions. The type

ABOVE: A potted flowering maple looks good with an understory of low-growing annuals.
RIGHT: Place potted gardenias in outdoor seating areas, where you can appreciate the perfume.

This sunny balcony garden includes a decorative, yet refreshing, display of mainly greenery and the soft pale-pink tones of the containerized roses.

of garden you can create using shrubs in containers is endless, so don't feel at all limited by the size of your garden—some of the prettiest gardens are those featuring traditional, cottage garden shrubs such as roses, pelargoniums, and lavender cotton (*Santolina chamaecyparissus*) spilling unhindered from containers. If conditions are tough—too shady, windy, or hot—you

can choose between tough shrubs such as Japanese aucuba (*Aucuba japonica*), heavenly bamboo (*Nandina domestica*), and yuccas, which are almost happy to look after themselves. Or you can create a tropical paradise using plants with lush-looking foliage that you'll be able to combine in exotic ceramic bowls placed near a water feature or garden sculpture. If

that's too flamboyant for your climate or nature, you could choose more sedate plants like box (*Buxus sempervirens*) that you can clip into formal balls, tripods, or—once you become addicted—into animal shapes.

Vines

Where space is really tight, vines provide the ideal solution as they scramble to great heights while not taking up too much ground space when

If you suspect that a shrub or tree may not be cold-hardy, move it to a protected place for the winter.

planted in large containers. There are a number of quick-growing annual vines that are ideal for summer color if you live in cold areas, but don't dismiss the more enduring climbers if you live in more temperate zones. Look for dense, evergreen screeners such as English ivy (*Hedera helix*), star jasmine (*Trachelospermum jasminoides*), or stephanotis (*Stephanotis floribunda*). There are also the more delicate clematis species which like their roots in the shade but climb to great heights looking for the sun. Bleeding glorybower (*Clerodendrum thomsoniae*) is very much at home in more humid conditions outdoors, or you can treasure it as a potted patio or conservatory plant in colder climates. And, remember, not all vines are meant to grow skyward. There are many that you can grow in a hanging basket to flow from above head height to eye level, including cup-and-saucer vine (*Cobaea scandens*), black-eyed Susan vine (*Thunbergia alata*), or sun-loving nasturtiums (*Tropaeolum majus*).

Annual Vines for Summer Screens

If you have a location where you need some fast summer shade or a screen for privacy, try growing annual vines in your containers.

Brilliant 'Heavenly Blue' morning glory (*Ipomoea tricolor* 'Heavenly Blue') will quickly grow to 10 feet (3 m) or more. Sweet peas (*Lathyrus odoratus*) won't grow quite as tall, but they'll produce loads of lusciously fragrant flowers for cutting. Or try an edible and ornamental bean like scarlet runner bean (*Phaseolus coccineus*). These annual vines don't need much to climb on—just get them started up some stakes, string, or twine, and they'll do the rest themselves.

Camellia

You don't have to restrict your container gardening to one plant per pot—you'll want to try to gain maximum benefit from your limited garden space, so join in the fun of experimentation. Try training a fuchsia (*Fuchsia* x *hybrida*) into a standard plant with a living mulch of a delicate creeper at its base. Or choose a rose to team with a clematis to produce a striking color display that will bloom for a long period over summer. Then, when you prune, take cuttings of your favorite geranium or hydrangea, place them in individual terracotta pots, and line them up a flight of sunny steps in summer. You'll have as much fun as a gardener with a large plot, but you'll have much more time to sit and enjoy the potted garden you took delight in growing.

Special Container Considerations

During the growing season, container trees, shrubs, and vines need basically the same attention you give to your other potted plants. In the winter, however, they'll require a little special care.

Roots of plants growing in containers are exposed to more cold than if they were growing in the ground, so a plant that is normally winter-hardy in the garden in your area might not survive a cold winter in a container. To ensure success, there are several things you can do.

First, if you want to leave the plants outside year-round, choose species and cultivars that are rated to be hardy to at least one zone colder than your area. If, for example, you live in Zone 6, choose

Support Your Vines

Vining plants also make great additions to container gardens. To keep them from sprawling, however, you'll need to provide some kind of support for them to climb on. You can buy trellises or make your own. Since wood or bamboo stakes may rot and break off after a year or two, plastic supports are a better choice for perennial vines. If you buy a ready-made wooden trellis, insert plastic or metal poles in the container soil, then attach the wooden trellis to this permanent support.

If your vines don't cling to the support on their own, you may need to help them out. Use string or plastic-coated wire ties to attach the vine stems to the support. Be careful not to fasten the stems too tightly, and check the ties several times during the season; you don't want them to cut into the stems.

1. Set the base of the trellis into the container, then fill in around it with the container mix.

2. Place the new vine next to the trellis at the same level that it was growing in its original container.

3. Fill in around the vine with container mix, then water well to settle the soil around the vine's roots.

plants that are hardy to at least Zone 5. (If you're not sure which hardiness zone you live in, see the USDA Plant Hardiness Zone map on page 276.)

Next, give the plants a well-blended, well-drained container mix to keep the roots healthy. Start with a mix that contains some real soil (not just a soil-less mix). Then add compost (for long-term nutrients) and composted bark pieces (to help maintain good drainage). If you can't get composted bark, use some perlite in the largest particle size you can find. (Some garden centers stock large bags of ready-made container mix designed specifically for this kind of long-term container planting, but you may need to ask around to find it.)

If you have plants that you know won't survive in your climate's winters, or if you have some that you really don't want to risk outdoors, move them indoors for the coldest months. If they are deciduous plants like fruit trees or roses, which go dormant in winter, you can put them in a cold, dark garage. Evergreen plants prefer

Container-grown vines can be an exciting, movable accent to garden beds and borders.

cold but bright spots in a sunroom or breezeway, but in a pinch some can spend a couple of months in a cold, dark spot.

Indoors or outdoors, your plants will still need some water during the winter. They aren't growing much, so they only need enough water to keep the soil from drying out completely. However, once summer comes remember to start a regular watering program or install a system of irrigation tubes, preferably operating on an automatic timer, to keep your plants nice and moist during the hot weather.

Maintaining Container Trees, Shrubs, and Vines

You'll need to keep container trees, shrubs, and vines in tip top condition as you'll want them to be on display over a

Protecting Delicate Root Systems

Too much sun can be just as detrimental to your plants as too much shade. When plants in containers are placed in the sun all day, especially if the container bears the brunt of reflected afternoon heat, the soil can reach very high temperatures, cooking the roots, which in turn will make the visible part of your plant look stressed. If your container is placed in such a position, try to create an insulating barrier between the roots and the container. To do this you can leave the shrub in its original black plastic pot and insert it into a slightly larger, more decorative container. Place a layer of coconut fiber over the surface area, pushing some down into the space between the two pots. Alternatively, you can cut up a discarded polystyrene box and place a layer of this effective insulating material against the inside of the container as you fill it with compost—much easier when you use a rectangular or square pot!

Evergreen shrubs such as boxwood (*Buxus* spp.) offer year-long garden interest, and can also be pruned into fun topiary shapes.

long period in prime positions. Whatever plants you grow in containers, you'll get a more even shape and uniform, healthy growth if you swivel the pot around every couple of weeks to give the plant an even amount of sunshine and light.

Feeding

Once the cold weather is over, and the container mix has warmed a little, give the trees and shrubs a generous mulch of homemade compost, if you have some available, otherwise a little organic fertilizer will get them unfurling their new spring growth in a healthy fashion. It's so easy to burn tender roots which are often near the surface in container-grown trees and shrubs, so always make sure the container mix is moist when using a pelleted organic fertilizer and then only use the barest minimum. It is much safer to use a slow-release or liquid fertilizer on potted plants— if you're not sure which fertilizer to use, ask for advice at your local garden center. You'll find it's a good idea to keep feeding them little amounts often, rather than giving these plants a huge amount in early spring and then forgetting about fertilizing them for the rest of the growing period. Every time you water them some of the fertilizer is leached out of the pot and

there's no way the roots of a containerized plant can forage for its own food outside the confines of the pot.

Deadheading

One of the reasons that you might select a tree, shrub, or vine is for the flowers it produces. However, fading flowers do not look good, so take a stroll in the garden on a summer evening to deadhead any flowers that may be past their prime.

Pruning

These larger container plants will need some pruning. Non-flowering shrubs can usually be trimmed anytime from late winter to midsummer. If you're growing a flowering shrub or vine, you'll need to determine whether it flowers on new wood each year (in which case you should prune it back hard) or if it flowers on older wood (in winter, prune right after it flowers). Not sure how your plant blooms? Check the entries in "A Guide to Popular Container Plants" starting on page 164, ask at your local garden center, or just make a point of watching where flower buds appear in spring.

Some plants, such as the maple cultivars (*Acer palmatum* Dissectum Group), make wonderful container plants and naturally grow into a graceful shape as they mature. These don't need any pruning. You can train gardenias (*Gardenia jasminoides*), azaleas, lantana (*Lantana camara*), and fuchsias (*Fuchsia* x *hybrida*) into standards with a little timely shaping and pruning.

Fuchsia

Edibles and Herbs for Containers

Containers are a great way to grow vegetables, herbs, and fruit crops without putting a lot of work into a full-scale garden. You can have a steady supply of fresh produce right outside your kitchen door, within easy reach for a finishing touch to any meal. Containers also offer ideal growing conditions for carrots, which can grow short and stunted if your garden soil isn't deep, loose, and rock-free. Mix some flowers in with your edibles, and you can have a container garden that's pretty as well as productive.

Patio-type tomatoes, such as 'Pixie', can give you a welcome harvest from a very small space.

Container Crop Basics

Growing vegetables, fruits, and herbs in containers is much like growing flowers, but there are a few special things you'll need to think about.

Choose Compact Crops

Most herbs adapt quite well to life in containers, but standard selections of some vegetables and fruits can get too big for successful container culture. Fortunately, plant breeders have worked with many crops to develop compact cultivars that are specifically suitable for container growing. For specific cultivar suggestions, check out the individual vegetable entries in "A Guide to Popular Container Plants," starting on page 164. You should also read the descriptions in your favorite seed and nursery catalogs to find cultivars that are recommended for container growing.

Consider the Container

You'll get better yields of edibles if you use a good-sized container—one that holds at least 2 gallons (9 l) of container mix. If you're more interested in production than beauty, 5-gallon (23 l) plastic buckets make excellent inexpensive and effective containers. (You may be able to find some used buckets you can recycle from a restaurant or delicatessen. Be sure to drill plenty of drainage holes in the bottom.)

Container Vegetables

The size of the container needed depends on which plants you grow, but it must have drainage holes.

Fill the container with a soil-based or soil-less mix. Don't use garden soil, which will pack down too tightly with repeated watering. You can make your own soil-based mix by blending 2 parts of garden soil with 1 part each of compost, peat moss, vermiculite, and perlite. If you don't have garden soil to spare, you can can buy commercial soil-less mixes, such as Jiffy Mix, or you can make your own soil-less mix of equal parts of compost, perlite, and peat moss.

When choosing which vegetable to grow, remember that compact or dwarf cultivars are generally the best choice for containers. Listed below are some vegetables that are well adapted to container culture.

Bean (bush types); carrot (short-rooted cultivars); corn salad; cucumber (bush cultivars); eggplant; kale; lettuce; onion; pea (needs a trellis); pepper, radish; silverbeet; summer squash (bush cultivars); tomato; watercress.

How about starting your crops with the following surefire favourites:

Tomatoes Tomatoes come in all sizes, from giant, vining types that may grow to 6 feet (180 cm) or more (they're called "indeterminate" types) to tiny, compact, cherry tomato cultivars that are perfect for growing in hanging baskets.

Peppers Hot and sweet peppers are excellent plants to grow in containers. Because they are perennials, you can cut them back at the end of each season, move them inside for the winter, and then move them back outside again next spring. (See

Peppers are decorative container plants, and come in a variety of colors, including purple.

"Inside Out and Outside In" on page 61 for tips on helping plants adapt to moves.)

Lettuce Lettuce is very easy to grow in containers and looks as great as it tastes. Try a packet of a "cutting mix," which contains several kinds of lettuce (with green and red leaves), along with other spicy salad greens such as mustard, mizuna, and arugula. With these cutting mixes, you just plant the seed rather thickly, then cut handfuls with scissors as the lettuce grows. After cutting, the plants will grow back quickly.

Fruits for Containers

If you enjoy growing edible plants, there's no need to stop with vegetables and herbs. Container gardens give you tremendous flexibility to experiment with fruit growing.

Combining ornamentals and edibles in a container is a decorative and effective way of utilizing space in your garden.

If your soil is so poor or hard that you have to dig it with a pick, containers give your crops better conditions for root growth. Containers also allow you to grow fruit on a deck, patio, or balcony and move plants around to take advantage of the available sunlight in a mostly shaded garden. In cold climates, containers let you grow tender plants—such as citrus and figs—indoors in a greenhouse or sunroom.

Choosing a Container

The ideal containers for fruit growing have thick walls that slow moisture loss and insulate the roots from extreme air

Greens such as chard and spinach add diverse leaf colors and textures to container gardens. Snip the leaves as needed for salads or garnishes.

Create a Container Salad Garden

A container garden can be perfect for one-stop salad gardening and harvesting. You can plant your salad greens in a container or window box outside the kitchen, and simply add some chives and basil. Hang a basket of cherry tomatoes above the pot or box, and you'll have salads literally at your fingertips!

Lettuce and spinach do best in cooler temperatures, so start some in early spring. Plant some again in late summer, and you'll enjoy months of delicious salads. If your greens are still going strong when hard frosts arrive, just move them inside—they'll grow nicely in a bright, south-facing window.

Most salad plants are decorative as well as functional. Plant flowers with the vegetables, or place flowering containers next to them. Zinnias, sweet alyssum, marigolds, and ageratum provide color and attract valuable pollinating insects.

The main requirements for growing salad vegetables in containers are correct drainage and containers that have sufficient depth for the particular plants. Because terracotta pots dry out more rapidly than plastic containers, you should line terracotta pots with plastic, making sure that you make holes in the bottom of the plastic for drainage. The size of the container will determine what can be planted in it, and the minimum depths required by common salad vegetables are given below:

Cabbage

4 inches (10 cm) Lettuce, radish, beetroot, chives, shallots.
6 inches (15 cm) Kohlrabi, baby carrots, turnips, Chinese cabbage, spinach, silverbeet, sorrel, endive.
8 inches (20 cm) Beans, cabbage, capsicum, cucumbers, zucchini, celery, peas.
10 inches (25 cm) Broccoli, cauliflower, deep-rooted carrots, tomatoes.

Chives

Radishes

Favorite Fruits for Containers

Strawberries You can buy strawberry plants from your local garden center in spring and pop them into pots for luscious, full-sized fruit. Or you might want to try the alpine types such as 'Mignonette', which can be grown from seed. Their great taste more than makes up for the smaller size of the berries.

Blueberries Blueberries are small shrubs that grow only a few feet high, so they don't need much pruning. They are ideal for containers as it's easier to meet the plants' need for acid soil by blending a special container mix. Use a soil mix that's at least one-quarter to one-half acidic peat moss and never add lime, and you'll have blueberries before you know it.

Citrus Citrus trees can't tolerate frost, but they grow nicely in containers, especially if you buy plants that have been grafted onto a special dwarfing rootstock to keep them small. The plants need plenty of sun and fertilizer in the summer

Dwarf peach tree

and a bright window in winter (except in very mild climates, where they can stay outside year-round). Not only will they give you fruit but the flowers are also wonderfully fragrant.´

Dwarf Fruit Trees You can even grow full-sized apples, peaches, and cherries from compact, container-sized, dwarf fruit trees. Provide ample rooting room by choosing a container at least 30 inches (75 cm) wide and deep. In cold climates (Zone 5 or colder), move the pots to an unheated garage during the coldest part of winter. In warmer zones, potted fruit trees can stay outside through winter. Some fruits—including apples and peaches— need to have a certain amount of cold to set fruit properly, so if you live in Zone 8 or warmer, be sure you get "low-chill" cultivars that will grow in your climate. For more tips on helping container trees get through the winter, see "Special Container Considerations" on page 86.

temperature swings. Clay pots are very attractive and work fine for strawberries, but they tend to dry out quickly, and they chip or crumble if left outdoors during a cold winter. For fruit trees, look for durable, thick-walled plastic pots that resemble clay but retain more moisture. You also can plant fruit trees in wooden half-barrels and planters.

Whatever container you choose, you should check that it has drainage holes so the roots won't get waterlogged. Also make sure that it has a wide, stable base so it won't tip over when the plant gets tall and heavy with fruit. The best size for the container varies, depending on which plant you want to grow. Here are some suitable pot sizes for different crops:

Dwarf apples, apricots, cherries, peaches, pears, citrus, plums Thick wooden or plastic tubs or barrels at least 2 feet (60 cm) wide and 3 feet (90 cm) deep.

Blueberries Large plastic, wooden, or ceramic pots that are at least 2 feet (60 cm) wide and deep.

Strawberries Plastic or clay pots, strawberry pots, hanging baskets, or strawberry towers or barrels that are at least 8 inches (20 cm) deep and 12 inches (30 cm) wide.

Caring for Fruit in Containers

Growing fruiting plants in containers isn't hard, but it does take some care to keep them in peak production. You'll find that regular watering is one of the most important aspects of care, especially in hot, dry weather. Here are some other care considerations to keep in mind.

It is important to provide the right rooting conditions. The roots of container plants are much more limited than those growing in the ground. Roots in containers can't stretch in search of moisture

Dwarf citrus tree

and nutrients, so you'll have to water and fertilize them much more often than you would for a garden plant.

You'll also need to provide a growing medium that will nourish and support the roots while still providing plenty of air and moisture. Not just any soil will do. You need to use specially blended mixes that can be either soil-less or soil based.

Fertilize for good growth. Even compost-rich mixes won't have enough nutrients to keep fruits growing for long. It helps to blend some fertilizers into the mix before planting. To every bushel-basket of mix, add a sprinkle of bloodmeal and a handful each of greensand, rock, or colloidal phosphate, and bonemeal.

After the first year, keep plants growing strong by fertilizing with a liquid material, such as fish emulsion. Dilute and apply the fertilizer according to the label directions. If there are no specific guidelines for containers, dilute the fertilizer to half the normal strength and use it twice as often. You can also use dry organic fertilizers for potted plants; just follow the label directions.

Check the pH. Since your plants may grow in the same container for several seasons, it pays to check the pH at least once a year. Peat-based mixes tend to become acidic over time. To check the pH, use litmus paper (usually available from garden centers and garden-supply catalogs). Unless you're growing blueberries, you'll want to raise the pH if it is below 6.0. Scatter a heaping tablespoon of limestone over the soil of a 5-gallon pot; use a smidge less than ⅛ cup for a half-barrel.

Protect pots in cold weather. Even thick-walled containers can expose roots to damaging temperature extremes, especially in the cold of winter. To protect the roots, surround the pot with leaf-filled garbage bags. If you can move the pot, you could sink it in well-drained

There are special planters, called strawberry barrels, with holes all around the sides, so you can cover the barrel with berry plants.

Common Fruit and Vegetable Pests and Diseases

Pest	Damage	Prevention and Control
Snails and slugs	Seedlings eaten, irregular holes in leaves	Place shallow containers of beer near containers, or trap pests under boards.
Aphids	Foliage wilted or curled, deformed buds and flowers	A short, sharp spray of water from the hose will dislodge them. Spray with insecticidal soap.
Cabbageworm	Leaves eaten	Spray or dust with BT.
Carrot fly	Carrot roots eaten	Plant crops in late spring to minimize damage.
Cutworms	Plant stem chewed at soil surface	Place cardboard or metal cutworm collars around the stems of the plants. Sprinkle moist bran mixed with BT on the soil surface in the evening.
Leaf miners	Winding or large, blotchy lines on leaves, especially on beet, spinach, and tomatoes	Pick and destroy infected leaves. Control adults with yellow sticky traps or a pyrethrin/rotenone mix.
European corn borer	Tunnels in corn stalks and ears	Spray with BT.
Beetles (Mexican bean, Japanese, cucumber)	Chewed foliage	Eliminate weeds. Spray with garlic or pyrethrin.
Red spider mite	Discoloration and bronzing	Use a garlic or pyrethrin/rotenone spray.

Disease	Damage	Prevention and Control
Powdery mildew	Downy patches on foliage	Provide good air circulation. Control weeds. Spray the foliage with compost tea.
Damping-off	Seedlings weaken and collapse because of decay at soil line	Start seeds in well-drained mix. Avoid overwatering, crowding, and poor air circulation. Disinfect any reused pots and trays.
Rust	Rust-colored powder on leaves	Provide good air circulation. Remove infected leaves.
Wilt (Fusarium and Verticillium)	Leaves yellow, plant gradually wilts	Rotate crops. Plant resistant cultivars. Destroy infected crops.

LEFT: A decorative hanging basket filled with herbs is practical for hanging outside the kitchen. The height also keeps the herbs safe from snails.

Mint is ideal for container growing because its runners can spread too rapidly in a garden bed. Mint likes moist soil, so add water-saving granules to the container mix and keep it well watered. Place bay in a large pot and clip it to create a standard. Plant coriander in a large trough, but not during the heat of summer, as it will bolt to seed. You can clip the leaves as required or harvest the whole plant if you want the root. Annual dill may be sown as soon as the danger of frost is over and you can clip fresh leaves as you need them.

Don't overwater your herb plants, since they prefer to be on the dry side rather than being continually moist. If the container mix is good quality and has adequate drainage, water will not accumulate in the container and the roots will not become waterlogged. How often to water depends on the size of the pot and the requirements of the particular

Shade-tolerant Herbs

The following herbs will tolerate part or dappled shade:

Agrimony, angelica, bay, bergamot, betony, catmint, chamomile, chervil, comfrey, coriander, costmary, feverfew, germander, ginger, horsetail, hyssop, lemon balm, lovage, Madagascar periwinkle, mint, parsley, pennyroyal, pipsissewa, plantain, sweet cicely, sweet woodruff, tansy, tarragon, thyme, valerian, violet, wormwood.

Violet   Coriander

soil amid your foundation plants and mulch over the top of the roots. Dormant hardy fruit trees will also survive well in a cool garage over winter. Bring cold-tender plants indoors to a greenhouse or sunroom until warm weather returns.

Rejuvenate overgrown plants. After a few years, fruiting trees and bushes will outgrow their containers and begin to decline. When the roots form a solid mass in the container, repot the plant in a larger pot with some fresh container mix. Or you can prune the larger roots and branches back so you can replant in the original pot with some fresh mix.

Herbs for Container Gardens

Herbs are a good choice since they don't require as much space as vegetables. Containers brimming with herbs look very attractive when grown near your kitchen door or in a window box. This way you can simply reach out and cut some basil leaves or a sprig of rosemary when you need it. A tub of chervil, with its feathery foliage, grown on a sunny balcony looks just as attractive as a potted fern, but chervil has practical uses, too.

Marjoram, oregano, rosemary, sage, mint, and thyme will all thrive in containers. Once you have successfully cultivated herbs that you use regularly in cooking, you can go on to grow some of the more exotic varieties.

You can plant sun-lovers such as basil, sage, rosemary, and thyme in the same container. If you have a partly shady area, plant lemon balm, lovage, and tansy. Basil, oregano, and parsley will tolerate as little as 4 hours of sun per day.

LEFT: Place a container of golden sage (*Salvia officinalis* 'Aurea') where you will often brush past the plant and release the aroma.

RIGHT: This hanging basket, which is attached to a garden fence, is an ideal, space-saving way of growing herbs in containers.

plant. Because unglazed clay pots are very porous and tend to dry out rapidly, they will require more frequent watering than ceramic or plastic pots.

A small pot will need to be watered more often than a large one, and plants with large leaves require more watering than those with small foliage. The general rule is that if the top inch (2.5 cm) of the soil is dry, the plant needs watering. A thorough soaking every 3 to 5 days is more effective than a daily light sprinkling. An effective watering method is to fill the drainage saucer with water and let the plant soak it up through the drainage holes. Let the plant soak for an hour, then remove any excess water.

Make Your Own Container Mix for Herbs

The container mix is very important for herbs, which generally prefer a slightly alkaline soil. It is thus essential to have a container mix that is more alkaline than acid. While there are some quite good commercial container mixes available, the most economical approach is to make up your own, which will specifically suit the requirements of your herbs. A good mix is: 2 parts good garden loam or well-rotted

Herbs are sun lovers, so place potted herbs in a sunny position on your patio or balcony.

compost, 1 part leaf mold, 1 part well rotted manure, and 2 parts coarse sand.

The manure makes the container mix alkaline. If you don't have any manure, a small amount of lime will be just as good.

Planting Herbs in Pots

By following these basic instructions, you will be able to pot and repot your herbs without trauma or setback:

1. Water the herb in its original pot (which is probably the one from the nursery) several hours before potting.
2. Ensure that the fresh container mix is moist, but not wet, before you begin.
3. Place gravel or stones in the base of the container to prevent container mix escaping through the drainage holes. If your pot doesn't have drainage holes, use a drill to make several holes in the bottom. If this isn't possible, choose another container.
4. Make sure the container is clean before starting. Rinse the pot with warm, soapy water if it has been used for other plants to prevent the transfer of disease.
5. Place some container mix on top of the gravel layer and gently remove the herb from its container. Do this by carefully tapping the pot against a table to loosen the soil and then inverting it while cradling the top and stem in your hand. The entire root ball should come out intact and undamaged. Run a knife gently around the inside of the pot if it still won't leave the original container.
6. Place the herb in its new pot and fill in around the sides with fresh container mix. Don't fill the container right to the top or it will be hard to water.
7. Water the container thoroughly once the plant is in place.
8. Keep the plant out of direct sunlight for several days until it has thoroughly recovered from the transplant.

Container Gardening Solutions

*Outdoor container gardening helps you bring plants closer to
your daily life. Pots, planters, and hanging baskets provide
movable accents of color and fragrance to brighten up balconies,
courtyards, patios, porches, decks, and other outdoor living spaces.
As you work with your container plants outdoors, you may find
that a few carefully placed flower pots, hanging baskets, window boxes,
or bonsai plants can enhance your yard more effectively and
easily than planting an entire new flower bed or border.*

Window Boxes

Well-planned window boxes can add a special touch to any home. Besides brightening up otherwise plain windows, boxes can dress up a deck or porch railing. The conventional use of window boxes is on the exterior sills of windows. However, there is no reason why the trend to indoor gardening should not include the window box—why not arrange window boxes on the inside of your windows, using the wide range of flowering and foliage plants to make a striking display?

Choosing the Container

Window boxes can be made of metal (usually copper or lead), wood (mostly redwood or cedar for good quality, durable boxes), terracotta, cement, or plastic. They can be simple, unadorned boxes or painted, stenciled, molded, or carved.

Many garden centers sell ready-made window boxes of plastic, wood, or metal, with special brackets that screw to the wall below the window to hold the box. Usually these boxes are not very large, so try not to overplant them; allow enough space for plants to grow larger through the season.

Experienced window box gardeners believe that one of the secrets of creating a really good-looking window box is to keep the box in proportion to the window

they decorate, so that it occupies about one-quarter of the height of a low window and about one-fifth the height of a tall one. Try to bear this in mind when choosing your window box container.

Building Your Own Window Boxes

If you build your own boxes, make them a little bigger than the typical garden-center sizes. A box about 8 inches (20 cm) wide and deep will give you enough additional

When planting your window box, choose compact plants that won't block your view.

soil for a range of plants to grow well. Be sure to put the box together with galvanized screws. Don't use nails—they won't hold as well as screws. It's also a good idea to reinforce the corners of the box to help them stay together.

Whether you choose to buy your window boxes or make your own, make

Creating a Window Box Display

You can improve the view from your window by simply planting a window box of beautiful flowers on the windowsill outside. Choose a container material that is in keeping with the style of your home. A simple material, such as terracotta, always looks good.

1. Line the window box with a layer of shards for good drainage. Add a 2-inch (5-cm) layer of container mix.

2. Arrange the plants in the window box to experiment with the design, until you are happy with the arrangement.

3. Plant the taller plants first and then the lower-growing plants. Firm the container mix around the plants.

Window boxes attract lots of attention, so make sure you can reach them for regular grooming.

Fragrant Favorites for Window Boxes

If you want some powerful nighttime fragrance wafting into your bedroom from your window boxes, pick up a packet of evening-scented stock (*Matthiola longipetala* subsp. *bicornis*) seeds and plant some in a corner of each window box. The stock isn't a showy flower, but it has a strong, sweet scent that fills the air at night. Other good choices for fragrance include petunias, sweet alyssum (*Lobularia maritima*), 'Lemon Gem' marigold (*Tagetes tenuifolia* 'Lemon Gem'), scented geraniums (*Pelargonium* spp.), mignonette (*Reseda odorata*), stock (*Matthiola incana*), and night phlox (*Zaluzianskya capensis*).

sure that there are adequate drainage holes in the bottom, so excess water can run out.

Cachepots

Window boxes can be surprisingly flexible, particularly if you decide to follow the practice of cachepot gardening—the use of containers (usually utilitarian) within more decorative outer containers.

Using a cachepot can make both outdoor, as well as indoor, gardening very versatile. As one group of plants finishes its display, it can be replaced by others held in readiness for the purpose. These can be loosely placed in the window box or held in place with container mix, peat, sphagnum moss, or some other material that will hold moisture.

Cachepots can be especially useful when you are planting window boxes since they need to be strongly secured to your windowsill or ledge. They can also be rearranged very easily if your original planting ideas need a little fine tuning.

Securing Window Boxes

While a window box can be a superb addition to your home, a little planning is needed to make sure the project is trouble-free. The weight of plants, container mix, window box, and water can be quite

substantial, and you need to be able to secure the window box and, at the same time, avoid having any moisture becoming trapped to damage the structure of your home. Allowing a gap of just half an inch (12 mm) lets air circulate and water escape.

Before you install your window boxes, fill one with soil and water it well. Then lift it carefully so you experience just how heavy it is. You need to use really sturdy supports to hold all that weight.

Since large window boxes can be cumbersome as well as heavy, you may want to secure them in such a way as they can be easily taken down from the window for cleaning and maintenance work.

Pay particular attention to supporting brackets as they can be under a lot of pressure and any loosening or damage has to be quickly repaired.

Picking the Plants

Top plant choices for window boxes include all of the low and medium-sized annuals, along with plenty of trailing plants, such as large periwinkle (*Vinca major*) and petunias. And if the window

Grow scented plants, such as herbs, in your window box. Not only are they practical, but the lovely fragrance will waft through the window.

above the box will be open to let in the summer breezes, be sure to include some fragrant plants; see "Fragrant Favorites for Window Boxes" for ideas.

Planting Your Window Box

Once you've selected the plants for your window box, it's time to start planting.

If you are planting directly into the window box, add a drainage layer of about an inch or so of coarse gravel, terracotta chips, or other suitable drainage material. If the window box has few drainage holes, the drainage layer is of even greater importance.

Fill the window box about half full with premium-quality container mix, adding some slow-release fertilizer.

Plant the most upright-growing plants first, to provide a kind of design backbone to your planting scheme. Then fill in the intermediate spaces with lower-growing specimens, allowing enough space for your flowers to grow. Once you're happy with the appearance of your window box, water it thoroughly.

To maintain the look of your window box, check it regularly as it will need watering more often than similar flowers planted in the open garden.

Hanging Baskets

To keep hanging baskets looking lush through the season, water them regularly, fertilize often, and pinch off any spent flowers.

Plant evergreens, such as Boston fern (*Nephrolepis exaltata*), for a basket with year-round interest.

Bring your container gardens to new heights with hanging baskets. Baskets look terrific on porches, beside a doorway, or hanging on an arbor over a patio. You can buy hanging baskets already planted and ready to hang, or you can easily plant them yourself (and probably save a bit of money). Some gardeners develop a real passion for hanging baskets and a well-planted basket can be a truly spectacular sight. Hanging baskets do not necessarily have to be hung up particularly high. It's up to you to decide what is the best height to display your favorite plants.

Preparing the Basket

Many garden centers and hardware stores stock lightweight, plastic baskets complete with drainage saucers and supporting light chains—these are certainly the most convenient and cheapest baskets. To some they can look a bit hard-edged, but if you are planting so that the container is hidden, this won't matter too match.

There are other ready-made hanging baskets made of ceramic, terracotta, wood, or metal, but weight may become an issue with these.

The true hanging garden enthusiast usually prefers a moss basket—a wire frame lined with sphagnum moss or a layer of similar fibrous material to hold the container mix and plants. At a pinch you can use good quality burlap—doubled over if it seems a little thin. Some adventurous folk even plant through slits in the fiber at the sides of the basket.

It is best to use a galvanized or otherwise rust-proofed wire basket frame. Most container mixes that are specially sold for hanging baskets are peat-based, which may be very tricky to remoisten if they dry out. Add some standard mix containing loam or humus to aid moisture retention. Slow-release fertilizer added to the mix will give your plants a boost and reduce feeding later.

Great Balls of Flowers

Petunias

If you want your basket to be a ball of color, plant the sides of the basket as well as the top. You can buy special baskets that have holes around the sides, or use wire baskets with fiber or moss liners, that allow you to cut holes for planting all around the sides.

To plant into the holes, first fill the basket with mix to just below where the holes begin. Then remove a plant from its cell pack, and wrap it loosely inside a little cylinder of newspaper. From the inside of the basket, slip the top part of the cylinder out through a hole, so the leafy top of the plant is on the outside and the roots are on the inside. Slip off the paper, then settle the roots in the container mix. When you have all the holes filled, add more soil to within 1 inch (2.5 cm) of the rim, then set in more plants on top. Water thoroughly to settle the mix around the roots.

As your hanging basket settles down, you may notice water running from thinner sections of the fiber. One of the great advantages of moss basket gardening is that you can add reinforcement from the outside by poking an extra piece of fiber through the wire frame.

Picking Plants for Hanging Baskets

Hanging baskets are great for annuals that grow quickly and bloom spectacularly. However, if you grow varieties that need full sun, this adds to the natural tendency of hanging baskets to dry out fast. Baskets look best with a combination of low, bushy plants to fill the top and trailing plants to spill over the sides. Good bushy plants include tuberous begonias (*Begonia* Tuberhybrida hybrids), browallia (*Browallia* spp.), and vinca (*Catharanthus roseus*). Around the edge of the basket include cascading plants, such as petunias, annual lobelia (*Lobelia erinus*), sweet alyssum (*Lobularia maritima*), nasturtium (*Tropaeolum majus*), and mints (*Mentha* spp.). Plants that are both bushy and trailing, such as ivy geranium (*Pelargonium peltatum*) and fuchsia (*Fuchsia* x *hybrida*), look good when planted by themselves to fill a hanging basket.

Perhaps the most dramatic effect is achieved by a hanging basket that is richly planted with a single type of plant. This is certainly the easiest way to meet one of the basic requirements of hanging basket—and indeed all container—planting. Plants in the same container must share identical (or very similar) soil, water, light, and temperature requirements.

Hanging Baskets for Herbs

You don't have to limit your choice of plants to the conventional, flowering annuals. The dry, warm conditions that are characteristic of hanging baskets can suit many Mediterranean plants, particularly the cooking herbs.

As herbs will be picked quite often, it is best to hang a herb basket within easy reach of the kitchen. Herbs to try include oregano, thyme, basil, and lemon balm.

Planting and Caring for Hanging Baskets

Most hanging basket containers look like regular containers, and you plant them in basically the same way. However, hanging baskets dry out faster than other container plants, so it's a good idea to use a container mix that holds plenty of water. Adding extra vermiculite will help. It also helps to use larger baskets which are at least 12 inches (30 cm) in diameter, because these will dry out more slowly.

One of the keys to lush-looking containers is regular fertilizing. Give hanging baskets a boost by misting or watering them with liquid fertilizer, such as fish emulsion.

Because hanging baskets allow you to display concentrated plantings of your favorite plants, it is a good idea to plant them more densely than you would in the open garden or in more conventional containers. The tangled, intertwining effect of such dense plantings is part of the appeal of the hanging basket.

Since most hanging baskets have a rounded base, steady them by placing them in a flower pot or kitchen mixing bowl.

Garden centers sell brackets that let you hang baskets anywhere you choose on a wall or post. Make sure you choose sturdy brackets and fasten them securely; they have to hold a lot of weight.

The easiest way of watering hanging baskets that are out of reach is to get a long extension nozzle for your garden hose and simply lift the water to the height of the basket. Alternatively, you can hang the basket on a rope or chain that can be lowered, so that you can water it as you would any other container, and carry out other necessary maintenance work at the same time.

You won't need to water too much at first, when the plants are small. But as the plants grow, the basket may need watering at least once and possibly twice a day by the end of the season.

If your hanging baskets are drying out too quickly, consider using water-retaining pellets to help you even out the moisture highs and lows in this miniature ecosystem.

If you're going to be away from home, even for one night, move your baskets to a shady spot until you return, or ask a neighbor to water them for you.

You can find a plant suitable for a hanging basket in any situation. Impatiens, or busy Lizzy, (*Impatiens wallerana*), is ideal for providing a burst of color to shady areas of the garden, such as under a veranda.

Basic Bonsai

Bonsai is an art that attempts to replicate, in a container, the look of an old tree that has been shaped by time and the elements. The process of training beautiful bonsai requires time and patience, but the results can be stunning and gratifying.

Japanese maple (*Acer palmatum*) is an attractive plant for bonsai, because the leaves turn a beautiful copper color during fall.

Caring for Bonsai

Before you buy or begin a bonsai project, be aware that these plants will need some special care. Hardy bonsai normally prefer to be outdoors during the growing season. They enjoy the shelter of a lath house or some other shade-producing structure, where they will receive bright indirect light and protection from the elements. One gust of wind can easily knock over small plants and undo months or years of care!

Bonsai generally grow in shallow pots, so you'll have to water them frequently—possibly twice a day in very hot weather—to keep the soil evenly damp. During the winter months, you'll need to protect bonsai from cold temperatures. Many overwinter best in a greenhouse, where they will get a dormant, or rest, period.

Without this cold period, many hardy plants will not bloom, and they'll gradually become weak and spindly. Bonsai created from houseplants are somewhat easier to care for: They can adapt easily to indoor culture on sunny windowsills or under lights year-round.

Picking a Plant

Generally, the species that adapt best to bonsai have small leaves, woody trunks, stout limbs, and flowers, fruit, or good fall color. Deciduous plants that make great bonsai subjects include azaleas, beeches (*Fagus* spp.), hawthorns (*Crataegus* spp.), flowering quince (*Chaenomeles* spp.), ginkgo (*Ginkgo biloba*), Japanese maple (*Acer palmatum*), hornbeams (*Carpinus* spp.), hardy orange (*Poncirus trifoliata*), and zelkova (*Zelkova serrata*). Good choices for

evergreens include arborvitaes (*Thuja* spp.), camellias, (*Camellia* spp.), cryptomeria (*Cryptomeria japonica*), junipers (*Juniperus* spp.), boxwoods (*Buxus* spp.), false cypress (*Chamaecyparis* spp.), pines (*P. mugo* and *P. parvifolia*), spruces (*Picea* spp.), and yews (*Taxus* spp.). If you want a bonsai that can grow indoors year-round, consider woody houseplants such as serissa (*Serissa foetida*) or weeping fig (*Ficus benjamina*).

When you are choosing a young plant for bonsai, you don't necessarily want a symmetrical specimen. Stems with bends, twists, scars, or stumps can give a bonsai real character; even some dead wood can be desirable! Ask the staff at your local nursery if they have any misshapen plants destined for the compost pile; with some trimming, these can have immediate impact as bonsai. Of course, potential bonsai specimens should otherwise be healthy and free of insects and disease.

Whatever you pick, start small, with a plant growing in a 1-gallon (4.5-l) or smaller container. If you start with a larger plant, you'll need to root prune it over time, getting the roots into successively smaller pots to control the growth.

Planting and Feeding

Choose a shallow pot that is in scale with the young plant. Cover drainage holes with a piece of wire screen to ensure good drainage. For soil, use 2 parts container mix and 1 part leaf mold (screened through a ¼-inch [6 mm] sieve).

Like all living things, these plants need to be nourished. Fertilizer can be incorporated into the container mix, or you can apply half-strength liquid fertilizer throughout the growing season—remembering, though, that you don't want the plant to have great growth spurts; you just want to keep it healthy, so don't overdo the feeding.

Shapes, Styles, and Settings

After planting, the next step is to decide what shape you want the plant to grow in. You may allow it to grow upright or encourage a leaning or cascading form.

Shaping Bonsai

Bonsai begins with pruning the branches and roots of the desired plant, in order to help restrict the growth of the plant. It is best to train and prune in early spring, just before new growth appears. Leaf pruning can be done throughout the season.

1. Remove plant from its pot and remove the excess container mix from the roots.

2. Prune the roots with clippers, to cut away about half the roots and any damaged growth.

3. Prune the top of the plant to reveal the natural structure of the original plant.

Part of choosing an appropriate style is knowing how a plant grows in its natural setting; books with photographs of the plant in the wild may help inspire you. Also consider how your particular plant is growing; it may naturally have a form that suggests a certain shape for easier training.

While most potted plants are placed in the center of their container, a bonsai can look effective when placed toward one end of a rectangular container and trained so that the foliage sweeps across the pot toward the other end, in what's known as a slanting or semi-cascade style. Similarly, some of the best effects are gained by growing three plants grouped together, or many of the same species almost filling the surface in the style of a mini forest. You can have lots of fun propagating plants for use in this way. Japanese maples are easy to grow from seed and are quick to give a good display. Some plants, such as figs have distinctive aerial roots and you can expose these in what is known as root-over-rock or clinging-to-a-rock settings.

Moss, too, plays a very important role in a bonsai setting, and you'll find that it helps to keep the surface of these shallow containers moist, while also adding to their overall visual appeal.

You can display your bonsai alone, or group them with other bonsai and container plants in rock gardens.

Training Bonsai

Pruning, pinching, wiring, and root pruning are standard training techniques you'll use to work with your bonsai. On deciduous plants, do most of your pruning during the dormant season, but don't hesitate to remove undesirable growth as soon as it appears. It's common to remove crossing or rubbing limbs, but you may choose to leave poorly placed branches, depending on the effect you're trying to create. On pines, spruces, and firs, pinch the "candles" (new shoots) back by about half in spring. Carefully trim other evergreens in summer. Pinch any plant through the growing season to direct its growth and to keep it compact.

To shape individual stems, it's best to use annealed (softened) #14- to #26-gauge copper wire. Coil the wire gently but firmly over the length of the stem or branch to shape and direct the growth. Check the wire frequently to make sure that it isn't cutting into the stem. Take the wire off after several months. To bring upward-pointing branches down to a more horizontal position, use twine or soft string to tie on small weights.

Root pruning is a scary but necessary aspect of bonsai. It is a key part of keeping the plants in their smaller scale. Do this every 4 to 5 years, in late winter before growth begins for the season, or when you need to repot the plant. Allow the soil to dry slightly more than usual and remove the plant from its pot. Loosen the roots and tease away the soil in the outer third of the root ball. Using thinning cuts, trim away the roots in this outer third. Repot the plant and keep it in a sheltered position for a couple of weeks—you certainly don't want heavy rain or wind buffeting the plant. To reduce the likelihood of a repotted, top-heavy plant toppling over, run wire or a cord across the top of the pot and between the slats of a bench to hold it firmly in position until normal maintenance is resumed.

The word bonsai basically means "plant in a tray." There are many different styles of bonsai in Japan, named according to the overall shape, as well as the angle of the trunk in the container.

Balconies, Courtyards, and Patio Gardens

Container plants are ideal for balconies, courtyards, patios, and other outdoor living areas. You can create many types of containerized gardens in these areas, even in the limited space of balconies. Whether your balcony is in a high-rise apartment or on the second floor of a suburban home, you can transform it quickly and simply into a peaceful patch of green.

Courtyards and patios are increasingly significant aspects of the modern lifestyle. As urban backyards become smaller, courtyards and patios are becoming popular as outdoor rooms, and are now home to everything from decorative trees, shrubs, and succulents to productive container vegetable and herb gardens.

Your Balcony Backyard

Just because you live in an apartment doesn't mean you have to be deprived of a garden. A clever use of containers can help you discover a lively new world. With a few containers brimming with

You can even grow a productive garden of fruits, herbs, and vegetables in the confined space of a balcony.

colorful flowers, your balcony can become a relaxing area for entertaining. Dwarf trees and small shrubs can be used to create interesting effects on a small scale, and you can even be productive with vegetables and herbs in containers and flowering fruit trees. Here are some ways to transform your balcony into a lush, green space.

Getting Started

Before you start your balcony garden, there are some important factors to consider. The first and most obvious consideration is the amount of weight your balcony can bear. Most condominium balconies have concrete floors, but some city houses have timber floors which will not support the

weight of concrete containers. It is best to avoid using heavy containers—use plastic and cedar wood where possible. Spread the load over a wide area and make sure brackets and hooks are capable of taking the weight of hanging pots or baskets.

Next, check the microclimate of your balcony. Note the direction the balcony faces and how much sun it receives. Some balconies are very sheltered and receive no direct sunlight or wind at all, while others have considerable wind exposure and scorching sunlight. Many balcony plants don't get much rain since they are situated beneath awnings, so you must ensure that the container mix is kept moist.

Balcony Design

Because balconies are usually small, space is a major design consideration. The main principle is to keep the design as simple as possible. The last thing you want is a cluttered, busy look. Using square or rectangular containers that suit the angles and edges of balconies will save space. And use hanging baskets, espaliered, and climbing plants to bring walls to life. One approach is to grow climbing plants on a trellis attached to the wall for that purpose. Don't forget to leave enough room for a small table and a couple of chairs.

Rooftop gardens are often blasted by wind and sun, so select suitable plants for the conditions.

Courtyards and Patios

Courtyards are areas that adjoin the house or are discrete, enclosed areas inside a garden. They are natural extensions of the house and provide areas for entertaining, relaxing, or barbecuing.

Courtyards are not a recent invention and have been elements of gardens from early times. A courtyard provides a small, confined area in which to create a unique atmosphere. The limitations of courtyards are part of their appeal. The walls, hedges, or buildings that create the space for a courtyard also define its boundaries.

Patios are the ideal areas for everything from barbecues to formal lunches and dinner parties. Building a patio is an ideal way to create a separate, private room somewhere in the garden.

While some patios adjoin the house or are close to the kitchen, these days many patios are located in the backyard. You can place your patio under a large tree, in an area where there is an attractive view, or simply in the section of the yard that receives the most sun. In hot climates, you may wish to place the patio in a cool area surrounded by greenery.

You can partially enclose the patio by surrounding it with a formal clipped hedge, clipped balls of box (*Buxus* spp.), or well-placed large pots.

The biggest challenge when designing and constructing your ideal separate area is coming to terms with space limitations. The small scale of courtyards and patios makes attention to detail a priority.

Courtyard and Patio Design

Think carefully about the style and function of your courtyard or patio. Do you want it to have a formal or an informal style? With a formal look you can create a modern, minimalist style with a few container plants. But perhaps you prefer the informal texture, softness, and color of carefully selected plants.

A vine-covered trellis and collection of potted plants transform this corner into an inviting alcove.

Be sure to use heavy, wide pots in windy areas, to prevent the pots from being blown over.

Details are very important in small areas because mistakes are more obvious. Space should be carefully allocated and the selection of materials to be used is a major consideration. Avoid using too many plants in small spaces. You can use repeat plantings to give a clean, uncluttered appearance. Several large containers or planter boxes can be more eye-catching than a collection of small pots.

How to Decorate Courtyard Walls

Courtyard walls cry out for climbing plants. You can attach wire to a wall in any pattern and train a potted climber to flesh out the design. Diagonal patterns

Shape up Your Balcony, Courtyard, or Patio

Terracotta pots filled with clipped shapes or standards create truly elegant effects and may be used as dominant features. You can create an exquisite look in a small space by using several pots of clipped shrubs. Box (*Buxus* spp.) can be clipped into spheres, squares, or any shape you desire. It is cheaper to buy a large, unclipped box and shape it yourself than to buy one already shaped. But keep in mind that it does take several years to obtain a good shape—which accounts for the relatively high cost of clipped box.

Containers filled with box make great portable hedges or screens. They are ideal for separating your courtyard or patio from the rest of the garden in order to create a separate garden room.

Correct pruning is a must when shaping container plants. The aim is to have compact, solid growth. Make sure you have a good pair of hedge clippers. The general rule is to prune in late spring after new growth has appeared. The next new growth should be pruned in late summer or fall. The main aim of pruning the new tips is to encourage the stem to branch two or three times in order to create denser growth.

Planning your courtyard carefully will help you to transform your ideas into a workable design.

look good, but the choice is yours. The first step is to drill holes for galvanized roofing screws and then pull the wire tight between the screws to create the pattern. You might consider accentuating your climber's flowers and foliage by painting the wall a contrasting color.

A suitable climber for this treatment is star jasmine (*Trachelospermum jasminoides*), which has glossy, evergreen leaves and perfumed, white flowers. You could also use clematis, cup-and-saucer vine (*Cobaea scandens*), ivy, or bleeding glorybower (*Clerodendrum thomsoniae*).

A trellis is another way of attaching climbers to walls. Fix a square, rectangle, or arch of trellis to the wall, plant a climber at the base and train it over the trellis. Choose an evergreen like ivy that can be clipped as it grows to the shape of the trellis. A clever approach is to incorporate this structure into a *trompe-l'oeil*. Stephanotis is also recommended for a trellis design and it has a perfume to die for. Mandevillas are easy to grow and have large, showy flowers.

What to Plant Where

Every inch of space counts in courtyards, patios, and balconies and every plant should fulfil its purpose well. Correct positioning of plants according to their cultivation needs is of great importance, as small spaces will magnify any problems or errors. Remember to choose plants for their foliage to ensure year-round appeal. You can check the basic needs and features of plants in "A Guide to Popular Container Plants," starting on page 164.

Sunny Balconies, Courtyards, and Patios

Colorful annuals are always eye-catching for sunny balconies. Scented geraniums (*Pelargonium* spp.) are ideal for container culture and provide bright color for weeks on end. Petunias and sages (*Salvia* spp.) are also good choices. Yuccas, heavenly bamboo (*Nandina domestica*), together with love-lies-bleeding (*Amaranthus caudautus*) will also grow well. For more plants

that grow well in the sun, see "The Right Container Plant for the Right Place," starting on page 114.

Succulents are particularly suitable for really hot balconies and courtyards where it is difficult to get anything to grow. The huge range of leaf shapes and sizes enables you to have a variety of interesting mixes.

You need not be deprived of essential kitchen ingredients such as herbs if you have a small but sunny courtyard or balcony. Plant a selection of herbs in a large trough or pot. You could grow chives, parsley, marjoram, thyme, oregano, and rosemary. A large tub of salad greens is also an interesting approach for a balcony or courtyard. Choose loose-leafed varieties of lettuce so you can pick the leaves as required. If you have the space, why not grow a lemon tree in a pot?

Water Features for Balconies, Courtyards, and Patios

You can cool hot and sunny balconies, courtyards, and patios with a water feature. Water spheres are popular. The sphere, over which water trickles from the top, can be placed in its own dish and surrounded by pebbles. It is as much a sculpture as a water feature. Even a birdbath will provide the presence of water and perhaps create a cool bathing spot for local birds. A large water bowl with a lotus or waterlily planted in it makes a stylish feature, or you could even add a small fountain.

Wall fountains are favorite courtyard features as they enhance both the wall and its surroundings. Creative gardeners can enliven a small courtyard or patio by combining mosaic and water in a Moorish style. A mosaic may be created on the ground or on a wall, or you can decorate your containers. There are some wonderful tiles and pebbles around, and when pieces of broken crockery or other brightly colored objects are added, the outcome can be quite stunning.

Shady Balconies, Courtyards, and Patios

There are many plants that grow well in shady positions. Impatiens gives displays of flowers for months on end, and there is a great color range. Bergenias (*Bergenia* spp.) give a good foliage display, as do ferns. For more shade-loving plants, see "The Right Container Plant for the Right Place," starting on page 114.

Don't forget the importance of the containers themselves. A grouping of colorful pots can bring a shaded balcony, courtyard, or patio garden to life.

Windy Balconies, Courtyards and Patios

For windy positions you should select low, sturdy pots that will not be blown over easily. Use hardy, compact plants that are strong enough to withstand strong gusts of wind, such as glossy abelia (*Abelia* x *grandiflora*), lavender, and rosemary.

Even on the shadiest of patios, you can always find attractive plants to suit the site.

This row of potted geraniums (*Pelargonium* spp.) forms a colorful, yet practical, privacy screen.

Scented Plants for Balconies, Courtyards, and Patios

Scented plants add another dimension to container gardens. By using a number of fragrant plants, you can create a "scent pocket" on your balcony or in a section of your courtyard. Here are some suggestions:

Gardenia (*Gardenia augusta*)
Sweet pea (*Lathyrus odoratus*)
Lavender (*Lavandula angustifolia*)
Lilies (*Lilium* hybrids)
Magnolia (*Magnolia* spp.)
Lemon balm (*Melissa officinalis*)
Sweet cicely (*Myrrhis odorata*)
Daffodils (*Narcissus* hybrids)
Four-o'clocks (*Mirabilis jalapa*)
Rosemary (*Rosmarinus officinalis*)
Roses (*Rosa* spp.)

Plants for Hanging Baskets

Hanging baskets are ideal for balconies and courtyard walls. Hanging baskets bring attractive, colorful plants to eye level and have the advantage of saving valuable floor and ground space. Here are some suggestions for plants to grow in baskets:

Ageratum (*Ageratum houstonianum*)
Basket-of-gold (*Aurinia saxatilis*)
Fuchsia (*Fuchsia* x *hybrida*)
Treasure flower (*Gazania rigens*)
Strawberries (*Fragaria* spp.)
Nasturtium (*Tropaeolum majus*)
Rock speedwell (*Veronica prostrata*)

Evening Stars

As twilight descends, your courtyard, patio or balcony takes on a very different aspect. It is transformed into another world in which the predominance of the visual gradually gives way to the scents and sounds of night. Many light-colored flowers and silver foliage look their best during this twilight transformation, while others actually open in a burst of activity. For nighttime fragrance consider the following plants:

Moonflower (*Ipomoea alba*)
Jasmine (*Jasminum* spp.)
Chilean jasmine (*Mandevilla suaveolens*)
Night-scented stock (*Matthiola bicornis*)
Four-o'clocks (*Mirabilis jalapa*)
Flowering tobacco (*Nicotiana* spp.)
Stephanotis (*Stephanotis floribunda*)
White-flowering star jasmine (*Trachelospermum jasminoides*)

Night-scented stock

Caring for Balcony, Courtyard, and Patio Plants

A good container mix is the key to success with pot plants for balconies, courtyards, and patios. For hot areas, make sure you purchase a container mix that will hold moisture. Adding water-storing granules to a container mix will assist with water retention. You can also buy mixes for specific purposes, such as those formulated especially for terracotta pots. Because of their porous nature, you should line the inside of terracotta or stone pots with black plastic. But don't line the bottom of the pot or drainage will be impeded.

Potted plants need regular feeding. Annuals benefit from fortnightly feeds of a soluble plant food at half strength. Add a slow-release fertilizer to shrubs.

Caring for Container Gardens

Your container plants need to be cared for properly if they are to look their best for the longest possible time. Unlike regular garden plants, which can search for moisture and nutrients in the soil with their roots, container plants require regular watering and feeding to remain healthy. By following the simple maintenance guidelines in this section, your container plants should remain happy and healthy all season long.

Container Garden Primer

When planting groups of flowers in a container, ensure their light requirements are compatible.

In many ways, caring for container gardens is the same as for houseplants. They all need good soil, periodic fertilizing, and regular watering. However, the main difference is that outdoor containers are exposed to more light and more wind, so they'll need more water and more fertilizer to stay in top shape. And since they can't spread their roots to search out water and nutrients, container plantings are completely at your mercy for their needs.

To keep your container plants healthy, you'll have to pay attention to them at least every other day—maybe every day in midsummer. But if you set everything up carefully at the beginning, your plant care chores won't amount to more than a few minutes a day. There are a few techniques you can use to make your container plantings as low maintenance as possible.

Starting with large containers and using a rich, moisture-retentive potting mix are the two key steps to success. You'll find that large containers will look better than smaller pots, and they won't need to be watered as often. Plastic pots tend to lose water more slowly than clay pots, so they're a good choice for reducing your watering chores. (You'll find everything you need to know about containers in "Choosing Containers" on page 18.)

Rich, organic soil is the foundation of any good garden. It is important to choose a commercial container mix that will provide good rooting conditions for your container plants. You can also learn how to blend your own potting mixes to create a growing medium that's perfectly suited to your plants and less expensive as well. (For more information, see "Selecting Container Mixes" on page 22.)

Once your container gardens are established, routine grooming, fertilizing, and watering will keep them growing strong. "Container Care," below, offers pointers on planting, pinching, and preventing pest problems to keep your container gardens in peak condition.

Container Care

You've got the pot, and you've got the soil— now it's time to get your container garden started! Planting containers is easy, and it's a fun chance to try out new flower and foliage

Use small stakes to keep weak-stemmed plants from sprawling.

combinations to create pleasing groupings. Once you have your potted plants settled in, you'll want to groom them occasionally to keep them looking their best through the season. You'll also want to keep an eye out for pest and disease problems so you can catch them before they get out of hand.

Planting

There's no special trick to planting containers; simply do it just as you would garden beds, spacing transplants according to the instructions on the seed packets or the transplant labels. You can space them a little closer in containers if you want, but don't overdo it and try to put too many plants into one container. Remember, the container won't look full and lush immediately, but the little transplants will grow up quickly. It's more likely that you'll need to trim them back than worry about them looking too sparse.

Grooming

Through the season, a little regular pruning will keep all of your container plants looking first-rate. Once a week, grab a bucket and your garden shears and visit each of your container plantings. Snipping back long shoot tips on annuals and removing spent flowers on perennials will stimulate bushy growth and more flowering. Removing any damaged or dead leaves or branches will keep the plants looking fresh and healthy. Collect the clippings in the bucket for later composting.

If you've included taller plants in your containers, you may need to stake them to support their upright growth. You can buy bamboo stakes in various heights, or just use small branches pruned from shrubs in your yard. (If you save a little pile of branches when you prune in late winter, you'll have a perfect source of free material for staking. And the branches actually work better than the bamboo stakes because all of the side twigs help to support the plants better.)

Coping with Container Problems

Keeping your container gardens well watered and fertilized will go a long way toward keeping the plants healthy and vigorous. Insects tend to attack plants that are weak or stressed, so if you prevent the stress, you protect the plants.

Occasionally, though, conditions may be right for insects or diseases to attack even healthy-looking plants. Once a week or so, take a few minutes to really look at your plants and see if you notice any problems developing. Turn over a few leaves, and check the shoot tips for any indications of pests.

If bugs do show up, the same sprays that protect your houseplants will also work well outside. Spraying plants thoroughly with water will keep aphids and spider mite levels down. Insecticidal soap is generally recommended primarily to control soft-bodied insects (such as aphids), although it also works against tough customers like Japanese beetles. Just be sure you spray plants thoroughly, hitting both the tops and bottoms of all leaves. Soap sprays must hit the insects directly to be effective. Handpicking or flicking pests into a tub of soapy water also works well for larger insects, such as caterpillars. But be sure you know what you're killing—some very nasty-looking bugs are actually beneficial insects that prey on plant-eating pests.

If you have trouble with slug or snail damage (the usual symptoms are large holes in the leaves), sprinkle some finely crushed eggshells over the surface of the container mix in the pots. The snails and slugs will be deterred since they won't want to

Snails cannot reach hanging baskets, but are a problem for pots on the ground, wall baskets, and window boxes.

crawl over the rough edges of the eggshells. (As a bonus, the empty eggshells will provide a slow-release source of calcium, an important plant nutrient.)

Diseases are seldom a problem on container plants. As long as there are holes in the bottom of the container, root rots due to poor drainage aren't too common. If you let the plants dry out often, the leaf tips may turn brown— make more effort to water regularly to prevent further damage. Pinch off and discard plant parts that show fuzzy, white or gray patches—signs of powdery mildew—or off-color spots. Brown or white scorched spots on indoor plants that you've recently moved outside for the summer indicate sunburn. Plants generally grow out of this damage, although they will be somewhat weakened for a while. To avoid this problem, follow the guidelines covered in "Inside Out and Outside In" on page 61.

LEFT: When planning container plantings, consider how they'll look through the whole season. Bulbs are great for spring, but you'll need to replace them with annuals for later color.

Japanese beetles feed on a wide range of edible plants and herbs, as well as ornamentals.

Watering Container Gardens

For indoor container plants, your most important concern is providing enough light; while outdoors, watering is usually the most critical factor. Plants growing in outdoor containers will need more water as the season grows warmer and as they grow larger in relation to their pots. If you live in a windy location, containers will dry out even more quickly.

Unlike plants growing in the ground, the roots of container plants have only a limited space from which to absorb water and nutrients. Plants in the ground may be stressed if they aren't watered during a drought, but they usually recover. If the soil in a container gets too dry, however, the plants may sicken and die.

Do not wait until plants are dry to water them—the container mix dries out it shrinks, leaving a gap for water to run through the pot. Peat-based mixes can also be difficult to remoisten.

Knowing How Much to Water

The rule for watering established container plants is to always wet the container mix thoroughly, until water runs out of the bottom of the pot. The exception to this is when your container plants are very young and haven't yet grown roots out into the container. In this case, water sparingly or less often until the top growth

Large pots tend to dry out more slowly than small pots, so they'll need watering less often.

Save Time with Self-watering Pots

When you're shopping for pots, you may find some labeled "self-watering." While these containers aren't totally self-watering—you do have to add water from time to time—they have a reservoir area built into the bottom to hold a supply of water. Some of these containers have a wick running down from the soil to the reservoir; others are designed so that a small column of soil extends down into the reservoir to soak up water as needed. There's usually a small hole in the side of the container where you can fill the reservoir and check the water level.

These pots tend to be a bit more expensive, but they definitely help to reduce the frequency of watering. If you want to place a container planting in a spot where it's difficult for you to check it daily, by all means consider using a self-watering pot.

begins to be about the same size as the container. Once the plant is established, water it as you would your other plants.

Use Pure Water

Water that has a high salt content can harm your plants, if it is used over a long period. Sodium, calcium, and magnesium salts can cause damage to your plants that will first show in the leaves. Leaf speckling, leaf burn, and leaf fall can be caused by excessively salinated water.

Over time, salts can accumulate and show up as a white or tan crust at the edges of plant pots, or actually soak through clay or terracotta pots. Crust may also form on the soil surface and around the plant stems.

If your tap water is hard or salty, you will probably know about it already—you will have trouble getting soap to lather and

It's generally not wise to keep saucers under pots, but they can help with pots that dry out quickly.

doing your laundry. Use distilled or purified water instead of tap water. The increasing popularity of water purifiers means that pure water is available in many households. However, this is not practical for larger quantities of water in which case you may have to buy water in large capacity bottles.

Do not use artificially "softened" water on your plants which merely replaces the magnesium and calcium salts with sodium. It is not actually pure water.

If your tap water is chlorinated, let it stand in a pan or bucket overnight before using it on your plants. Alternatively, fill your bucket with the hose nozzle set to a fine spray. Both methods disperse chlorine.

Choosing Equipment for Easier Watering

There are several pieces of equipment that are quite helpful in making container watering as easy and efficient as possible. A watering can will be fine if you have only one or two pots to water. But if you have a collection of many containers, you'll save a lot of time and energy by using a hose with a special attachment called a water breaker. The breaker provides a soft, steady flow that won't wash the soil out of the pots as you water. You can buy the breaker alone, or attached to a long-handled watering wand that lets you reach all of your pots and hanging baskets easily.

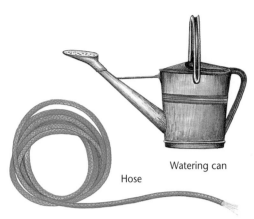

Watering can

Hose

These wands usually come with a shut-off valve so you don't have to leave the hose running when you go to turn it on or shut it off—a very handy feature.

If you live in an apartment and don't have access to an outside faucet, you can buy special attachments for your kitchen faucet and special lightweight hoses that you can run from your kitchen out to your balcony or rooftop garden.

Reducing Watering Chores

Besides having the right equipment, there are also several things you can do to keep your watering chores to a minimum.

Use large pots. The bigger the pots you use, the less often you will need to water—

Covering exposed soil with mulch while plants are young keeps it from drying out as quickly.

since large pots dry out more slowly—and the better your container garden will look.

Choose plastic or wood over clay. Clay pots dry out much faster than plastic or wood, so you may want to avoid using clay containers if you live in a hot, dry climate.

Arrange plants with similar watering needs into groups. This will make watering easier and reduce overall water loss.

Cover the soil with mulch. Mulching plants with shredded bark or grass clippings will help to reduce evaporation and keep moisture in the container mix.

Amend your container mix. Adding extra compost or vermiculite to the mix will help it hold more moisture. Or you may want to try the new synthetic water-absorbing polymers now on the market. These polymers aren't organic, but they are apparently nontoxic. You just combine the polymer granules with the container mix before planting, and the granules work by absorbing large amounts of water and holding it until the plant's roots need it.

Use a long-necked spout or wand if you are watering plants from the top. By doing this you can avoid splashing leaves and be able to direct water more carefully all over the surface of your container mix.

If you follow all of these tips and your plants are drying out so fast that they need watering twice a day, either move them to larger pots or prune them back to bring the top growth into better balance with the roots. (Pruning off older growth also helps to stimulate fresh new flowers on annuals and many perennials.)

Watering Wisdom

In general, you should not keep saucers under outdoor plants because they will fill up with water during rainstorms and could cause the soil to become waterlogged and the roots to rot. If you are concerned about pots leaving stains where they sit on your deck or patio, just set them up on small scraps of wood. (This is especially a good idea for large containers to ensure that water drains well from the bottom holes.)

There are two instances where it can be all right to put saucers under your outdoor

A Quick Fix for Parched Plants

It's bound to happen—one day you accidentally skip a container while you're watering, and you come home the next day to find a pot of wilted plants. Before you throw the whole thing away, first try reviving the plants with a deep soaking.

Submerge the whole pot or basket in a large bucket or tub of water, and leave it there for an hour or two. Take it out and set or hang it in a cool, shady place for a day or two to see if the plants perk up. If they do revive, move the container back to its previous spot, and pay extra-careful attention to watering and fertilizing to help the plants make a full recovery.

plants. The first is when a plant should be moved to a bigger container and needs a little extra water until you have time to repot it. The other time you may want to use saucers is when you are going away for a day or two and want your plants to get by without extra watering. Water as normal and add some extra water to the saucers to sustain the plants; remove the saucers when you return.

Never water your plants with icy cold water, as it might shock the root system. It is safer to use tepid water.

Fungus and molds like cool, wet conditions. If you water in the mornings, you avoid leaving your plants wet all night and minimize fungal problems.

Shallow watering is no help, especially in hot conditions. Water deeply so that the entire soil mass is wet to encourage deeper root growth.

One soaking might not be enough for large pots. Wait until you see water running through the bottom of the pot.

Fertilizing Container Gardens

To keep your container plantings in great shape from spring through fall, you'll need to supply extra nutrients sometime during the growing season. You can choose from a variety of solid or liquid materials to fertilize your plants and flowers.

Choosing Fertilizers

Whether you should use organic or chemical fertilizers is a hot topic among gardeners. However, the choice you make has environmental implications that you might want to consider. Excess nitrogen and other chemical salts from inorganic fertilizers seep into groundwater and waterways degrading the environment.

You can buy organic fertilizers, such as fish emulsion, bloodmeal, and bonemeal, at most local garden centers. Or you can combine these ingredients with wood ashes, coffee grounds, and other recyclable organic "wastes" to make your own organic fertilizer blends. For complete details on selecting and blending various organic fertilizers, see "Understanding Organic Fertilizers" on page 43.

Whatever fertilizer you choose, be sure to read and thoroughly understand the instructions on labels and packaging so that you can apply just the right amount for the specific plants you are growing. If in any doubt, it is better to under-fertilize plants. In fact, some experienced gardeners prefer to use fertilizer at half strength but twice as often.

A similar effect can be achieved by using slow-release fertilizers—chemical fertilizers that have been coated with a type of resin that breaks down and releases small doses of fertilizer over a longer period of time. Some gardeners mix in slow-release fertilizers at planting time and, for plants with limited nutrient needs, they may be enough to support the plant throughout its life. For other plants, further applications of liquid fertilizers throughout the growing season may still be needed.

Organic fertilizers release nutrients slowly, promoting steady, healthy plant growth.

Regular feedings with liquid fertilizer will keep annuals vigorous and blooming all season long.

Necessary Nutrients

Plants can't really tell the difference between an organic fertilizer and one made in a chemical factory. More important is the range of elements available to the plant and the balance between them. It may be a good idea to try out different fertilizers on various specimens of a plant, experimenting to find out which fertilizer produces the best results for you.

These days, chemical and many organic fertilizers will let you know the ratio of the most important elements plants need for healthy growth. The numbers represent the proportion by weight of the most important plant nutrients contained in the fertilizer: nitrogen (N), phosphorus (P), and potassium (K).

Nitrogen

Nitrogen is the most important element, since plants use it to build proteins, enzymes, chlorophyll, and hormones. Adequate nitrogen gives a plant healthy, green leaves and strong growth. Too little nitrogen results in a pale, slow-growing plant. Too much nitrogen can give you a plant that is very green and sappy, and attractive to pests and disease. Nitrogen is always on the move through the soil, atmosphere, and living things, and can be rapidly leached away in irrigation water. Therefore, it's the element most likely to be in short supply. Bloodmeal (12-1-1) can give your plants a quick jolt of nitrogen but you may prefer to use more balanced fertilizers such as fish emulsion (5-2-2) or cottonseed meal (7-2-2).

Phosphorus

Phosphorus is essential to the plant's metabolic processes, seed production, and root development. A phosphorus deficiency shows up as stunted growth, sometimes with a reddish or purplish cast to the leaves. Phosphorus becomes available to plants when there is plenty of water and organic matter, and the soil pH is close to neutral. Bonemeal (1-11-0) is the classic organic source for phosphorus.

Potassium

Potassium is necessary in fairly large quantities to regulate metabolic reactions within the plant, including photosynthesis. Some plants need potassium more than any other nutrient. A plant deficient in potassium might be soft and weak, and its leaf margins might appear scorched. There isn't much potassium in organic matter so if your plants need it, you should add granite dust or another rock powder.

Using Fertilizers

Meeting the nutrient needs of your container plants starts at planting time. Adding compost to commercial or homemade container mixes is one of the best things you can do to promote good root growth. Compost provides millions of live microorganisms, which feed on other organic fertilizers and make the nutrients available to your plants. (Organic fertilizers will still work in soils without compost, but they are much more effective with it.)

If you're growing annual flowers, herbs, and vegetables, mixing extra organic fertilizers into the compost-enriched soil is not really necessary. However, for long-term container plantings, such as perennials, shrubs, and trees, supplementing the container mix with kelp (seaweed) meal, greensand, and other organic

RIGHT: It is a good idea to add some compost to container perennials, shrubs, and trees every spring.

Successful Containers Start with Compost

Hopefully, you have enough space for a small compost pile. You just need an area that's at least 3 feet (90 cm) long, wide, and high. You can buy a commercial compost bin, build your own out of old pallets or chicken wire, or just heap the material in a pile. Good compost ingredients include most organic garden and kitchen wastes. Avoid oils, fats, and bones—all of which break down slowly and attract scavengers—and human and pet wastes, which carry diseases. Also avoid adding diseased or insect-infested materials.

Mix a balance of dry materials, such as leaves or shredded newspaper, with moist materials, such as grass clippings or vegetable peelings. The pile should feel damp but not soggy. If it's dry, add water; if it's too wet, mix in more dry material. Keep adding more materials as you gather them until the pile fills its space or bin. About once a week, use a pitchfork to turn over, or at least stir up, the mix. Eventually—after a few weeks or months—the original ingredients will break down into dark, crumbly compost. Before using the finished compost, sift it through ½-inch (12-mm) wire mesh to screen out any lumps that are left.

If you don't have the space for outdoor composting, try worm composting. You can keep worms in an indoor bin and feed them your food scraps to make a very rich compost. Several garden-supply catalogs offer bins, instructions, and even the worms themselves.

Of course, if you just need a little compost now and then, or if you need more than you can make, you can buy it in bags at your garden center. If your community has a composting program, you may also be able to get it at no charge from your local yard waste composting site.

Compost tea

If you want to turn your compost from a solid nutrient source into a quick-acting liquid fertilizer, make it into tea. Add one or two shovelfuls of compost (or farm manure) into a burlap or woven-mesh bag. Tie the bag securely and submerge it into a large bucket or barrel of water. Let it steep for 1 week, then remove the bag. Dilute the remaining liquid until it is the color of weak tea if you plan to spray or sprinkle it directly on your perennials, or use it full strength to drench the ground around the base of the plants.

nutrients will help ensure a steady supply of nutrients for the developing roots. "Making Your Own Container Mixes," on page 22, offers a recipe for a well-balanced, nutrient-enriched, deluxe growing medium that's great for the needs of these "permanent" plantings. Once your plants are established, after a few weeks, it's time to start adding extra nutrients. Begin with a liquid fish product, using it at half the recommended strength every 2 weeks. Most fish

fertilizers are higher in nitrogen than in potassium or phosphorus. This is fine until it's time for flowering plants to begin blooming. Then you may want to treat flowering plants to a handful of bonemeal (for extra phosphorus) and kelp meal or wood ashes (for plenty of potassium). Mix these materials with a little compost and scratch them into the soil surface.

You can keep feeding most container plants through late summer; after that, the cooler temperatures of fall will naturally slow their growth. For outdoor potted trees and shrubs, stop fertilizing by midsummer to give the new growth a chance to "harden up" before frost.

The Right Container Plant for the Right Place

For successful container gardening, it is important to match plants with their preferred conditions. To help you make the best choices for the conditions you have, the following chart summarizes the specific needs of over 330 perennials, annuals, bulbs, groundcovers, ornamental grasses, trees and shrubs, vines, edible plants, and herbs. You can see at a glance exactly which plants prefer sun, and which prefer shade, and you can check if the plant will thrive in your particular climatic zone. In addition, the chart notes the main season of interest for the plant, as well as other useful comments to guide you in your plant choices.

Plant	Light Needs	Hardiness	Season of interest	Comments
PERENNIALS				
Woolly yarrow (*Achillea tomentosa*)	Full sun	Zones 3–7	Yellow flowers bloom from early to midsummer.	Ideal for low-maintenance containers.
Bicolor monkshood (*Aconitum x bicolor*)	Full sun to light shade	Zones 3–7	Dark blue or two-toned flowers bloom in summer and fall.	All parts of the plant are poisonous if ingested.
Azure monkshood (*Aconitum carmichaelii*)	Full sun to light shade	Zones 3–7	Blue flowers bloom in late summer and fall.	Dislikes disturbance once established.
White baneberry (*Actaea alba*)	Partial to full shade	Zones 3–9	Fuzzy white flowers bloom in spring; white berries occur in late summer to fall.	Plant in a large (2-foot/60-cm wide) container.
Ajuga (*Ajuga reptans*)	Full sun to partial shade	Zones 3–8	Blue or purple flowers bloom in spring or early summer.	Looks great growing under a Japanese maple (*Acer palmatum*).
Lady's-mantle (*Alchemilla mollis*)	Partial shade	Zones 3–9	Greenish-yellow flowers bloom in late spring.	Plant is especially pretty in a cool, moist, partly shady spot.
Peruvian lily (*Alstroemeria aurea*)	Full sun to partial shade	Zones 7–10	Orange or yellow flowers bloom throughout summer.	Achieves best performance after the third year.
Willow blue star (*Amsonia tabernaemontana*)	Full sun to partial shade	Zones 3–9	Blue flowers bloom in spring with some secondary shoots appearing in early summer.	Plant in a large (2-foot/60-cm wide) container.
Three-veined everlasting (*Anaphalis triplinervis*)	Full sun to partial shade	Zones 3–8	A profusion of white flowers in July, August, and September.	Flowers dry on the plant and last for weeks.
Italian bugloss (*Anchusa azurea*)	Full sun to light shade	Zones 3–8	Blue flowers bloom in late spring.	Plant in a large (2-foot/60-cm wide) container.
Grape-leaved anemone (*Anemone tomentosa* 'Robustissima')	Full sun to light shade	Zones 3–8	Pink flowers bloom in summer and fall.	Plant in a large (2-foot/60-cm wide) container.
Hybrid columbine (*Aquilegia x hybrida*)	Full sun to partial shade	Zones 3–9	Flowers of many colors, including yellow, red, purple, white, and pink, bloom in early summer.	In light shade, combine with wildflowers, ferns, and hostas in a large container.
Marguerite (*Argyranthemum frutescens*)	Full sun	Zones 7–10	White, pink, or yellow flowers bloom from spring to fall and in winter.	Plant in a large (2-foot/60-cm wide) container.
Thrift (*Armeria maritima*)	Full sun	Zones 4–8	Pink flowers bloom in spring and summer.	Drought-tolerant once established.

Plant	Light Needs	Hardiness	Season of interest	Comments
Butterfly weed (*Asclepias tuberosa*)	Full sun to light shade	Zones 3–9	Orange flowers bloom profusely in May and June.	The flowers attract butterflies.
Frikart's aster (*Aster x frikartii*)	Full sun to light shade	Zones 6–8	Lavender-blue flowers bloom from midsummer to fall.	Flowers are ideal for floral arrangements.
New England aster (*Aster novae-angliae*)	Full sun to light shade	Zones 3–8	The white, pink, rose, lavender and purple flowers bloom from summer through fall.	Plant in a large (2-foot/60-cm wide) container.
Astilbe (*Astilbe x arendsii*)	Full to partial shade	Zones 3–9	Red, pink, and white blooms in spring and early summer.	Pots may be placed in shallows of ponds during summer.
Dwarf Chinese astilbe (*Astilbe chinensis* var. *pumila*)	Partial shade	Zones 5–8	Pinkish-blue flowers bloom from mid- to late summer.	Flowers dry well and are good for winter arrangements.
Masterwort (*Astrantia major*)	Partial to full sun	Zones 6–9	Pink or white daisies bloom in early to late summer.	If plant is in full sun, ensure its roots are kept moist.
Rock cress (*Aubrieta deltoidea*)	Full sun to light shade	Zones 4–8	White, rose, or purple flowers bloom in early spring.	Ideal for hanging baskets or urns.
Basket-of-gold (*Aurinia saxatilis*)	Full sun	Zones 3–7	Brilliant yellow flowers bloom in early spring.	Avoid excessively hot and humid conditions.
Blue false indigo (*Baptisia australis*)	Full sun or partial shade	Zones 3–9	Deep blue flowers bloom in spring and early summer.	Plant in a large (2-foot/60-cm wide) container.
Heart-leaved bergenia (*Bergenia cordifolia*)	Partial shade	Zones 3–9	Pink, rose, or white flowers bloom in spring.	Avoid slug and snail damage by placing pot in a high place.
Siberian bugloss (*Brunnera macrophylla*)	Partial shade	Zones 3–8	Forget-me-not-blue flowers bloom in spring.	Plant in a large (2-foot/60-cm wide) container.
Carpathian harebell (*Campanula carpatica*)	Full sun to light shade	Zones 3–8	Blue-purple or white flowers bloom in early summer.	Looks great combined with yellow daylilies.
Dalmation bellflower (*Campanula portenschlagiana*)	Sun or partial shade	Zones 5–9	Blue-purple flowers bloom in spring and early summer.	Plant is ideal for window boxes or hanging baskets.
Cupid's dart (*Catananche caerulea*)	Full sun	Zones 4–9	Blue-purple flowers bloom in summer.	Plants may be short-lived in badly drained container mixes.
Knapweed (*Centaurea hypoleuca*)	Full sun	Zones 3–7	Pink flowers bloom in spring and early summer.	Remove faded flower heads to promote rebloom.
Red valerian (*Centranthus ruber*)	Full sun	Zones 4–8	Deep coral red flowers bloom in spring and summer.	Plants perform best in areas with dry summers.
Leadwort (*Ceratostigma plumbaginoides*)	Full sun to partial shade	Zones 5–9	Cobalt blue flowers appear from late summer until frost.	Plant in a large (2-foot/60-cm wide) container.
Pink turtlehead (*Chelone lyonii*)	Full sun to partial shade	Zones 3–8	Rosy pink flowers bloom from late summer into fall.	Plant in a large (2-foot/60-cm wide) container.
Lily-of-the-valley (*Convallaria majalis*)	Partial to full shade	Zones 2–8	Waxy, white flowers appear in spring.	Glossy, orange-red berries may appear in summer.

Plant	Light Needs	Hardiness	Season of interest	Comments
Hybrid delphinium (*Delphinium* x *elatum* hybrids)	Full sun	Zones 4–7	Flowers from white to true blue to lavender and purple appear in spring.	Plant in a large (2-foot/60-cm wide) container.
Garden mum (*Dendranthema* x *grandiflorum*)	Full sun to light shade	Zones 3–9	White, pink, red, gold, or yellow flowers bloom from summer through fall.	Plant in a large (2-foot/60-cm wide) container.
Cheddar pinks (*Dianthus gratianopolitanus*)	Full sun	Zones 3–9	White, rose, or pink flowers bloom from early to midsummer and often continue until frost.	Looks good cascading out of a hanging basket.
Cottage pinks (*Dianthus plumarius*)	Full sun	Zones 3–9	Fragrant white or pink flowers bloom from early to midsummer.	This sweet-scented plant is ideal for hanging baskets and window boxes.
Bleeding heart (*Dicentra spectabilis*)	Partial shade; full sun in Northern gardens	Zones 3–9	Pink flowers bloom in spring.	Combine with bulbs, primroses, and wildflowers for a spring display.
Leopard's bane (*Doronicum orientale*)	Full sun to shade	Zones 3–8	Bright yellow flowers bloom in spring and early summer.	Plant in a large (2-foot/60-cm wide) container.
Globe thistle (*Echinops ritro*)	Full sun	Zones 3–8	Steel-blue flowers bloom in midsummer.	Good drainage is essential, especially in winter.
Daisy fleabane (*Erigeron speciosus*)	Full sun or light shade	Zones 2–9	Flowers in white, pink, rose, or purple bloom in early to midsummer.	Hardy container plant.
Amethyst sea holly (*Eryngium amethystinum*)	Full sun	Zones 2–8	Steel-blue flowers bloom in summer.	Plant is extremely drought-tolerant once established.
Queen-of-the-prairie (*Filipendula rubra*)	Full sun to light shade	Zones 3–9	Peach-pink flowers bloom in late spring and early summer.	Plant in a large (2-foot/60-cm wide) container.
Blanket flower (*Gaillardia* x *grandiflora*)	Full sun	Zones 4–9	Yellow and orange flowers bloom throughout summer.	Drought-tolerant container plant.
Endres cranesbill (*Geranium endressi*)	Full sun to partial shade	Zones 4–8	Soft pink flowers bloom from early to midsummer.	The pale pink flowers become darker with age.
Baby's breath (*Gypsophila paniculata*)	Full sun to light shade	Zones 3–9	Masses of small, dainty, white flowers appear in summer.	Plant in a large (2-foot/60-cm wide) container.
Common sneezeweed (*Helenium autumnale*)	Full sun to light shade	Zones 3–8	Yellow flowers bloom in late summer and fall.	Plant in a large (2-foot/60-cm wide) container.
Lenten rose (*Helleborus* x *hybridus*)	Light to partial shade	Zones 4–8	Reddish purple, pink, or white flowers bloom from early winter through spring.	Established plants tolerate dry container mix and deep shade.
Daylilies (*Hemerocallis* hybrids)	Full sun to light shade	Zones 3–9	Orange, yellow, red, pink, buff, apricot, or green flowers appear from spring through summer.	Most modern hybrids need 8 hours of direct sunlight to flower well.
Coral bells (*Heuchera* spp.)	Full sun to light shade	Zones 3–8	White, red, purplish, or pink flowers bloom during summer.	Heat-tolerant container plant.

Plant	Light Needs	Hardiness	Season of interest	Comments
Hostas (*Hosta* hybrids)	Light to moderate shade	Zones 4–9	Purplish or white flowers appear in summer.	Avoid slug and snail damage by placing pot in a high place.
Perennial candytuft (*Iberis sempervirens*)	Full sun to light shade	Zones 3–9	White flowers bloom in early spring.	Shear after flowering to promote compact growth.
New Guinea impatiens (*Impatiens* New Guinea hybrids)	Full sun to filtered light	Zones 5–10	Orange, red, purple, lavender, or pink flowers bloom in summer.	Can bring pots indoors during winter.
Impatiens (*Impatiens wallerana*)	Partial to full shade	Zones 5–10	White, pink, red, orange, or lavender blooms from late spring until frost.	Good for window boxes and hanging baskets.
Crested iris (*Iris cristata*)	Partial shade	Zones 3–8	Lavender flowers bloom in midspring.	Looks great combined with ferns.
Shasta daisy (*Leucanthemum* x *superbum*)	Full sun	Zones 3–10	White flowers with bright yellow centers appear during summer.	Deadhead plants to promote continued bloom.
Spike gayfeather (*Liatris spicata*)	Full sun	Zones 3–9	Pinkish purple flowers bloom in midsummer.	Plants tend to flop in partial shade.
Creeping lilyturf (*Liriope spicata*)	Full sun to deep shade	Zones 5–10	Lavender to whitish flowers bloom mid- to late summer.	Drought-tolerant container plant.
Cardinal flower (*Lobelia cardinalis*)	Full sun to partial shade	Zones 2–9	Scarlet flowers bloom in late summer to fall.	Plant in a large (2-foot/60-cm wide) container.
Persian nepeta (*Nepeta mussinii*)	Full sun	Zones 3–8	Lavender-blue flowers bloom from spring to midsummer.	A relative of catnip, this plant may attract cats.
Showy sundrops (*Oenothera speciosa*)	Full sun to very light shade	Zones 3–8	White flowers bloom in summer.	Plant in a large (2-foot/60-cm wide) container.
Prickly pear (*Opuntia humifusa*)	Full sun	Zones 5–9	Yellow flowers with white stamens bloom in late spring or early summer.	Plant in a large (2-foot/60-cm wide) container.
Allegheny pachysandra (*Pachysandra procumbens*)	Partial to full shade	Zones 5–9	White or purplish flowers bloom in early spring.	Plant in a large (2-foot/60-cm wide) container.
Common garden peony (*Paeonia lactiflora*)	Full sun to light shade	Zones 2–8	Flowers from white, cream, and yellow to pink, rose, burgundy, and scarlet bloom from April to June.	Plant in a large (2-foot/60-cm wide) container.
Oriental poppy (*Papaver orientale*)	Full sun to light shade	Zones 2–7	Flowers in shades of pink through red bloom in summer.	Plant in a large (2-foot/60-cm wide) container.
Foxglove penstemon (*Penstemon digitalis*)	Full sun to light shade	Zones 4–8	White flowers with purple lines bloom from late spring to early summer.	Plant in a large (2-foot/60-cm wide) container.
Garden phlox (*Phlox paniculata*)	Full sun to light shade	Zones 3–8	Flowers of magenta to pink and white bloom from mid- to late summer.	Dense flower heads are fragrant and useful for cutting.

Plant	Light Needs	Hardiness	Season of interest	Comments
Obedient plant (*Physostegia virginiana*)	Full sun to light shade	Zones 3–9	Rose pink to lilac-pink flowers bloom in late summer.	Plant in a large (2-foot/60-cm wide) container.
Balloon flower (*Platycodon grandiflorus*)	Full sun to light shade	Zones 3–8	Rich blue flowers appear in summer.	Established plants are drought-tolerant.
Fragrant Solomon's seal (*Polygonatum odoratum*)	Partial to full shade	Zones 3–9	Pale green flowers in spring. Blue-black fruits in summer.	Plant in a large (2-foot/60-cm wide) container.
Japanese primrose (*Primula japonica*)	Light shade	Zones 4–8	Cultivars flower in pink, rose, red, purple, and white in late spring to early summer.	Place containers near the edges of ponds.
Polyanthus primrose (*Primula* x *polyantha*)	Light to partial shade	Zones 3–8	Flowers vary from white, cream, and yellow to pink, rose, red, and purple in spring and early summer.	Good hanging basket plant.
English primrose (*Primula vulgaris*)	Light to partial shade	Zones 4–8	Pale yellow flowers bloom in spring and early summer.	Plants may go dormant if container mix dries out in summer.
Pasque flower (*Pulsatilla vulgaris*)	Full sun to light shade	Zones 3–8	Purple flowers with yellow centers bloom from early to midspring.	Plant does not tolerate a soggy container mix.
Orange coneflower (*Rudbeckia fulgida*)	Full sun	Zones 3–9	Gold flowers with dark central cones bloom during summer and fall.	Drought-tolerant container plant.
Violet sage (*Salvia* x *superba*)	Full sun to light shade	Zones 4–7	Violet-blue flowers appear in early to midsummer.	Drought-tolerant container plant.
Pincushion flower (*Scabiosa caucasica*)	Full sun to light shade	Zones 3–7	Flowers in pink, red, purple, or blue hues bloom in summer.	Plants are sensitive to high temperatures.
Sedum (*Sedum spectabile*)	Full sun	Zones 3–9	Small bright pink flowers bloom in mid- to late summer.	Plant is extremely drought-tolerant.
Dusty miller (*Senecio cineraria*)	Semi-shade	Zones 7–9	Yellow flowers bloom in summer.	The silvery foliage looks good at night.
Solomon's plume (*Smilacina racemosa*)	Light to full shade	Zones 3–8	White flowers bloom in late spring.	Grow in a large (2-foot/60-cm wide) container.
Lamb's-ears (*Stachys byzantina*)	Full sun to light shade	Zones 4–8	Rose-pink flowers bloom in spring.	The silvery foliage looks good at night.
Stoke's aster (*Stokesia laevis*)	Full sun to light shade	Zones 5–9	Blue flowers bloom in summer.	Established plants tolerate dry conditions.
Allegheny foamflower (*Tiarella cordifolia*)	Light shade	Zones 3–8	White flowers bloom in midspring.	Ideal container plant for shady gardens.
Common spiderwort (*Tradescantia* x *andersoniana*)	Full sun to partial shade	Zones 3–9	Blue, purple, or white flowers appear in spring and summer.	Plants in dry containers go dormant in summer.
Great merrybells (*Uvularia grandiflora*)	Partial to full shade	Zones 3–8	Lemon-yellow flowers bloom in spring.	Spring sun is important for bloom, but plant needs summer sun.

Plant	Light Needs	Hardiness	Season of interest	Comments
Nettle-leaved mullein (*Verbascum chaixii*)	Full sun to light shade	Zones 4–8	Yellow flowers bloom in summer.	Plant in a large (2-foot/60-cm wide) container.
Spike speedwell (*Veronica spicata*)	Full sun to light shade	Zones 3–8	Pink, blue, or white flowers bloom in summer.	Plant in a large (2-foot/60-cm wide) container.
Sweet violet (*Viola odorata*)	Sun or shade	Zones 6–9	Purple flowers bloom in spring.	Perfume is sweet and quite strong.

✺ ANNUALS

Plant	Light Needs	Hardiness	Season of interest	Comments
Ageratum (*Ageratum houstonianum*)	Full or half-day sun	Zones 5–10	Lavender, blue, pink, or white flowers from early summer until frost.	Protect plant from hot midday sun.
Love-lies-bleeding (*Amaranthus caudatus*)	Full sun	Zones 6–10	Crimson flowers bloom from midsummer until frost.	Grow in a very large container, such as a half-barrel.
Snapdragon (*Antirrhinum majus*)	Full sun to light shade	Zones 6–10	Flowers bloom in wide range of colors, except true blue, in late summer.	Remove spent flower spikes to promote more flowers.
Wax begonia (*Begonia* Semperflorens-Cultorum hybrids)	Half-day of sun with shade in hottest hours	Zones 5–10	Small white, pink, or red flowers bloom from spring to fall.	Can bring pots indoors for winter.
Hybrid tuberous begonias (*Begonia* Tuberhybrida hybrids)	Half-day of sun or filtered sun	Zones 6–10	Flowers in all colors except blue bloom from summer until frost.	Reduce watering in fall and bring pots indoors before or just after the first frost.
English daisy (*Bellis perennis*)	Full sun to partial shade	Zones 3–9	White, pink, or red flowers bloom from April to June.	Looks great combined with forget-me-nots and spring bulbs.
Swan River daisy (*Brachyscome iberidifolia*)	Full sun	Zones 6–10	Blue, white or rose-colored flowers bloom from spring.	Excellent hanging basket plant.
Strawflower (*Bracteantha bracteatum*)	Full sun	Zones 5–10	White, pink, rose, orange, red, or yellow flowers from midsummer until frost.	The long lasting flowers are ideal for drying.
Ornamental cabbage (*Brassica oleracea*)	Full sun to light shade	Zones 6–9	Leaves are marked with pink, purple, cream, or white in fall.	Looks good in window boxes.
Browallia (*Browallia speciosa*)	Full to filtered sun	Zones 6–9	White, blue, or lilac flowers bloom from summer.	Ideal for window boxes and baskets in partial shade.
Pot marigold (*Calendula officinalis*)	Full sun	Zones 4–9	Orange and yellow flowers bloom from summer to fall.	Flowers tend to close during cloudy weather and at night.
China aster (*Callistephus chinensis*)	Full sun	Zones 4–9	White, cream, pink, red, purple, or blue flowers bloom from late summer to frost.	Renew mix and change pot each year to minimize disease.
Madasgar periwinkle (*Catharanthus roseus*)	Full sun	Zones 5–10	White, rose, or pink flowers bloom throughout the year.	Tolerates heat, pollution, and drought.
Celosia (*Celosia cristata*)	Full sun	Zones 5–10	Flowers of red, pink, orange, or yellow bloom all summer.	Tricky to get started, but easy once plant is established.

Plant	Light Needs	Hardiness	Season of interest	Comments
Cornflower (*Centaurea cyanus*)	Full sun	Zones 5–9	White, blue, pink, purple, or red flowers bloom in summer.	Pinching off spent blooms can prolong the flowering season.
Cleome (*Cleome hasslerana*)	Full sun to light shade	Zones 4–10	White, pink, or lavender flowers from midsummer to midfall.	Plant in a large (2-foot/60-cm wide) container.
Rocket larkspur (*Consolida ambigua*)	Full sun	Zones 4–9	Purple-blue, rose, pink, or white flowers bloom from late spring through summer.	The spiky blooms make great cut flowers.
Dwarf morning glory (*Convolvulus tricolor*)	Full sun	Zones 5–10	Blue flowers with a yellow throat and a white central band bloom all summer.	Great for hanging baskets.
Coreopsis (*Coreopsis tinctoria*)	Full sun	Zones 6–10	Yellow flowers with maroon centers, plain yellow, or orange flowers bloom from midsummer until frost.	Cutting plants back by one third in summer can prolong flowering.
Cosmos (*Cosmos bipinnatus*)	Full sun to partial shade	Zones 4–10	White, pink, or red flowers bloom from late summer through fall.	Remove spent flowers to encourage more blooms.
Yellow cosmos (*Cosmos sulphureus*)	Full sun	Zones 4–10	Yellow, orange, or red blooms appear from late summer until frost.	Seed can be collected from mature flowers at the end of the season.
Sweet William (*Dianthus barbatus*)	Full sun to partial shade	Zones 6–9	Red, pink, or white flowers bloom from early to midsummer.	Start new plants each year for the best results.
China pink (*Dianthus chinensis*)	Full sun	Zones 6–9	White, pink, or red flowers appear through summer.	Fragrant container plant.
Wallflower (*Erysimum cheiri*)	Full sun to partial shade	Zones 6–9	Red, pink, or creamy white flowers bloom from midspring to early summer.	Fragrant container plant.
California poppy (*Eschscholzia californica*)	Full sun	Zones 6–10	Orange, yellow, white, pink, or red flowers appear from summer to fall.	Pinch off developing seedpods to prolong bloom.
Snow-on-the-mountain (*Euphorbia marginata*)	Full sun	Zones 6–9	Tiny flowers with white bracts appear in summer.	Cut stems leak a milky sap that can irritate mouth, eyes, and skin.
Prairie gentian (*Eustoma grandiflorum*)	Full sun to partial shade	Zones 6–9	White, cream, rose, and purple-blue blooms appear in summer.	Bring pot indoors for winter.
Blanket flower (*Gaillardia pulchella*)	Full sun	Zones 5–9	Red, yellow, or orange flowers bloom in summer.	Plant is heat- and drought-tolerant.
Treasure flower (*Gazania rigens*)	Full sun	Zones 6–10	The mainly red, orange, or yellow blooms appear from midsummer until frost.	For winter bloom, bring plants indoors before frost.

Plant	Light Needs	Hardiness	Season of interest	Comments
Globe amaranth (*Gomphrena globosa*)	Full sun	Zones 6–10	Magenta, pink, or white flowers from midsummer until frost.	Compact cultivars are best suited to container culture.
Licorice plant (*Helichrysum petiolatum*)	Full sun	Zones 6–10	Yellow-white flowers bloom in spring.	Great for window boxes and hanging baskets.
Annual candytuft (*Iberis umbellata*)	Full sun to partial shade	Zones 5–9	White, pink, pinkish-purple, rose, or red flowers appear from spring through midsummer.	In hot-summer areas, pull out plants after bloom.
Garden balsam (*Impatiens balsamina*)	Full sun to partial shade	Zones 5–10	White, pink, purple, rose, or red flowers appear from midsummer until frost.	Good container plants for shady areas.
Sweet pea (*Lathyrus odoratus*)	Full sun	Zones 6–10	Flowers in white, pink, red, or purple bloom from midspring into summer.	Provide a tepee of bamboo stakes for plant to climb on. Looks good in a hanging basket.
Annual statice (*Limonium sinuatum*)	Full sun	Zones 6–10	Flowers in white, pink, peach, red, orange, yellow, purple, and blue bloom in summer and early fall.	Flowers are pretty in dried or fresh arrangements.
Edging lobelia (*Lobelia erinus*)	Partial to full sun	Zones 5–10	Blue, violet, pink, or white flowers appear in summer.	Looks good in strawberry jar planters.
Sweet alyssum (*Lobularia maritima*)	Full sun	Zones 5–9	White, pink, or purple flowers appear from summer to fall.	Great for edging large containers.
Honesty (*Lunaria annua*)	Partial shade	Zones 7–10	Purple-pink flowers bloom in spring and early summer; followed by silvery seedpods.	Blooms are lightly fragrant.
Virginia stock (*Malcomia maritima*)	Full sun to partial shade	Zones 6–10	Purple, pink, or white flowers appear from midsummer until frost.	Ideal for window boxes.
Common stock (*Matthiola incana*)	Full sun	Zones 6–9	White, pink, red, yellow, or purple flowers appear in summer.	Fragrant container plant.
Monkey flower (*Mimulus x hybridus*)	Partial shade	Zones 5–9	Orange, yellow, or red blooms appear in summer.	Bring containers indoors to overwinter.
Four-o'clock (*Mirabilis jalapa*)	Full sun to partial shade	Zones 6–10	Flowers in white or shades of pink, magenta, red, and yellow appear from midsummer until frost.	Fragrant container plant. Flowers open in the late afternoon.
Forget-me-not (*Myosotis sylvatica*)	Partial shade to a half-day of sun	Zones 5–9	The tiny blue or pink, white-centered flowers bloom from May to June.	Can bloom in the first year if started early indoors.
Baby-blue-eyes (*Nemophila menziesii*)	Full sun to partial shade	Zones 5–9	Sky blue flowers with a white center bloom in summer.	Looks great trailing out of pots and planters.

Plant	Light Needs	Hardiness	Season of interest	Comments
Flowering tobacco (*Nicotiana* spp.)	Partial shade to full sun	Zones 6–10	White, pink, or red flowers bloom from summer until frost.	Plant in large (2-foot/60-cm wide) container.
Love-in-a-mist (*Nigella damascena*)	Full sun to partial shade	Zones 5–9	Blue, pink, or white flowers bloom in summer.	Established plants are care-free.
Iceland poppy (*Papaver nudicaule*)	Full sun	Zones 2–10	White, pink, red, orange, or yellow flowers bloom in early to midsummer.	Easiest to grow from seed sown directly into the container.
Corn poppy (*Papaver rhoeas*)	Full sun	Zones 4–9	Scarlet, red, white, pink, and bicolor flowers bloom during summer.	Remove spent blooms to extend the flowering season.
Petunia (*Petunia* x *hybrida*)	Full sun; tolerates half-day sun	Zones 6–10	Red, salmon, pink, deep purple, blue, yellow, orange cream, or white blooms appear from early summer.	Ideal for hanging baskets and window boxes.
Annual phlox (*Phlox drummondii*)	Full sun	Zones 6–10	Flowers of various colors, some with a contrasting eye, bloom from midsummer.	If plant stops flowering, cut back by half and water thoroughly.
Rose moss (*Portulaca grandiflora*)	Full sun	Zones 6–10	White, pink, red, orange, yellow, and magenta flowers bloom in summer and fall.	Ideal for hot, dry spots.
Black-eyed Susan (*Rudbeckia hirta*)	Full sun to light shade	Zones 3–10	Golden-yellow flowers bloom from summer into fall.	Flowers are excellent in fresh arrangements.
Mealy-cup sage (*Salvia farinacea*)	Full sun	Zones 6–9	Purple-blue flowers bloom from midsummer until frost.	Too much shade will lead to spindly growth and poor flowers.
Scarlet sage (*Salvia splendens*)	Full sun	Zones 6–10	Mostly red flowers bloom from early summer until frost.	Tall types bloom longer than dwarf cultivars.
Creeping zinnia (*Sanvitalia procumbens*)	Full sun	Zones 5–10	Yellow or orange flowers bloom from midsummer until frost.	Ideal for hanging baskets.
Coleus (*Solenostemon scutellarioides*)	High, indirect light to moderate shade	Zones 8–10	Pale blue flowers appear from late spring to early summer.	Dwarf types are ideal for window box culture.
Marigolds (*Tagetes* spp.)	Full sun to a half-day of sun	Zones 5–10	Yellow, orange, gold, cream, brown, or maroon blooms appear in summer.	Pinching off spent flowers prolongs bloom season.
Feverfew (*Tanacetum parthenium*)	Full sun to partial shade	Zones 4–9	White or yellow flowers bloom in early to midsummer.	Removing spent flower stalks will promote new leafy growth.
Mexican sunflower (*Tithonia rotundifolia*)	Full sun	Zones 5–10	Glowing orange flowers bloom in early summer.	Plant in a large (2-foot/60-cm wide container).
Wishbone flower (*Torenia fournieri*)	Partial shade	Zones 6–9	Purplish-blue flowers with a yellow throat bloom from summer to fall.	Bring pots indoors to enjoy the blooms during winter.

Plant	Light Needs	Hardiness	Season of interest	Comments
Nasturtium (*Tropaeolum majus*)	Full sun	Zones 5–9	Flowers in a range of colors appear from early summer through fall.	Tends to grow poorly in hot-summer areas.
Large periwinkle (*Vinca major*)	Light shade	Zones 5–9	Brilliant violet flowers bloom in spring.	Ideal for hanging baskets and window boxes.
Pansy (*Viola* x *wittrockiana*)	Partial shade	Zones 5–9	Pink, red, orange, yellow, blue, purple, and near-black flowers bloom in spring and fall.	Plants do not like hot weather.
Zinnia (*Zinnia* spp.)	Full sun	Zones 5–10	Flowers of nearly every color, except true blue, bloom from midsummer to frost.	Fertilize monthly and pinch off spent blooms.

BULBS

Plant	Light Needs	Hardiness	Season of interest	Comments
Star of Persia (*Allium christophii*)	Full sun	Zones 4–8	Metallic, lilac-pink flowers bloom in summer.	Striking in a container with tall ornamental grasses and sedums.
Grecian windflower (*Anemone blanda*)	Full sun to partial shade	Zones 5–8	Blue, pink, or white flowers bloom in mid- to late spring.	Ideal for window boxes.
Italian arum (*Arum italicum*)	Partial shade	Zones 6–10	Greenish-yellow flowers bloom in mid- to late spring.	Columns of reddish-orange berries appear in fall.
Showy autumn crocus (*Colchicum speciosum*)	Full sun to partial shade	Zones 4–9	Pink flowers bloom in late summer to early fall.	Corms may bloom before planting if planting is delayed.
Crocosmia (*Crocosmia* x *crocosmiiflora*)	Full sun	Zones 6–9	Red or orange flowers bloom in summer and early fall.	Foliage resembles that of gladiolus.
Hardy cyclamen (*Cyclamen hederifolium*)	Partial shade	Zones 5–9	Pink or white flowers bloom in early fall.	Grows well in containers placed under trees and shrubs.
Dahlias (*Dahlia* hybrids)	Partial to full sun	Zones 9–10	Red, orange, pink, purple, white, and yellow flowers bloom from midsummer through fall.	The dwarf cultivars are best for container gardening.
Crown imperial (*Fritillaria imperalis*)	Full sun	Zones 5–9	Yellow, orange, or red blooms appear in mid- to late spring.	Plant has a musky (skunk-like) odor.
Checkered lily (*Fritillaria meleagris*)	Partial shade	Zones 3–8	Flowers from white to deep purple bloom in spring.	Combine with daffodils for a pretty feature.
Common snowdrop (*Galanthus nivalis*)	Full sun to partial shade	Zones 3–9	White flowers bloom in late winter and early spring.	Established bulbs are trouble-free.
Spanish bluebells (*Hyacinthoides hispanica*)	Full sun to partial shade	Zones 4–8	White, pink, and purple-blue flowers bloom in spring.	One of the easiest of all spring bulbs to grow in containers.
Hyacinth (*Hyacinthus orientalis*)	Full sun	Zones 4–8	White, pink, red, orange, yellow, blue, and purple flowers bloom in spring.	Suitable for winter forcing indoors.
Reticulated iris (*Iris reticulata*)	Full sun	Zones 5–9	Blue, purple, or white flowers bloom in early spring.	Suitable for winter forcing indoors.

Plant	Light Needs	Hardiness	Season of interest	Comments
Siberian iris (*Iris sibirica*)	Full sun to partial shade	Zones 3–9	Summer flowers range from pure white to purple.	Head- and cold-tolerant.
Summer snowflake (*Leucojum aestivum*)	Full sun to partial shade	Zones 4–9	White flowers bloom in mid- to late spring.	Interplant with summer- and fall-blooming annuals.
Lilies (*Lilium* hybrids)	Full sun to partial shade	Zones 4–8	Lilies bloom in early summer in a huge variety of colors.	Dwarf hybrids are best for smaller containers.
Grape hyacinth (*Muscari armeniacum*)	Full sun to light shade	Zones 3–10	Purple-blue, white-rimmed flowers bloom in early spring.	Allow foliage to turn yellow before storing the pot, dry, over summer.
Daffodils (*Narcissus* hybrids)	Full sun to partial shade	Zones 4–8	The mostly yellow or white flowers bloom in spring.	For the best display, grow daffodils in a pot for a single season only.
Siberian squill (*Scilla sibirica*)	Full sun to partial shade	Zones 3–8	Deep blue flowers bloom in spring.	Established bulbs are trouble-free.
Tulips (*Tulipa* hybrids)	Full sun to partial shade	Zones 3–8	Flowers in orange, pink, purple, red, white, green, and yellow bloom in spring.	For a great display every year, plant new bulbs each fall.
Kaufmanniana tulip (*Tulipa kaufmanniana*)	Full sun to light shade	Zones 4–8	Pink, yellow, red, and white flowers bloom in early spring.	Can withstand considerable drought and shade.

🌸 GROUNDCOVERS

Plant	Light Needs	Hardiness	Season of interest	Comments
Wall rock cress (*Arabis caucasica*)	Full sun	Zones 3–7	White flowers bloom in spring.	Plant smothered in clusters of fragrant flowers.
Mountain sandwort (*Arenaria montana*)	Full sun	Zones 4–8	White flowers with a yellow eye bloom in spring and early summer.	Ideal for trough culture.
Snow-in-summer (*Cerastium tomentosum*)	Full sun	Zones 2–7	White flowers bloom in spring and early summer.	Looks good in a hanging basket.
Hardy iceplant (*Delosperma cooperi*)	Full sun	Zones 7–9	Rosy purple flowers bloom from summer until frost.	Looks good cascading from hanging baskets and urns.
Sun rose (*Helianthemum nummularium*)	Full sun	Zones 6–8	Yellow, pink, or white flowers bloom in late spring and early summer.	Plant blooms for many weeks, although each flower lasts for only one day.
Yellow archangel (*Lamium galeobdolon*)	Partial to full shade	Zones 4–9	Yellow flowers bloom in late spring.	Ideal for hanging baskets.
Spotted lamium (*Lamium maculatum*)	Partial to full shade	Zones 3–8	Lavender-pink flowers bloom throughout summer.	Perfect for low-maintenance containers and hanging baskets.
Creeping Jenny (*Lysimachia nummularia*)	Full sun to full shade	Zones 3–8	Yellow flowers bloom throughout summer.	Grow in window boxes or hanging baskets.
Mazus (*Mazus reptans*)	Full sun to partial shade	Zones 5–8	Light blue-violet flowers bloom in spring and summer.	Ideal for a shallow container or trough.
Blue-eyed Mary (*Omphalodes verna*)	Partial shade	Zones 5–8	Lavender-blue flowers bloom in spring.	Mulch in hot climates to prolong bloom period.

Plant	Light Needs	Hardiness	Season of interest	Comments
Creeping phlox (*Phlox stolonifera*)	Partial to full shade	Zones 2–8	Lavender, pink, blue, or white flowers bloom in late spring.	Purple cultivars look good combined with yellow primroses.
Bethlehem sage (*Pulmonaria saccharata*)	Partial to full shade	Zones 3–8	Pink to medium blue flowers bloom in spring.	Foliage remains attractive all season unless in a dry mix.
Rock soapwort (*Saponaria ocymoides*)	Full sun	Zones 4–10	Bright pink flowers bloom in early to midsummer.	May be grown in a hanging basket.
Two-row stonecrop (*Sedum spurium*)	Light to partial shade	Zones 3–8	Flat, pink clusters of flowers appear in midsummer.	A tough, durable spreader for dry containers or hanging baskets.
Hens-and-chickens (*Sempervirum tectorum*)	Full sun	Zones 5–9	Small, purple-red, aster-like flowers bloom in summer.	Low-maintenance container plant.
Mother-of-thyme (*Thymus serpyllum*)	Full sun	Zones 4–7	Rose-purple flowers bloom in summer.	Combine in shallow containers with succulents.
Rock speedwell (*Veronica prostrata*)	Full sun	Zones 4–8	Deep blue flowers bloom in late spring.	Perfect for containers in sunny courtyards.
Barren strawberry (*Waldsteinia fragarioides*)	Partial shade	Zones 5–8	Yellow flowers bloom in late spring.	Grow in hanging baskets.

ORNAMENTAL GRASSES

Plant	Light Needs	Hardiness	Season of interest	Comments
Bushy bluestem (*Andropogon glomeratus*)	Full sun to light shade	Zones 5–10	Fluffy, white flowers in late summer; seed heads and leaves turn purple in late fall.	Plant in a large (2-foot/60-cm wide) container.
Side oats grammagrass (*Bouteloua curtipendula*)	Full sun	Zones 4–9	Purple or reddish flowers bloom in early summer.	Plant is drought-tolerant.
'Bowles Golden' sedge (*Carex elata* 'Bowles Golden')	Half-day sun or light, all-day shade	Zones 5–9	Bright golden evergreen leaves attractive year-round.	Pots may be placed in shallow water.
Northern sea oats (*Chasmanthium latifolium*)	Full sun	Zones 5–9	Green flower spikes bloom in summer.	Plant is salt-tolerant.
Job's tears (*Coix lacryma-jobi*)	Full sun	Zones 9–10	Short, tassel-like, gray flowers bloom in midsummer.	The light green seeds turn white or black when ripe.
Blue fescue (*Festuca glauca*)	Full sun to light shade	Zones 4–9	Silver-blue spiky evergreen foliage attractive year-round.	Thrives near the seaside.
Bottlebrush grass (*Hystrix patula*)	Full sun to light shade	Zones 5–9	Greenish flowers bloom throughout summer.	Grows poorly in dry, sunny locations.
'Red Baron' blood grass (*Imperata cylindrica* 'Red Baron')	Full sun	Zones 6–9	Green, red-tipped foliage becomes more red in spring and blood-red by late summer.	Makes a dramatic mass planting in a large container.
Large blue hairgrass (*Koeleria glauca*)	Full sun	Zones 6–9	Blue-green flower clusters bloom in late spring.	Flowers are beautiful in arrangements.
Snowy woodrush (*Luzula nivea*)	Full sun to light shade	Zones 4–9	Creamy white flowers bloom in spring.	Makes a wonderful companion for spring bulbs.

Plant	Light Needs	Hardiness	Season of interest	Comments
Fountain grass (*Pennisetum alopecuroides*)	Full sun to light shade	Zones 5–9	Creamy white to pink flowers bloom in midsummer.	Wind-tolerant container plant.
White-striped ribbon grass (*Phalaris arundinacea* var. *picta*)	Light shade	Zones 4–9	Pretty white flower spikes bloom in early summer.	Plant one per pot, as plant is very invasive.

TREES AND SHRUBS

Plant	Light Needs	Hardiness	Season of interest	Comments
Glossy abelia (*Abelia* x *grandiflora*)	Full sun	Zones 6–10	Pinkish-purple or white flowers in late spring to early summer.	Flowers are lightly fragrant.
Japanese maple (*Acer palmatum*)	Filtered light or morning sun	Zones 2–9	Leaves turn scarlet or orange, in fall.	Can live in the same pot for years.
Japanese aucuba (*Aucuba japonica*)	Light to full shade	Zones 7–10	If you have both both male and female plants, red berries will form in fall and winter.	Some cultivars have yellow markings on the leaves.
Boxwood (*Buxus sempervirens*)	Full sun to partial shade	Zones 6–10	Tiny, pale green blooms appear in early spring.	Easy to clip into a variety of topiary shapes.
Heather (*Calluna vulgaris*)	Full sun to partial shade	Zones 5–7	Tiny, pinkish flowers bloom from late summer to fall.	Plant different cultivars together in a large container.
Camellia (*Camellia japonica*)	Partial shade	Zones 8–10	White, pink, or red flowers bloom in winter.	Plant in a large (2-foot/60-cm wide) container.
Sasanqua camellia (*Camellia sasanqua*)	Full sun	Zones 7–9	Pink, red, white, or lavender flowers bloom in fall.	Cultivars range from small sizes for hanging baskets to large types for tubs.
Hybrid bluebeard (*Caryopteris* x *clandonensis*)	Full sun	Zones 5–9	Purple-blue flowers bloom in mid- to late summer.	Ideal in a sheltered position near a sunny wall.
False cypress (*Chamaecyparis* spp.)	Full sun	Zones 5–8	Evergreen foliage provides year-round interest.	Underplant with grape hyacinths (*Muscari* spp.) for spring interest.
Smoke tree (*Cotinus coggygria*)	Full sun	Zones 5–9	Pink, purple, or gray plumes from midsummer to fall.	Water frequently until plants are established.
Rose daphne (*Daphne cneorum*)	Full sun	Zones 4–9	Pink flowers bloom in late spring, and sometimes in fall.	Keep container raised on feet to ensure good drainage.
Slender deutzia (*Deutzia gracilis*)	Full sun	Zones 5–9	White flowers bloom in late spring or early summer.	Prefers a moist, semi-shaded site, away from drying winds.
Redvein enkianthus (*Enkianthus campanulatus*)	Full sun to full shade	Zones 4–8	Creamy yellow flowers, lightly tinged with red, bloom in late spring.	Plant in a large (2-foot/60-cm wide) container.
Wintercreeper (*Euonymus fortunei*)	Full sun to full shade	Zones 5–9	On some cultivars, the evergreen foliage is variegated.	Variegated or trailing types are easy-care container plants.
Fuchsia (*Fuchsia* x *hybrida*)	Filtered light	Zone 7	White, red, or pink with violet, purple, or red flowers bloom during summer.	Best planted alone in hanging baskets. Place away from winds.
Common gardenia (*Gardenia augusta*)	Partial shade	Zones 8–10	White flowers bloom in early to midsummer.	The creamy-white flowers are extremely fragrant.

Plant	Light Needs	Hardiness	Season of interest	Comments
Veronica (*Hebe speciosa*)	Full sun to light shade	Zones 7–10	Deep magenta flower spikes bloom during summer.	Plant in a large (2-foot/60-cm wide) container.
Rose-of-Sharon (*Hibiscus syriacus*)	Full sun	Zones 5–9	Flowers in white, pink, red, lavender, or purple bloom from late summer.	Plant in a large (2-foot/60-cm wide) container.
Big-leaved hydrangea (*Hydrangea macrophylla*)	Partial shade	Zones 6–9	Blue flowers in acid container mix, or pink flowers in alkaline mix, bloom in midsummer.	Plant in a large (2-foot/60-cm wide) container.
Common juniper (*Juniperus communis*)	Full sun	Zones 2–9	Inconspicuous green or yellow flowers bloom in spring.	Best grown in its own container.
Mountain laurel (*Kalmia latifolia*)	Full sun	Zones 4–7	White, pink, or rose flowers from late spring to early summer.	One of the most valued evergreen shrubs for a cold-climate garden.
Lantana (*Lantana camara*)	Full sun	Zones 8–10	Yellow, orange, red, or bi-colored flowers bloom in summer.	Looks good in hanging baskets.
Magnolia (*Magnolia* spp.)	Partial shade	Zones 7–10	White, pink, or purple flowers bloom from late spring to midsummer.	For container culture, choose the small, more compact cultivars.
Heavenly bamboo (*Nandina domestica*)	Full sun to partial shade	Zones 6–10	White flowers bloom in midsummer.	Easy-care container plant.
Ivy geranium (*Pelargonium peltatum*)	Full sun to light shade	Zones 9–10	Single or double white, pink, red, or lavender flowers bloom all summer.	An excellent choice for hanging baskets and window boxes.
Zonal geranium (*Pelargonium* Zonal Hybrids)	Full sun to light shade	Zones 5–10	White, pink, red, salmon, or bi-colored flowers bloom from late spring until frost.	A popular choice for window boxes.
Shrubby cinquefoil (*Potentilla fruticosa*)	Full sun to very light shade	Zones 2–8	Yellow flowers bloom in early summer to early fall.	Plant in a large (2-foot/60-cm wide) container.
Rhododendrons and azaleas (*Rhododendron* spp.)	Filtered shade	Zones 4–9	White, yellow, pink, orange, or red flowers appear over the colder months.	Don't disturb the roots by planting annual companions.
Rose (*Rosa* Large-flowered)	Full sun	Zones 4–10	White, pink, orange, yellow, red, lavender, or multi-colored flowers bloom from late spring to late summer.	Plant in a large (2-foot/60-cm wide) container.
Miniature roses *Rosa* Miniature hybrids	Full sun	Zones 4–9	Blooms of all colors except blue and green; some flower year-round.	More than 200 types of miniature rose are now available.
Rugosa rose (*Rosa rugosa*)	Full sun	Zones 2–9	Pink, red, or white flowers bloom in summer.	Tolerant of seaside conditions.
Lavender cotton (*Santolina chamaecyparissus*)	Full sun	Zones 5–9	Bright gold flowers bloom in profusion in midsummer.	Does not like humidity.

Plant	Light Needs	Hardiness	Season of interest	Comments
Lace shrub (*Stephanandra incisa*)	Full sun	Zones 5–9	Greenish-white flowers bloom in spring.	Leaves turn purple or red in fall.
Yucca (*Yucca filamentosa*)	Full sun	Zones 5–9	White flowers bloom in late spring and early summer.	Spectacular spires of white flowers.
VINES				
Jackman clematis (*Clematis x jackmanii*)	Full sun	Zones 5–9	Violet-purple flowers bloom from mid- to late summer and fall.	Add a trellis to the container so the plant can climb.
Bleeding glorybower (*Clerodendrum thomsoniae*)	Partial shade	Zones 9–10	Red and white flowers bloom from summer to fall.	Makes an excellent hanging basket plant.
Cup-and-saucer vine (*Cobaea scandens*)	Full sun	Zones 5–10	From late summer until frost, flowers bloom yellow-green before turning purple or white.	Plant in a large (2-foot/60-cm wide) container.
English ivy (*Hedera helix*)	Full sun to full shade	Zones 5–10	Insignificant cream flowers in fall, followed by black berries.	Grow in a hanging basket.
Crimson starglory (*Ipomoea lobata*)	Full sun to light shade	Zones 8–10	Reddish buds fade to yellow and orange through summer.	Easy-care plant for patio or hanging basket.
Common morning glory (*Ipomoea purpurea*)	Full sun	Zone 10	Purple, white, pink, red, blue, or variegated flowers bloom from summer to early fall.	Provide support such as a trellis against a wall, or a tepee of bamboo stakes.
Morning glory (*Ipomoea tricolor*)	Full sun	Zones 4–10	Purple flowers bloom in summer.	Can be very rampant in warm areas.
Chilean jasmine (*Mandevilla laxa*)	Full sun to light shade	Zones 9–10	White flowers bloom in late spring to summer.	Makes an excellent hanging basket plant.
Stephanotis (*Stephanotis floribunda*)	Full sun to light shade	Zone 10	White flowers bloom from midspring to fall.	Ensure adequate air circulation.
Black-eyed Susan vine (*Thunbergia alata*)	Full sun to partial shade	Zone 10	White, yellow, or orange flowers, bloom in midsummer.	Looks lovely cascading from a hanging basket.
Star jasmine (*Trachelospermum jasminoides*)	Full sun to partial shade	Zones 8–10	White flowers bloom in late spring to early summer.	Perfume can be overpowering in a semi-enclosed area.
EDIBLE PLANTS				
Onion (*Allium cepa*)	Full sun	Zones 3–10	Harvest bulbs after tops turn brown.	Pick the young greens for scallions.
Swiss chard (*Beta vulgaris* subsp. *cicla*)	Full sun to light shade	Zones 5–10	Can provide a full season of fresh greens.	Available with rich yellow or red stalks.
Kale (*Brassica oleracea*, Acephala Group)	Full sun	All Zones	Provides tasty greens late into the season.	Mature plants will tolerate severe frost.
Bell pepper (*Capsicum annuum*)	Full sun	Zones 4–10	Produces fruit from summer until frost.	The fully ripe bell pepper's color will depend on the cultivar.

Plant	Light Needs	Hardiness	Season of interest	Comments
Calamondin (x *Citrofortunella microcarpa*)	Full sun	Zones 9–10	Harvest when the fruits are fully colored.	Plant in a large (2-foot/60-cm wide) container.
Winter squash (*Cucurbita* spp.)	Full sun	Zones 4–10	Harvest in winter, when shell cannot be dented by fingernail.	Provide the plant with a trellis for support.
Carrot (*Daucus carota* var. *sativus*)	Full sun	All Zones	Harvest at 45–70 days. Pull a few to see if they are ready.	Try the short-rooted kinds in standard-sized pots.
Arugula (*Eruca sativa*)	Full sun, half-day of sun to partial shade.	Zones 7–10	In mild climates, grow as a winter vegetable.	The flowers can be added to salads.
Kumquat (*Fortunella* spp.)	Full sun	Zones 9–10	Edible orange fruits appear from summer to fall.	The skin is edible and sweet, but the juicy flesh is tart.
Strawberries (*Fragaria* spp.)	Full sun to partial shade	Zones 3–9	Juicy, red berries are produced during summer.	Strawberries grow best when planted alone.
Lettuce (*Lactuca sativa*)	Full sun	All Zones	In warm climates, fall sowing can give you an early spring harvest.	Red or frilly-leaved types can double as ornamentals.
Tomato (*Lycopersicon esculentum*)	Full sun	All Zones	Pick fruit when evenly colored but still firm.	Dwarf tomatoes can produce tasty fruit even in small containers.
Watercress (*Nasturtium officinale*)	Full sun to partial shade	Zones 3–10	Plant is at its best in fall and early spring.	Flavor deteriorates while plant is flowering.
Beans (*Phaseolus* spp.)	Full sun	Zones 3–10	Pods appear about 60 days after sowing.	Pick beans any size, but before seeds swell noticeably.
Radish (*Raphanus sativus*)	Full sun	All Zones	Radishes can be harvested in winter, spring, and fall.	Young radish leaves can be used in salads.
Garden sorrel (*Rumex acetosa*)	Full sun	Zones 3–9	Plant produces abundantly during spring and fall.	Plant is less productive during hot weather.
Eggplant (*Solanum melongena*)	Full sun	Zones 5–10	Harvest fruit before it over-matures and becomes bitter.	Plant produces pretty, lavender flowers.
Potato (*Solanum tuberosum*)	Full sun	Zones 3–10	Harvest when foliage turns yellow and begins to die back.	Potatoes are available with gold, purple, red, or brown flesh.
Spinach (*Spinacia oleracea*)	Full sun	All Zones	Pick leaves or cut entire plant when it forms a full rosette, but before it sends up a flower spike.	Spinach freezes well for use as a cooked vegetable.
Blueberries (*Vaccinium* spp.)	Full sun	Zones 3–9	Harvest berries from late spring when they first become sweet.	Most blueberries produce better berries if cross-pollinated.
Corn salad (*Valerianella locusta*)	Full sun to partial shade	Zones 2–9	Plant in fall to harvest in spring for salads.	Avoid plantings that will mature in hot weather.

HERBS

Plant	Light Needs	Hardiness	Season of interest	Comments
Anise hyssop (*Agastache foeniculum*)	Full sun	Zones 6–10	Spikes of lavender flowers bloom from midsummer to fall.	Leaves have a licorice scent and flavor.
Garlic (*Allium sativum*)	Full sun	Zones 6–10	White to pinkish flowers bloom in early summer.	Garlic dies back in winter and reshoots in warmer months.

Plant	Light Needs	Hardiness	Season of interest	Comments
Chives (*Allium schoenoprasum*)	Full sun to light shade	Zones 3–10	Pink, pompon-like flowers bloom in spring.	The leaves and flowers have a mild onion flavor.
Aloe (*Aloe vera*)	Full sun to light shade	Zones 9–10	Yellow flowers appear during summer.	Leaves contain a medicinal and cosmetic gel. Grow as an ornamental pot plant on a sunny windowsill.
Lemon verbena (*Aloysia triphylla*)	Full sun	Zones 9–10	White to pale mauve flowers appear in late summer and early fall.	Strongly lemon-scented leaves. Dried leaves will retain their scent for a number of years.
Dill (*Anethum graveolens*)	Full sun	Zones 6–10	Flattened umbels of yellow flowers bloom in summer.	Sow at 2- or 3-week intervals for continuous harvest through to fall.
Chervil (*Anthriscus cerefolium*)	Full sun or shade	Zones 6–10	White flowers bloom in summer.	Loses flavor quickly when heated, so add to recipes at the end.
Common wormwood (*Artemisia absinthium*)	Full sun	Zones 3–9	Yellow flowers bloom in late summer and fall.	Dried leaves can be used in potpourri.
French tarragon (*Artemisia dracunculus* var. *sativa*)	Full sun to partial shade	Zones 6–9	Yellowish-green flowers bloom in late summer.	Has a heavy licorice flavor that holds well in cooking.
Borage (*Borago officinalis*)	Full sun to partial shade	Zones 6–10	Pink, purple, lavender, or blue flowers bloom from midsummer.	Leaves have a cucumber flavor.
Mustard (*Brassica* spp.)	Full sun	Zones 6–10	Yellow flowers bloom in early summer.	Seedings in the seed-leaf stage can be added to salads.
Caraway (*Carum carvi*)	Full sun	Zones 6–10	White or pink flowers bloom in summer of the second year.	The aromatic seeds are used for flavoring foods, as well as for their carminative effect.
Roman chamomile (*Chamaemelum nobile*)	Full sun	Zones 3–8	White flowers bloom in mid- to late summer.	The small, white daisies can be used to make a soothing tea.
Coriander (*Coriandum sativum*)	Full sun	Zones 6–10	White flowers bloom in early to late summer.	The seeds and leaves are used in cooking. Stems and roots used in Thai cooking.
Purple coneflower (*Echinacea purpurea*)	Full sun	Zones 3–8	Reddish-purple to rose-pink flowers bloom in summer.	The roots are used in medicine that helps to increase the body's resistance to infection.
Fennel (*Foeniculum vulgare*)	Full sun	Zones 6–9	Yellow flowers bloom from July to September.	Licorice-scented plant.
Sweet woodruff (*Galium odoratum*)	Partial to full shade	Zones 3–8	White flowers bloom in late spring.	The leaves may be toxic when taken internally.
St. John's wort (*Hypericum calycinum*)	Full sun to partial shade	Zones 6–8	Yellow flowers with showy stamens bloom in summer.	Flowers more profusely if plant is in sunny spot.
Hyssop (*Hyssopus officinalis*)	Full sun	Zones 6–9	Blue or violet-blue flowers bloom from June to August.	Leaves add a minty aroma to salads and soups.
Bay (*Laurus nobilis*)	Full sun to filtered shade	Zones 7–9	Yellow flowers bloom in late spring.	North of Zone 8, bring container indoors for winter.

Plant	Light Needs	Hardiness	Season of interest	Comments
English lavender (*Lavandula angustifolia*)	Full sun	Zones 6–9	Lavender-blue flowers bloom from June to July.	Extremely drought-tolerant. Good for topiary.
Lovage (*Levisticum officinale*)	Full sun to partial shade	Zones 6–9	Greenish-yellow flowers bloom from June to July.	Roots and shoots used as a vegetable, and the seeds for flavoring foods.
Lemon balm (*Melissa officinalis*)	Full sun to partial shade	Zones 4–9	White flowers bloom in late summer and fall.	There is season-long interest from the foliage.
Mint (*Mentha* spp.)	Full sun to partial shade	Zones 5–9	Tiny, pink or purple flowers bloom from July to August.	Picking the leaves or brushing by them will release their fragrance.
Bee balm (*Monarda didyma*)	Full sun to partial shade	Zones 4–8	Red, tubular flowers bloom in summer.	The flowers are favored by hummingbirds.
Sweet cicely (*Myrrhis odorata*)	Partial shade	Zones 5–9	White flowers bloom from May to June.	Sweet cicely has a scent like lovage and a sweet licorice taste.
Catmint (*Nepeta cataria*)	Full sun to partial shade	Zones 4–9	White, purple-dotted flowers bloom from summer to fall.	The bruised foliage releases a scent that cats love.
Basil (*Ocimum basilicum*)	Full sun	Zones 6–10	White flowers bloom continuously from midsummer.	Plant near tomatoes and peppers to enhance their growth.
Sweet marjoram (*Origanum majorana*)	Full sun	Zones 6–9	White or pink flowers bloom from August to September.	The dried leaves retain their flavor well and may aid digestion.
Greek oregano (*Origanum vulgare* subsp. *hirtum*)	Full sun	Zones 5–10	Clusters of small, pink or white flowers appear from August to September.	Lower growing and with more flavor than common oregano.
Scented geranium (*Pelargonium* spp.)	Full sun	Zones 9–10	Rose, rosy-white, or white flowers bloom in clusters from spring to summer.	Add the fragrant leaves to potpourri.
Parsley (*Petroselinum crispum*)	Full sun to partial shade	Zones 5–9	Greenish yellow umbels flower in early spring of the second year.	Cut leaf stalks at the base for fresh foliage all summer.
Anise (*Pimpinella anisum*)	Full sun	Zones 6–10	White flowers bloom in summer.	Licorice-scented leaves and seeds. Anise is the base of some alcoholic drinks.
Rosemary (*Rosmarinus officinalis*)	Full sun	Zones 7–10	Blue flowers appear in spring and sometimes in fall.	Trailing types are great around the edge of large containers. In Zone 7 and north, bring the pot inside in the fall.
Sage (*Salvia officinalis*)	Full sun	Zones 4–8	Purple-lavender flowers appear in early summer.	Aromatic foliage. Place in a spot where you can brush by and release fragrance.
Comfrey (*Symphytum officinale*)	Full sun to partial shade	Zones 6–9	Purple-pink, white, or cream flowers bloom in early to late summer.	Shaded plants will be smaller, with few blossoms.
Tansy (*Tanacetum vulgare*)	Full sun to partial shade	Zones 6–9	Yellow flowers bloom from July to September.	Aromatic foliage. Place in a spot where you can brush by and release fragrance.
Thyme (*Thymus vulgaris*)	Full sun	Zones 5–9	Lavender blooms appear from May to October.	Great for carpeting the soil in containers.

A Guide to Popular Houseplants

Growing indoor plants is a fun hobby, but you'll get the most satisfaction if you choose plants that are best adapted to the growing conditions in your home. To help you make an informed buying decision, we've included this handy guide to some of the most popular foliage and flowering houseplants. Individual entries are arranged alphabetically by botanical name, with the common name displayed prominently. If you don't know the botanical name, look up the common name in the index, and you'll be directed to the right place. Each entry provides a color photograph, a description of the plant, as well as details on the plant's light, temperature, water, and humidity needs. Growing guidelines are also included along with propagation pointers. With this kind of practical information at your fingertips, you'll be able to provide the right care to keep your indoor plants happy and healthy.

Abutilon hybrids
MALVACEAE

FLOWERING MAPLES

Flowering maples are old-fashioned favorites for indoors. These hibiscus relatives bloom year-round in a bright spot; they enjoy spending summer outdoors.

Other common names Chinese lantern, parlor maples.

Description These South American shrubs have maple-like, green leaves and papery, 1-inch (2.5-cm) blooms in white, yellow, orange, or red. These fast-growing bushy or trailing plants grow up to 6 feet (1.8 m) tall.

Light needs Bright sun 4–6 hours a day.

Best temperatures Average room temperature during the day; intermediate to cool nights (50°–60°F [10°–16°C]). A 10°F (6°C) difference between day and night temperatures is ideal.

Water and humidity needs Keep moist while in active growth. Allow soil to dry out slightly between waterings in winter.

Growing guidelines Grow in pots or hanging baskets in all-purpose potting soil. Repot in late winter, if needed. Stake for upright growth. Feed with fish emulsion twice a month. Prune off one-third of the plant in winter.

Common problems Spider mites can cause yellowish stippling or browning on the leaves; increase the humidity and treat affected plants with superior oil.

Propagation Take tip cuttings at any time or grow plants from seed.

Comments For best flowering, pinch back new growth once six leaves appear.

Acalypha hispida
EUPHORBIACEAE

CHENILLE PLANT

Fluffy, red or purplish cattails highlight these heirloom plants year-round. The puffed plumes are reminiscent of chenille piling on bedspreads.

Other common names Red hot cattails.

Description In ideal conditions, chenille plants are rampant growers. They grow up to 15 feet (4.5 m) tall, although 6 feet (1.8 m) is more likely in containers. Their leaves can reach 9 inches (22.5 cm) long. The 12–18-inch (30–45-cm), dense, pendent flower clusters are typically red or purplish.

Light needs Full to medium light in winter; medium light (with some shade against direct sun) in summer.

Best temperatures Warm, not below 60°F (16°C).

Water and humidity needs Keep moist. Provide high humidity and mist daily.

Growing guidelines A self-watering pot with all-purpose potting soil works well for chenille plants. Fertilize monthly with a 1-2-1 mix. Prune heavily in spring to promote bushy new growth.

Common problems If spider mites cause yellow stippling on leaves, spray plant with superior oil. Dry air and lack of water can cause plants to drop their leaves; increase humidity around the plant and water more often to keep the soil evenly moist.

Propagation Take tip cuttings in early spring or late summer. If you have trouble getting tip cuttings to root, try taking a piece with a bit of older growth at the base.

Anthurium spp.
ARACEAE

FLAMINGO FLOWER

The lacquered-looking, puckered blooms of flamingo flower often fool people into thinking they must be artificial. Each flower can last for 2–3 months.

Description This plant grows to 20 inches (50 cm) tall, with long, leathery, green leaves. Each flower has a curved, tail-like spadix and a heart-shaped spathe, ranging from deep red to pink, salmon, white, and speckled. Miniature types are available.

Light needs Medium indirect light.

Best temperatures Warm year-round. Ideal conditions are 85°F (29°C) days and 65°F (18°C) nights. To encourage plants to bloom, reduce nighttime temperature to 60°F (16°C) for 6 weeks.

Water and humidity needs Provide constant moisture and high humidity while plants are actively growing. Let the soil dry out a bit between waterings in winter, but never allow it to get bone dry.

Growing guidelines Grow flamingo flower in a mix of equal parts potting soil and sphagnum moss. Repot plants in spring if needed. Fertilize with an all-purpose, organic fertilizer twice a month from early spring to early fall; do not fertilize in winter.

Common problems Flamingo flower does not like cold temperatures or hard water. Keep the temperature at least 60°F (16°C).

Propagation Divide in spring or summer, remove offshoots at the base, or grow new plants from seed.

Begonia spp.
BEGONIACEAE

FLOWERING BEGONIAS

The thousands of begonia hybrids and species provide a wealth of indoor houseplant choices. Those grown for flowers often have beautiful foliage as well.

Description Begonias have asymmetrical leaves with a waxy texture. The leaves grow alternately along the stems. Flowers are borne on short stems arising from or near the leaf axils.

Angelwing begonias belong to the cane-stemmed group and have pairs of large, pointed leaves that resemble extended wings and come in an amazing variety of shapes and colors, often beautifully marked. They grow to 6 feet (1.8 m) tall, with fibrous roots and straight, upright stems bearing regularly spaced, swollen nodes and long-lasting flowers in large pendent clusters in spring, summer, and fall. Tall plants may need staking.

Reiger begonias offer huge flowers and medium to dark green leaves on 12–18-inch (30–45-cm) stems. The natural flowering period is winter, but there are varieties that flower almost year-round.

Wax begonias are compact, 6–12-inch (15–30-cm) plants with thick, waxy leaves. The white, pink, or red single or double flowers form in small clusters. This plant is excellent for decorating windowsills. Many wax begonias have bronze-colored foliage.

Begonia Lorraine hybrids are winter flowering, with clusters of small white or pink flowers. *Begonia* x *cheimantha* 'Gloire de Lorraine' is a popular variety, which grows up to 12 inches (30 cm).

Begonia sutherlandii is a trailing plant with small, lance-shaped leaves and many single, orange flowers that bloom in loose clusters during summer.

The Begonia Tuberhybrida group have large single or double flowers in a wide range of colors produced from early summer to early fall. They form bushy plants with pointed, glossy bright to dark green leaves. Pendula hybrids carry their flowers on long, thin, cascading stems and are often grown in hanging baskets.

Light needs Protect from hot sun.
Best temperatures Warm room temperature; prefers at least 60°F (16°C).
Water and humidity needs Let dry slightly between waterings. Provide extra humidity.
Growing guidelines Grow in humus-rich, soil-less mix. Repot in spring as needed. Fertilize twice a month from spring through fall. Pinch off stem tips every month to encourage branching. To reflower, Reiger begonias need a 3-month, cool, dry rest period after bloom.
Common problems Lower leaves drop if plants get too little or too much water; over-watering can also lead to rot and mildew.
Propagation Begonias root easily from tip cuttings. You can also grow them from seed.

Bougainvillea spp.
NYCTAGINACEAE

BOUGAINVILLEA

The beautiful papery blooms of this South American vine can be orange, red, yellow, pink, or white. The flowers appear on the new growth.

Other common names Paper flower.
Description Bougainvilleas are woody vines, usually with large thorns. The foliage can be solid green or mottled with white or yellow. The true flowers are small white blooms surrounded by colorful single or double bracts; appearing in fall and winter.
Light needs High.
Best temperatures Warm, at least 60°F (16°C); can adapt to 50°F (10°C) nights.
Water and humidity needs While plants are actively growing, water thoroughly, then let soil surface dry out before watering again. Reduce watering after bloom until new growth starts again in spring.
Growing guidelines Use small pots and all-purpose potting mix enriched with sphagnum moss. Repot in spring as needed. Feed plants twice a month while they are actively growing. Pinch off shoot tips regularly from spring through midsummer to encourage a compact, well-branched, 2–3-foot (60–90-cm) plant. Prune heavily after bloom. Bougainvilleas enjoy spending the summer outdoors in full sun.
Common problems If not flowering, increase light and cut back on water.
Propagation Take stem or root cuttings in late spring and early summer.

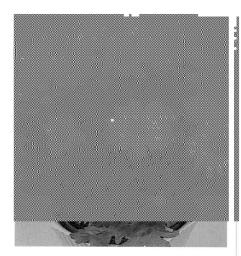

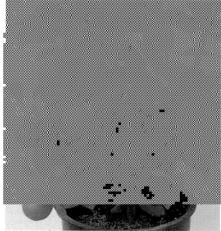

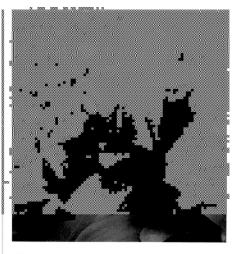

Chrysanthemum spp.
COMPOSITAE

CHRYSANTHEMUMS

Potted chrysanthemums provide a magnificent, if brief, show. Plant spring-blooming kinds outdoors for another set of flowers before frost.

Other common names Florist's chrysanthemum.

Description These 15-inch (37.5-cm) tall, bushy plants have divided, aromatic, green leaves. They come in a wide array of flower colors and shapes—often daisy-like, button, or pompon—and may bloom for 2–3 weeks. Unlike garden mums, many of the chrysanthemums for indoor bloom will not survive the winter outdoors in cold climates.

Light needs Medium, indirect light.

Best temperatures Flowers last longest in cool 55°F (13°C) temperatures.

Water and humidity needs Water frequently to keep the soil evenly moist.

Growing guidelines Grow in well-drained, all-purpose mix. Discard fall-flowering potted mums after bloom. For a late-season display from spring bloomers, cut back by one-half to two-thirds after bloom and plant them in the ground. Pinch off shoot tips every 2 weeks until mid-July, then stop pinching to allow flower buds to form. Plants may not live through the winter.

Common problems Aphids may feed on leaves, shoots, and buds, causing distorted growth. Knock them off with a strong spray of water, or spray with insecticidal soap, superior oil, or neem.

Propagation Take tip cuttings in spring.

Citrus spp.
RUTACEAE

CITRUS

In return for giving citrus plants lots of light and space, you'll be rewarded with the thrill of picking your own oranges, lemons, limes, and grapefruits.

Description Citrus are tree-like or shrubby branched plants that grow to 8 feet (2.4 m) indoors. They have glossy leaves, perfumed, white blooms, and brightly colored fruits. Easy-to-grow calamondin or panama orange (*Citrofortunella mitis*) produces 2–4-foot (60–120-cm) plants; its sour fruit is good for culinary uses. Spring-blooming, 8-foot (2.4-m) tall key lime (*C. aurantiifolia*) has tart, greenish yellow fruit.

Light needs A spot against a window with at least 4 hours of full sun is best.

Best temperatures Average room temperature during the day; approximately 50°F (10°C) nights.

Water and humidity needs Let the top 1 inch (2.5 cm) of soil dry out between waterings. Provide extra humidity.

Growing guidelines Pot in large tubs with extra drainage in African violet-type mix (or a mixture of sand, peat moss, and fine bark). Spread coffee grounds on soil to maintain acidity and add nutrients. Put plants outdoors for summer. If stems get leggy, cut back by one-third in midwinter.

Common problems Spider mites can cause yellow stippling on leaves; raise humidity around the plant and spray with superior oil.

Propagation Take citrus cuttings during spring or summer.

Clivia miniata
AMARYLLIDACEAE

CLIVIA

Clusters of trumpet-shaped blooms and glossy leaves make this flowering plant a favorite of many indoor gardeners. Clivias may take several years to flower.

Description The strap-like, leathery, green leaves of clivia emerge from a bulbous base. Mature plants can reach 2 feet (60 cm) tall and 3 feet (90 cm) wide. Clusters of 12–20 winter blooms are usually orange-red with yellow interiors.

Light needs Medium to high indirect light.

Best temperatures Average room temperature in spring and summer; much cooler (to 40°F [4.5°C]) in fall and winter.

Water and humidity needs Keep soil moist in spring and summer; allow it to dry between waterings in fall and winter.

Growing guidelines Start clivias in small clay pots. Use a blend of 3 parts all-purpose potting mix and 1 part sand, with a handful of bonemeal. Clivias grow best when crowded, so leave them in their pot for about 3 years before repotting in late winter. Feed with liquid fertilizer twice a month in spring and summer. Give plants a cool, dry rest period without fertilizer in winter.

Common problems Mealybugs produce white clusters on leaves. Knock them off with a strong spray of water, or spray with insecticidal soap, superior oil, or neem.

Propagation Divide overgrown plants when you repot them, or remove offsets in late winter.

Coffea arabica
RUBIACEAE

COFFEE PLANT

While coffee plant won't supply you with enough beans for your morning brew, it's worth growing for its glossy, green leaves and scented, white flowers.

Description These shrubby plants grow 3–4 feet (90–120 cm) tall and have shiny, green leaves up to 6 inches (15 cm) long. Clusters of many small, white flowers appear in spring to summer, turning to pulpy, red berries by winter.

Light needs High indirect light; provide at least 4 hours of filtered sun a day.

Best temperatures Warm; at least 60°F (16°C) at night.

Water and humidity needs Keep moist and provide high humidity.

Growing guidelines Grow coffee plant in a humus-rich all-purpose mix. Repot in spring as needed. Fertilize with fish emulsion and add coffee grounds to the soil twice a month from spring to fall.

Common problems Set coffee plant where it won't be disturbed; the leaves tend to turn brown when touched. It grows very slowly and must be several years old before it will bloom.

Propagation Take tip cuttings from soft, upright shoots. You can grow coffee plants from seeds removed from the fresh berries.

Comments Coffee plants perform best in humid greenhouses but can adapt to life in the home if you're willing to provide some special care.

Cuphea ignea
LYTHRACEAE

CIGAR PLANT

The summer blooms of this Mexican native look like bright red cigarettes or firecrackers. The plants will bloom generously if you give them plenty of light.

Other common names Firecracker flower.

Description This pretty little shrub grows 12–24 inches (30–60 cm) tall. The leafy green stems are dotted with slender, tubular, red flowers that are tipped with purple and white. Each flower is about 3 inches (7.5 cm) long.

Light needs High light.

Best temperatures Average room temperature; cooler in winter.

Water and humidity needs Allow the soil surface to dry between waterings. Mist regularly.

Growing guidelines Grow cigar plant in all-purpose mix in a pot with plenty of drainage holes. Fertilize twice a month in spring through fall, while the plant is actively growing. Water less and hold back on the fertilizer during the winter to give the plant a rest period. If an older plant looks scraggly, take cuttings to start new plants and throw away the old one.

Common problems Cottony, white masses on leaves and stems are signs of mealybugs. You can knock these pests off with a strong spray of water, or spray the plant with insecticidal soap, superior oil, or neem.

Propagation Take stem or tip cuttings during fall.

Cyclamen persicum
PRIMULACEAE

FLORIST'S CYCLAMEN

The butterfly-like blooms of florist's cyclamen flutter gracefully over beautiful silver-marked leaves. The flowers come in pink, red, lavender, and white.

Description Florist's cyclamen forms 12-inch (30-cm) clumps of deep-green, heart-shaped leaves often with silver and light green marbling on the upper surface. The single-stemmed, waxy flowers emerge from leafy clumps from early winter to early spring. Each flower has five reflexed and erect petals often with a darker color at the throat. Many beautiful forms of florist's cyclamen exist, including those with double, fringed, or ruffled-edged flowers. 'Scentsation' cultivars have fragrant flowers in a wide range of colors.

Miniature cyclamen have normal-sized leaves but smaller flowers. They come in a wide range of colors from deep or light shades of salmon and pink, to lilac, purple, or white and tend to be longer flowering and often more strongly scented than the larger varieties.

Light needs High indirect light while in bloom; medium light after bloom.

Best temperatures During the day, florist's cyclamen prefers 60°–72°F (16°–22°C); at night, keep temperatures at 40°–60°F (4.5°–16°C). High temperatures will shorten the flowering period.

Water and humidity needs Keep soil moist while plants are in bloom. When flowering ends, allow soil to dry between

Cyclamen persicum continued

Euphorbia milii
EUPHORBIACEAE

CROWN OF THORNS

Crown of thorns blooms freely with minimal care in bright light. Give it an out-of-the-way spot so you won't have to deal with the thorny stems!

Euphorbia pulcherrima
EUPHORBIACEAE

POINSETTIA

This Mexican native is the quintessential winter holiday plant. Its showy blooms last for months, with petal-like bracts in red, pink, yellow, or cream.

waterings. Keep away from dry heat. Mist the plants when not in bloom.

Growing guidelines Grow in all-purpose soil-based mix. Repot crowded plants to a larger container only when nights are above 55°F (13°C). Fertilize twice a month from fall to early spring. Plants need a cool, dry rest period in summer to rebloom—put plants outdoors in the shade and turn pots on their side; keep them barely moist until new leaves begin to appear. Remove the first few flowers and their stems, since the buds appear to strengthen the plants.

Common problems Spider mites and cyclamen mites can cause distorted growth. Discard infested plants. A cyclamen receiving too little light will develop yellow leaves and spindly new growth.

Propagation Sow cyclamen seed in September and keep it dark until the seedlings appear. Put seedlings in a cool, bright spot for the winter; repot them in May. Plant with the tops of the tubers just above the soil surface.

Comments The many beautiful varieties of cyclamen grown in pots for indoor decoration, have all been developed from *C. persicum*. Despite its botanical name, it has no Persian origin, but comes from the eastern Mediterranean region, Lebanon, and North Africa.

Description The spiny, woody stems of crown of thorns sport scattered green leaves, mostly on the young growth. The stems may reach 4 feet (1.2 m) tall. The tiny flowers are surrounded by showy red, yellow, pink, or salmon-colored, petal-like bracts. They bloom mostly in summer but can appear at any time.

Light needs Needs high light, with some direct sun.

Best temperatures Average room temperature.

Water and humidity needs Water thoroughly, then let dry before the next watering. In winter, reduce watering somewhat.

Growing guidelines Grow crown of thorns in clay pots; use all-purpose potting mix with some added sand. Fertilize twice a month, except in winter. When the plants get leggy, cut the stems back to a pleasing shape in spring.

Common problems Crown of thorns will sulk if it's in a drafty spot.

Propagation Take tip cuttings and allow them to dry for 24 hours before placing the cut ends in moist sand.

Comments The stems produce an irritating, milky sap when you cut them; apply cold water to stop it from flowing.

Description These shrubby plants grow to 2 feet (60 cm) tall in containers. The sturdy stems carry broad, green leaves up to 7 inches (17.5 cm) long. In winter, the stems are tipped with tiny flowers surrounded by leafy bracts.

Light needs High light.

Best temperatures Cool conditions, with days not over 70°F (21°C) and nights around 55°F (13°C).

Water and humidity needs Allow to dry between waterings.

Growing guidelines Poinsettias prefer well-drained, all-purpose mix. If you buy a blooming plant and plan to discard it when the season's over, it won't need care. If you want to it to bloom again, repot and cut stems back to 6 inches (15 cm). Water as needed and fertilize weekly from Labor Day to Thanksgiving. Give the plant 14 hours of darkness at night for 8 weeks from mid-September, with temperatures of 75°F (24°C) during the day and 60°F (16°C) at night. Once blooming, display the plant as desired. Do not fertilize while flowering.

Common problems Leaves will drop due to low light, drafts, or overwatering.

Propagation Take tip cuttings in late spring and early summer; allow to dry overnight before rooting in moist sand.

Gardenia jasminoides
RUBIACEAE

GARDENIA

For gorgeous fragrance, few houseplants surpass the gardenia. Even when your plant isn't in bloom, you'll still enjoy the glossy foliage and shrubby form.

Other common names Cape jasmine.
Description This woody shrub bears pointed, 4-inch (10-cm), glossy, dark green leaves on stems that can reach 6 feet (1.8 m) tall. Creamy, 3-inch (7.5-cm) wide flowers appear in spring to fall.
Light needs High light, especially in winter, with 4 hours of full sun per day.
Best temperatures Between 65° and 80°F (18° and 26°C) during the day; around 60°F (16°C) at night.
Water and humidity needs Keep soil moist. Mist regularly for high humidity.
Growing guidelines Grow gardenias in all-purpose potting mix with added peat moss and sand. Feed monthly from spring to fall with acid fertilizer. Adding used coffee grounds to the soil several times a year stimulates flower production.
Common problems Spider mites can cause yellow stippling on leaves; raise humidity and spray plant with superior oil. Drafts and/or low temperatures can cause leaves to yellow and drop. Dry air and/or too little light causes buds to wilt and drop before opening; move the plant to a brighter location and increase the humidity.
Propagation Take cuttings of ripe (firm but still green) stems with a bit of mature wood at the base.

Hibiscus rosa-sinensis
MALVACEAE

HIBISCUS

Fabulous huge flowers in white, pink, rose, red, yellow, and orange are open just a single day, but they bloom successively and almost continuously.

Other common names Rose-of-China.
Description Tree-like hibiscus can reach 8 feet (2.4 m) tall, with glossy, green, oval leaves to 6 inches (15 cm) long. The dramatic, single or double flowers can be 5–6 inches (12.5–15 cm) wide.
Light needs High light with some sun.
Best temperatures Warm conditions; at least 70°F (21°C) during the day and at least 60°F (16°C) at night.
Water and humidity needs Keep soil moist, but don't allow pot to sit in water.
Growing guidelines Grow hibiscus in a well-drained, soil-based mix. Repot every 2 or 3 years in spring. Fertilize with a 3-1-2 fertilizer twice a month. Pinch new growth to keep plants bushy.
Common problems Catch whiteflies on yellow sticky traps, vacuum them off leaves, or spray with insecticidal soap, superior oil, or neem. Wash mealybugs off plants with a strong spray of water, or treat leaves and stems with insecticidal soap, superior oil, or neem. If leaves turn yellow, use a higher nitrogen fertilizer, such as fish emulsion.
Propagation Take stem cuttings in spring.
Comments Rejuvenate leggy plants by cutting the stems down to 4 inches (10 cm) in spring.

Hippeastrum hybrids
AMARYLLIDACEAE

AMARYLLIS

Spectacular and easy to bring into bloom, amaryllis makes a perfect winter gift plant. Keep the plant cool when it is in bloom so the flowers last longer.

Description Amaryllis sends up a 2-foot (60-cm) hollow bloom stalk, along with or slightly before the strap-like leaves. One to 10 trumpet-shaped, single or double flowers bloom atop the stalk for up to a month.
Light needs Medium light when first planted; increase to a half-day of sun when the flower stalk is 6 inches (15 cm) tall.
Best temperatures Warm conditions: 70°F (21°C) days and 60°F (16°C) nights.
Water and humidity needs Moisten soil thoroughly at planting time, then wait until growth starts before watering again. Keep soil moist while the plant is growing.
Growing guidelines Set bulb in well-drained, all-purpose potting mix. Choose a pot that is 1 inch (2.5 cm) wider than the bulb. Position bulb in the pot so the top quarter is sticking out of the soil. Feed monthly while the plant is growing; stop fertilizing and watering when leaves turn yellow. Allow bulb to rest for a month, then repot or replace the top inch (2.5 cm) of potting soil with fresh mix and 1 teaspoon of bonemeal. Water thoroughly and place bulb in a warm spot to promote new growth.
Common problems If plant produces leaves but no flowers, pot may be too large.
Propagation Remove offsets from the parent bulb.

Hoya carnosa
ASCLEPIADACEAE

WAX VINE

Wax vine's long stems can climb up trellises or trail around window frames. This milkweed relative produces clusters of fragrant, starry blooms.

Other common names Honey plant, porcelain flower.

Description Wax vine has 3-inch (7.5-cm), silvery green leaves atop trailing vines that climb to 20 feet (6 m). Clusters of small, pinkish, red-centered flowers dangle from the stems in summer.

Light needs High light.

Best temperatures Intermediate to warm conditions not below 50°F (10°C).

Water and humidity needs From spring through fall, let the soil dry out between waterings. In winter, reduce water drastically, just enough to prevent shriveling. Do not use cold water.

Growing guidelines Grow wax vine in a peat-moss-based mix in a pot or in a hanging basket lined with sphagnum moss. Provide potted plants with a support; wind the stems counterclockwise around support. Fertilize once in spring with an all-purpose fertilizer. Once buds form, avoid moving the vine. Wax vine must be 3 feet (90 cm) long to bloom, so avoid pruning, or you'll remove the stubby flowering spurs.

Common problems Wash off white cottony mealybugs with a strong spray of water, or spray with insecticidal soap or neem.

Propagation Take cuttings of the previous year's growth in spring.

Jasminum spp.
OLEACEAE

JASMINES

To get the best from your jasmines, give them lots of light and provide extra humidity. They'll reward you with masses of fragrant blossoms.

Other common names Jessamine.

Description Jasmines are shrubby or vining climbers with small, white blooms almost all year long. Poet's or french perfume jasmine (*J. officinale* var. *grandiflorum*) has double, white flowers on twining stems. Let it trail from a hanging basket, train it to climb up a trellis, or shape it into a bush form. Another good basket plant is winter jasmine (*J. polyanthum*). This robust vine bears pink-blushed, white blooms from February onward if you keep it cool (40°–55°F [4.5°–13°C]) in fall to early winter. In warmer conditions, try *J. tortuosum* instead.

Light needs High light, with a half-day of direct sun.

Best temperatures Warm conditions between 60° and 80°F (16° and 26°C).

Water and humidity needs Keep the soil very moist. Extra humidity is very helpful.

Growing guidelines Grow in humus-rich mix in pots or hanging baskets. Fertilize with fish emulsion twice a month in spring through summer. Prune after bloom season.

Common problems If spider mites cause yellow stippling on leaves, it usually means that the air is too dry. Spray with superior oil and raise humidity around the plant.

Propagation Take cuttings of half-ripe (green but somewhat firm) stem tips.

Kalanchoe blossfeldiana
CRASSULACEAE

KALANCHOE

This Madagascar native has beautiful glossy foliage and huge clusters of winter flowers held high above the leaves. Remove the stalks when the flowers fade.

Other common names Flaming Katy.

Description Kalanchoe forms clumps of succulent, 3-inch (7.5-cm), deep green leaves. Plants bloom for 2–3 months with clusters of red, pink, yellow, orange, or white flowers on 12-inch (30-cm) stems.

Light needs High light.

Best temperatures Provide cool conditions—50°–60°F (10°–16°C)—in fall while buds are forming, then move to average room temperature.

Water and humidity needs Let the soil dry between waterings. Do not overwater.

Growing guidelines Grow kalanchoe in all-purpose potting mix with added sand. Fertilize with fish emulsion once a month from when bloom ends until late summer. Put the plant outdoors for the summer, then give it a cool, drier rest period in fall to encourage bud formation.

Common problems Knock aphids and mealybugs off with a strong spray of water, or spray with insecticidal soap or neem.

Propagation Take stem cuttings in summer, or grow plants from seed.

Comments It may be challenging to get kalanchoe to rebloom. If you just want to enjoy the flowers, you should treat kalanchoe as a seasonal plant and discard it after flowering.

Murraya paniculata
RUTACEAE

ORANGE JASMINE

This easy-to-grow little shrub blooms on and off year-round. Its white flowers smell strongly of orange blossoms.

Other common names Chinese box.
Description Orange jasmine is a compact shrub that bears small, glossy, green leaves. Waxy, white flowers appear several times per year, followed by bright red berries.
Light needs Best in high light, with some direct sun.
Best temperatures Warm conditions, at least 60°F (16°C).
Water and humidity needs Keep the soil very moist.
Growing guidelines Grow orange jasmine in all-purpose potting mix. Fertilize twice a month with an all-purpose fertilizer. Clip as desired to shape the plant. It adapts well to training as a topiary or bonsai.
Common problems Leaves drop and plants wilt if the soil gets too dry; otherwise, orange jasmine is fairly trouble-free.
Propagation Grow new plants from seed.
Comments Do not eat the berries.
Related plants *M. exotica*, mock orange, is another easy, fragrant windowsill plant.

Various genera
ORCHIDACEAE

ORCHIDS

Some 25,000 species and 100,000 hybrids make this the largest flowering plant group on Earth, with something for every grower.

Description Most orchids are tropical epiphytes (plants that grow on the sides of trees instead of in the ground). There are two types of growth habits: sympodial and monopodial. A sympodial orchid grows along a horizontal rhizome, producing new growing points along its length. Monopodial orchids originate from a single growing point, producing leaves from a central rosette or single stem. The flowers have three sepals and three petals, with one petal modified into a showy "lip." Indoor orchids usually bloom in winter.

Cattleyas (*Cattleya* spp. and hybrids) are among the most recognizable orchids, with big, showy, fragrant flowers that are often used for corsages. Brightly colored, new "mini-catts" such as 'Hazel Boyd' are better for windowsills. These miniatures grow only 4–10 inches (10–25 cm) tall, as compared to 3 feet (90 cm) for standard types. These sympodial orchids adapt to intermediate temperatures and medium light. Many Cattleya hybrids have other related genera in their parentage such as the Brasso-cattleyas, which are a cross between Brassavola and Cattleya orchids. These evergreen epiphytic types have showy, often fragrant flowers with conspicuous frilled or ruffled lips and are

borne in spring or fall. Warmer conditions generally bring better growth and flowering.

Dendrobiums (*Dendrobium* spp. and hybrids) include a wide range of tropical and subtropical orchids. Two are common houseplant types, both sun-lovers with long, sympodial cane growth and sprays of flowers. Brilliantly bloomed *D. nobile* types (Yamamoto hybrids) are deciduous, needing a cool, dry rest period; evergreen *D. phalaenopsis* prefers warmer conditions.

Moth orchids (*Phalaenopsis* spp. and hybrids) have a monopodial growth habit. They are low-growing, with green or silver-mottled leaves. They produce arching, 3-foot (90-cm) tall sprays of large, striped and spotted blooms in white, pink, yellow, green, and red. Moth orchids are excellent beginner's plants for a warm, low-light spot.

The Odontoglossum group of orchids has some of the most fantastically shaped, spotted, fringed, and colored orchids. Flowering is from early spring to fall depending on the variety. They are fairly easy to grow as houseplants and most are cool growing. They need plenty of water while in growth and little during the dormant season, although they must not be allowed to dry out completely.

Oncidiums (*Oncidium* spp. and hybrids) include a wide range of tropical and subtropical orchids from a variety of habitats. The most prominent feature of each flower is the broad yellow lip. They

Orchids continued

Osmanthus fragrans
OLEACEAE

SWEET OLIVE

Sweet olive is one of the most fragrant houseplants you can grow. The small flowers have a scent reminiscent of ripe apricot.

Oxalis spp.
OXALIDACEAE

OXALIS

Oxalis boasts beautiful blooms up to 3 inches (7.5 cm) wide, in just about every color except blue. Some of the new hybrids flower nearly year-round.

generally prefer warmer intermediate conditions and dislike being overwatered.

Some of the most striking of all orchid flowers are those of the Vandas. Often flowering throughout the year, they are generally robust-growing plants needing lots of bright light, warm conditions, and good air circulation.

Light needs Low to high light, depending on the type of orchid.

Best temperatures Cool to warm conditions, depending on the type of orchid. A 10°–15°F (6°–9°C) temperature drop at night is essential, especially in fall, to set buds.

Water and humidity needs Allow pots to dry between waterings; overwatering is deadly. Extra humidity results in better growth and bloom.

Growing guidelines Grow in small pots of a well-drained epiphytic mix: three-quarters fir bark chips to one-quarter perlite. Repot after bloom with fresh mix to maintain good drainage. Fertilize twice a month with a weak solution of fish emulsion, manure tea, or all-purpose fertilizer.

Common problems Aphids, mealybugs, and scale may feed on orchids; treat with insecticidal soap, superior oil, or neem.

Propagation Divide sympodial types, leaving three stems on each. Remove rooted offshoots from monopodial types.

Other common names Fragrant olive, tea olive.

Description Sweet olive's leathery, elliptical, finely toothed leaves grow on woody, shrubby branches to 6 feet (1.8 m) tall. Clusters of small, creamy white, fragrant flowers appear mainly in fall and winter; they occasionally bloom in spring and summer as well.

Light needs High, indirect light.

Best temperatures Cool conditions, between 40° and 65°F (4.5° and 15°C).

Water and humidity needs Keep moist, allowing the soil to dry out slightly between waterings during bloom. Extra humidity is essential.

Growing guidelines Grow sweet olive in soil-based container mix with leaf mold or compost. Repot every second year in spring; top-dress with compost during spring in the years you don't repot. Fertilize monthly. Prune in spring after bloom. Put plants outdoors for the summer.

Common problems Leaf tip browning indicates plant is lacking phosphorus and potash; look for a fertilizer that contains more of these nutrients.

Propagation Take stem cuttings, set them in sand, and keep the humidity very high for good rooting.

Other common names Wood sorrel.

Description These bushy, shamrock-leaved plants grow 4–20 inches (10–50 cm) tall. Pink-leaved, lavender-flowered *O. regnellii* var. *atropurpurea* from Brazil is especially easy. It blooms almost continually, even in a low-light, northern window. Pink-flowered *O. rubra* (*O. crassipes*) is also a good choice.

Light needs High light, with full sun.

Best temperatures Intermediate conditions, at or above 50°F (10°C).

Water and humidity needs Keep evenly moist; reduce water somewhat after bloom.

Growing guidelines Add sand and peat moss to all-purpose mix. Repot in fall as needed. Trim everblooming kinds in summer to tidy them up. If your plant flowers only in one season (winter blooming is common), water less after flowering to give the plant a rest period.

Common problems Spindly growth results from too little light.

Propagation Separate offsets from the parent plant and pot them up. You can also divide types that grow from rhizomes.

Comments Leaves can be poisonous if eaten. Flowers close and leaves fold up at night and on cloudy days.

Passiflora spp.
PASSIFLORACEAE

PASSIONFLOWERS

Passionflowers are coveted for their large, gorgeous, fringed flowers. They often bloom in rare shades of blue, and some are delightfully scented.

Description Passionflowers have robust vines that grow to 20 feet (6 m). White, purple, red, and blue flowers bloom almost continuously. Orchid passionflower (*P. x alatocaerulea*) is one of the longest bloomers, with 4-inch (10-cm) flowers in a blend of purple, white, and pink. The best edible type is *P. edulis* 'Compact Purple Granadilla'.
Light needs High light, with at least 4 hours of sun.
Best temperatures Relatively warm at 60°F (16°C) or warmer.
Water and humidity needs Keep the soil moist while plants are actively growing; reduce watering slightly in fall and winter.
Growing guidelines Grow in all-purpose mix in a large container. Replace the top 1–2 inches (2.5–5 cm) of soil every year. Fertilize twice a month from spring to late summer with an all-purpose fertilizer.
Common problems Without enough light, buds wilt and drop before opening.
Propagation Take stem cuttings at any time, or grow new plants from seed.
Comments To produce fruits, most passionflowers must be hand pollinated. Use a small artist's brush to transfer the powdery pollen from the downward-facing, narrow, yellow anthers to the tips of the stigmas, at the center of the flowers.

Pelargonium spp.
GERANIACEAE

GERANIUM

Geraniums aren't just for outdoor gardens! You can bring some types indoors to enjoy their colorful flowers and scented or patterned leaves all winter.

Description Geraniums are shrubby or trailing plants that can grow up to to 4 feet (1.2 m) tall. Their leaves may be round, scalloped, or intricately cut; some have pleasant scents or multicolored markings. Flowers generally appear in spring and summer, although some bloom year-round—usually in white, pink, red, or bicolors.

Ivy geraniums (*P. peltatum*) have trailing stems that make them ideal for hanging baskets.

Zonal geraniums have almost circular leaves with scalloped or shallowly lobed margins, often with dark rings or zones on the leaves. Flowers are single, semi-double, and double and come in a vast number of color variations and flower shapes. Flowers appear almost continuously.

Regal geraniums, also called Martha Washington geraniums, have large, throat-marked, rhododendron-like blooms.

As their flowers are quite large in comparison to the plants' size, the Unique and Angel geraniums make delightful small houseplants. They rarely exceed 10 inches (25 cm) in height and have scented, rounded, or lobed leaves. Often flowers are borne freely for several months.
Light needs High light, with full sun during winter.

Best temperatures Average room temperature for most geraniums; cooler for ivy and regal types (not over 70°F [21°C]).
Water and humidity needs Allow to dry between waterings. For best results, use distilled water or rainwater.
Growing guidelines Grow geraniums in heavy, sandy mix in small pots. Repot in spring as needed. Fertilize monthly with an all-purpose fertilizer in spring to summer only. After bloom, cut the stems of zonal geraniums back to 3 inches (7.5 cm). Regal geraniums can suffer from shock if they are pruned too hard and it is preferable to only cut back top growth by one-third at any one time. Set the plants in a cool, bright spot, and keep them fairly dry until spring.
Common problems Low light or too much or too little water can cause leaves to yellow; give the plant more light and try to water more evenly. A lack of flowers may mean that the plant is over-fertilized. They bloom best when slightly potbound.
Propagation Take tip cuttings in summer.

Saintpaulia hybrids
GESNERIACEAE

AFRICAN VIOLETS

The colorful blooms of African violets make them the most popular of all flowering houseplants. Grow them on windowsills or under fluorescent lights.

Description African violets have velvety, green or variegated, fleshy leaves that grow between 3 and 12 inches (7.5 and 30 cm) tall. Trailing forms may develop stems to 4 inches (10 cm) long and will cascade over the side of the pot. Single or double blooms to 2 inches (5 cm) wide appear just above the leaves on and off year-round. The blooms can be blue, purple, pink, red, white, or green; some are multicolored or marked with a white edge or star.

Light needs Medium to high indirect light is best. Use fluorescent lights if natural light is inadequate.

Best temperatures Warm conditions, with a steady temperature of around 65°F (18°C).

Water and humidity needs Allow the soil to dry out slightly between waterings. Water carefully to avoid getting water directly onto the leaves.

Growing guidelines Grow in soil-based African violet mix in shallow pots, repotting once a year. Fertilize every 2 weeks in spring and summer with quarter-strength African violet-type fertilizer, or add bonemeal or aged manure each time you repot. Leaves should be kept dust-free with a soft brush.

Common problems Aphids and mealybugs may feed on leaves and stems. Wash the pests off the plants with tepid water, or dab them with a cotton swab soaked in witch hazel. A lack of flowers may mean that the plant isn't getting enough light, that the temperature is too high, or that the soil is too dry. Cold water can cause spots on leaves. Extremes of heat and cold will affect growth and reduce flowers.

Propagation You can take leaf cuttings by removing a mature leaf where it joins the stem, then planting the leaf with its stem in a moist but loose medium. Each leaf should produce several plantlets which, when they are large enough, are potted on individually.

Comments African violets were discovered and collected in the higher elevations of tropical East Africa in 1892 by Baron Walter von Saint Paul-Illaire and were later named Saintpaulia in his honor.

Schlumbergera bridgesii
CACTACEAE

CHRISTMAS CACTUS

The showy flowers and distinctive, segmented, trailing stems make Christmas cactus an attractive choice for hanging baskets.

Description This shrubby, 12-inch (30-cm) cactus has arching, flat-jointed, thornless, green leaves and stems. It blooms abundantly in winter with starry, 3-inch (7.5-cm) flowers. Red is a traditional favorite, although you can also find types with pink, white, or yellow flowers.

Light needs Medium to high, indirect light.

Best temperatures Average room temperature for most of the year; provide 55°F (13°C) nights in fall to set buds.

Water and humidity needs Keep the soil evenly moist. Reduce watering in fall until buds form.

Growing guidelines Grow in small pots with a well-drained mixture of soil, sand, peat moss, and compost. Repot with fresh mix in spring. Bring indoors before frost in fall, and set in a cool room that is not lighted at night to promote bud formation.

Common problems Control aphids by knocking them off with a strong spray of water, spraying plants with insecticidal soap, or spot-treating with isopropyl alcohol on a cotton swab. Too much or too little water, or water that is too cold, can cause leaves to drop. Leaves may turn yellow if the light is too bright; move plants to a spot with less light.

Propagation Take tip cuttings at any time.

Sinningia hybrids
GESNERIACEAE

GLOXINIAS

Gloxinias' velvety leaves make a beautiful background for the showy blooms. The plants thrive in the same conditions as African violets.

Description Clusters of hairy, succulent, green leaves range in height from a scant 1 inch (2.5 cm) tall to 6-inch (15-cm) miniatures and 12-inch (30-cm) standards. The trumpet-shaped, wavy-edged flowers range from reds, pinks, and white to purples and blues. They bloom primarily in summer but may flower year-round.
Light needs Medium to high, diffused light, or fluorescent light.
Best temperatures Warm conditions, around 65°–70°F (18°–21°C); cooler dormancy after bloom.
Water and humidity needs Keep the soil evenly moist. Provide high humidity.
Growing guidelines Pot in African violet mix, positioning tubers with cupped side up. Repot yearly when new growth begins. Fertilize as for African violets (see African violets entry on page 144). If the leaves start to die down after bloom, give plants a rest period; cut down on watering and reduce temperatures to 50°–60°F (10°–16°C).
Common problems Cold water can stain leaves; use tepid water and avoid getting it on foliage. If leaves produce long stems and the leaf edges curl under, the plant isn't getting enough light.
Propagation Propagate as for African violets; see the African violets entry.

Stephanotis floribunda
ASCLEPIADACEAE

STEPHANOTIS

Stephanotis has starry blooms that are traditional favorites for bridal bouquets. Their intoxicating scent can be overwhelming in a small space.

Other common names Bride's flower, Madagascar jasmine.
Description Stephanotis has waxy, 3-inch (7.5-cm), green leaves along twining vines that can reach 20 feet (6 m). Waxy, white, tubular, 2-inch (5-cm) flowers appear from late spring through fall.
Light needs High light with direct sun during winter.
Best temperatures Average to warm conditions—around 70°F (21°C)—in spring and summer; cooler—around 55°F (13°C)—in fall and winter.
Water and humidity needs During active growth, keep soil moist; keep barely damp in winter. Provide extra humidity.
Growing guidelines Pot in well-drained, all-purpose mix, and provide a trellis. Fertilize monthly between February and October with an all-purpose fertilizer.
Common problems Insufficient light can lead to few or no blooms. If spider mites cause yellow stippling on leaves, raise the humidity and spray the plant with superior oil. Leaf yellowing can be a sign of soggy roots; hold off a bit on watering.
Propagation Take 4-inch (10-cm) stem cuttings of half-matured (still green but somewhat firm) stems during spring and early summer.

Streptocarpus hybrids
GESNERIACEAE

CAPE PRIMROSE

These African violet relatives boast a long period of colorful bloom; try them in a north window or under fluorescent lights.

Description The hairy-leaved rosettes of cape primrose grow up to 12 inches (30 cm) tall. They produce 2-inch (5-cm) wide trumpets of red, pink, blue, or purple blooms atop 6-inch (15-cm) stalks nearly all year.
Light needs Medium, indirect light.
Best temperatures Intermediate conditions, with a 5°F (3°C) drop at night; adapts to average room temperature.
Water and humidity needs Keep the soil moist but not soggy. After bloom, allow it to dry somewhat between waterings.
Growing guidelines Grow cape primrose in shallow pots in African violet mix, repotting only when absolutely necessary. Fertilize twice a month with African violet fertilizer, or add bonemeal or aged manure to the growing mix when you repot. Provide a drier rest period after bloom.
Common problems Limp stems and leaves indicate too little light. Wilted, yellowed leaves may also indicate root rot from overwatering; plants may recover if you let the soil dry out a bit between waterings.
Propagation Take leaf cuttings by slicing a leaf into three or four parts crossways; stand the pieces upright in a moist growing medium, and keep them warm until they produce roots and new growth. You can also divide plants in spring.

Agave spp.
AGAVACEAE

CENTURY PLANTS

This succulent seems to take a century to bloom, hence its name; actually, though, 15 years is more typical. Give it plenty of light, but water sparingly.

Description Century plant grows in a rosette of long, upright foliage. The silvery or blue-gray leaves are narrow, with spiny edges. Some can reach 4 feet (1.2 m) across. The most popular indoor species is *A. victoriae-reginae*, with blue-green leaves edged and lined in white; it grows to 10 inches (25 cm) wide. *A. desmettiana* grows to 2 feet (60 cm) wide, with dark green to blue-green leaves.
Light needs High light, with full sun.
Best temperatures Average temperature.
Water and humidity needs Allow to dry somewhat between waterings, especially in winter. Century plant can tolerate dry air.
Growing guidelines Century plants grow well in a mix of sand and soil; add a pinch or two of ground limestone to the mix, too. Plants like being potbound, so move them to a bigger container only if they outgrow their pot. Fertilize just once yearly, in spring, with an all-purpose fertilizer.
Common problems Too much water will cause rot.
Propagation Remove offsets from the base of the plant and pot them up to root. You can also grow plants from seed. (Flowers will produce seed if you hand-pollinate them with a fine brush.)

Aglaeonema spp.
ARACEAE

CHINESE EVERGREENS

Chinese evergreen offers gorgeous foliage marked with a mixture of green, pewter, silver, cream, and white; some kinds may even show a bit of pink.

Description These shrubby, many-stemmed plants can reach 3 feet (90 cm). They are notable for their patterned, elliptic foliage, which grows up to 1 foot (30 cm) long and 4 inches (10 cm) wide. *A. commutatum* is the source of many cultivars: the 10-inch (25-cm) tall *A. costatum* has dark green leaves marked with creamy blotches. *A. roebellinii* produces elongated, oval, green leaves and has an upright habit.
Light needs Low (even dark).
Best temperatures Warm, 65°F (18°C) nights to 85°F (29°C) days.
Water and humidity needs Keep just moist. Use unchlorinated water, allowing tap water to stand overnight before use for best results. Provide extra humidity.
Growing guidelines Pot in a peat-based mix, repotting when the plant looks tired. Fertilize three times a year, or less if in low light. Periodic showers will clean leaves.
Common problems Brown leaf edges indicate dry air, bad drainage, or too much minerals or salts from tap water. Leaf variegation fades in too much light. Mealybugs hide at leaf bases. Wash off with a sharp stream of water or drench with insecticidal soap, horticultural oil, or neem.
Propagation Take stem cuttings, divide the stalks, or air layer at any time.

Aloe spp.
ALOEACEAE

MEDICINE PLANTS

These cactus-like houseplants can live for years on benign neglect. Water thoroughly when you think of it, then let the soil dry out before you water again.

Other common names Aloe, burn plant.
Description Medicine plants have sword-like leaves filled with gel-like juice. The leaves may be plain green or variegated or spotted with white or gray. Plants range from 1 inch (2.5 cm) to several feet tall. In bright light, medicine plants may produce spikes of orange, yellow, or red flowers in fall to winter. Burn plant (*A. vera*) has sword-like leaves, with pale cream spots, that grow to 2 feet (60 cm) long. Grow it on a kitchen windowsill, since the sap inside the leaves relieves burns and cuts. Tiger aloe (*A. variegata*) grows to 9 inches (22.5 cm) tall, with clumps of lance-like, green leaves that have wavy, ivory striping.
Light needs High light, with at least a half-day of full sun, is best; adapts to less.
Best temperatures Intermediate conditions; approximately 70°F (21°C) days and 50°F (10°C) nights.
Water and humidity needs Allow to dry between waterings.
Growing guidelines Grow medicine plants in clay pots and all-purpose mix with added sand for best drainage. Fertilize lightly once a year, in fall.
Common problems Overwatering can cause rotting.
Propagation Remove offsets at any time.

Aphelandra squarossa
ACANTHACEAE

ZEBRA PLANT

For dramatic foliage, it's hard to beat the highly striped leaves of zebra plant. It can also produce bright yellow flowers in late summer and fall.

Other common names Saffron spike.
Description Zebra plant produces dark stems and oval, glossy, green leaves with cream-colored veins that can reach 1 foot (30 cm) long. The shrubby plants grow to 3 feet (90 cm) tall.
Light needs High, indirect light.
Best temperatures Warm conditions, at least 65°F (18°C).
Water and humidity needs Provide abundant water in spring through fall; allow to dry somewhat during winter rest. Provide high humidity.
Growing guidelines Grow zebra plant in all-purpose potting mix, and fertilize twice a month from spring through fall. After flowering, cut the stem back drastically to just above the lowest node (where the lowest pair of leaves join the stem). Pinch out the tips of new growth when it reaches 6 inches (15 cm) to encourage bushiness.
Common problems Spider mites can cause stippling on leaves; raise humidity and spray the plant with superior oil. Knock mealybugs off with a strong spray of water, or spray the plant with insecticidal soap, superior oil, or neem. It is normal for leaves to fall after the plant blooms.
Propagation Take tip cuttings in late winter to early summer.

Araucaria heterophylla
ARAUCARIACEAE

NORFOLK ISLAND PINE

Norfolk Island pine is a winning houseplant. Purchase full, dense plants, since sparse-looking specimens will stay that way when you get them home.

Description This pyramidal, tiered tree has bright green, soft needles. It can grow up to 200 feet (60 m) tall in nature. Fortunately for indoor gardeners, it usually only reaches about 7 feet (2.1 m) tall as a houseplant. The branches have resinous sap.
Light needs High light, with full sun, is best, but plants can live with less.
Best temperatures Ideal conditions are 70°F (21°C) during the day and 50°–55°F (10°–13°C) at night (particularly in winter). However, Norfolk Island pine can adapt to a range of temperatures from 45°–85°F (7°–29°C).
Water and humidity needs Keep the soil evenly moist.
Growing guidelines Grow Norfolk Island pine in African violet mix. Repot every 3 years. Fertilize four times a year.
Common problems Needles drop if the air is too hot and dry; move the plant to a cooler spot and increase the humidity. Lower branches fall as the plant ages.
Propagation Buy new plants or start them from seed. Taking cuttings will ruin the shape of your plant.
Comments Many gardeners enjoy using their Norfolk Island pine as a small Christmas tree during the holiday season.

Asparagus densiflorus
ASPARAGACEAE

ASPARAGUS FERN

Show off asparagus fern's arching stems by displaying the plant in a hanging basket. The needle-like leaves are actually flattened stems.

Other common names Emerald feather.
Description This plant has feathery, arching, green plumes on distinctive, woody, spiny stems to 3 feet (90 cm) long. Tiny, pink flowers may form, followed by small berries that turn successively from white to green to red to black.
Light needs High, indirect light.
Best temperatures Average to cool conditions (55°–70°F [13°–21°C]).
Water and humidity needs Keep the soil just moist.
Growing guidelines Grow asparagus fern in a humus-rich mix. Fertilize four times a year. Repot whenever the fast-growing roots start creeping out of the pot.
Common problems Yellowed foliage means too much light or a lack of nitrogen; reduce the light slightly and fertilize with fish emulsion. Brittle stems and dropping leaves usually indicate that the plant has outgrown its pot and depleted the available nutrients; move the plant to a larger pot with fresh mix.
Propagation Divide large plants by cutting all the stems down to the soil, then slicing the root ball into 4-inch (10-cm) wide wedges; plant the wedges in individual pots. You can also grow asparagus ferns from seed.

Aspidistra elatior
CONVALLARIACEAE

CAST-IRON PLANT

Known since the Victorian age, this Chinese native is renowned for its "cast-iron" constitution. It's suitable for even the most black-thumbed gardener.

Other common names Barbershop plant.
Description Usually between 18 and 24 inches (45 and 60 cm) tall, cast-iron plant has an upright growth habit. Its leaves grow to 30 inches (75 cm) long and 4 inches (10 cm) wide. The foliage is generally dark green, although you can occasionally find variegated forms. Small, bell-shaped, purple blooms may form at the base of the plant.
Light needs Tolerates low light, even very dim corners.
Best temperatures Average room temperature during the day; around 50°F (10°C) at night.
Water and humidity needs Keep the soil evenly moist.
Growing guidelines Repot this slow grower in all-purpose potting mix only every 5 years. Fertilize once in spring (and again in fall if the plant gets medium light).
Common problems Spider mites occasionally attack the foliage. Control these pests by washing the leaves monthly with plain water or with a solution of insecticidal soap.
Propagation Divide the roots in early spring and replant in fresh mix; plant two or three pieces together in each pot.

Begonia spp.
BEGONIACEAE

FOLIAGE BEGONIAS

Who needs flowers when you can have leaves like these! Actually, some foliage begonias do produce flowers, but the blooms tend to be inconspicuous.

Other common names Painted begonia.
Description Foliage begonias mostly grow from rhizomes to a height of about 16 inches (40 cm). The leaves are often hairy and heart-shaped, with bold or subtle markings in the form of marbling, mottling, spots, or zones. Leaf colors range from green to silver, bronze, purple, red, pink, and black; a silvery overlay is common. Iron cross begonia (*B. masoniana*) has a chocolate-colored cross in the center of each leaf.
Light needs Medium to high, indirect light; protect from direct sun. Plants also grow well under fluorescent lights.
Best temperatures Warm—75°F (24°C) during the day and at least 60°F (16°C) at night; slightly cooler in winter.
Water and humidity needs Allow soil surface to dry between waterings, especially in winter. Provide extra humidity.
Growing guidelines Grow in all-purpose mix in shallow pots. Repot only when the plant outgrows its container. Fertilize monthly from spring to fall, allowing a slight dormancy in winter.
Common problems Leaf drop in winter is not unusual. If leaf colors fade, move the plant to a brighter spot.
Propagation Take stem or leaf cuttings at any time. Divide the rhizomes in spring.

Brassaia actinophylla
ARALIACEAE

SCHEFFLERA

This elegant indoor tree has handsome foliage and can adapt to a range of growing conditions. Prune frequently to keep plants bushy.

Other common names Umbrella tree; Australian umbrella tree.
Description Scheffleras are shrubby plants with large, compound leaves. Each leaf is composed of seven or more glossy, green leaflets combined in an umbrella-like cluster. Scheffleras can grow to 40 feet (12 m) tall in their native home of Australia and Indonesia; when they're grown indoors in pots, 8 feet (2.4 m) tall is more likely.
Light needs High light; will tolerate some direct sun.
Best temperatures Average to warm conditions, around 60°–70°F (16°–21°C).
Water and humidity needs Allow the soil to dry between waterings.
Growing guidelines These fast growers need big pots and all-purpose mix; repot at any time. Fertilize monthly in spring and summer, while plants are actively growing.
Common problems Spider mites may cause stippling on leaves. Control problems by increasing the humidity around the plant and washing the leaves monthly with water; spray serious infestations with insecticidal soap.
Propagation Take cuttings, air layer the stems, or grow new plants from seed.
Related plants *B. arboricola*, Hawaiian elf, is a more compact species.

Various genera
BROMELIACEAE

BROMELIADS

Bromeliads include a variety of striking, slow-growing tropical plants. They may take several years to bloom; but they have beautifully marked leaves.

Other common names Air plants, living vase plants.
Description Bromeliads produce rosettes of leaves that range in height from 1 inch (2.5 cm) to 3 feet (90 cm) tall. Flower spikes may arise from the center of a rosette, in red, yellow, pink, and green.

Air plant (*Tillandsia cyanea*) has long, narrow, arching, green leaves and flat plumes of deep pink or red bracts and violet-blue flowers.

Flaming sword (*Vriesia splendens*) has vases of brown-banded, green leaves and gorgeous, long, red flower spikes that can grow to 3 feet (90 cm) tall.

Guzmanias (*Guzmania* spp. and hybrids) grow in a vase shape with strap-like, arching, green leaves to 18 inches (45 cm). *G. musaica* has mottled foliage and orange-yellow spires of flowers.

Living vases (*Aechmea* spp. and hybrids) include some of the most well-known houseplant bromeliads. They often have strap-shaped, blue-green leaves marked with silvery bands. The spiny-edged, silvery-green urn plant (*A. fasciata*) grows to 3 feet (90 cm), with fat spikes of blue flowers and showy, pink, petal-like bracts.

Neoregelias (*Neoregelia* spp. and hybrids) form somewhat flattened rosettes of green

leaves. As the flowers appear, the center of the plant takes on a colorful blush.

Pineapple (*Ananas comosus*) has a vase-shaped habit and narrow, toothed, gray-green leaves. The flower stalk that eventually emerges from the center of the plant is topped with a miniature pineapple.
Light needs High light with some direct sun; protect from midday sun.
Best temperatures 60°F (16°C) or warmer conditions.
Water and humidity needs Keep the center cups of vase-shaped types filled with rainwater; drain and refill the cups every week or two. Let other types dry between waterings. Provide extra humidity.
Growing guidelines Most bromeliads grow best in clay pots and an epiphytic wood chip mix (as you would use for orchids). Pineapples can grow in well-drained cactus potting soil. Provide liquid fertilizer twice a month in spring and summer and once a month during the rest of the year. Put plants outdoors for the summer.
Common problems Too much light can burn leaves; move plants outdoors or to high light areas gradually. If you have hard water or if you allow the leaf cups to dry out, you may notice white stains (salt or lime buildup) on leaves; flush the cups weekly with rainwater to remove the stains.
Propagation Remove and pot up offsets, or grow plants from seed.

Various genera
CACTACEAE

CACTI

Cacti are generally rugged enough for even black-thumbed gardeners. Their brilliant flowers are often surprisingly large compared to the size of the plant.

Description Cacti have no leaves to speak of, just thickened, water-storing, spiny stems. They come in a wide variety of shapes and sizes.

The bishop's cap (*Astrophytum myriostigma*) is a quirky, odd-looking species from Mexico with a grayish-green spineless body up to 12 inches (30 cm) high and 4 inches (10 cm) across in the shape of a bishop's miter. Yellow fragrant flowers appear in summer.

Barrel cacti (*Echinocactus* spp.) are spiny, clumping, and barrel-shaped, with showy, bell-shaped flowers that are often yellow. The plants are particularly pretty and colorful while young and are fun to grow from seed.

Chin cactus (*Gymnocalycium mihanovichii*) is globe-shaped with prominent ribs and long-lasting blooms. You may see red or yellow forms of this cactus grafted atop a green stem. The popular cultivar 'Red Head' has brilliant red stems and bears pinkish-red flowers in early summer.

Cob cactus (*Lobivia leucomalla*) has huge flowers on compact, 1-inch (2.5-cm) plants.

Mammillarias (*Mammillaria* spp.) include many species of easy-to-grow, clustering cacti with showy hairs or spines. They tend to have a ring of small flowers around the

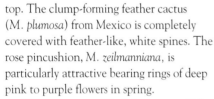

Cacti continued

Chlorophytum comosum
ANTHERICACEAE

SPIDER PLANT

One of the most common hanging basket plants, spider plant is beloved for its graceful habit. It produces baby plants at the ends of long stems.

top. The clump-forming feather cactus (M. *plumosa*) from Mexico is completely covered with feather-like, white spines. The rose pincushion, M. *zeilmanniana*, is particularly attractive bearing rings of deep pink to purple flowers in spring.

Old man cactus (*Cephalocereus senilis*) looks like a hunched man covered with long, white "hair." It blooms at night with rose-pink flowers.

Peanut cactus (*Chamaecereus silvestri*) forms 6-inch (15-cm) long clusters of green branches with soft, white spines. It produces orange-red flowers.

Prickly pear cacti (*Opuntia* spp.) are among the most recognized cactus groups, with their flat "pads" and glossy flowers. Rabbit ears (*O. microdasys*) reaches 12 inches (30 cm) tall, with green pads dotted with small clusters of tiny, spine-like glochids. The clump-forming dwarf, *O. verschaffeltii*, reaches about 6 inches (15 cm) tall and produces red or orange-red flowers 1 inch (2.5 cm) across from spring to summer, followed by round red fruit.

Rattail cactus (*Aporocactus flagelliformis*) is good for hanging baskets, with 3-foot (90-cm) long stems and bright red blooms.

The sea urchin cacti (*Echinopsis* spp.) include many popular species native to South America with funnel-shaped, brilliantly colored flowers up to 8 inches (20 cm) long in summer.

Light needs High light, with direct sun.

Best temperatures Average room temperature for most of the year; cool conditions—approximately 65°F (18°C) days and 40°F (4.5°C) nights—in winter.

Water and humidity needs In late March and April, water thoroughly and wait until the soil surface feels dry before watering again. Begin decreasing water steadily from May through December; give almost no water in winter. Cacti can tolerate dry air.

Growing guidelines Keep cacti potbound in well-drained clay pots of all-purpose mix with added sand. Fertilize just once a year during early spring. Put cacti outdoors for the summer. Provide a cool, dry rest period during winter.

Common problems Plants that do not get a winter rest period may produce weak, spindly growth. Overwatering can lead to wilting and root rot.

Propagation Take stem or leaf cuttings, remove and repot offsets, or grow new plants from seed. Any cactus can be grafted to another by placing the cut bottom of one atop a cut tip of another and tying them firmly until they unite.

Other common names Ribbon plant, spider ivy.

Description Spider plant grows from rhizomes to produce arching, narrow, 12–18-inch (30–45-cm) long, green leaves. It also sends out long, pale yellow stems, with small white flowers along their length.

Light needs Medium light; avoid strong, direct sun.

Best temperatures Average room temperature during the day; approximately 50°F (10°C) at night.

Water and humidity needs Allow soil to dry between waterings. Plants can take dry air but prefer extra humidity and rainwater.

Growing guidelines Use all-purpose mix in small hanging baskets, leaving 1 inch (2.5 cm) between the rim of the pot and the top of the soil. Fertilize twice a month in spring and summer.

Common problems High temperatures can cause brown leaves; move the plant to a cooler spot. Some kinds of tap water can cause brown leaf tips; if this is a problem, snip off the tips and use rainwater.

Propagation Divide parent plant or grow new plants from seed. Make new plants by removing plantlets from ends of stems. Set the base of the plantlet in water until roots begin to form, then move it to a pot.

Cissus spp.
VITACEAE

GRAPE IVY

Grape ivies make splendid foliage vines, adapting to low light and dry air without too much fuss. Provide some kind of trellis so vines can climb.

Other common names Kangaroo vine.
Description These tendril-climbing vines can grow to 10 feet (3 m). The fleshy, green leaves grow to 4 inches (10 cm) long; they are sometimes fuzzy underneath. Grape ivy (*C. rhombifolia*), from tropical America, has large, metallic green, lobed leaves; it is easy to grow. Kangaroo vine (*C. antarctica*) is a vigorous grower with shiny, leathery leaves; it hails from Australia. Dwarf grape ivy (*C. striata*), from Chile, is a compact climber with small, five-lobed leaves.
Light needs Medium to high light, but keep the plant out of direct sun.
Best temperatures Warm conditions but cooler than 75°F (24°C).
Water and humidity needs Keep evenly moist, but don't let the plant sit in water. Provide extra humidity.
Growing guidelines Provide all-purpose mix in very well-drained baskets. Repot as needed. Fertilize twice a month in spring and summer. Pinch sideshoots back frequently to encourage dense growth.
Common problems Grape ivies are generally problem-free.
Propagation Take stem cuttings at any time, or grow new plants from seed.

Codiaeum variegatum var. *pictum*
EUPHORBIACEAE

CROTON

These tropical Indian and Malaysian plants provide some of the most brilliantly colored houseplant foliage. Their colors often change as the plants age.

Other common names Variegated laurel.
Description These shrubby, 4-foot (1.2-m) plants boast spectacular, oak-leaf-shaped to oval-shaped leaves. The foliage color ranges through yellow, red, pink, orange, green, and brown, with markings often different from leaf to leaf on the same plant.
Light needs High light; some direct sun.
Best temperatures Warm conditions between 65° and 80°F (18° and 26°C).
Water and humidity needs Keep evenly moist for most of the year; allow the surface to dry between waterings in winter. Provide extra humidity.
Growing guidelines Repot in spring into soil-based mix. Fertilize twice a month except in winter. Set outside for summer. If plants get leggy, cut stems back to 6 inches (15 cm) above the soil, just above a node.
Common problems If spider mites cause stippling on leaves, raise the humidity and spray with superior oil. Knock cottony white mealybugs off the plant with a strong spray of water, or spray with insecticidal soap, superior oil, or neem. Lack of light can cause leaf colors to fade. Cold temperatures can cause leaf drop.
Propagation Air layer the stems, or take cuttings from half-ripe (green but somewhat firm) sideshoots.

Crassula argentea
CRASSULACEAE

JADE PLANT

This slow-growing, easy-care succulent is one of the most widely grown houseplants. Its fleshy, emerald green leaves branch off of thick, trunk-like stems.

Other common names Baby jade.
Description Jade plant grows slowly to reach 4 feet (1.2 m) tall, with thick branches and a shrubby form. The smooth, oval, 2-inch (5-cm) long leaves are usually bright green. Jade plant seldom blooms when grown indoors.
Light needs High light.
Best temperatures Intermediate; 50°–80°F (10°–26°C).
Water and humidity needs Allow to dry between waterings; don't overwater.
Growing guidelines Grow jade plant in a blend of half perlite and half all-purpose potting mix. Fertilize every 3 months, except in winter. Pinch new growth to encourage bushiness. If you keep it cool and allow it to get potbound, the plant may flower in winter.
Common problems Mealybugs like to hide along stems and under leaves. Knock them off the plant with a strong spray of water, or spray with insecticidal soap, superior oil, or neem. Weak or leggy growth tells you the plant isn't getting enough light; move it to a brighter spot.
Propagation Take stem or leaf cuttings.
Comments Leaf margins take on a reddish tinge when the plant is getting the ideal amount of light.

Dieffenbachia seguine
ARACEAE

DUMBCANE

Bold, fancy leaves are the trademark of this plant. It gets its name from its irritating sap, which causes swelling and pain of the tongue if eaten.

Other common names Mother-in-law's tongue.

Description The upright stems of dumbcane grow to 6 feet (1.8 m) tall, with elliptical leaves that can reach 18 inches (45 cm) long by 12 inches (30 cm) wide. The green foliage is marked and spotted in various shades of green, cream, and yellow. 'Amoena' has broad, lance-shaped, glossy leaves to 6–14 inches (15–35 cm) long with a tracery of creamy-white between the veins. 'Exotica' is heavily and irregularly marked with creamy-white blotches between the veins and on the midribs. 'Memoria Corsii' has gray-green leaves, marked dark green and lightly speckled white. 'Rudolph Roehrs' has yellowish-green or creamy-yellow leaves with green midribs and green margins. 'Tropic Marianne' has green-edged leaves that are almost entirely cream. 'Tropic Snow' is a stout, almost stemless plant to 4 feet (1.2 m) tall with thick green and white leaves.

Light needs High, indirect light is best, although the plant can adapt to less.

Best temperatures Warm conditions (at least 60°F [16°C]). Keep out of drafts.

Water and humidity needs Allow the soil to dry a bit between waterings. Provide extra humidity.

Growing guidelines Grow dumbcane in all-purpose mix, and keep it potbound. Fertilize lightly with fish emulsion twice a month in warm seasons. Rinse dust off of the leaves several times a year.

Common problems As they age, plants tend to drop their lower foliage, leaving you with a bare stem topped with a tuft of leaves. To rejuvenate the plant, cut the stem to about 6 inches (15 cm) tall. Control spider mites by raising the humidity and spraying with superior oil. Knock mealybugs off the plant with a strong spray of water, or treat the plant with insecticidal soap, superior oil, or neem. Overwatering and lack of light can produce thin stems and widely spaced leaves.

Propagation Air layer the stems, or take tip or stem cuttings.

Dizygotheca elegantissima
ARALIACEAE

FALSE ARALIA

False aralia sports upright stems clad in lacy leaves. This South Pacific native is a good choice for warm, shaded, humid spots with low to medium light.

Description This shrubby tree grows to 6 feet (1.8 m) tall, with serrated, fern-like leaves. Young foliage is coppery bronze, sometimes mottled with cream; the leaves change to dark greenish black as they age.

Light needs Low to medium, indirect light.

Best temperatures Warm conditions; at least 60°F (16°C) in winter.

Water and humidity needs Allow the soil surface to dry between waterings. Provide extra humidity.

Growing guidelines Grow false aralia in all-purpose potting mix. Repot every few years as needed. Fertilize twice a month in spring and summer.

Common problems Control spider mites by raising the humidity and spraying the plant with superior oil. Leaves may drop as the plant ages or because of overwatering or moving the plant from place to place. Age, cold, and lack of humidity can cause the plant to get scraggly; take cuttings to rejuvenate the plant and keep in a warm, humid location.

Propagation Take stem cuttings during warm seasons.

Comments For the best-looking false aralias, you should treat them as short-lived specimens and replace them when they start looking shabby.

Dracaena spp.
AGAVACEAE

DRACAENA

Dracaenas are tough, adaptable plants that are easy to find and easy to grow. With age, they produce a thick trunk and lose their bottom leaves.

Description Dracaenas are tree-like plants that can grow anywhere from 18 inches (45 cm) up to 8 feet (2.4 m) tall. They are noted for their distinctively marked, bold, often sword-like foliage. Most dracaenas shed their lower leaves as they increase in height, and therefore develop a somewhat palm-like appearance.

Corn plant (*D. fragrans*) has green, corn-like foliage. The popular cultivar, 'Massangeana' has broad, gracefully curved green leaves with a yellowish-green central stripe attached to stout central stems. Panicles of small creamy-white flowers are strongly scented and are followed by orange-red berries. 'Victoria' has brighter creamy-gold coloring.

Dragon tree (*D. marginata*), which is also known as red-margined dracaena, has narrow, dark green leaves that are edged with maroon. 'Tricolor' has slender, pointed, cream-striped, green leaves prominently edged with red. It needs bright light to maintain color.

Slow-growing golddust dracaena (*D. godseffiana*) has rounded gold-and-white spotted leaves. It has a shrubby appearance and grows up to 3 feet (90 cm).

Striped dracaena (*D. deremensis*) can reach 15 feet (4.5 m) with arching, glossy green leaves usually striped with white and gray to 18 inches (45 cm) long. 'Warneckii' has dark gray-green leaves with narrow lighter streaks running lengthwise.

Light needs High, indirect light is best, but dracaena tolerates less.

Best temperatures Warm conditions (65°–70°F [18°–21°C]).

Water and humidity needs Keep evenly moist most of the year; allow it to dry somewhat between waterings in winter. Provide extra humidity.

Growing guidelines Grow dracaenas in all-purpose potting mix. Fertilize twice a month in warm seasons. Rejuvenate leggy plants by cutting back to within 6 inches (15 cm) of the base in spring.

Common problems Low light causes thin stems and faded leaves. Browned leaf edges indicate overdrying and/or salt buildup. Mealybugs may be a nuisance. If the plant is badly infested knock the pests off with a strong spray of water, or spray the plant with insecticidal soap, superior oil, or neem.

Propagation Take tip or stem cuttings, or air layer the trunk.

Fatsia japonica
ARALIACEAE

ARALIA

This ivy relative is a fast-growing plant ideal for cool spots. Wipe the broad leaves with a damp cloth several times a year to keep them clean and glossy.

Other common names Formosa rice tree, Japanese aralia.

Description Aralia's large, green, lobed leaves can grow up to 12 inches (30 cm). The shrubby plant may reach 5 feet (1.5 m) tall.

Light needs High light.

Best temperatures Cool conditions, with days around 65°F (18°C) and nights around 50°F (10°C).

Water and humidity needs Keep soil just moist in spring and summer; reduce watering in fall and winter, but don't let soil dry out. Provide extra humidity.

Growing guidelines Grow aralia in large pots in all-purpose mix. Repot as needed in spring. Fertilize twice a year in early spring and early summer. Set plants outdoors for the summer. Keep them bushy by trimming stems lightly in spring.

Common problems If the stems get leggy, cut them back by half in spring.

Propagation Take cuttings in late winter and spring, or grow new plants from seed.

Related plants *Fatshedera lizei*, tree ivy (a cross between *Fatsia japonica* and *Hedera helix* var. *hibernica*—English ivy) has five-lobed leaves. Its upright stems grow to 3 feet (90 cm) tall. Tree ivy appreciates the same growing conditions as its parents.

Various genera

FERNS

Loved for their graceful, arching, feathery fronds, ferns are a mainstay for houseplant growers. Ferns grow from rhizomes and reproduce via spores.

Description Ferns are a broad group of plants that includes many different genera.

Bird's-nest fern (*Asplenium nidus*) produces broad, glossy, bright green fronds with a black midrib and wavy margins in an attractive radial arrangement somewhat resembling a bird's nest.

Boston fern (*Nephrolepis exaltata* 'Bostoniensis') has been grown in cultivation for over 100 years for its graceful, arching fronds. It is a long-time favorite hanging basket fern.

The creten brake (*P. cretica* 'Albolineata') which produces attractive, divided, pale green fronds, centrally variegated with a creamy-white band is one of the easiest ferns to care for. 'Mayi' is very similar to 'Albolineata' but has crested frond tips.

Holly fern (*Cyrtomium flacatum*) has toothed, glossy, dark green leaves. It tolerates low humidity and poor light.

Maidenhair ferns (*Adiantum* spp.) produce thin, dark stems and lacy, light green fronds. Australian maidenhair (*A. hispidulum*) is the most rugged species for indoor growing.

Mother fern (*Asplenium bulbiferum*) has feathery, bright green fronds that may reach 4 feet (1.2 m). It develops tiny new

plantlets on mature fronds that can be removed and potted to form new plants.

Rabbit's foot fern (*Davallia fejeensis*) is an unfussy, feathery fern with "furry-footed" rhizomes.

Light needs Medium to high light, but not direct sun.

Best temperatures Average conditions, with day temperatures up to 75°F (24°C) and nights between 55° and 65°F (13° and 18°C).

Water and humidity needs Keep evenly moist; water daily if necessary. Extra humidity is a plus. Never allow your fern to stand in water.

Growing guidelines Grow ferns in small pots in light, well-drained, all-purpose mix with added peat moss and perlite. Repot in spring as needed. Fertilize twice a year—in early spring and early summer—with fish emulsion.

Common problems Scales may produce small, irregularly spaced spots on the fronds; scrape them off with your fingernail or with a cotton swab.

Propagation Divide clump-forming ferns, grow new plants from spores, or pin the runners to the soil and repot them when they are rooted.

Ficus spp.
MORACEAE

FIGS

Figs are a large group of attractive tropical plants that have produced some of our best-known and easiest-to-grow houseplants.

Other common names Ficus, rubber plant.

Description Figs can be trees, shrubs, or woody vines, with milky sap and usually thick leaves. Many species make good houseplants.

Creeping fig (*F. pumila*) is a fast-growing, dark, oval-leaved vine suitable for baskets. Trim regularly and pinch out growing tips to encourage branching and help retain dainty juvenile leaves. The tiniest types, such as quilted creeping fig (*F. pumila* var. *minima*), are excellent growing on moss-stuffed topiary forms.

Edible fig (*F. carica*) grows to 8 feet (2.4 m) tall in big tubs, producing large leaves and edible fruits. It drops its leaves in winter, when it needs a cool, dry rest period.

Fiddle-leaf fig (*F. lyrata*) is a handsome robust fig with heavily veined, large, dark green, lustrous leaves shaped like a violin and up to 18 inches (45 cm) or more long. Indoors it may reach up to 6 feet (1.8 m) tall and may be pruned at the top to make the plant bushy.

Hill's weeping fig (*F. microcarpa* var. *hillii*) has small, shiny, pointed, oval leaves with a slightly weeping habit. This is a popular species for training as a standard fig with plaited stems.

Fittonia verschaffeltii
ACANTHACEAE

Mistletoe fig (F. *deltoidea*) has flat, green leaves that are oval at the tips and pointed at the base. It produces small, yellowish fruits on plants shorter than 6 feet (1.8 m).

Mosaic fig (F. *aspera* 'Parcellii') produces wide, bright green, oval leaves that are mottled with white and rather hairy underneath.

Rubber plant (F. *elastica*), with its large, elliptical, dark green leaves, is a common sight in houseplant collections. It normally reaches about 6 feet (1.8 m) tall indoors. 'Burgundy' is the purple rubber tree. 'Doescheri' has deep green leaves patterned with gray-green, cream, and white with light pink stalks and midribs.

Weeping or java fig (F. *benjamina*) is one of the best species of fig for indoor gardens. It grows in a tree-like form up to 8 feet (2.4 m) tall, with dainty, 2–5-inch (5–12.5-cm), oval leaves and cinnamon-colored bark. Weeping fig is easy to grow even in low light, although the more light it gets, the more leaves it produces. The variegated form has rich green leaves splashed with white.

Light needs Medium to high light.

Best temperatures Average room temperature; avoid moving plants from high to low light.

Water and humidity needs Allow the soil of most figs to dry somewhat between waterings. Keep creeping types evenly damp.

Growing guidelines Grow figs in all-purpose mix that's been enriched with compost. Keep them potbound to prevent overwatering; repot only every 3–4 years. Feed twice a year, occasionally providing a very dilute vinegar solution. Wipe large-leaved types periodically with a damp sponge. Fresh air is very beneficial. When plants outgrow your house, do not be tempted to plant them in the garden as the roots can become very invasive.

Common problems Spider mites and scale can attack if the air is hot and dry; control them by raising the humidity and decreasing the temperature. Treat scale by spraying with insecticidal soap or superior oil, or by dabbing them with a cotton swab dipped in isopropyl alcohol. Treat spider mites by spraying with superior oil. Lower leaves may drop due to temperature or light changes, drafts, or too much or too little water. If the bottom of a weeping fig becomes too bare, cut it back to 5 inches (12.5 cm) above the soil and withhold water until new growth begins.

Propagation Sow seed in spring. Air layer the stems of upright types. Root creeping types from tip cuttings or divide the rooting stems.

FITTONIA

The green leaves of fittonia are etched in an intricate mosaic pattern with rosy white veins. This plant can be finicky, especially with regard to humidity.

Other common names Mosaic plant, red-nerved plant.

Description These low, creeping or trailing plants have olive green, oval leaves veined in rose, cream, or red, depending on the cultivar.

Light needs Medium to high light. Fittonia grows well under fluorescent lights.

Best temperatures Warm conditions, with both day and night temperatures at least 65°F (18°C).

Water and humidity needs Keep the soil evenly moist. High humidity is essential; mist often.

Growing guidelines Grow fittonias in African violet mix. Feed monthly with a half-strength, all-purpose fertilizer. Pinch the stem tips often to keep the plant dense.

Common problems Plants get scraggly with age; so it's best to take cuttings and discard old plants.

Propagation You can root stem or tip cuttings in sand.

Comments Fittonias thrive in terrariums.

Related plants F. *verschaffeltii argyroneura* 'Stripes Forever', or silver-nerved fittonia, has bright white veins on very small, light green leaves.

Haworthia margaritifera
ALOEACEAE

PEARL PLANT

This small African native has spiky rosettes of upright, spotted or striped, succulent leaves. It's a great choice for a beginner, since it's practically indestructible.

Description Pearl plant forms 4-inch (10-cm) tall rosettes of fat, green leaves that are decorated with small, white, raised spots. You may occasionally see the plant produce slender stems topped with small, white blooms.

Light needs Medium light, without direct sun. Pearl plant also grows well under fluorescent lights.

Best temperatures Average room temperature.

Water and humidity needs Allow the soil to dry a bit between waterings. Water less often in winter, but don't let the soil get completely dry. Pearl plants can tolerate dry air.

Growing guidelines Grow pearl plant in cactus soil in shallow pots. Do not fertilize.

Common problems This plant is virtually trouble-free and tough to kill.

Propagation Separate offsets and pot them up.

Related plants *H. fasciata*, zebra plant, has 2-inch (5-cm) leaves that are wonderfully striped in dark green and black. *H. retusa*, cathedral window cactus, has flat, spade-shaped leaf tips windowed with pale lines.

Hedera helix
ARALIACEAE

ENGLISH IVY

English ivy leaves come in just about any shape and markings you can imagine. Train them to climb trellises or let them cascade from hanging baskets.

Description These woody vines bear green or mottled, lobed leaves in a variety of oval, pointed, and heart shapes. The young leaves tend to have the most attractive forms and colors; older leaves often lose their lobes and revert to solid color forms. The stems can climb by means of clinging roots.

Light needs Medium to high, indirect light is best, although English ivy can adapt to a range of light conditions.

Best temperatures Keep plants around 65°F (18°C) during the day and 50°F (10°C) at night, but they can tolerate lower temperatures.

Water and humidity needs Allow the soil surface to dry somewhat between waterings. English ivy appreciates misting.

Growing guidelines Grow in all-purpose mix in pots or hanging baskets or provide a trellis for climbing. Fertilize twice a year (spring and summer). Pinch off the tips of new growth to keep the plant bushy.

Common problems To control spider mites, raise humidity and rinse plant in the shower every few weeks.

Propagation Take tip cuttings any time.

Cultivars 'Filigran', filigree ivy, has green leaves with fluted edges. 'Sagittaefolia Variegata', bird's foot ivy, forms mounds of white-frosted leaves.

Hypoestes phyllostachya
ACANTHACEAE

POLKA DOT PLANT

Who could believe that something this colorful is actually real? Polka dot plant is a striking and unique addition to bright indoor gardens.

Other common names Freckleface.

Description Polka dot plant is a woody-based shrub that can grow up to 3 feet (90 cm) tall, although it is normally smaller when grown indoors. Its 2½-inch (7-cm) long, pointed, dark green leaves are liberally spotted in lavender-rose or white.

Light needs High light.

Best temperatures Average room temperature.

Water and humidity needs Allow soil surface to dry slightly between waterings.

Growing guidelines Grow in all-purpose, soil-based mix. Fertilize twice a month in spring and summer. Pinch off the shoot tips to promote bushy growth; the plant is best at about 18 inches (45 cm) tall.

Common problems The colorful leaf spots tend to fade if the plant isn't getting enough light; move it to a brighter location. Plants get leggy with age, so it is best to replace them with new plants or cut the old ones back to 1 inch (2.5 cm) tall and repot them.

Propagation Take tip cuttings, or grow new plants from seed.

Comments *H. phyllostachya* is often sold as *H. sanguinolenta*.

Maranta leuconeura
MARANTACEAE

PRAYER PLANT

Prayer plant has unique markings that look as though a rabbit left tracks down the leaves. Its leaves fold upward at night.

Other common names Rabbit tracks.
Description Prayer plant's branching stems form clumps to 12 inches (30 cm) tall, with 5-inch (12.5-cm) long, oval leaves. The bright green, satiny foliage is distinctively marked with brownish purple "rabbit tracks" on either side of the midrib. Each leaf has large, rosy pink veins and a red-purple underside.
Light needs Medium, indirect or artificial light. Avoid direct sun.
Best temperatures Warm conditions, between 60° and 70°F (16° and 21°C).
Water and humidity needs Keep the soil evenly moist through most of the year and somewhat drier in winter. Mist often and provide extra humidity.
Growing guidelines Grow prayer plant in soil-less mix. Repot into fresh mix each year during early spring. Fertilize twice a month from spring to fall; do not fertilize in winter.
Common problems Prayer plant likes fresh air, but cold drafts can lead to poor growth and a gradual decline in health.
Propagation Divide in spring.
Cultivars The variety Kerchoveana is deep green and chocolate without rosy veins; 'Variegata' has yellow and pink spots.

Monstera deliciosa
ARACEAE

SPLIT-LEAVED PHILODENDRON

These sometimes enormous and very popular houseplant vines offer spectacularly notched, perforated leaves. Sponge leaves to keep them clean.

Other common names Hurricane plant.
Description This vine grows to 30 feet (9 m) in the jungle, although it grows to 6 feet (1.8 m) indoors. The dark green leaves can reach 3 feet (90 cm) wide, with many indented notchings.
Light needs Medium to high, indirect or artificial light.
Best temperatures Warm conditions, with daytime temperatures to 85°F (29°C) and nights from 65°–70°F (18°–21°C).
Water and humidity needs Keep the plant barely moist.
Growing guidelines Grow in all-purpose mix, and provide a trellis for support. Repot as needed. Fertilize twice a year (early spring and mid-summer). Pinch back regularly to encourage side branching. To rejuvenate overgrown plants, air layer the tops and drastically cut back the remaining stems.
Common problems Split-leaved philodendron will not grow in cold temperatures. Weak growth, sparse foliage, or solid, unsplit leaves tell you that your plant is not getting enough light. It's natural for bottom leaves to drop as the plant ages.
Propagation Take leaf bud cuttings by slicing the stem into sections, each with one leaf, and placing the stem pieces into soil; or air layer stems.

Nolina recurvata
AGAVACEAE

PONYTAIL PALM

Native to Mexico, ponytail palm has a thick, swollen base that can store up to a year's supply of water. It's a good choice if you tend to forget to water!

Other common names Elephant foot palm.
Description When young, ponytail palm is just a grassy clump of narrow leaves growing from a swollen, enlarged base. As it ages, the base expands, and the plant develops a greenish brown trunk topped with a tuft of thin, leathery, strap-like, green leaves. Mature plants can reach 3 feet (90 cm) tall.
Light needs High light.
Best temperatures Average room temperature but cooler than 75°F (24°C) in winter.
Water and humidity needs Water thoroughly, then allow the soil to dry before you water again. Ponytail palm can tolerate dry air.
Growing guidelines Grow ponytail palm in a well-drained cactus mix. Wait several years between repottings. Fertilize annually in early spring.
Common problems Too little sun causes limp, pale leaves; move the plant to a brighter location. Otherwise, ponytail palm is generally easy.
Propagation Separate and repot offsets.
Comments Ponytail palm produces only one flush of growth a year in spring.

Various genera
ARECACEAE

PALMS

Palms appreciate a summer vacation outdoors; just make sure they're sheltered from direct sun. If you notice brown leaf tips, trim them off with scissors.

Description Indoor palms range in size from 3–15 feet (0.9–4.5 m), with stiff trunks and fan-like or feathery, compound leaves.

Butterfly palm (*Chrysalidocarpus lutescens*) has clustered stems and long, drooping fronds of numerous slender, yellowish-green leaflets.

Chamaedoreas (*Chamaedorea* spp.) are small palms. The popular parlor palm (*C. elegans*, also known as *Neanthe bella* or *Collinia elegans*) is a true dwarf, with 2-foot (60-cm) long, medium to light green leaves and a single, 3–4-foot (90–120-cm), dark green, ringed trunk.

Chinese fan palm (*Livistona chinensis*) has a single trunk and almost circular, bright green, shiny leaves deeply divided into narrow segments that attractively droop at the tips. It likes bright indirect light.

Clustered fishtail palm (*Caryota mitis*) has finely divided fronds with leaflets flattened and split which somewhat resemble the tail of a fish.

Kentia palm (*Howea forsterana*) is the easiest and most popular indoor palm, enduring drought and low light. It produces gorgeous, arching, dark green fronds to a height of about 7 feet (2.1 m).

Lady palm (*Rhapis excelsa*) is a small, clump-forming palm with deep green

fan-shaped fronds divided into finger-like segments. The slender, bamboo-like stems are covered with a net of dark, fibrous hair. It is slow-growing and tolerant of poor light, dust, and drought.

Miniature date palm (*Phoenix roebelenii*) will attain a height of around 5 feet (1.5 m) indoors. It has arching, dark green, feathery fronds and makes an elegant pot plant.

Light needs Medium, indirect light.

Best temperatures Average room temperature, not below 55°F (13°C).

Water and humidity needs Water abundantly while the plant is in active growth; allow the soil surface to dry just slightly between waterings. Don't let pots stand in water.

Growing guidelines Grow in a mixture of equal parts all-purpose potting soil and sandy, organic topsoil. Provide fish emulsion from late spring to early fall. Repot as needed in spring or summer. Put plants outdoors for the summer. Wash foliage frequently with a hose or in the shower.

Common problems If spider mites attack, raise humidity and spray with superior oil.

Propagation Grow new palms from seed.

Peperomia spp.
PIPERACEAE

PEPEROMIAS

Peperomias thrive in warm, bright spots with extra humidity. These compact plants come in a wide range of leaf textures and patterns.

Description Most peperomias have vining or bushy stems that usually grow to about 6 inches (15 cm) tall. Their fleshy, oval leaves may be flat and smooth, or puckered and wrinkled. Some species have plain green leaves; others may be edged or veined with cream, gray, or silver. The plants occasionally produce thin, pink stems topped with narrow, creamy white flower spikes.

Light needs High light, with some full sun (especially for variegated types); peperomias also grow well under fluorescent lights.

Best temperatures Average room temperature.

Water and humidity needs Keep evenly moist in spring and summer; allow to dry slightly between waterings in fall and winter. Extra humidity is necessary.

Growing guidelines Grow peperomias in clay pots in light, well-drained mix. Repot with fresh mix each spring. Give dilute fertilizer monthly in spring and fall.

Common problems Peperomias rot easily if you overwater them or if water stands on the leaves. Tan patches on leaves are a sign of sunburn; pinch off damaged leaves and move the plant to a spot out of direct sun.

Propagation Divide clump-forming types; take leaf or stem cuttings from upright or vining types.

Philodendron spp.
ARACEAE

PHILODENDRON

If you're nervous about growing houseplants, start with philodendrons—they're durable plants that don't take much fussing to stay looking good.

Description Philodendrons produce climbing or bushy growth that can eventually reach 9 feet (2.7 m) tall. Their stems carry thin, aerial roots and usually lobed, green leaves that can be marked with gold, red, or white. The young leaves are often not as distinctively shaped or colored as the older ones. Bushy, self-heading types of philodendron grow from a single crown near the ground. Heart-leaved philodendron (*P. scandens* subsp. *oxycardium*, also known as *P. cordatum*) is a small-leaved, silky, green vine that can trail or be trained upright. Of the bushy, self-heading types, slow-growing *P. bipinnatifidum* is best. The species has green leaves and can grow to 8 feet (2.4 m) tall; miniature cultivars are available. Red-leaf philodendron (*P. erubescens*) is a climbing species with broadly arrow-shaped, glossy green leaves attached to sturdy, red stalks. New growth, flower bracts, and the undersides of the leaves are coppery-red. The plant will need a supporting frame. *P. melanochrysum* is a slow-growing climber. It has dark green, velvety, heart-shaped leaves to 30 inches (75 cm) long with pale green veins. Elephant's ear (*P. domesticum*) is a sparsely branched climber with large, rich green, arrow-shaped leaves to 24 inches (60 cm) long with wavy margins.

Light needs Medium to high, indirect light; bushy types tolerate lower light.
Best temperatures Warm conditions, with nights around 65°–70°F (18°–21°C).
Water and humidity needs Keep the soil just moist.
Growing guidelines Philodendron grows fine in almost any mix; it will even root and grow in water! Repot at any time. Fertilize every 3 months. Aerial roots form on some varieties. These can be trained around a support, pushed into the soil or cut off. Leaves can be occasionally wiped with a damp cloth to clean them.
Common problems Direct sun can produce tan patches of sunburn on leaves; move the plant out of the sun to prevent further damage.
Propagation Take tip or stem cuttings from vining types at any time. Grow self-heading (bushy) types from seed, or separate and pot up the offsets.
Comments All parts of plant are poisonous.

Pilea spp.
URTICACEAE

PILEAS

Pileas are excellent terrarium plants. To keep them looking good, take cuttings each year to start new plants, then dispose of the old, scraggly ones.

Other common names Aluminum plant.
Description These low-growing, tropical, shrubby plants are distinguished by their textured and sometimes puckered leaves. Ferny, bright green, 12-inch (30-cm) artillery plant (*P. microphylla*) is so named because it releases its pollen in puffs. It has tiny, dense leaves on thick stems and inconspicuous greenish-yellow flowers in summer. Cat's tongue (*P. mollis*) has green-and-brown, puckered leaves. The Pan-American friendship plant (*P. involucrata*) from Peru grows 6–8 inches (15–20 cm) tall. It offers wonderful oval, quilted, chocolate-veined, hairy leaves, as well as tiny, creamy or greenish flowers on occasion. Trailing creeping Charlie (*P. nummulariifolia*) is a lovely little rooting groundcover, making it ideal for a hanging basket. The rounded, light green leaves to ¾ inch (2 cm) long have a crinkled surface and minutely toothed edges that turn slightly inwards. Aluminum plant (*P. cadieri*) is the most popular species, growing to 12 inches (30 cm) tall with silver-painted, green, oval leaves that appear quilted. Clusters of tiny, greenish flowers form at the stem tips. 'Minima' is a dwarf compact variety. Originally from China, *P. peperomioides* is a widely cultivated houseplant. It forms an

Pilea spp. continued

Plectranthus australis
LAMIACEAE

SWEDISH IVY

Swedish ivy's trailing stems make it a perfect choice for hanging baskets. Pinch off the stem tips frequently to promote full growth.

Raphidophora aurea
ARACEAE

POTHOS

Pothos is a trailing or climbing houseplant that's often confused with philodendron. It's a real survivor that can take some neglect.

erect dome-shaped plant to 12 inches (30 cm) in diameter with elongated stems and succulent, almost rounded pale green leaves like those of peperomia. From Jamaica, *P. grandifolia* produces textured, ovate, toothed leaves with pointed tips to 8 inches (20 cm) long.

Light needs Medium to high, indirect light.

Best temperatures Warm conditions, with 65°–70°F (18°–21°C) nights.

Water and humidity needs Water to moisten the soil, then let the surface dry before you water again. Provide extra humidity. Do not overwater in winter.

Growing guidelines Grow in all-purpose potting mix with added peat moss. Fertilize twice a month in spring and summer. Pinch out tips in the growing season to encourage a neat, bushy appearance.

Common problems Plants get leggy with age. Discard pilea plants each year after taking cuttings.

Propagation Take tip cuttings or divide in spring.

Description The scalloped, round, green, fleshy leaves of Swedish ivy grow along trailing stems that can reach 8 inches (20 cm) long. Occasionally, small, light purple flowers will appear.

Light needs Medium to high light.

Best temperatures Average temperature.

Water and humidity needs Keep the soil evenly moist.

Growing guidelines Grow Swedish ivy in hanging pots in all-purpose mix. Repot yearly. Fertilize twice a month from spring to fall (or less often if you don't want your plant to grow quite so fast). Pinch off the tips of new growth often.

Common problems Wash mealybugs off plants with a strong spray of water; you could also spray with insecticidal soap, superior oil, or neem. Strong sun can cause tan patches on leaves; move the plant out of direct sun to prevent further damage. Swedish ivy tends to get scraggly with age; root new plants from young stem pieces and discard the old plants.

Propagation Take tip cuttings and stick them in all-purpose potting mix to root.

Related plants *P. oertendahlii*, candle plant, has dark green, silver-veined leaves that are red underneath. It may also produce lacy white flowers.

Other common names Devil's ivy.

Description This vining plant produces long stems that can climb to 40 feet (12 m) if left unpruned. The stems will trail out of a hanging basket or climb a support, clinging with aerial roots. The leathery, heart-shaped leaves grow to 4 inches (10 cm) long. The foliage and stems are bright green and richly splashed with yellow and/or white.

Light needs High, indirect light is best, although the plant adapts to less.

Best temperatures Average temperature.

Water and humidity needs Let soil dry somewhat between waterings, especially for plants growing in low light. Avoid keeping the soil very wet or very dry.

Growing guidelines Grow pothos in a soil-based potting mix in hanging baskets or trained on wire wreath forms. Fertilize twice a year, while the plant is producing new growth. Cut the stems back if they get leggy. Wash the leaves occasionally to keep them clean.

Common problems If you notice the leaf and stem markings are fading, move the plant to a brighter spot.

Propagation Take tip cuttings any time.

Cultivars 'Marble queen' has ivory-and-white variegated leaves and stems. 'Orange moon' has apricot markings.

Rhoeo spathacea
COMMELINACEAE

MOSES-IN-A-BOAT

This plant's common name refers to the small flowers, which are cradled in boat-like bracts. But the real highlight is the colorful, two-toned foliage.

Other common names Moses-in-the-cradle.
Description Upright, lance-shaped, 8-inch (20-cm) leaves grow from a rosette to 1 foot (30 cm) tall. The foliage is dark green on the upper sides and purple underneath. At the base of the plant, small, white flowers are cradled in cupped, purple bracts.
Light needs High light with some direct sun; adapts to less light.
Best temperatures Average conditions but not over 70°F (21°C).
Water and humidity needs Water often to keep soil evenly moist while the plant is in active growth; allow to dry between waterings in winter. Provide extra humidity.
Growing guidelines Grow moses-in-a-boat in all-purpose potting mix. Repot only when the plant is really crowded in its current container. Fertilize twice a month in spring and summer.
Common problems Too little light will make the plant lanky and not as colorful. Older plants tend to look shabby; start new plants and discard the old ones.
Propagation Take offsets or divide any time; repot seedlings that appear in the pot.
Comments *R. spathacea* is also known as *R. bermudensis*.
Cultivars The leaves of 'Variegata' are striped with pale yellow.

Sansevieria trifasciata
AGAVACEAE

SNAKE PLANT

The extraordinarily striped leaves make snake plants very popular. They can look dreadful if neglected but are handsome if you give them just a little care.

Description Snake plant's tall, upright, stemless, spear-like leaves can grow to 4 feet (1.2 m) tall. The green foliage is crossbanded in darker green, yellow, white, and/or black. Plants sometimes produce tall sprays of green-white, fragrant flowers.
Light needs Plants can tolerate almost any level of light.
Best temperatures Average conditions, with 65°F (18°C) nights.
Water and humidity needs Allow the soil surface to dry between waterings in spring to fall. In winter, water only enough to prevent shriveling. Snake plant endures drought well.
Growing guidelines Grow snake plant in cactus or all-purpose mix in a well-drained pot. This slow-growing plant can wait 3–4 years between repottings. Fertilize infrequently, perhaps once a year.
Common problems Cold temperatures can cause leaf edges to turn brown.
Propagation Divide plants at any time, or separate and pot up offsets. Propagate green-leaved types by leaf cuttings: remove a leaf, slice it crosswise into 3-inch (7.5-cm) sections, and insert the bottom side of each section into moist sand. (Leaf cuttings from yellow-edged types will root, but the plants they produce will be all green.)

Saxifraga stolonifera
SAXIFRAGACEAE

STRAWBERRY BEGONIA

Show off strawberry begonia's trailing habit by growing it in a hanging basket. 'Tricolor' has green leaves marked with cream, pink, rose, or white.

Other common names Mother-of-thousands, strawberry geranium.
Description This creeping plant grows in compact rosettes to about 4 inches (10 cm) tall. The leaves are silver-veined, dark green above and pinkish purple underneath. Clusters of small, white flowers appear on 9-inch (22.5-cm) stalks. The thread-like stolons, reminiscent of strawberry-plant runners, carry baby plantlets.
Light needs Medium light.
Best temperatures Cool conditions, around 50°–60°F (10°–16°C); can take temperatures to 72°F (27°C).
Water and humidity needs Provide abundant water to keep the soil evenly moist from spring through fall; in winter, allow soil surface to dry between waterings.
Growing guidelines Grow in all-purpose mix with added compost. Fertilize monthly from spring to fall.
Common problems Plants tend to get scraggly as they age; repot plantlets and discard the old plants.
Propagation Pot plantlets in a mix of peat moss and sand; repot them into all-purpose mix when they've rooted.
Comments Strawberry begonia can also grow outdoors to form a groundcover as far north as Zone 5.

Sedum morganianum
CRASSULACEAE

BURRO'S TAIL

A basket of burro's tail adds a unique accent to a sunny window. To keep the trailing stems full, hang the plant where it won't be disturbed.

Other common names Donkey tail.
Description Burro's tail offers succulent, grayish blue-green, 1-inch (2.5-cm) leaves densely strung on hanging stems to 4 feet (1.2 m) long. Coral to red flowers sometimes appear.
Light needs High light; can tolerate some direct sun.
Best temperatures Average temperature.
Water and humidity needs Keep moderately moist in spring to fall; in winter, water only to prevent shriveling. Burro's tail tolerates dry air.
Growing guidelines Grow burro's tail in all-purpose mix with sand added for better drainage. Repot only when absolutely necessary, since the leaves break easily when the plant is handled. Fertilize three times a year: in early spring, late spring, and late summer.
Common problems Roots rot if you provide too much water; otherwise, these plants are fairly trouble-free.
Propagation Tip or leaf cuttings root easily in damp sand.
Comments An easy, slow-growing conversation piece.

Soleirolia soleirolii
URTICACEAE

BABY'S TEARS

The tiny, oval leaves of this little creeper are delicate enough to have inspired the name "baby's tears." It's an excellent groundcover for terrariums.

Other common names Irish moss.
Description Baby's tears grows in creeping, dense mats to 4 inches (10 cm) tall. The tiny, juicy, green stems and leaves can become nicely mounded.
Light needs Medium light, with no direct sun.
Best temperatures Average temperature.
Water and humidity needs Water often to keep the soil evenly moist. Extra humidity is a must; mist plants often.
Growing guidelines Grow baby's tears in a mix of peat moss and soil, with no lime. Rainwater is beneficial. Fertilize infrequently, perhaps just once a year. Trimming plants with scissors encourages new growth.
Common problems The center of the plant will turn brown if the soil dries out or if the plant gets direct sun.
Propagation It's easy to divide the clumps. You can also grow baby's tears from cuttings.
Comments Also known as *Helxine soleirolii.*

Spathiphyllum hybrids
ARACEAE

PEACE LILY

Peace lily is popular for its graceful, shiny, green leaves, as well as its curious, hooded flower spikes. This tolerant plant adjusts to many conditions.

Other common names Spathe flower.
Description Peace lily grows to 2 feet (60 cm) tall, with sword-like leaves. The plant blooms occasionally throughout the year, first in white, then turning green. The flowers can last for 6 weeks.
Light needs Low to medium, indirect light.
Best temperatures Warm to average conditions (around 65°–70°F [18°–21°C]).
Water and humidity needs Keep the soil evenly moist. Provide extra humidity.
Growing guidelines This easy grower thrives in all-purpose potting mix enriched with compost or other organic material. Fertilize twice a month. Repot in early spring as needed. Provide monthly showers to keep the leaves clean.
Common problems Too much light actually inhibits bloom. If you want flowers but none are appearing, try moving your plant to a slightly darker spot. Too much fertilizer or too little water can cause brown leaf tips; keep the soil evenly moist and try fertilizing only every other month.
Propagation Remove and repot offsets, or divide the clumps in spring.
Related plants *S. wallisii,* at 12 inches (30 cm), is a more compact, spring to late-summer bloomer.

Syngonium podophyllum
ARACEAE

SYNGONIUM

Syngonium has lovely, arrow-shaped leaves on climbing or trailing stems. The species has plain green foliage, but there are several variegated cultivars.

Other common names Nephthytis.
Description Syngonium's long-stalked, green leaves grow to 1 foot (30 cm) long and are arrow-shaped when young. They can climb or trail, with vining stems up to 15 feet (4.5 m) long.
Light needs Medium light.
Best temperatures Average room temperature (60°–70°F [16°–21°C]).
Water and humidity needs Water green-leaved types often so the soil stays evenly moist. Keep variegated forms slightly dry for best coloration.
Growing guidelines Grow syngonium in all-purpose potting mix in a hanging basket, or give it a wooden slab to climb. Prune frequently to promote the growth of young, arrow-shaped leaves.
Common problems Mealybugs may be a problem. If the plant is badly infested, cut the whole thing back to 1 inch (2.5 cm); otherwise, knock the pests off with a strong spray of water, or spray the plant with insecticidal soap, superior oil, or neem. If new growth is spindly, give the plant more light. Leaf markings tend to fade as the plant gets older or if it gets too much fertilizer; remove green reverted leaves.
Propagation You can grow new plants from cuttings.

Tolmiea menziesii
SAXIFRAGACEAE

PIGGYBACK PLANT

Piggyback plant is a favorite for its unique growth habit. Try it in a hanging basket to show off the baby plantlets that form at the base of older leaves.

Other common names Pickaback.
Description Piggyback plant grows in rosettes to 12 inches (30 cm) tall and 18 inches (45 cm) wide. Its hairy, scalloped, green leaves grow to 5 inches (12.5 cm) wide. New plantlets form where the leaf stalk meets the blade.
Light needs Medium to low indirect light.
Best temperatures Prefers cool conditions (50°–60°F [10°–16°C]) but will take average room temperature.
Water and humidity needs Water and mist frequently in spring to fall. Provide extra humidity.
Growing guidelines Grow in hanging baskets in all-purpose potting mix. Repot in spring. Fertilize twice a month in spring and summer. Wash the plant off in the shower every month or two.
Common problems Knock mealybugs off the plant with a strong spray of water, or spray the plant with insecticidal soap or neem. Warm, dry conditions may encourage spider mites, so move the plant to a cooler spot and raise the humidity. Older plants tend to look scraggly; discard them and start with new ones.
Propagation Root plantlets by pinning the parent leaf to the soil; when rooted, dig up the plantlet and pot it up separately.

Zebrina pendula
COMMELINACEAE

WANDERING JEW

Wandering Jew's green and purple iridescence, along with its ability to root quickly from cuttings, has long made this Mexican vine a favorite.

Other common names Inch plant.
Description This trailing vine has 2-inch (5-cm), green leaves colored or striped with red, purple, yellow, pink, and/or silver.
Light needs Medium to high light, but not direct sun.
Best temperatures Average conditions during the day with cool nights (50°–60°F [10°–16°C]).
Water and humidity needs Allow the soil surface to dry a bit between waterings. Provide extra humidity.
Growing guidelines Grow wandering Jew in all-purpose potting mix. Provide dilute fertilizer twice a month. Pinch back new growth often to keep the plant full.
Common problems If your plant's leaves are fading, try moving it to a brighter spot. Older plants tend to get scraggly; take cuttings to start new plants and discard the old ones.
Propagation Cuttings root easily. Pot several together, arranging them around the rim and also in the center of the container, to create a bushy new plant.
Comments Wandering Jew is easy to grow. Variegated types need higher light.
Cultivars 'Purpusii' has dark, greenish red leaves.

A Guide to Popular Container Plants

Almost any plant that you could enjoy in the garden will also grow just fine in a container. The key to success is providing the right growing conditions. To get you started, we've included this guide to a wide variety of garden plants for containers, including perennials, annuals, bulbs, groundcovers, ornamental grasses, trees and shrubs, vines, edible plants, and herbs. Individual entries are arranged alphabetically by botanical name, with the common name displayed prominently. If you don't know the botanical name, look up the common name in the index, and you'll be directed to the right place. Each entry provides a color photograph and a description of the plant. You'll also find information on the height and spread, flower color and season, the best climate and site, along with growing guidelines. Refer to these encyclopedic entries when you're choosing your plants, and again through the season to make sure you're giving them the best care possible, and you'll enjoy great results with your container gardens.

Achillea tomentosa
ASTERACEAE

WOOLLY YARROW

Woolly yarrow is a low-growing plant suited to large containers. Combine in large pots with other drought-tolerant perennials such as coreopsis (Coreopsis spp.) and butterfly weed (Asclepias tuberosa).

Description Woolly yarrow forms spreading mats of aromatic, hairy, gray-green foliage. The leaves may be evergreen in warm climates. Small flowers bloom in flat, 1-inch (2.5-cm) clusters.
Height and spread Height of foliage to 2 inches (5 cm); spread to 1 foot (30 cm). Flower height 6–8 inches (15–20 cm).
Flower color and season Vivid yellow flowers bloom from early summer to midsummer.
Best climate and site Zones 3–7. Grows poorly in hot, humid areas. Full sun. Plant in a well-drained container mix.
Growing guidelines Set plants 1 foot (30 cm) apart in spring or fall. Woolly yarrow is ideal for low-maintenance containers. Cut down the flowering stems after bloom to keep the planting neat and to encourage new flowers. Propagate the species by seed or division and the cultivars by division in spring.
Possible problems No serious problems.
Other common names Milfoil.

Aconitum x bicolor
RANUNCULACEAE

BICOLOR MONKSHOOD

Bicolor monkshood is a showy, fall-flowering perennial that makes a pretty show in a container. Bicolor monkshood thrives in climates with cool summer nights and warm days with low humidity.

Description Lush, five- to seven-lobed, dissected leaves clothe sturdy stems topped with dense flower spikes. Plants grow from thickened, spidery roots. All parts of the plant are poisonous if eaten. The foliage is attractive before flowering.
Height and spread Height 3–4 feet (90–120 cm); spread 2 feet (60 cm). Habit is variable, but generally open and vase-shaped, especially in shade.
Flower color and season Dark blue or two-toned flowers bloom in late summer and fall.
Best climate and site Zones 3–7. Full sun or light shade; afternoon shade is advised in warmer zones. Plant in an all-purpose container mix.
Growing guidelines Space plants 2–3 feet (60–90 cm) apart, with the crowns just below the surface. Divide in fall or early spring only if plants become overcrowded and bloom diminishes.
Possible problems Keep container mix moist. Not suitable for hot, humid areas.
Other common names Wolfsbane, aconite.
Comments Combine in a large container with other late-summer- and fall-blooming perennials like *Helenium* spp. and grasses.

Aconitum carmichaelii
RANUNCULACEAE

AZURE MONKSHOOD

Azure monkshood is a graceful plant with lush, three-lobed, dissected leaves, sturdy stems, and hooded flowers. All parts of the plant are poisonous.

Description Azure monkshood is one of the most popular monkshoods because of its beautiful, deep violet-blue flowers in dense spikes. The leaves are thick, glossy, and deeply veined and grow on woody stems.
Height and spread Height 2–3 feet (60–90 cm); spread 2 feet (60 cm).
Flower color and season The blue flowers bloom in late summer and fall.
Best climate and site Zones 3–7. Prefers climates with cool summer nights and warm days with low humidity. Full sun to light shade; afternoon shade in warmer zones. Plant in an all-purpose container mix.
Growing guidelines Azure monkshood dislikes disturbance once established. Plant with the crowns just below the surface. Take care not to damage the brittle roots. Divide if plants become overcrowded. Divide crowns in fall or early spring. Replant strong, healthy divisions into new containers in potting mix that has been enriched with organic matter.
Possible problems Keep container mix moist. Not suitable for hot, humid areas.
Comments Plant in a large container with orange coneflowers (*Rudbeckia* spp.) and ornamental grasses for striking effect.

Actaea alba
RANUNCULACEAE

WHITE BANEBERRY

Mature clumps of white baneberry in full fruit are stunning in the fall. The red-stalked berries are poisonous to people but savored by birds.

Description White baneberries are shrubby, woodland plants noted for their showy, fall fruit. The spring flowers lack petals and are composed of a fuzzy cluster of broad stamens. The blooms are carried on sturdy stems above deeply dissected, compound leaves. The oval, white fruits are ¼ inch (6 mm) long and borne on showy stalks. Plants grow from a woody crown with wiry, yellow roots.
Height and spread Height 2–4 feet (60–120 cm); mature clumps may reach 3 feet (90 cm) across.
Flower color and season The fuzzy, white flowers bloom in spring; the white berries occur in late summer to fall.
Best climate and site Zones 3–9. Partial to full shade. Plant in an all-purpose container mix enriched with compost.
Growing guidelines Grow in large containers and top-dress with compost or shredded leaves in spring or fall. Plants seldom need division. Sow seed outdoors in early fall to midfall after removing the pulp.
Possible problems Container mix must be kept moist throughout the growing season or plants will decline.
Comments In fall, the berried plants look terrific with ferns, cardinal flower (*Lobelia cardinalis*), and monkshoods (*Aconitum* spp.).

Ajuga reptans
LAMIACEAE

AJUGA

The short, spinach-like leaves of this excellent, low-growing perennial spread rapidly to form a solid carpet. Many colorful cultivars of ajuga are available.

Description The leaves of ajuga are usually dark green; cultivars are available with purple, bronze, or variegated foliage. Ajuga is evergreen in warm areas but tends to turn brown by midwinter in cold climates. The plant sends up spikes of ¼-inch (6-mm) blue or purple flowers.
Height and spread Height of foliage to 3 inches (7.5 cm); spread unlimited. Flower height to about 6 inches (15 cm).
Flower color and season Blue or purple flowers bloom in spring or early summer.
Best climate and site Zones 3–8. Full sun to partial shade (shade is especially important in hot climates). Grow in a well-drained, all-purpose container mix.
Growing guidelines Set plants about 12–15 inches (30–37.5 cm) apart anytime during the growing season. They need little maintenance. Don't give them fertilizer or the lush growth will be prone to fungal disease. Propagate by division anytime during the growing season.
Possible problems Bronze and variegated forms require sun to color well.
Other common names Common bugleweed.
Comments Grow in a large, shallow container underneath a small tree like a Japanese maple (*Acer palmatum*).

Alchemilla mollis
ROSACEAE

LADY'S-MANTLE

Grow lady's-mantle for its soft, rounded leaves and tall-stalked clusters of chartreuse blooms. The plant is especially pretty when growing in a cool, moist, partly shady spot.

Description Lady's-mantle's grayish, rounded, lobed, hairy leaves grow on long stems in a clump. Each clump produces starry, 2–3-inch (5–7.5-cm) wide sprays of greenish-yellow flowers.
Height and spread Grows to a height and spread of about 16 inches (40 cm).
Flower color and season Greenish-yellow flowers bloom in late spring.
Best climate and site Zones 3–9. Partial shade. Grow in an all-purpose container mix with added compost. Keep evenly moist, especially during hot weather.
Growing guidelines Set plants 8 inches (20 cm) apart; three clumps together make a nice show. Remove the flowers before they go to seed to prevent rampant spreading. Divide clumps as needed in early winter or early spring. Lady's-mantle also self-sows if you don't remove the flowers.
Possible problems Lady's-mantles may suffer during hot weather. It is especially important to keep the container mix moist during that time.
Comments Grow lady's-mantle in a large, shallow container under a Japanese maple (*Acer palmatum*), or combine it with other perennials, such as cranesbills (*Geranium* spp.) and hostas.

Alstroemeria aurea
ALSTROEMERIACEAE

PERUVIAN LILY

Peruvian lilies have tall, leafy stems crowned by open clusters of flaring, saucer-shaped flowers. The gray-green leaves are narrow and pointed.

Description This is the most commonly grown and popular species of *Alstroemeria*. Its heads of showy orange or yellow flowers are flared with brown on the upper petals and tipped with green. The lance-shaped leaves are narrow and twisted.

Height and spread Height 2–3 feet (60–90 cm); spread 2 feet (60 cm).

Flower color and season Orange or yellow flowers bloom throughout summer.

Best climate and site Zones 7–10. Full sun to partial shade; protect from strong winds. Grow in an all-purpose, well-drained container mix.

Growing guidelines Plant dormant roots in early spring or fall. Growth begins early in the season, and plants may be damaged by late frost. Mulch with organic matter in fall to avoid frost heaving or move pots to a protected position. Achieves best performance after the third year. Divide clumps in early spring or fall. Take care not to damage the brittle roots. Sow fresh seed indoors after 4–6 weeks of cold (35°–40°F/ 4°–5°C), moist stratification.

Possible problems Do not overwater in winter while dormant or tubers may rot.

Comments Peruvian lilies' flowering season makes them invaluable container plants. Combine with blue Dutch irises.

Amsonia tabernaemontana
APOCYNACEAE

WILLOW BLUE STAR

Willow blue star is a tough, shrubby plant with lance-shaped leaves, stout stems, and terminal clusters of tiny blue flowers.

Description Willow blue star has stiff 2–3-foot (60–90-cm) stems, topped by clusters of steel blue, ½-inch (12-mm), five-petaled, starry flowers. The lance-shaped leaves are narrow to elliptical.

Height and spread Height 1–3 feet (30–90 cm); spread 3 feet (90 cm).

Flower color and season Blue flowers in spring, with some secondary shoots blooming in early summer.

Best climate and site Zones 3–9. Full sun to partial shade. Plant in a large container in all-purpose container mix. Heat- and cold-tolerant.

Growing guidelines Plants in full shade may be floppy. If necessary, prune stems back to 6–8 inches (15–20 cm) after flowering. Divide plants in early spring or fall. Take 4–6-inch (10–15-cm) stem cuttings in early summer. Sow ripe seed outdoors in fall or indoors after soaking in hot water for several hours before planting. Mulch with organic matter to keep the container mix evenly moist.

Possible problems No serious problems.

Other common names Willow amsonia, blue dogbane.

Comments Combine with orange Peruvian lilies (*Alstroemeria aurea*) or yellow marigolds for a striking display.

Anaphalis triplinervis
ASTERACEAE

THREE-VEINED EVERLASTING

Unlike most silver-leaved plants, three-veined everlasting grows well in moist container mix. The papery, white flowers and soft leaves add bright spots to late-summer containers.

Description Three-veined everlasting has soft, silver-gray leaves and papery, white, double flowers that dry right on the plant and persist for weeks. The flowers have dark centers and are borne in open, flattened clusters. Plants form broad clumps from creeping stems.

Height and spread Height 1–1½ feet (30–45 cm); spread 1 foot (30 cm).

Flower color and season Plants produce a profusion of white flowers in July, August, and September.

Best climate and site Zones 3–8. Full sun to partial shade. Plant three-veined everlasting in all-purpose container mix.

Growing guidelines Divide the vigorous clumps every 2–4 years. Cuttings root freely in early summer. Prune back hard in winter.

Possible problems No serious problems.

Other common names Pearly everlasting.

Comments Combine with the vertical leaves of Siberian iris (*Iris sibirica*). Ornamental grasses are excellent companion plants, as are astilbes, daylilies, and garden phlox (*Phlox paniculata*).

Anchusa azurea
BORAGINACEAE

ITALIAN BUGLOSS

Italian bugloss has lush, oblong leaves covered in stiff hair. The long branches bear terminal clusters of small, blue flowers.

Description This delightful plant, which grows wild around the Mediterranean, has lance-shaped, gray-green foliage. It has tiers of brilliant blue, ¾-inch (18-mm), five-petaled flowers.
Height and spread Height 2–5 feet (60–150 cm); spread 2 feet (60 cm).
Flower color and season Blue flowers bloom in late spring.
Best climate and site Zones 3–8. Full sun to light shade. Plant in a large container in all-purpose container mix.
Growing guidelines Choose a named cultivar for better performance and longevity. Cut plants back after blooming to encourage more flowers. Divide every 2–3 years to keep plants vigorous. Divide clumps after flowering. Replant strong, healthy divisions into fresh container mix. Take root cuttings in early spring. Plants freely self-sow. Transplant during winter.
Possible problems In hot climates plant in partial shade to maintain flower color. Otherwise no serious problems.
Other common names Alkanet, summer forget-me-not.
Comments Plant with bright flowers such as shasta daisies (*Leucanthemum* x *superbum*) and yarrows (*Achillea* spp.).

Anemone tomentosa 'Robustissima'
RANUNCULACEAE

GRAPE-LEAVED ANEMONE

Grape-leaved anemone lights up the fall garden with pink flowers atop tall stems. Once established, plants spread by creeping underground stems to form broad clumps.

Description Grape-leaved anemone produces clouds of fragile, soft rosy pink flowers atop slender stems. The foliage is mostly basal, with three-lobed, thrice-divided, hairy leaves. Plants grow from thick tuberous roots.
Height and spread Height 3–5 feet (90–150 cm); spread 2–3 feet (60–90 cm).
Flower color and season Pink flowers bloom in summer and fall.
Best climate and site Zones 3–8. Sun or light shade. In warmer zones, protect plants from hot afternoon sun. Plant in a large container in all-purpose container mix.
Growing guidelines Divide overgrown clumps in spring if bloom was sparse the previous fall. Propagate by division or sow fresh seed outdoors in summer or fall. Provide a winter mulch for plants in Northern gardens.
Possible problems No serious problems.
Other species *A.* x *hybrida*, Japanese anemone, is similar but grows taller and comes in a variety of colors with single or double flowers. Zones 5–8.
Comments For fall displays, combine in a large container with garden phlox (*Phlox paniculata*), asters, and monkshoods (*Aconitum* spp.).

Aquilegia x *hybrida*
RANUNCULACEAE

HYBRID COLUMBINE

Hybrid columbines are graceful plants with curious, nodding flowers. The blooms may be bicolored or of a single color.

Description Each flower has five spurred petals surrounded by five petal-like sepals. The spurs may be ½–4 inches (12–100 mm) long. The ferny foliage has many fan-shaped leaflets. Plants grow from a thick taproot.
Height and spread Height 2–3 feet (60–90 cm); spread 1–2 feet (30–60 cm).
Flower color and season Flowers in many shades, including yellow, red, purple, white, or pink, bloom in early summer.
Best climate and site Zones 3–9. Full sun or partial shade. Plant in a well-drained, all-purpose container mix.
Growing guidelines Hybrid columbines self-sow prolifically, so new plants are always developing. Sow seed outdoors in spring or summer; indoors, place pot-sown seeds in a refrigerator for 4–6 weeks before moving them to room temperature.
Possible problems Leafminers create pale tunnels and blotches in the leaves. Remove and destroy damaged foliage. In severe cases spray weekly with insecticidal soap. Borers cause the plant to collapse. Remove and destroy all portions of affected plants.
Other common names Granny's bonnets.
Comments Combine with spring and early-summer perennials, tulips, and daffodils. In light shade, grow them with wildflowers, ferns, and hostas.

Argyranthemum frutescens
ASTERACEAE

MARGUERITE

Marguerites have ferny foliage covered with dainty daisies almost all summer. They are perennial in warm climates, but grown as annuals north of Zone 9.

Description This shallow-rooted, shrubby plant has bright green or bluish leaves and abundant, daisy-like, 2-inch (5-cm) blooms. It is often covered in a mass of flowers for a long period, if spent blooms are removed.
Height and spread Grows to about 3 feet (90 cm) tall; spread 4 feet (120 cm).
Flower color and season White, pink, or yellow flowers bloom from spring to fall, and also in winter.
Best climate and site Zones 7–10. Full sun. Plant in a large container in all-purpose container mix.
Growing guidelines Keep container mix evenly moist. Fertilize twice a month. Prune plants lightly every month or two for best flowering. Take cuttings anytime.
Possible problems If leafminers are a problem, remove and destroy infested leaves and spray with insecticidal soap.
Other common names Paris daisy.
Comments Large-flowered types are not as prolific as those with small blooms. You can bring pots of marguerites indoors for the winter and move them back outdoors the following spring. Marguerites combine well with many other sun-loving plants, including verbenas and dusty millers (*Senecio cineraria*).

Armeria maritima
PLUMBAGINACEAE

THRIFT

Thrift forms dense tufts of grass-like, gray-green, evergreen leaves. The taller bloom stalks arise from the centers of the tightly packed rosettes.

Description Native in the northern hemisphere, thrift has a mound-like mass of narrow, dark green leaves and dense flower heads of small, pink flowers crowded into rounded 1-inch (2.5-cm) heads.
Height and spread Height 10–14 inches (25–35 cm); spread 8–10 inches (20–25 cm).
Flower color and season Pink flowers bloom in spring and summer.
Best climate and site Zones 4–8. Full sun. Prefers cool nights and low humidity. Plant in an all-purpose container mix.
Growing guidelines Drought-tolerant once established. Tolerates air-borne salt; perfect for seaside gardens. Divide clumps in early spring or fall. Sow seed indoors in winter on a warm (70°F/21°C) seedbed.
Possible problems No serious problems.
Other common names Common thrift, sea pink.
Cultivars 'Alba' has white flowers on 5-inch (12.5-cm) stems. 'Dusseldorf Pride' has wine-red flowers on 6–8-inch (15–20-cm) stems. 'Robusta' has 3-inch (7.5-cm), pink flower heads on 12–15-inch (30–37.5-cm) stems.
Comments Combine with ageratum or ornamental grasses for a pretty display.

Asclepias tuberosa
ASCLEPIADACEAE

BUTTERFLY WEED

The bright flowers of butterfly weed are perfect for container plantings. The plants can even tolerate seaside conditions. The sap is poisonous.

Description Butterflies adore the masses of brilliant orange flowers that crown the mounded, shrub-like clumps of butterfly weed in summer. The fuzzy, lance-shaped leaves densely clothe sturdy stems that arise from a thick, deep-seated taproot.
Height and spread Height 2–3 feet (60–90 cm); spread 2 feet (60 cm).
Flower color and season The orange flowers open in profusion in May and June. The seedpods explode in the fall, releasing clouds of silken parachutes carrying the flattened seeds aloft.
Best climate and site Zones 3–9. Full sun or light shade. Plant in all-purpose container mix. Plants tolerate seaside conditions.
Growing guidelines Established plants are extremely drought-tolerant and thrive for years with little care. Take tip cuttings in late spring or early summer; they root quickly. Sow fresh seed outdoors directly into containers.
Possible problems No serious problems.
Other common names Milkweed.
Other species *A. speciosa* has deep pink and white flowers. It grows to 3 feet (90 cm) and has oval leaves. Zones 2–9.
Comments Combine in large containers with blue and purple flowers such as sages (*Salvia* spp.) and lavenders (*Lavandula* spp.).

Aster x frikartii
ASTERACEAE

FRIKART'S ASTER

Frikart's aster produces open clusters of flowers on loosely branched stems. Plants grow from short, slow-creeping rhizomes with fibrous roots.

Description These vibrant, fragrant, lavender-blue, 2½-inch (6-cm) daisies with bright yellow centers provide a constant source of flowers for floral arrangements.
Height and spread Height 2–3 feet (60–90 cm); spread 2–3 feet (60–90 cm).
Flower color and season Lavender-blue flowers bloom from midsummer to fall.
Best climate and site Zones 6–8; in Zone 4 place under cover in winter or mulch with leaf mold. Full sun to light shade. Grow in all-purpose container mix.
Growing guidelines Frikart's aster may be short-lived. Clumps spread slowly. Divide plants as necessary in spring or fall. Take stem cuttings in spring. Divide in early spring or fall.
Possible problems Plant in well-drained container mix to deter root rot. Don't overwater during winter.
Other species *A. lateriflorus* reaches a height of 4 feet (120 cm) with small leaves which turn copper-purple in fall when the lilac flowers appear. Zones 2–9.
Comments Combine Frikart's aster with late-summer and fall perennials garden phlox (*Phlox paniculata*), coneflowers (*Rudbeckia* spp.), and ornamental grasses.

Aster novae-angliae
ASTERACEAE

NEW ENGLAND ASTER

New England aster is a tall, stately plant with hairy stems and clasping, lance-shaped leaves. Most selections are best planted in large pots. There are many different cultivars in a variety of colors.

Description New England aster grows in vigorous clumps. The lavender to purple, 1½–2-inch (3.5–5-cm) flowers have bright yellow centers.
Height and spread Height 3–6 feet (90–180 cm); spread 3 feet (90 cm). Matures into broad clumps.
Flower color and season The mostly lavender to purple flowers bloom from summer through fall. Flowers may vary in color from white to pink and rose.
Best climate and site Zones 3–8. Full sun to light shade. Plant in an all-purpose container mix.
Growing guidelines Clumps become quite large with age. Divide every 3–4 years in spring. Plants may need staking. Take 4–6-inch (10–15-cm) stem cuttings in late spring or early summer. Divide in early spring or fall.
Possible problems Powdery mildew turns leaves dull gray. Thin stems to promote air circulation. Dust plants with sulfur.
Cultivars 'Purple Dome' is a dwarf selection with royal purple flowers on 2-foot (60-cm), late-flowering clumps.
Comments Plant in large pots with ornamental grasses for an arresting effect.

Astilbe x arendsii
SAXIFRAGACEAE

ASTILBE

Astilbes have showy flower clusters and ferny, dissected leaves with shiny, broad leaflets. The emerging spring shoots are often tinged with red.

Description The foliage of astilbe often has a coppery tinge. The upright, often-plumed flower clusters bear tightly packed, fuzzy blooms in a range of colors.
Height and spread Height 2–4 feet (60–120 cm); spread 2–3 feet (60–90 cm).
Flower color and season Flowers, ranging from red through pink to white, bloom in spring and early summer.
Best climate and site Zones 3–9. Full to partial shade. Grow in an all-purpose container mix enriched with compost. Dry container mix results in shriveled foliage.
Growing guidelines Astilbes benefit from an annual application of balanced organic fertilizer. Divide clumps every 3–4 years and replant into container mix that has been enriched with organic matter. Keep plants well watered. Propagate true species by sowing fresh seed outdoors in summer or early fall. Propagate cultivars by division in spring or fall only.
Possible problems Spider mites may be a problem in warm areas. Spray with insecticidal soap. Control root rot with good drainage and good air circulation.
Other common names False spirea.
Comments Pots may be placed in the shallows of ponds during summer but remove to a drier position in winter.

Astilbe chinensis var. *pumila*
SAXIFRAGACEAE

DWARF CHINESE ASTILBE

The ferny leaves of dwarf Chinese astilbe form in elegant, spreading clumps that are attractive from spring through fall. The pink, summer flower plumes are an added bonus.

Description This dwarf astilbe spreads slowly but steadily with attractive, fern-like, shiny leaves. Plumes of flowers—rosy pink with a hint of blue—grow on spikes above the foliage.

Height and spread Height of foliage 8–12 inches (20–30 cm); spread 1–2 feet (30–60 cm). Flower stalks to 1½ feet (45 cm) tall.

Flower color and season Pinkish-blue flowers bloom in mid- to late summer.

Best climate and site Zones 5–8. Partial shade; grows in full sun in cool-summer climates. Plant in all-purpose container mix.

Growing guidelines Set plants 1–2 feet (30–60 cm) apart during the growing season. Work plenty of compost or other organic matter into the container mix before planting to hold moisture and add nutrients. Propagate by division in spring or fall.

Possible problems Slugs and snails may be a problem; trap pests under cabbage leaves (destroy trapped slugs daily).

Other common names Chinese astilbe.

Comments Astilbe flowers dry well and are good for winter arrangements. Combine them with hostas.

Astrantia major
APIACEAE

MASTERWORT

Masterwort is a trouble-free perennial that thrives in cool-summer areas. Its button-like flower heads are surrounded by starry, pointed bracts.

Description Masterwort is a showy perennial with bold, deeply lobed leaves rising directly from a stout, fibrous-rooted crown. Leafy, branched flower stalks rise from the center of the clumps. The flower heads are surrounded by stiff bracts that remain after the flowers fade, prolonging the display.

Height and spread Height 2–3 feet (30–60 cm), spread 1–2 feet (30–60 cm).

Flower color and season Pink or white, daisy-like flowers bloom in early to late summer; reblooms frequently if deadheaded. The foliage is attractive all season.

Best climate and site Zones 6–9. Will tolerate full sun, as long as the roots are kept moist. Grow in an all-purpose container mix.

Growing guidelines Sow fresh seed outdoors in late summer. Propagate by division in early spring.

Possible problems Leaves will burn and dry out if insufficient water is given.

Other species *A. maxima* is a species that reaches a height of 3 feet (90 cm). It has pink flowers and bracts.

Comments Grow with astilbe or hostas. Pots may be placed in the shallows of ponds.

Aubrieta deltoidea
BRASSICACEAE

ROCK CRESS

Rock cress is a low, mounding, spring-blooming plant with weak stems clothed in sparsely toothed, evergreen leaves.

Description Rock cress is a profusely flowering plant. Its flowers appear in loose clusters held above the foliage. The four-petaled, ¾-inch (18-mm) flowers may be single or double. The grayish-green, downy leaves form a spreading mat which can be invasive if not trimmed.

Height and spread Height 6–8 inches (15–20 cm); spread 8–12 inches (20–30 cm).

Flower color and season The white, rose, or purple flowers bloom in early spring.

Best climate and site Zones 4–8. Full sun to light shade. Grow in a well-drained, all-purpose container mix.

Growing guidelines Plants tend to flop after flowering. Shear clumps to promote compact growth and to encourage repeat bloom. Divide in fall. Take stem cuttings after flowering. Sow seed indoors or outdoors from spring to fall.

Possible problems Do not overwater and plant in well-drained container mix to avoid root rot, especially where nighttime temperatures are high.

Cultivars 'Aurea Variegata' has yellow-variegated leaves and blue-violet flowers. 'Carnival' produces a profusion of violet flowers. 'Royal Blue' has dark blue flowers.

Comments Rock cress looks good in hanging baskets or urns.

Aurinia saxatilis
BRASSICACEAE

BASKET-OF-GOLD

Basket-of-gold produces mounds of 6-inch (15-cm), oblong, gray-green leaves from a thick crown. Hairy leaves and deep roots help the plant endure dry container mix and warm temperatures.

Description Basket-of-gold is a small, mounding perennial with hairy, gray-green leaves. The yellow flowers have four rounded petals and are carried in upright, branched clusters.
Height and spread Height 10–12 inches (25–30 cm); spread 1 foot (30 cm).
Flower color and season The brilliant yellow flowers bloom in early spring.
Best climate and site Zones 3–7. Full sun. Avoid excessively hot and humid climates. Plant in a well-drained, all-purpose container mix. Tolerates hot, dry conditions.
Growing guidelines Clumps spread by creeping stems and may flop after flowering. Cut stems back by two thirds after flowering to encourage compact growth. Divide in fall. Take stem cuttings in spring or fall. Sow seed in fall.
Possible problems High humidity will encourage root rot.
Other common names Yellow alyssum.
Cultivars 'Citrinum' has lemon-yellow flowers. 'Compactum' forms tight clumps only 8 inches (20 cm) tall. 'Sunny Border Apricot' has peach-colored flowers.
Comments Combine with rock cresses (*Aubrieta* spp.) and pinks (*Dianthus* spp.).

Baptisia australis
FABACEAE

BLUE FALSE INDIGO

Combine blue false indigo in large containers with tall grasses for striking effect. It forms dense, rounded mounds that reach shrub-like proportions.

Description The stout, branching stems bear 1–3-inch (2.5–7.5-cm), three-lobed, blue-green leaves. The 1-inch (2.5-cm) lupine-like flowers are carried in narrow, open clusters. Plants grow from a thick, deep taproot.
Height and spread Height 2–4 feet (60–120 cm); spread 3–4 feet (90–120 cm).
Flower color and season The deep blue flowers bloom in spring and early summer. The foliage looks lovely all season, and the dried pods persist well into the winter.
Best climate and site Zones 3–9. Full sun or partial shade. Grow in an all-purpose container mix.
Growing guidelines Space the young plants 3–4 feet (90–120 cm) apart. Division is seldom necessary except for propagation; then divide clumps in fall using a sharp knife or shears. Keep at least one eye (bud) per division. Take tip cuttings after flowering or sow fresh seed outdoors in summer.
Possible problems No serious problems.
Other common names Baptisia.
Other species *B. alba* is slightly taller, with bluish-gray foliage and white flowers.
Comments Combine with Siberian iris (*Iris sibirica*), peonies, and other bold-textured plants.

Bergenia cordifolia
SAXIFRAGACEAE

HEART-LEAVED BERGENIA

If you want to add year-round interest to a container planting, it's hard to beat heart-leaved bergenia. This rugged perennial has glossy, evergreen leaves that turn red in fall.

Description Heart-leaved bergenia bears thick, waxy, wavy-edged leaves in dense clumps. In spring, the clumps are accented by sturdy, 1-foot (30-cm) stems topped with drooping flowers.
Height and spread Height 1–1½ feet (30–45 cm), width 1 foot (30 cm).
Flower color and season Pink, rose, or white flowers bloom in spring.
Best climate and site Zones 3–9. Partial shade. Grow in all-purpose container mix.
Growing guidelines You may need to divide plants every year or two to keep them from getting overcrowded. Keep container mix evenly moist.
Possible problems Snails and slugs love to feed on bergenia leaves. Keep damage to a minimum by putting the container up high—perhaps on a table or pedestal.
Other common names Heartleaf saxifrage.
Cultivars The leaves of 'Purpurea' are tinged purple; the flowers are magenta pink.
Comments Combine heart-leaved bergenia with other shade-lovers, such as ferns, hostas, rhododendrons, edging lobelia (*Lobelia erinus*), and forget-me-nots (*Myosotis sylvatica*).

Brunnera macrophylla
BORAGINACEAE

SIBERIAN BUGLOSS

The attractive heart-shaped leaves of Siberian bugloss are a perfect foil for fine-textured plants such as astilbes, ferns, and grasses.

Description The 8-inch (20-cm), heart-shaped leaves rise in a tight mound from a short, fibrous-rooted rhizome. Sprays of ¼-inch (6-mm), starry flowers cover the plants in spring.
Height and spread Height 1½ feet (45 cm), spread 2 feet (60 cm).
Flower color and season Forget-me-not-blue flowers bloom in spring. The foliage is stunning all season long.
Best climate and site Zones 3–8. Plants are tolerant of short dry spells once established; if drought persists, plants will go dormant. In Northern gardens, bugloss can take considerable sun. Grow in a large container in all-purpose container mix.
Growing guidelines This tough perennial seldom needs division. Self-sown seedlings will appear regularly around the parent clumps. Divide clumps in early spring or fall, or take 3–4-inch (7.5–10-cm) root cuttings in fall or early winter. Transplant self-sown seedlings to their desired position. Water containers regularly.
Possible problems No serious problems.
Comments Combine in a large container with tulips, daffodils, and other spring bulbs, along with wildflowers such as phlox and foamflower (*Tiarella cordifolia*).

Campanula carpatica
CAMPANULACEAE

CARPATHIAN HAREBELL

Carpathian harebell spreads to form tidy mounds of dark green leaves topped with cup-shaped, blue-purple flowers. It looks pretty in a container with yellow flowers and gray-leaved grasses.

Description Quick-growing Carpathian harebell grows in clumps. The large, lively, purple-blue flowers are bell-shaped and the leaves are oval.
Height and spread Height to 9 inches (22.5 cm); slightly wider spread.
Flower color and season Blue-purple or white flowers bloom in early summer.
Best climate and site Zones 3–8. Full sun; light shade in hotter sites. Grow in an all-purpose container mix.
Growing guidelines Short-lived unless you divide and renew every couple of years. Mulch with compost during summer. Water in drought. Deadhead for an extended bloom period, but let some flowers set seed so the plant can self-sow.
Possible problems Watch out for slugs and snails.
Other common names Tussock bellflower.
Cultivars 'Blue Clips' and 'White Clips' are more compact. 'Wedgwood Blue' has violet-blue flowers.
Comments Combine in a container with yellow daylilies for a bright display.

Campanula portenschlagiana
CAMPANULACEAE

DALMATIAN BELLFLOWER

Dalmatian bellflower is a free-flowering, easy-care perennial. Its blue-purple spring flowers look most attractive in a hanging basket or window box combined with yellow basket-of-gold.

Description Dalmatian bellflower forms low, creeping mats of small, triangular leaves. At bloom time, the leaves are practically obscured by scads of starry, blue-purple, bell-shaped flowers. Plants grow from fibrous-rooted crowns and root along the stems as they rest on the ground.
Height and spread Height 3–6 inches (7.5–15 cm); spread 10–12 inches (25–30 cm).
Flower color and season Blue-purple flowers bloom in spring and early summer.
Best climate and site Zones 5–9. Sun or partial shade. Grow in an all-purpose container mix.
Growing guidelines For propagation, divide plants in spring or fall or take tip cuttings in late spring. Plants are also easy to grow from seed sown indoors or out.
Possible problems No serious problems.
Other species *C. rotundifolia*, harebell, has lilac-blue summer flowers. Zones 3–9.
Comments Combine Dalmatian bellflower with spring bulbs, purple rock cress (*Aubrieta deltoidea*), columbines (*Aquilegia* spp.), basket-of-gold (*Aurinia saxatilis*), sedums, and ornamental grasses.

Catananche caerulea
ASTERACEAE

CUPID'S DART

Cupid's dart is a hardy container plant that produces tufts of narrow, woolly leaves. The straw-like flowers look great in summer containers and dry easily for flower arrangements.

Description A romantic flower, as its common name implies, cupid's dart was once used as an ingredient in love potions. A cornflower-like plant, its 2-inch (5-cm) flower heads are protected by silvery bracts and carried singly on wiry stems.
Height and spread Height 1½–2 feet (45–60 cm); spread 10–12 inches (25–30 cm).
Flower color and season The blue-purple flowers bloom in summer.
Best climate and site Zones 4–9. Full sun. Grow in an all-purpose container mix. Heat-tolerant.
Growing guidelines Plants may be short-lived in badly drained container mixes. Divide plants every year to promote longevity. Divide in fall. Take 2–3-inch (5–7.5-cm) root cuttings in fall or winter. Sow seed indoors in early spring. Plants will bloom the first year.
Possible problems Good drainage is imperative for healthy growth.
Cultivars 'Blue Giant' is a stout cultivar with dark blue flowers.
Comments Combine with yarrows (*Achillea* spp.), ornamental grasses, and sundrops (*Oenothera* spp.).

Centaurea hypoleuca
ASTERACEAE

KNAPWEED

Knapweed is a bushy, fast-spreading perennial that makes an ideal low-maintenance container plant. It bears a profusion of fringed, pink flowers in late spring and early summer.

Description Knapweed grows from a fibrous-rooted crown to produce a clump of pinnately lobed leaves with eight to 10 woolly divisions. The leaves clothe thick, weakly upright, flowering stems. The fringed, pink flowers have broad, white centers and are borne one to a stem. The flowers are long-lasting in dried or fresh arrangements.
Height and spread Height 1½–2½ feet (45–75 cm); spread 1½ feet (45 cm).
Flower color and season Pink flowers bloom in spring and early summer.
Best climate and site Zones 3–7. Full sun. Plants become lanky in too much shade. Plant in all-purpose container mix.
Growing guidelines Remove flower heads as they fade to promote rebloom. When flower production wanes, cut plants back to remove floppy stems. Divide clumps every 2–3 years to keep plants vigorous. Sow seed outdoors in fall or indoors in late winter.
Possible problems No serious problems.
Cultivars 'John Coutts' has rosy purple flowers on 2-foot (60-cm) stems.
Comments Combine with ornamental grasses, orange coneflowers (*Rudbeckia* spp.), and yarrows (*Achillea* spp.).

Centranthus ruber
VALERIANACEAE

RED VALERIAN

The bright red flowers of red valerian add vibrant color to spring and summer containers. Pink, rose, and white-flowered selections are also available.

Description Red valerian is an upright perennial with opposite, gray-green, oval leaves on branching stems. Plants grow from a fibrous-rooted crown. The flowers are carried in branched clusters.
Height and spread Height 1–3 feet (30–90 cm); spread 2 feet (60 cm).
Flower color and season Deep coral-red flowers bloom in spring and summer.
Best climate and site Zones 4–8. Full sun. Plant in all-purpose container mix. Plants perform best where summers are dry.
Growing guidelines Plants may become floppy after blooming; shear them back to promote compact growth and reblooming. Sow seed outdoors in summer. Plants often self-sow prolifically, but seedlings may not be the same color as their parents. To reproduce plants of specific color, remove basal shoots and treat them like tip cuttings.
Possible problems No serious problems.
Other common names Jupiter's beard, kiss-me-quick.
Cultivars 'Albus' has white flowers.
Comments The often harsh coral-red flower color combines well with the neutral colors of stone containers and creamy yellow flowers.

Ceratostigma plumbaginoides
PLUMBAGINACEAE

LEADWORT

Blue flowering leadwort is slow to emerge in spring but eventually forms mats of shiny, green leaves that turn reddish in fall.

Description Leadwort has deciduous foliage that appears in late spring; then it quickly forms a tufted mat of shiny, green, 3-inch (7.5-cm) long leaves with pointed ends. The cobalt blue flowers are ½ inch (12 mm) wide. The stems and leaves turn reddish bronze in fall.
Height and spread Height 8–12 inches (20–30 cm); spread 1–1½ feet (30–45 cm).
Flower color and season Cobalt blue flowers appear in late summer and often last till frost.
Best climate and site Zones 5–9. Full sun to partial shade. Plant in all-purpose container mix.
Growing guidelines Set plants 8–12 inches (20–30 cm) apart in spring for a quick result in a large container. In Zone 5, place under the eaves or mulch for winter protection. Propagate by division in spring or take cuttings in summer.
Possible problems No serious problems.
Other common names Chinese plumbago, dwarf plumbago.
Comments Suitable for a large container. Interplant the creeping stems with spring bulbs. Plant with summer-flowering orange coneflowers (*Rudbeckia* spp.).

Chelone lyonii
SCROPHULARIACEAE

PINK TURTLEHEAD

Pink turtlehead is ideal for a large container combined with other summer-flowering perennials. A bushy perennial, it has tall, leafy stems that grow from a stout, fibrous-rooted crown.

Description Pink turtlehead is a popular summer-flowering plant because of its dark, glossy foliage and its slightly hooded, tubular, rosy pink flowers borne on a terminal spike, which somewhat resemble the head of a turtle with its jaws open. The 4–7-inch (10–17.5-cm) leaves have toothed margins.
Height and spread Height 1–3 feet (30–90 cm); spread 1–2 feet (30–60 cm).
Flower color and season Rosy pink flowers bloom late summer into fall.
Best climate and site Zones 3–8. Full sun to partial shade. Grow in all-purpose container mix. Intolerant of excessive heat.
Growing guidelines Divide crowns to reduce large clumps in aged plants. Divide in spring or after flowering. Take stem cuttings in early summer; remove any flower buds. Sow seed outdoors in fall or indoors in late winter after stratification.
Possible problems No serious problems.
Other species *C. glabra*, white turtlehead, has narrow leaves and white flowers.
Comments Combine in a container with asters and phlox for late-summer color.

Convallaria majalis
CONVALLARIACEAE

LILY-OF-THE-VALLEY

Grow lily-of-the-valley in containers and bring them indoors in spring to enjoy their beautiful perfume. Or grow in a large container as a groundcover underneath a Japanese maple (Acer palmatum).

Description Lily-of-the-valley is popular for its fragrant, bell-shaped flowers. Each crown (known as a "pip") produces two large, oblong, green leaves and one upright flower spike. The flowers may be followed by glossy, orange-red berries in summer.
Height and spread Height of foliage 6–8 inches (15–20 cm); spread unlimited.
Flower color and season Waxy, white flowers appear in spring.
Best climate and site Zones 2–8. Partial to full shade. Grow in all-purpose container mix enriched with compost.
Growing guidelines Set plants 4–6 inches (10–15 cm) apart in late fall or very early spring. The deciduous leaves turn brown in mid- to late summer, so place them where their unsightly appearance isn't a problem. If desired, you can cut down the brown leaves to tidy up the planting. Lily-of-the-valley benefits from an application of compost or leaf mold each fall. Thin out crowded plantings if they stop blooming well. Propagate by division after flowering or in fall.
Possible problems No serious problems.
Comments Combine lily-of-the-valley in pots with other spring-flowering bulbs.

Delphinium x *elatum hybrids*
RANUNCULACEAE

HYBRID DELPHINIUM

The name "delphinium" comes from the Greek word for "dolphin," which the flower buds were thought to resemble. Hybrid delphiniums are stately plants with dense flower clusters atop tall stems.

Description The stately, candle-like flowers have petal-like sepals that surround two to four small, true petals, which are often called the "bee." The top sepal has a long spur. The palmate leaves are deeply cut. Plants grow from stout crowns with thick, fleshy roots.

Height and spread Height 4½–6 feet (1.35–1.8 cm); spread 2–3 feet (60–90 cm).

Flower color and season Flowers range in color from white through all shades of true blue to lavender and purple and bloom in late spring through summer, depending on the hybrid group. Remove spent flower-heads to encourage fall blooms.

Best climate and site Zones 4–7. Many hybrids are hardy to Zone 3. Full sun. Grow in a large container in all-purpose container mix.

Growing guidelines Often short-lived in warm climates. Hybrid delphiniums are particularly sensitive to high night temperatures. The wild species are often longer-lived than the hybrids. Delphiniums are heavy feeders and benefit from an annual spring topdressing of a balanced organic fertilizer or well-rotted manure. Set out new plants in spring, taking care not to damage the thick roots. Mature

plants produce many stems. Thin clumps to three to five stems as they emerge to promote strong growth and to reduce the chance of disease. To encourage plants to rebloom, cut off old flowering stems above the foliage below the flower spike. New shoots often emerge from the crown. When they develop, cut the old shoots to the ground to enable the new ones to flower by fall. Divide overgrown plants and replant into fresh container mix. Divide in spring. Sow fresh seed in summer or fall. Take cuttings in spring from the new shoots; use the stems removed from thinning the clumps for propagation.

Possible problems Exclude slugs, which attack leaves and stems, with a ring of diatomaceous earth, wood ashes, or sand around the clumps. Powdery mildew causes white blotches on the leaves. Dust affected parts with sulfur. Plant resistant cultivars and thin stems to avoid the problem.

Hybrids Hundreds of hybrid delphiniums are available, many of which have *D. elatum* in their parentage.

Other species *D.* x *belladonna* hybrids are hardy, heat-resistant, compact plants. 'Casa Blanca' has pure white flowers. 'Clivedon Beauty' has sky-blue flowers. To Zone 3.

Comments The juice of the delphinium plant is poisonous if ingested.

Dendranthema x *grandiflorum*
ASTERACEAE

GARDEN MUM

The bright flowers of garden mums signal the end of summer and the return of cold weather. The height and spread can be quite variable.

Description Garden mums have stout stems clothed in lobed leaves and grow from creeping stems with tangled, fibrous roots. Flower size ranges from 1–6 inches (2.5–15 cm).

Height and spread Height 1½–5 feet (45–150 cm); spread 1–3 feet (30–90 cm).

Flower color and season White, pink, red, gold, or yellow flowers bloom from summer through fall.

Best climate and site Zones 3–9. Full sun or light shade. Grow in a large container in all-purpose container mix.

Growing guidelines Pinch stems once or twice in May or June to promote compact growth. Divide the fast-growing clumps in spring every 1–2 years to keep them vigorous. Take tip cuttings in late spring or early summer.

Possible problems To deal with aphids or spider mites, spray with insecticidal soap or a botanical insecticide such as pyrethrin.

Other common names Florist's chrysanthemum, hardy chrysanthemum, hardy mum, mum.

Comments Combine garden mums with asters, sedums, ornamental grasses, and anemones for a showy fall display. Use them with foliage plants such as yuccas and ornamental grasses.

Dianthus gratianopolitanus
CARYOPHYLLACEAE

CHEDDAR PINKS

Cheddar pinks are sweet-scented flowers that are similar to carnations, but with simpler blooms. Plant them in raised containers or hanging baskets so they can cascade over the side.

Description These broad, mounded plants produce dense clusters of 3-inch (7.5-cm), blue-green, linear leaves with fibrous roots. The fragrant flowers, with toothed ("pinked") edges are borne on wiry stems.
Height and spread Height 9–12 inches (22.5–30 cm); spread 1 foot (30 cm).
Flower color and season The white, rose, or pink flowers bloom from early- to midsummer and often continue until frost.
Best climate and site Zones 3–9. Full sun. Plant in an all-purpose container mix. The container mix should be neutral or only slightly acid for the best growth.
Growing guidelines Divide clumps every 2–3 years to keep them vigorous. Remove flowers as they fade to promote continued bloom. Take stem cuttings from the foliage rosettes in summer.
Possible problems Pinks are susceptible to rust, a fungus that causes yellow blotches on the upper surface. Thin clumps to promote air circulation, and dust affected plants with sulfur.
Comments Interplant cheddar pinks with spiky foliage, such as yuccas, as well as ornamental grasses.

Dianthus plumarius
CARYOPHYLLACEAE

COTTAGE PINKS

Cottage pinks are popular, sweet-scented plants for hanging baskets and window boxes. The broad, mounded plants produce dense clusters of 3-inch (7.5-cm), blue-green, grass-like leaves.

Description *D. plumarius* is thought to be the parent of the old-fashioned and modern pinks. The fragrant flowers add an old-fashioned touch. They make pretty posies indoors.
Height and spread Height 1½–2 feet (45–60 cm); spread 1 foot (30 cm).
Flower color and season Fragrant white or pink flowers are borne in open clusters on wiry stems from early to midsummer.
Best climate and site Zones 3–9. Full sun. Plant cottage pinks in all-purpose container mix. The container mix should be neutral or only slightly acid for best growth. Tolerates extreme heat and cold.
Growing guidelines Plants may be short-lived, especially in warmer zones. Divide clumps every 2–3 years to keep them vigorous. Remove flowers as they fade to promote continued bloom. Layer or take stem cuttings from the foliage rosettes in summer. Strip leaves from the lower third of a 2–3-inch (5–7.5-cm) cutting. Place cutting in a medium of one part vermiculite and two parts sand or perlite to allow excellent drainage and air circulation.
Possible problems Rust causes yellow blotches on the upper surface of the leaves and raised orange spots on the lower

surface. To discourage rust, thin clumps for better air circulation and dust with sulfur.
Cultivars 'Essex Witch' has rose-pink flowers. 'Helen' has double, salmon-pink flowers. 'Mrs. Sinkins' has fragrant, double white flowers. 'Spring Beauty' is a seed-grown strain of clove-scented, semidouble to double flowers in white, pink, rose, and red.
Other species
D. armeria has rosettes of hairy, dark green leaves that are up to 2 inches (5 cm) long. Flowers have narrow, rose-pink petals that are dotted with pale pink.

D. carthusianorum is a tufted plant with pale green, grass-like foliage and deep pink to purple flowers that are borne in flattened, terminal clusters.

D. deltoides, maiden pink, is a mat-forming pink with green leaves and a mass of single, rose-colored flowers borne one to a stem. Zones 3–9.

D. gallicus is a loose-tufted plant that grows to 1½ feet (45 cm) tall, when in flower. Pink, fragrant flowers bloom in summer at the tips of stems.
Comments Plant pinks in window boxes so you can appreciate their perfume.

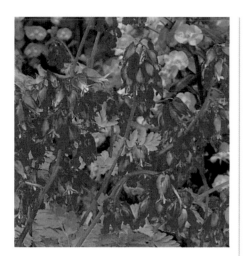

Dicentra spectabilis
FUMARIACEAE

BLEEDING HEART

The heart-shaped flowers of old-fashioned bleeding hearts are loved by bees. The ferny foliage looks great in containers from spring through fall.

Description Bleeding hearts bear a profusion of small clusters of heart-shaped flowers held above finely divided, blue-green foliage. Plants form dense rosettes of deeply cut foliage from thick, fleshy roots.
Height and spread Height 1–2½ feet (30–75 cm); spread 2–3 feet (60–90 cm).
Flower color and season The pink flowers bloom in spring, but flowers can appear anytime during the growing season.
Best climate and site Zones 3–9. Partial shade; plants tolerate full sun in Northern gardens. Protect plants with a winter mulch in colder zones or place the container under the eaves. Plant in an all-purpose container mix.
Growing guidelines Top-dress with compost in early spring. If plants lose vigor, lift and divide clumps and replant into container mix. For propagation, sow fresh seed outdoors in summer or divide plants in fall. Plants often self-sow.
Possible problems No serious problems.
Other common names Common bleeding heart.
Comments The plants are exquisite and delicate in foliage and flower, so place them where they are easy to admire. Combine with bulbs, primroses, and wildflowers for a striking spring container display.

Doronicum orientale
ASTERACEAE

LEOPARD'S BANE

Leopard's bane is a brightly colored, spring daisy. Plant it in a large container with blue-flowering clustered bellflower for a striking spring display.

Description Leopard's bane is grown for its attractive, single, 1–2-inch (2.5–5-cm), daisies that bloom above bright green, slender, leafless stems. The deep green, triangular leaves grow in open clusters from a fibrous-rooted crown.
Height and spread Height 1–2 feet (30–60 cm); spread 1 foot (30 cm).
Flower color and season Bright yellow flowers bloom in spring and early summer.
Best climate and site Zones 3–8. Full sun to shade. Prefers all-purpose container mix with added compost. Container mix must not dry out while plant is actively growing.
Growing guidelines Leopard's banes emerge early in spring and may be damaged by late frosts. Plants go dormant after flowering in warmer zones. In colder zones, the foliage remains all season, so moist container mix is imperative. Mulch will help keep the container mix cool. Divide clumps every 2–3 years to keep them vigorous. Divide in spring or fall. Sow seed indoors in late winter or early spring.
Possible problems No serious problems.
Cultivars 'Magnificum' has showy 2-inch (5-cm) flowers.
Comments Combine with spring bulbs. Foliage plants such as hostas can fill the void when plants go dormant.

Echinops ritro
ASTERACEAE

GLOBE THISTLE

Globe thistles are stout, coarse perennials with spiky, steel-blue, round flower heads, erect stems, and spiny, lobed leaves. They grow from thick, deep-branched taproots.

Description This handsome, old-world, thistle-like plant has white, woolly foliage and small flowers that are packed into 1–2-inch (2.5–5-cm) spherical heads.
Height and spread Height 2–4 feet (60–120 cm); spread 2–3 feet (60–90 cm).
Flower color and season Steel-blue flowers bloom in midsummer.
Best climate and site Zones 3–8. Full sun. Grow in all-purpose container mix. Good drainage is essential, especially in winter. Heat-tolerant.
Growing guidelines Globe thistles are tough, long-lived perennials. They are drought-tolerant once established and thrive for many years without staking or division. Remove sideshoots from main clump without disturbing the crown in fall or late winter. Take root cuttings in spring or fall.
Possible problems Plant in a well-drained container mix to avoid root rot.
Comments Combine showy globe thistles in a large container, such as a half-barrel, with other drought-tolerant perennials like Russian sages (*Perovskia* spp.), sedums, catmints (*Nepeta* spp.), and oriental poppy (*Papaver orientale*). Globe thistle flowers are perfect for cutting fresh or for drying.

Erigeron speciosus
ASTERACEAE

DAISY FLEABANE

Daisy fleabane is a hardy container plant that looks lovely combined with low grasses. The blooms make pretty, long-lasting cut flowers for indoor arrangements.

Description The floriferous fleabanes form leafy clumps of hairy, 6-inch (15-cm), lance-shaped leaves that spring from fibrous-rooted crowns. The 1½-inch (3.5-cm) blooms are aster-like.
Height and spread Height 1½–2½ feet (45–75 cm); spread 1–2 feet (30–60 cm).
Flower color and season Flowers in white, pink, rose, or purple bloom in early to midsummer with occasional rebloom.
Best climate and site Zones 2–9. Full sun or light shade. Plant in all-purpose container mix. Tolerant of heat and cold.
Growing guidelines Fleabanes are long-lived perennials that benefit from fall division every 2–3 years. If division isn't enough to increase your stock, take tip cuttings in spring before the flower buds form. Another option is to sow seed outdoors in fall or indoors in spring.
Possible problems No serious problems.
Other common names Oregon daisy.
Comments Combine with summer-blooming perennials such as pinks (*Dianthus* spp.), cranesbills (*Geranium* spp.), cinquefoils (*Potentilla* spp.), sundrops (*Oenothera* spp.), and phlox.

Eryngium amethystinum
APIACEAE

AMETHYST SEA HOLLY

The rounded flower clusters and spiny bracts of amethyst sea holly add excitement to any container planting. These trouble-free plants tolerate heat, cold, and drought.

Description Amethyst sea holly has stiff, flowering stems and mostly basal, pinnately divided leaves. Plants grow from thick taproots. The small, blue, globose flower heads are surrounded by thin, spiny bracts. The flowering stems are also blue.
Height and spread Height 1–1½ feet (30–45 cm); spread 1–2 feet (30–60 cm).
Flower color and season Steel-blue flowers bloom in summer. The glossy foliage is attractive all season.
Best climate and site Zones 2–8. Full sun. Plant in a large container in all-purpose container mix. Sea holly is extremely drought-tolerant once established.
Growing guidelines Set plants out in their permanent location while they are young; older plants resent disturbance. Division is seldom necessary. For propagation, sow fresh seed outdoors in fall. Self-sown seedlings may be plentiful.
Possible problems No serious problems.
Comments Combine with asters, phlox, and ornamental grasses. Surround the colorful heads with fine-textured plants such as sea lavenders (*Limonium* spp.), baby's-breath (*Gypsophila paniculata*), and coral bells (*Heuchera* spp.).

Filipendula rubra
ROSACEAE

QUEEN-OF-THE-PRAIRIE

Queen-of-the-prairie is a towering perennial with huge flower heads on stout, leafy stalks. The showy 1-foot (30-cm) leaves are deeply lobed and star-like. Plants grow from creeping stems.

Description The small, five-petaled flower heads of queen-of-the-prairie form airy clusters on this tall, feathery plant, and resemble cotton candy.
Height and spread Height 4–6 feet (120–180 cm); spread 2–4 feet (60–120 cm).
Flower color and season Peach-pink flowers bloom in late spring and early summer.
Best climate and site Zones 3–9. Full sun to light shade. Grow in a large container in all-purpose container mix with added peat. Plants will not tolerate prolonged dryness.
Growing guidelines If leaves become tattered after bloom, cut plants to the ground; new leaves will emerge. Plants spread quickly in moist container mix. Divide every 3–4 years. Division is the best method. Lift clumps in spring or fall, or dig crowns from the edge of the clump. Sow seed indoors in spring.
Possible problems No serious problems.
Cultivars 'Venusta' has deep rose-pink flowers, but many plants sold as the cultivar are seed-grown and vary in color.
Other species *F. vulgaris*, dropwort, has fern-like foliage and white flowers.
Comments Grow in large pots on the edge of ponds.

Gaillardia x *grandiflora*
ASTERACEAE

BLANKET FLOWER

Give blanket flowers a sunny spot, and they'll bear dazzling orange and yellow blooms all summer. They look good in large containers with grasses.

Description Hybrid blanket flower blooms on loose stems with hairy, lobed leaves. The larger basal leaves are 8–10 inches (20–25 cm) long. Plants grow from fibrous-rooted crowns. The ragged daisies have single or double rows of toothed, petal-like rays surrounding a raised center.
Height and spread Height 2–3 feet (60–90 cm); spread 2 feet (60 cm).
Flower color and season Yellow and orange flowers bloom throughout summer.
Best climate and site Zones 4–9. Full sun. Plant in all-purpose container mix. Rich, moist container mix causes plants to overgrow and flop.
Growing guidelines Blanket flowers are very hardy. Cut back stems in late summer in cool climates. Propagate from seed in spring or early summer. Divide in spring.
Possible problems No serious problems.
Other common names Gaillardia.
Cultivars 'Bremen' has copper-red flowers tipped in yellow. 'Burgundy' has deep red flowers. 'Goblin' is 1 foot (30 cm) tall with red and yellow flowers.
Comments Combine with other drought-tolerant perennials such as coreopsis (*Coreopsis* spp.), butterfly weed (*Asclepias tuberosa*), yarrows, and yuccas.

Geranium endressii
GERANIACEAE

ENDRES CRANESBILL

Endres cranesbill is a mounding plant with deeply cut, five-lobed leaves arising from a slow-creeping, fibrous-rooted crown.

Description This rhizomatous perennial forms clumps. The leaves are deeply lobed and toothed. The saucer-shaped, five-petaled flowers are carried above foliage in sparse clusters and are pale pink but become darker with age.
Height and spread Height 15–18 inches (37.5–45 cm); spread 1½ feet (45 cm).
Flower color and season Soft pink flowers bloom from early to midsummer.
Best climate and site Zones 4–8. Full sun to partial shade. Protect from hot afternoon sun in warmer zones. Grow in an all-purpose container mix.
Growing guidelines Heat slows blooming. In cooler zones plants may bloom all summer. Divide crowded plants and replant into fresh container mix. Divide in spring or fall. Sow seed outdoors in fall or indoors in spring on a warm (70°F/21°C) seedbed. Take stem cuttings in summer.
Possible problems No serious problems.
Cultivars 'A. T. Johnson' has dozens of silvery pink flowers. 'Claridge Druce', a hybrid with G. *versicolor*, has lilac-pink flowers with violet veins. 'Wargrave Pink' has pure pink flowers.
Other species G. *cinereum*, gray-leaved cranesbill, is a low, spreading plant with small, deeply incised leaves and saucer-

shaped, pink flowers veined with violet. 'Ballerina' is a hybrid with large, lilac-pink flowers that have striking veins and purple eyes. 'Splendens' has bright pink flowers with dark eyes. Zones 4 (with protection) or, preferably, 5–8.

G. *clarkei*, Clark's geranium, is a floriferous species with white, pink, or lilac, dark-veined flowers. The rounded leaves are deeply divided into seven lobes. This plant was recently separated from G. *pratense*. 'Kashmir Purple' has purple-blue flowers. 'Kashmir White' has white flowers with violet veins. Zones 4–8.

G. *dalmaticum*, Dalmatian cranesbill, is a low, rounded plant with small, curly, lobed leaves and 1-inch (2.5-cm), mauve flowers. Plants spread rapidly by creeping stems. The variety 'Album' has white flowers. 'Biokovo' is a hybrid with pale pink flowers. Zones 4–8.

G. *himalayense*, lilac cranesbill, is an open, mounding plant with deeply incised leaves and 2-inch (5-cm), violet-blue flowers. 'Birch Double' has double, lavender flowers. 'Gravetye' is a compact grower with violet-centered, blue flowers. Zones 4–8.

G. *ibiricum*, Caucasus cranesbill, is a robust plant with large, seven- to nine-lobed leaves and 2-inch (5-cm), purple-blue flowers on stout stems. Zones 3–8.

G. *macrorrhizum*, bigroot cranesbill, is a fast-spreading plant with fragrant, seven-lobed leaves and bright pink flowers.

Geranium endressii continued

Gypsophila paniculata
CARYOPHYLLACEAE

Helenium autumnale
ASTERACEAE

'Album' has white flowers with pink sepals. 'Ingwersen's Variety' has light pink flowers and glossy leaves. 'Spessart' has white flowers with pale pink sepals. Zones 3–8.

G. *maculatum*, wild cranesbill, is a woodland plant with five-lobed leaves and tall, sparsely flowering stalks of clear pink or white flowers. Zones 4–8.

G. *pratense*, meadow cranesbill, has deeply incised leaves and 1½-inch (3.5-cm), purple flowers with red veins. 'Mrs. Kendall Clarke' has lilac-blue flowers. Zones 3–8.

G. *sanguineum*, blood red cranesbill, is a low, wide-spreading plant with deeply cut, starry leaves and flat, magenta flowers held just above the foliage. 'Album' is more rambling than the species and has white saucer-shaped flowers. 'Shepherd's Warning' is low growing with deep rose-pink flowers. The variety G. *sanguineum* var. *striatum* (also sold as G. *sanguineum* var. *lancastriense*) is prostrate with pale pink, rose-veined flowers. Zones 3–8.

G. *sylvaticum*, wood cranesbill, is an early-spring bloomer with lobed leaves and pink or white flowers. Zones 3–8.

Comments Combine with sundrops (*Oenothera* spp.), bellflowers (*Campanula* spp.), phlox, and irises.

BABY'S BREATH

Clouds of baby's breath look great in combination with perennials that have spiky leaves or flowers, such as delphiniums or yuccas.

Description Baby's breath produces dense tufts of intricately branched stems covered in a froth of tiny, star-like flowers. The plant's cloud-like appearance makes a great contrast with other more striking plants.
Height and spread Height 3–4 feet (90–120 cm); spread 2–3 feet (60–90 cm).
Flower color and season Masses of small, dainty, white flowers appear in summer.
Best climate and site Zones 3–9. Full sun or light shade. Grow in a large container in all-purpose container mix. Tolerates heat and cold.
Growing guidelines Set baby's breath plants out in spring and do not disturb the crowns once plants are established. Good drainage is essential for longevity. Tall cultivars may need staking. Take stem cuttings in summer and place them in a high humidity environment. Sow seed outdoors in spring or fall.
Possible problems No serious problems.
Cultivars 'Bristol Fairy' has double, white flowers. 'Compact Plena' has double, white or soft pink flowers.
Other species G. *repens* forms low 8-inch (20-cm) mounds with lilac, white, or pale purple flowers during summer.
Comments For a dramatic effect, combine baby's breath with spiky perennials.

COMMON SNEEZEWEED

Sneezeweeds prefer cool temperatures and tend to "stretch" in warm weather; either stake them or pinch the stem tips in early summer to promote compact growth.

Description Common sneezeweed is a late-season perennial with tall, leafy stems that spring from a fibrous-rooted crown. The hairy, lance-shaped leaves have a few large teeth along the margins. The 2-inch (5-cm) daisies have broad, petal-like rays and spherical centers.
Height and spread Height 3–5 feet (90–120 cm); spread 2–3 feet (60–90 cm).
Flower color and season Yellow flowers bloom in late summer and fall. Some cultivars bloom in midsummer and again in fall if cut back.
Best climate and site Zones 3–8. Full sun or light shade. Grow in a large container in all-purpose container mix with added compost. Tolerates wet container mix.
Growing guidelines Cut plants back by half after flowering to promote a second bloom. Divide the clumps every 3–4 years to keep them vigorous. For propagation, take stem cuttings in early summer, or sow seed of that species outdoors in fall. Propagate cultivars by division or cuttings only.
Possible problems No serious problems.
Comments Combine with boltonias, asters, garden phlox (*Phlox paniculata*), and ornamental grasses.

Helleborus x *hybridus*
RANUNCULACEAE

LENTEN ROSE

Lenten roses may take 2 or 3 years to get established; after that, they'll bloom dependably every spring. They look pretty in a container with hostas, ferns, and spring bulbs.

Description Lenten roses are classic winter or early-spring perennials with deeply lobed, leathery leaves growing from a stout crown with fleshy roots. The flowers have five petal-like sepals surrounded by green, leafy bracts.

Height and spread Height 1–1½ feet (30–45 cm); spread 1–2 feet (30–60 cm).

Flower color and season The reddish purple, pink, or white flowers bloom from early winter through spring. The flowers fade to soft pink with age. The evergreen foliage is attractive year-round.

Best climate and site Zones 4–8. Light to partial shade. Plant in all-purpose container mix. Established plants tolerate dry container mix and deep shade.

Growing guidelines In spring, remove any damaged leaves. Divide only if needed for propagation. Lift clumps after flowering in spring and separate crowns. Replant divisions immediately. Plant fresh seed outdoors in late summer. Self-sown seedlings usually appear.

Possible problems No serious problems.

Other common names Winter rose.

Comments Combine Lenten roses with early-spring bulbs, wildflowers, lungworts (*Pulmonaria* spp.), and ferns.

Hemerocallis hybrids
HEMEROCALLIDACEAE

DAYLILIES

Daylilies make excellent container plants, since they have attractive, arching foliage as well as showy flowers. They adapt to a range of conditions.

Description Daylilies grow in clumps of arching, sword-like, green leaves. In summer, these leafy mounds are accented by 2–8-inch (5–20-cm) wide blooms on 12–42-inch (30–95-cm) stalks. Some cultivars rebloom later in the season.

Height and spread Height 1–5 feet (30–150 cm); spread 2–3 feet (60–90 cm). There are miniature and standard sizes as well as extremely tall types.

Flower color and season Daylily flowers may be orange, yellow, red, pink, buff, apricot, or green, sometimes with a contrasting band or throat. They bloom from spring through summer.

Best climate and site Zones 3–9 for most hybrids. Full sun to light shade. Most modern hybrids need at least 8 hours of direct sun to flower well. Grow in an all-purpose container mix.

Growing guidelines Plant container-grown or bareroot plants in spring or fall. Place crowns just below the container mix surface. Plants take a year to become established and then spread quickly to form dense clumps. Most hybrids and species can remain in containers for many years without disturbance. Some hybrids have so many bloom stalks that the flowers crowd together and lose their beauty. Divide these plants every 3 years. Lift the clumps and pull or cut the tangled crowns apart. Deadhead the plants regularly to keep them looking their best. The foliage of most daylilies remains attractive all season. If leaves are yellow, grasp them firmly and give them a quick tug to remove them from the base. Hybrids must be propagated by division only in fall or spring. Seed-grown plants will be variable and are often inferior to the parent plant.

Possible problems Flower color tends to fade in full sun; move plant to a shadier spot. Although daylilies are usually pest-free, aphids and thrips may attack foliage and flower buds. Wash off aphids with a stream of water or spray with insecticidal soap. Spray thrips with insecticidal soap or a botanical insecticide such as pyrethrin.

Cultivars Hundreds of cultivars are available in a full range of colors. 'Catherine Woodbery' is shell pink with a yellow throat. 'Chicago Royal' is purple with a green throat. 'Hyperion' has fragrant yellow flowers. 'Stella d'Oro' is a repeat-blooming plant with creamy gold flowers.

Other species *H. fulva*, tawny daylily, bears rich, orange-red flowers.

Comments "Mini" classifications often refer to flower size; the actual plant may still be large. To extend the season of interest, combine daylilies with spring bulbs or pansies.

Heuchera spp.
SAXIFRAGACEAE

CORAL BELLS

Some coral bells have green leaves and colorful flowers; others have dull blooms but strikingly colored foliage. Both kinds are heat-tolerant and adapt well to container growing.

Description Coral bells produce neat, compact clumps of rounded, scalloped leaves. The clumps are topped by airy spires of small, bell-shaped blooms in red, rose, green, or white through summer.

Height and spread Height 1–2 feet (30–60 cm); spread 1–2 feet (30–60 cm).

Flower color and season Flowers can be white, red, purplish, or pink and bloom during summer.

Best climate and site Zones 3–8. Full sun to light shade. Plant in an all-purpose container mix.

Growing guidelines Set plants 6 inches (15 cm) apart. When flowers fade, pinch off flower stalk at the base. Divide clumps in fall or spring, or sow seed indoors in spring. Keep the container mix evenly moist.

Possible problems Knock mealybugs off with a strong spray of water, or spray with insecticidal soap.

Other common names Alumroot.

Cultivars 'Palace Purple' (*H. micrantha* var. *diversifolia* 'Palace Purple') has maple-like, purplish leaves and pinkish white flowers on 20-inch (50-cm) stems.

Comments Coral bells look especially pretty edged with pink or white sweet alyssum (*Lobularia maritima*).

Hosta hybrids
HOSTACEAE

HOSTAS

Hostas are one of the most popular perennials for shady containers. Most gardeners grow them for their strikingly colored and textured leaves.

Description Hostas grow in leafy mounds in shades and markings of green, blue, gold, and/or white. The leaves can be rounded, heart-shaped, or lance-shaped. Flower spires are sometimes fragrant.

Height and spread Height 6 inches to 3 feet (15–90 cm); spread 6 inches to 5 feet (15–150 cm).

Flower color and season Purplish or white flowers appear in summer.

Best climate and site Zones 4–9. Light to moderate shade is best, although some can tolerate full sun. Grow in all-purpose container mix with added compost to help hold moisture.

Growing guidelines Fertilize once in spring with fish emulsion. Mulch container in winter to protect crown and roots; remove mulch in spring. During growing season, keep container mix evenly moist. Water less in winter, so container mix is barely moist.

Possible problems Hungry slugs and snails can quickly turn hosta leaves into lacy skeletons. Minimize problems by putting the container up on a table or pedestal. Or catch the pests in beer traps.

Other common names Plantain lily.

Comments Grow hostas with ferns, forget-me-nots (*Myosotis sylvatica*), and lady's-mantle (*Alchemilla* spp.).

Iberis sempervirens
BRASSICACEAE

PERENNIAL CANDYTUFT

Perennial candytuft is a floriferous, semi-woody subshrub with persistent stems tightly clothed in 1½-inch (3.5-cm), narrow, deep green leaves. Plants grow from fibrous-rooted crowns.

Description Usually evergreen, perennial candytuft becomes covered in a mass of tight, rounded clusters of many ¼-inch (6-mm), four-petaled flowers.

Height and spread Height 6–12 inches (15–30 cm); spread 1–2 feet (30–60 cm).

Flower color and season The white flowers bloom in early spring.

Best climate and site Zones 3–9. Full sun to light shade. Plant in all-purpose container mix.

Growing guidelines Space plants 1 foot (30 cm) apart, or 6 inches (15 cm) apart if edging a container. Shear after flowering to promote compact growth. Mulch plants or move to under the eaves in Zones 3 and 4 to protect stems from winter damage. Layer or take cuttings in early summer. Sow seed outdoors in spring or fall.

Possible problems No serious problems.

Cultivars 'Autumn Snow' has large, white flowers in spring and fall.

Comments Combine in a container with bleeding hearts (*Dicentra* spp.), basket-of-gold (*Aurinia saxatilis*), rock cresses (*Arabis* spp. and *Aubrieta* spp.), and columbines (*Aquilegia* spp.).

Impatiens New Guinea hybrids
BALSAMINACEAE

NEW GUINEA IMPATIENS

New Guinea impatiens do not bloom as abundantly as their shade-loving relatives. But this isn't a drawback, since it allows you to see the beautiful foliage more easily.

Description New Guinea impatiens are upright, mounded spreaders. Their pointed, green leaves can be brilliantly variegated in red, cream, or bronze. The 2-inch (5-cm) wide, flat flowers come in a variety of colors. New Guinea impatiens are perennial in frost-free areas; elsewhere, grow as annuals.
Height and spread Height and spread of 8–24 inches (20–60 cm).
Flower color and season The orange, red, purple, pink, and lavender flowers appear all summer.
Best climate and site Zones 5–10. Full sun to filtered light. Grow New Guinea impatiens in an all-purpose container mix.
Growing guidelines Space plants 1 foot (30 cm) apart. Fertilize twice a month. Sow seed indoors 6–8 weeks before the last frost date. Take cuttings anytime.
Possible problems Dry winds can cause plants to wilt, particularly in full sun. Water often to keep the container mix moist, and move container to a more sheltered location.
Other species *I. repens* has golden flowers. Zones 10–12.
Comments You may be able to hold over favorite plants by bringing their pots into a sunny room for the winter.

Impatiens wallerana
BALSAMINACEAE

IMPATIENS

Impatiens are justifiably popular for pots, planters, window boxes, and hanging baskets. They add plenty of color to shady spots and don't demand much care in return.

Description Impatiens are tender perennials usually grown as tender annuals. Plants form neat, shrubby mounds of well-branched, succulent stems; the lance-shaped, green or bronze-brown leaves have slightly scalloped edges. The plants are covered with flat, spurred flowers up to 2 inches (5 cm) wide. Some of the single or double blooms, in a variety of colors, have an eye, or swirls of contrasting colors. The flowers are followed by swollen, ribbed seedpods that burst open when ripe, flinging seeds far and wide.
Height and spread Height 6–24 inches (15–60 cm), depending on the cultivar; similar spread.
Flower color and season Flowers may be white, pink, red, orange, or lavender and bloom from late spring until frost.
Best climate and site Zones 5–10. Partial to full shade. Grow in an all-purpose container mix.
Growing guidelines Transplants of these plants are usually available for sale in spring in a variety of plant heights and flower colors. Sow seed indoors 8–10 weeks before your last frost date. Don't cover the seed; just press it lightly into the soil surface. Enclose the pot in a plastic bag and keep it

in a warm place until seedlings appear. Young seedlings tend to grow slowly. Set transplants out about 2 weeks after last frost date. Space compact types 6–8 inches (15–20 cm) apart and tall cultivars 1 foot (30 cm) apart. Mulch to keep roots moist and water during dry spells. Feed sparingly. Otherwise, these low-maintenance plants don't need much care to keep blooming through the season. Summer stem cuttings root quickly in water.
Possible problems Too little light can lead to leggy growth; move the container to a brighter spot. Plants wilt dramatically if they dry out but usually spring back if you water them right away.
Other common names Busy Lizzie.
Cultivars 'Sparkles Mixed' has colorful flowers and bronzy green leaves on 1-foot (30-cm) tall plants. 'Super Elfin Hybrid Mixed' blooms in a range of colors on 8–10-inch (20–25-cm) tall, well-branched plants. 'Super Elfin Swirl' has soft pink flowers that have deep rose pink edges.
Comments Double-flowered, rosebud types are beautiful, but they tend to bloom sparsely and can be disappointing.

Iris cristata
IRIDACEAE

CRESTED IRIS

Crested iris forms spreading clumps of spiky leaves and delicate spring flowers. Grow in a large container with foamflowers (Tiarella spp.) and other shade-loving wildflowers.

Description Crested iris has slightly fragrant flowers with toothed crests on the falls (three outer sepals). The blooms nearly hide the broad, dagger-shaped, green leaves that carpet the ground. Each bloom is short-lived, but the foliage remains attractive until dormancy in late summer.

Height and spread Height 6–8 inches (15–20 cm); spread unlimited.

Flower color and season Lavender flowers with white patches and yellow crests bloom in midspring.

Best climate and site Zones 3–8. Partial shade; will thrive in full sun if container mix is moist. Grow in all-purpose container mix.

Growing guidelines Set plants 1 foot (30 cm) apart. Barely cover roots with container mix. Each spring, top-dress plantings with 1 inch (2.5 cm) or so of compost. Crested irises don't need frequent division, but you can divide crowded clumps directly after blooming. This is also the best method of propagation.

Possible problems Trap slugs under cabbage leaves (remove pests daily).

Comments Crested iris look arresting in a container combined with ferns.

Leucanthemum x superbum
ASTERACEAE

SHASTA DAISY

Shasta daisies are hardy, summer-blooming plants that combine well with ornamental grasses and other plants in large containers.

Description Shasta daisies are showy plants with dense clusters of shiny, 10-inch (25-cm), deep green, toothed leaves from short, creeping, fibrous-rooted stems. The 3-inch (7.5-cm) daisies are carried on stout, leafy stems.

Height and spread Height 1–3 feet (30–90 cm); spread 2 feet (60 cm).

Flower color and season Produces white flowers with bright yellow centers freely throughout the summer months.

Best climate and site Zones 3–10; exact zones vary by cultivar. Full sun. Plant in an all-purpose container mix.

Growing guidelines Deadhead plants to promote continued bloom. These easy-care plants grow quickly but may be short-lived, especially in warmer zones. Divide and replant clumps every 3–4 years to keep them vigorous. For propagation, remove offsets from the main clump or divide in spring.

Possible problems No serious problems.

Cultivars 'Little Miss Muffet' is a dwarf 8–12-inch (20–30-cm) tall selection with single flowers.

Comments Combine with yarrows (*Achillea* spp.) and daylilies. For seaside containers combine with blanket flowers (*Gaillardia* spp.), coreopsis (*Coreopsis* spp.), and ornamental grasses.

Liatris spicata
ASTERACEAE

SPIKE GAYFEATHER

Spike gayfeather is a tall perennial with slender flower spikes. The erect stems arise from basal tufts of grass-like, medium green foliage.

Description This quick-growing perennial produces tall spikes of pink flowers like fluffy feather dusters carried in small heads that are crowded together into dense spikes. The spikes open from the top down. The grass-like leaves grow in tufts.

Height and spread Height 2–3 feet (60–90 cm); spread 1–2 feet (30–60 cm).

Flower color and season Pinkish purple flowers bloom in midsummer.

Best climate and site Zones 3–9. Full sun. Plants tend to flop in partial shade. Grow in an all-purpose container mix.

Growing guidelines Clumps increase slowly and seldom need division. Divide plants in spring or early fall. Sow seed outdoors in fall or indoors in late winter after stratification. To stratify, mix seed with moist peat moss or seed-starting medium in a plastic bag. Close bag with a twist-tie and place in refrigerator for 4–6 weeks. Then sow mixture as you would normal seed.

Possible problems No serious problems.

Other common names Blazing star, gayfeather.

Comments Combine with purple coneflowers (*Echinacea* spp.), coreopsis (*Coreopsis* spp.), and ornamental grasses.

Liriope spicata
CONVALLARIACEAE

CREEPING LILYTURF

Creeping lilyturf with its evergreen, strap-like leaves makes an attractive and hardy container plant. Lavender to white flower spikes appear above the foliage in summer.

Description The thick, long, narrow, grass-like leaves have tiny teeth on their margins. The foliage is evergreen in warm climates; it often becomes yellow and unsightly during Northern winters. Spikes of ¼-inch (6-mm) flowers bloom above foliage in mid- to late summer, followed by black berries.

Height and spread Height of foliage to 10 inches (25 cm); spread to 18 inches (45 cm). Flower spikes grow 16–18 inches (40–45 cm) tall.

Flower color and season Lavender to whitish flowers bloom mid- to late summer.

Best climate and site Zones 5–10. Full sun to deep shade. Grow creeping lilyturf in an all-purpose container mix. The plant tolerates drought.

Growing guidelines Set plants 1 foot (30 cm) apart in spring. Cut the foliage of established plants in early spring to encourage new growth. Propagate by division in spring or fall.

Possible problems No serious problems.

Comments Creeping lilyturf can tolerate seaside conditions.

Lobelia cardinalis
CAMPANULACEAE

CARDINAL FLOWER

Cardinal flowers have fiery colored flower spikes on leafy stems and grow from a fibrous-rooted crown. The lance-shaped leaves may be either fresh green or red-bronze.

Description This clump-forming plant has brilliant scarlet, tubular flowers with three lower and two upper petals that look like delicate birds in flight. The flowers bloom on branching stems above green or deep bronze-purple foliage.

Height and spread Height 2–4 feet (60–120 cm); spread 1–2 feet (30–60 cm).

Flower color and season Scarlet flowers bloom in late summer to fall.

Best climate and site Zones 2–9. Full sun to partial shade. Grow in a large container in all-purpose container mix.

Growing guidelines Plants are shallow-rooted and subject to frost heaving. Where winters are cold, mulch plants to protect the crowns. In warmer zones winter mulch may rot the crowns. Replant in spring if frost has lifted them. Plants may be short-lived, but self-sown seedlings are numerous. Divide in late fall or spring. Sow seed uncovered outdoors in fall or spring or indoors in late winter. Seedlings grow quickly and will bloom the first year from seed.

Possible problems No serious problems.

Comments Combine cardinal flower in a large container with crested iris, hostas, and ferns.

Nepeta mussinii
LAMIACEAE

PERSIAN NEPETA

Persian nepeta is an easy-to-grow, old-fashioned, trouble-free, container perennial. Cutting it back after flowering promotes compact growth and encourages rebloom.

Description Persian nepeta grows in mounds of gray-green, aromatic, toothed, evergreen leaves on square stems. It is a relative of catnip (*N. cataria*); it too may attract cats.

Height and spread Height of foliage to about 1 foot (30 cm); spread to 20 inches (50 cm). Flowering stems to 1½ feet (45 cm) tall.

Flower color and season Lavender-blue flowers bloom from spring until midsummer.

Best climate and site Zones 3–8. Full sun. Grow Persian nepeta in an all-purpose container mix.

Growing guidelines Set plants 20 inches (50 cm) apart in spring. Trim back halfway after blooming for compact appearance and to encourage reblooming. Plants that are 2 years old or more are not as vigorous as young ones and don't bloom as readily, so you may need to divide or replace them. Propagate by division in spring or by cuttings in summer.

Possible problems No serious problems.

Other common names Catmint.

Comments Persian nepeta looks pretty in a container with ornamental grasses and showy sundrops (*Oenothera speciosa*).

Oenothera speciosa
ONAGRACEAE

SHOWY SUNDROPS

The white blooms of showy sundrops appear in early summer during the day, unlike the many night-blooming species of the Oenothera genus.

Description Showy sundrops produce wiry stems clothed in toothed, green leaves and topped with 2-inch (5-cm), cup-shaped flowers that turn toward the sun.
Height and spread Height to 1½ feet (45 cm); spread to 2 feet (60 cm) or more.
Flower color and season White flowers bloom in summer.
Best climate and site Zones 3–8. Full sun to very light shade. Grow in a large container in all-purpose container mix.
Growing guidelines Set plants about 2 feet (60 cm) apart in spring or fall. They are ideal for containers as they can be invasive in the garden. Propagate by division or seed in spring or fall.
Possible problems No serious problems.
Other common names White evening primrose, showy evening primrose.
Cultivars 'Rosea' grows to 15 inches (37.5 cm) with clear pink, 3-inch (7.5-cm) blooms. 'Siskiyou' is similar to 'Rosea' but has larger flowers.
Other species *O. tetragona*, common sundrops, grows 1–2 feet (30–60 cm) tall. It has bright yellow, cup-shaped flowers that bloom on reddish stems in early summer. Spreads quickly. Zones 5–8.
Comments Showy sundrops are ideal low-maintenance plants for containers.

Opuntia humifusa
CACTACEAE

PRICKLY PEAR

Prickly pear is a surprisingly cold-tolerant cactus that looks stunning in a large, terracotta container. The yellow flowers give way to purplish fruits in fall.

Description This spreading, cold-hardy cactus bears prickly bristles on fleshy, oval pads. Attractive, cup-shaped, 3–4-inch (7.5–10-cm), yellow flowers bloom on short stems. Fleshy, purplish, 2-inch (5-cm), pear-shaped fruits form in fall; the fruits are edible but not very tasty. This species is also listed as O. *compressa*.
Height and spread Height 4–10 inches (10–25 cm); spread unlimited.
Flower color and season Yellow flowers with white stamens bloom in late spring or early summer.
Best climate and site Zones 5–9. Full sun. Grow in a large container in all-purpose container mix with added river sand.
Growing guidelines Set plants at least 1½ feet (45 cm) apart in spring. Handle with leather gloves to avoid the spines. Do not overwater. Prickly pear can become invasive in the South because any portion of stem roots quickly and birds scatter seed; be prepared to remove unwanted plants. Propagate by seed or division in spring.
Possible problems No serious problems.
Comments Makes a low-maintenance container plant for hot, dry areas.

Pachysandra procumbens
BUXACEAE

ALLEGHENY PACHYSANDRA

The new spring leaves of Allegheny pachysandra are upright and light green. By winter, they are dark green mottled with silver, and they tend to rest on the ground.

Description A native of the southeastern United States, this species of pachysandra has clumps of whorled, 3-inch (7.5-cm) leaves which are toothed at the ends. The leaves are evergreen in the South but often deciduous in the North. Brush-like spikes of white or purplish flowers spring from the base of the plant. Allegheny pachysandra spreads by rhizomes (underground runners).
Height and spread Height 6–10 inches (15–25 cm); spread to 1 foot (30 cm).
Flower color and season White or purplish flowers bloom in early spring.
Best climate and site Zones 5–9. Partial to full shade. Grow in a large container in all-purpose container mix. Established plants are drought-tolerant.
Growing guidelines Set plants 6–12 inches (15–30 cm) apart in spring. Mulch with compost or top-dress with aged manure in fall. Cut down all the leaves in early spring to clean up the planting and make it easier to see the flowers. Propagate by division in early spring or by cuttings in summer.
Possible problems No serious problems.
Other common names Allegheny spurge.
Comments Grown in a large pot, it makes a low-maintenance container plant.

Paeonia lactiflora
RANUNCULACEAE

COMMON GARDEN PEONY

Common garden peonies are shrub-like with sturdy stalks clothed in compound, shiny, green leaves. Plants grow from thick, fleshy roots and may live 100 years or more.

Description This species of peony, with large, fragrant, single or double flowers, is the parent of many garden peony hybrids. These cultivars offer great variety in shape and color and are easy to grow given the right conditions.

Height and spread Height 1½–3 feet (45–90 cm); spread 3–4 feet (90–120 cm).

Flower color and season Ranges in color from white, cream, and yellow to pink, rose, burgundy, and scarlet. Common garden peonies are classified by their bloom time; early May blooming (April in the South); mid-May blooming; and late May blooming (early June in the North).

Best climate and site Zones 2–8. Winter temperatures in the deep South are not cool enough to initiate flowering. Full sun to light shade. Grow in a large container in all-purpose container mix. Good drainage is important to avoid root rot.

Growing guidelines Plant container-grown peonies in spring or fall. Plant bareroot plants in September and October. Dig a hole 8–10 inches (20–25 cm) deep in well-prepared container mix. Place the "eyes" (buds) 1–1½ inches (2.5–3.5 cm) below the container mix surface. Mulch new plants to protect from frost heaving.

An annual winter mulch is advised where winter temperatures dip below 0°F (–18°C). Taller selections and those with double flowers may need staking. Plants may grow undisturbed in containers for years, but if roots become too crowded, flowering will drop off. Divide in fall: Lift plants and divide the roots, leaving at least one eye (bud) per division, then replant into fresh container mix.

Possible problems Spray or dust foliage with sulfur or bordeaux mix to discourage the fungal disease Botrytis.

Other common names Chinese peony.

Cultivars Many cultivars are available in a range of colors and forms. 'Beacon Flame' has deep red, semidouble flowers. 'Bowl of Beauty' grows to 3 feet (90 cm) tall and bears dense clusters of creamy pink flowers with creamy white centers in spring and midsummer. 'Coral Charm' has deep apricot buds fading to soft orange. 'Festiva Maxima' is an early white double flecked with red that is good for Southern gardens. 'Nippon Beauty' is a garnet red Japanese type.

Comments Combine the deep red, new shoots of common garden peony with early spring bulbs such as snowdrops (*Galanthus* spp.) and squills (*Scilla* spp.). Spring and early-summer perennials, such as irises and columbines (*Aquilegia* spp.), are also excellent companions.

Papaver orientale
PAPAVERACEAE

ORIENTAL POPPY

Oriental poppies are prized for their colorful, crepe paper-like flowers. Combine them in large containers with bushy perennials to fill the gap when the poppies go dormant in summer.

Description The 3–4-inch (7.5–10-cm) flowers have crinkled petals with black spots at their bases. They surround a raised knob that becomes the seedpod. Plants produce rosettes of coarse, hairy, lobed foliage from a thick taproot. Plants usually go dormant and die back to the ground soon after flowering.

Height and spread Height 2–3 feet (60–90 cm); spread 2–3 feet (60–90 cm).

Flower color and season Flowers in shades of pink through red bloom in summer.

Best climate and site Zones 2–7. Full sun or light shade. Plant oriental poppies in a large container in all-purpose container mix.

Growing guidelines In most areas, the plants go dormant after flowering. In fall, new foliage rosettes emerge; divide overgrown plants at this time.

Possible problems No serious problems.

Cultivars 'Snow Queen' is pure white with large black spots. 'Watermelon' is rosy pink.

Comments Combine oriental poppies with bushy plants such as catmints (*Nepeta* spp.), cranesbills (*Geranium* spp.), yarrow (*Achillea* spp.), and asters to fill the gap left by the declining foliage.

Penstemon digitalis
SCROPHULARIACEAE

FOXGLOVE PENSTEMON

Foxglove penstemons look wonderful In large containers combined with cardinal flowers (Lobelia cardinalis). Enjoy the flowers in late spring and the seed heads in winter.

Description Showy foxglove penstemon has upright flower spikes clothed in shiny, broadly lance-shaped leaves. The 1–1½-inch (2.5–3.5-cm) irregular, tubular flowers have two upper and three lower lips. Flowering stems and basal foliage rosettes rise from fibrous-rooted crowns.

Height and spread Height 2–4 feet (60–120 cm), occasionally larger; spread 1–2 feet (30–60 cm).

Flower color and season White flowers with purple lines bloom from late spring to early summer.

Best climate and site Zones 4–8. Full sun or light shade. Plant penstemons in a large container in all-purpose container mix.

Growing guidelines Plants benefit from division every 4–6 years. Plants may need more frequent division if they're growing in rich, moist container mix. Sow seed outdoors in fall.

Possible problems No serious problems.

Other common names Penstemon.

Cultivars 'Husker's Red' is attractive to hummingbirds.

Comments Combine foxglove penstemon with rounded plants such as cranesbills (*Geranium* spp.), yarrows (*Achillea* spp.), and coral bells (*Heuchera* spp.).

Phlox paniculata
POLEMONIACEAE

GARDEN PHLOX

Garden phlox is a popular summer-blooming perennial with domed clusters of fragrant, richly colored flowers atop stiff, leafy stems. Plants grow from fibrous-rooted crowns.

Description The many cultivars of this species are easy to grow and provide masses of long-lasting color. The dense flower heads are fragrant and useful for cutting.

Height and spread Height 3–4 feet (90–120 cm); spread 2–4 feet (60–120 cm).

Flower color and season Varies from magenta to pink and white. Hybrids have a wide color range, including purples, reds, and oranges. Bicolored and "eyed" forms are also popular. The bloom time is mid- to late summer.

Best climate and site Zones 3–8. Prefers full sun to light shade. Grow in an all-purpose container mix. Cold-hardiness varies with cultivars.

Growing guidelines Divide clumps every 3–4 years, in spring, to keep them vigorous. Take stem cuttings in late spring or early summer. Take root cuttings in the fall.

Possible problems Powdery mildew is the bane of phlox growers. It causes white patches on the leaves or, in bad cases, turns entire leaves white. To avoid problems, thin the stems before plants bloom to increase air circulation. Select resistant cultivars, especially hybrids with *P. maculata*.

Other common names Summer phlox, perennial phlox.

Cultivars Dozens of named selections are available. They vary in bloom time, mildew resistance, flower size, and cold-hardiness. 'Bright Eyes' has pink flowers with crimson eyes and is mildew-resistant. 'Caroline van den Berg' has purple flowers. 'David' has large heads of white flowers and is mildew-resistant. 'Dodo Hanbury Forbes' has large, clear pink flowers with rose eyes. 'Mt. Fujiyama' is a compact, late-summer white. 'Sandra' is a compact plant with scarlet flowers. 'The King' has red-violet flowers.

Other species

P. carolina, thick-leaved phlox, has glossy oval leaves and elongated clusters of lavender, pink, or white flowers in early summer. 'Miss Lingard' has white flowers with yellow eyes. 'Rosalinde' has bright pink flowers. Zones 4–9.

P. maculata, wild sweet William, is similar to *P. carolina* but the foliage is lance-shaped. 'Alpha' has rose-pink flowers with a darker eye. 'Omega' has white flowers with lilac-pink eyes. Zones 3–9.

P. ovata, mountain phlox, is an upright but spreading species with shiny, oval leaves and open clusters of pink to magenta flowers. 'Spring Delight' has deep rose pink flowers in late spring and early summer. Zones 4–8.

Comments Combine with summer daisies, bee balms (*Monarda* spp.), daylilies, asters, and ornamental grasses.

Physostegia virginiana
LAMIACEAE

OBEDIENT PLANT

Fast-spreading obedient plant is named for the tendency of its flowers to remain in any position when shifted in their four-ranked clusters.

Description This is an easy-to-grow herbaceous perennial with leafy, upright stems and spikes of tubular, bilobed flowers. The individual flowers have hinged stalks and will remain in any position they are moved to. The leaves are long and tapered and toothed around the margins.
Height and spread Height 3–4 feet (90–120 cm); spread 2–4 feet (60–120 cm).
Flower color and season The rose pink to lilac-pink flowers bloom in late summer.
Best climate and site Zones 3–9. Full sun to light shade. Grow in an all-purpose container mix.
Growing guidelines Wild forms of obedient plant tend to flop in rich container mix. Stake the plants or choose a compact cultivar. Divide every 2–4 years in spring. Take stem cuttings in early summer.
Possible problems No serious problems.
Other common names False dragonhead.
Cultivars 'Summer Snow' has white flowers on compact, 3-foot (90-cm) stems. 'Variegata' has leaves edged in creamy white and pale pink flowers. 'Vivid' has vibrant rose-pink flowers.
Comments Combine with asters, garden phlox (*Phlox paniculata*), boltonia (*Boltonia asteroides*), and ornamental grasses.

Platycodon grandiflorus
CAMPANULACEAE

BALLOON FLOWER

Balloon flowers are showy, summer-blooming plants with saucer-shaped flowers on succulent stems clothed in toothed, triangular leaves. Plants grow from thick, fleshy roots.

Description This compact, clump-forming, herbaceous perennial sends up numerous leafy flower stems. The balloon-like buds open to form wide, cup-shaped flowers with five-pointed petals. It is an easy plant to grow provided it has a sunny position and the right container mix.
Height and spread Height 2–3 feet (60–90 cm); spread 1–2 feet (30–60 cm).
Flower color and season The rich blue flowers bloom in summer.
Best climate and site Zones 3–8. Full sun to light shade. Grow in an all-purpose container mix. Established plants are drought-tolerant.
Growing guidelines New shoots are slow to emerge in spring. Take care not to damage them by mistake. Remove spent flowers to encourage more bloom. Established clumps seldom need division. Lift and divide clumps in spring or early fall; dig deeply to avoid root damage. Take basal cuttings of non-flowering shoots in summer, preferably with a piece of root attached. Sow seed outdoors in fall.
Possible problems No serious problems.
Comments Combine balloon flower with yellow yarrows (*Achillea* spp.), sages (*Salvia* spp.), and bee balms (*Monarda* spp.).

Polygonatum odoratum
CONVALLARIACEAE

FRAGRANT SOLOMON'S SEAL

Greenish flowers dangle from the arching stems of fragrant Solomon's seal in spring. The cream-edged leaves of the variegated form extend the interest through the season.

Description Fragrant Solomon's seal has graceful, arching stems with broadly oval, blue-green leaves arranged like stairsteps up the stem. The tubular, fragrant flowers hang in clusters below the leaves from the nodes (leaf joints). Showy blue-black fruits form in late summer. The leafy stems are attractive all season.
Height and spread Height 1½–2½ feet (45–75 cm); spread 2–4 feet (60–120 cm).
Flower color and season The pale green flowers bloom in spring.
Best climate and site Zones 3–9. Prefers partial to full shade. Plant in all-purpose container mix.
Growing guidelines Divide in spring or fall to control spread or for propagation. Sow fresh seed outdoors in fall. Seedlings may not appear for 2 years and will not bloom for several years.
Possible problems No serious problems.
Other common names Japanese Solomon's seal.
Cultivars The variety *P. thunbergii* 'Variegatum' is prized for its broad, oval leaves with creamy white margins.
Comments Combine in a large container with hostas, lungworts (*Pulmonaria* spp.), irises, and ferns.

Primula japonica
PRIMULACEAE

JAPANESE PRIMROSE

Japanese primrose is a tough, hardy, easy-to-grow plant in the right conditions. It looks pretty in pots combined with hostas, placed at the edge of a pond.

Description Japanese primroses are grown mainly for their blooms, which are up to 1 inch (2.5 cm) wide. They bloom one tier above the other on strong, upright stems over large clumps of oblong, 10-inch (25-cm) leaves.

Height and spread Height of foliage to 1 foot (30 cm); spread to 1½ feet (45 cm).

Flower color and season Cultivars come in many flower colors, including pink, rose, red, purple, and white, with "eyes" of varying shades. Flowers bloom in late spring and early summer.

Best climate and site Zones 4–8. Light shade. Grow in all-purpose container mix with added compost.

Growing guidelines Set the plants out 12–20 inches (30–75 cm) apart in spring in a spot that gets no direct sunlight. Top-dress plantings yearly with leaf mold, aged manure, or compost. Divide clumps when they become overcrowded—usually every 3–5 years—to promote better flowering. Propagate by seed or division in spring.

Possible problems No serious problems.

Other common names Candelabra primrose.

Comments Japanese primrose are especially attractive when combined with ferns and hostas.

Primula x polyantha
PRIMULACEAE

POLYANTHUS PRIMROSE

Polyanthus primroses are hybrids with large, showy flowers in a rainbow of colors. Grow them in window boxes and containers for a bright spring display.

Description These perennials, sometimes grown as annuals, have large, flat, five-petaled, scented flowers in every color but green. The flowers bloom on dense umbels. The broad, crinkled leaves rise directly from stout crowns with thick, fibrous roots.

Height and spread Height 8–12 inches (20–30 cm); spread 1 foot (30 cm).

Flower color and season Flowers vary in color from white, cream, and yellow to pink, rose, red, and purple. Many bicolored and eyed forms are available. They bloom in spring and early summer.

Best climate and site Zones 3–8. Light to partial shade. Grow in all-purpose container mix with added compost. Plants can tolerate dryness in the summer if they go dormant.

Growing guidelines In cooler zones mulch plants to avoid frost heaving and crown damage. Divide overgrown clumps after flowering and replant into container mix that has been enriched with compost. Species are easy to grow from fresh seed sown outdoors or indoors in early spring.

Possible problems No serious problems.

Other common names Polyanthus.

Comments Combine with early-blooming perennials such as hellebores (*Helleborus* spp.), forget-me-nots (*Myosotis* spp.), and cranesbills (*Geranium* spp.).

Primula vulgaris
PRIMULACEAE

ENGLISH PRIMROSE

The pale yellow flowers of English primroses are excellent companions for spring-blooming bulbs. Use them as a groundcover in containers under a Japanese maple.

Description English primroses have flat, five-petaled, pale yellow flowers. The broad, crinkled leaves rise directly from stout crowns with thick, fibrous roots.

Height and spread Height 6–9 inches (15–22.5 cm); spread 1 foot (30 cm).

Flower color and season Pale yellow flowers bloom in spring and early summer.

Best climate and site Zones 4–8. Light to partial shade. Plant in all-purpose container mix. Plants may go dormant if container mix dries out in summer.

Growing guidelines In Northern zones, mulch plants in winter to minimize the alternate freezing and thawing that can push plants out of the soil. Divide overgrown clumps after flowering. English primroses are easy to grow from fresh seed sown outdoors or indoors in early spring.

Possible problems No serious problems.

Other common names Primrose.

Other species *P. denticulata*, drumstick primrose, bears round heads of small pink, lavender, or white flowers on tall stalks.

Comments Combine with early-blooming perennials such as hellebores (*Helleborus* spp.), forget-me-nots (*Myosotis* spp.), and cranesbills (*Geranium* spp.). Wildflowers and ferns are other excellent companions.

Pulsatilla vulgaris
RANUNCULACEAE

PASQUE FLOWER

Pasque flowers are early-blooming perennials with cupped flowers over rosettes of deeply incised, lobed leaves clothed in soft hairs.

Description Pasque flower has ferny leaves and nodding flowers on erect, hairy stems. The flowers have five starry petals surrounding a central ring of fuzzy, orange-yellow stamens. The flowers are followed by clusters of fuzzy seeds. Its common name was given because the plant comes into bloom around Easter in the northern hemisphere.
Height and spread Height 6–12 inches (15–30 cm); spread 10–12 inches (25–30 cm).
Flower color and season Purple flowers with yellow centers bloom from early to midspring.
Best climate and site Zones 3–8. Full sun to light shade. Grow in all-purpose container mix with a little added sand. Does not tolerate a soggy mix.
Growing guidelines Pasque flowers begin blooming in spring and continue for several weeks. After seed is set, plants go dormant unless conditions are cool. Seldom needs division. Divide clumps after flowering or in fall. Sow seed outdoors in fall or spring. Self-sown seedlings are plentiful.
Possible problems No serious problems.
Other species *P. patens*, prairie pasque flower, has white or pale blue flowers.
Comments Combine with spring-flowering bulbs.

Rudbeckia fulgida
ASTERACEAE

ORANGE CONEFLOWER

A mass of orange coneflowers makes an eye-catching show in containers. Combine with blue-flowering Russian sage (Perovskia atriplicifolia) for stunning effect.

Description Orange coneflower is a sturdy and hardy plant with rough, narrow leaves and tall stems of flowers. The large daisies last for a long time and are suitable for cutting. It looks its best in bold groups.
Height and spread Height to 3 feet (90 cm); spread 2–4 feet (60–120 cm).
Flower color and season Gold flowers with dark central cones bloom during summer and fall.
Best climate and site Zones 3–9. Full sun. Grow in an all-purpose container mix. Tolerates drought.
Growing guidelines Start with divisions or nursery transplants. Deadhead after flowering or leave the seed heads on for winter interest and self-sown seedlings. Divide every 4 years to renew.
Possible problems No serious problems.
Other common names Black-eyed Susan.
Cultivars 'Goldsturm' black-eyed Susan (*R. fulgida* var. *sullivantii* 'Goldsturm') is compact and especially long-blooming.
Other species *R. hirta*, black-eyed Susan, is an annual with large, gold flowers and purplish-brown central cones.
Comments Combine with 'Autumn Joy' sedum (*Sedum* 'Autumn Joy') and violet sage (*Salvia* x *superba*).

Salvia x *superba*
LAMIACEAE

VIOLET SAGE

The spiky blooms of violet sage combine wonderfully with rounded perennials, such as cranesbills (Geranium spp.). Cut the stems back after flowering to promote rebloom.

Description Violet sage is covered with colorful flower spikes in summer. The violet-blue flowers are carried in narrow spikes; below each flower is a leaf-like bract. The bushy, well-branched plants have aromatic, triangular leaves. They grow from a fibrous-rooted crown.
Height and spread Height 1½–3½ feet (45–105 cm); spread 2–3 feet (60–90 cm).
Flower color and season Early to midsummer bloom for the violet-blue flowers; often reblooms later in the season.
Best climate and site Zones 4–7. Full sun or light shade. Plant violet sage in all-purpose container mix. Plants are drought-tolerant once they are established.
Growing guidelines Plants bloom nonstop for a month. After flowering wanes, shear off the spent flowers to promote fresh growth and renewed bloom. Plants seldom need division. Propagate by cuttings in late spring or early summer; remove any flowers that form on unrooted cuttings.
Possible problems No serious problems.
Comments Combine violet sage with yarrows (*Achillea* spp.), lamb's-ears (*Stachys byzantina*), daylilies, coreopsis (*Coreopsis* spp.), and ornamental grasses.

Scabiosa caucasica
DIPSACACEAE

PINCUSHION FLOWER

Pincushion flowers are old-fashioned perennials that are regaining the popularity they had in Victorian gardens. Combine them in pots with other summer-flowering perennials.

Description The stems of pincushion flowers are loosely clothed in lance-shaped to three-lobed leaves. The flowers are packed into flat, 2–3-inch (5–7.5-cm) heads. The flowers increase in size as they near the margins of the heads.
Height and spread Height 1½–2 feet (45–60 cm); spread 1–1½ feet (30–45 cm).
Flower color and season Flowers in pink, red, purple, or blue hues bloom in summer.
Best climate and site Zones 3–7. Prefers full sun to light shade. Plant in all-purpose container mix. Plants are sensitive to high temperatures.
Growing guidelines Plants form good-sized clumps in 1–2 years. Divide in spring if they become overcrowded. Remove spent flowers to promote continued bloom. Propagate by division in spring, or sow fresh seed outdoors in fall or indoors in late winter.
Possible problems No serious problems.
Other common names Scabiosa.
Cultivars 'Butterfly Blue' is a long-blooming plant with lilac-blue flowers. 'Miss Wilmott' has white flowers.
Comments Combine with cranesbills (*Geranium* spp.), phlox, pinks (*Dianthus* spp.), yarrows (*Achillea* spp.), bee balms (*Monarda* spp.), and daylilies.

Sedum spectabile
CRASSULACEAE

SEDUM

Sedums are late-summer perennials with clusters of pink flowers that bloom atop thick stems clothed in broad, gray-green leaves. Plants grow from fibrous-rooted crowns.

Description Much loved by butterflies and bees, sedum is grown for its showy, plate-like heads of starry, pink flowers, borne in 4–6-inch (10–15-cm) domed clusters on sturdy stems. The oval, succulent leaves help the plant withstand long dry periods.
Height and spread Height 1–2 feet (30–60 cm); spread 2 feet (60 cm).
Flower color and season Small bright pink flowers bloom in mid- to late summer.
Best climate and site Zones 3–9. Full sun. Grow in all-purpose container mix. Extremely drought-tolerant.
Growing guidelines Clumps get quite full with age and may fall open. Divide overgrown plants from spring to mid-summer. Take cuttings of non-flowering shoots in summer. Sow seed in spring or fall.
Possible problems No serious problems.
Other common names Showy stonecrop.
Hybrids Several hybrid cultivars are available. 'Autumn Joy' is a stout sedum similar to *S. spectabile* but more robust with darker flowers.
Comments Combine with yarrows (*Achillea* spp.), purple coneflowers (*Echinacea* spp.), cranesbills (*Geranium* spp.), coreopsis (*Coreopsis* spp.), and ornamental grasses.

Senecio cineraria
ASTERACEAE

DUSTY MILLER

"Senex" is Latin for "old man," referring to the white whiskers that give this very useful foliage plant its woolly, silver-white appearance.

Description The silvery gray leaves are a useful foil for other plants in a mixed container planting. Like so many gray-leaved plants, it grows well near the seaside and can survive dry conditions, but not frost. Plants may survive winter outdoors and produce yellow flowers their second year, but they're really best as annuals.
Height and spread The clumps grow 8–24 inches (20–60 cm) tall and wide.
Flower color and season Yellow flowers bloom in summer.
Best climate and site Zones 7–9. Semi-shaded spots. Grow in well-drained, all-purpose container mix. Does poorly in high humidity or excessive rain.
Growing guidelines Set plants 8–10 inches (20–25 cm) apart. Pinch off shoot tips in early summer to encourage branching. If plants get leggy, shear them back by half to two-thirds to promote bushy new growth. Allow container mix to dry between waterings. Sow seed indoors 8–10 weeks before the last frost; leave it uncovered.
Possible problems No serious problems.
Comments The silvery foliage is especially effective at nighttime. Combine with ivy geranium (*Pelargonium peltatum*), edging lobelia (*Lobelia erinus*), and rose moss (*Portulaca grandiflora*).

Smilacina racemosa
CONVALLARIACEAE

SOLOMON'S PLUME

Solomon's plume is a showy woodland wildflower. The erect, arching stems bear broad, glossy green leaves arranged like ascending stairs. It looks magnificent in a large container in a shady position.

Description This plant has erect to ascending stems of fresh green leaves and spikes of starry, white flowers borne in terminal, plume-like clusters, which are deliciously lemon-scented. As flowers age, they become tinged with pink and can be followed by red berries. Plants grow from a thick, creeping rhizome.

Height and spread Height 2–4 feet (60–120 cm); spread 2–3 feet (60–90 cm).

Flower color and season White flowers bloom in late spring.

Best climate and site Zones 3–8. Light to full shade. Plants burn in full sun. Plant in a large container in all-purpose container mix with added organic matter.

Growing guidelines Divide the tangled rhizomes if plants overgrow their container. Divide in spring or fall. Sow fresh seed outdoors in fall.

Possible problems No serious problems.

Other common names False Solomon's seal, false spikenard.

Comments Plant Solomon's plumes with hostas, bleeding hearts (*Dicentra* spp.), lungworts (*Pulmonaria* spp.), columbines (*Aquilegia* spp.), wildflowers, and ferns.

Stachys byzantina
LAMIACEAE

LAMB'S-EARS

The silvery, felted foliage is especially effective at nighttime. Combine in large pots with red zonal geraniums, ivy geranium (Pelargonium peltatum), and petunias for a colorful display.

Description Lamb's-ears are appealing low-growing plants with felted, silvery leaves forming dense rosettes from a creeping, fibrous-rooted rhizome. The small, two-lipped flowers are carried in whorls on woolly stems; they are secondary to the foliage.

Height and spread Height to 15 inches (37.5 cm) in flower, leaves 6–8 inches (15–20 cm) high. Plants are 12–24 inches (30–60 cm) high.

Flower color and season The rose-pink flowers bloom in spring. The foliage provides season-long interest.

Best climate and site Zones 4–8. Full sun or light shade. Grow in well-drained all-purpose container mix.

Growing guidelines Divide in spring or fall to control spread or for propagation. Take cuttings in summer. In wet, humid weather, rot may occur. Cut back plants to remove the affected portions and improve air circulation. Proper planting in well-drained container mix is the best defense.

Possible problems No serious problems.

Comments Combine lamb's-ears with bearded irises, ornamental onions (*Allium* spp.), grasses, yuccas, sedums, and cranesbills (*Geranium* spp.).

Stokesia laevis
ASTERACEAE

STOKE'S ASTER

Stoke's aster is attractive in foliage and flower. The broad, lance-shaped leaves are deep green with a white midvein. The leaves form a rosette from a crown with thick, fibrous roots.

Description From a basal rosette of plain, green leaves, the flower stems emerge with 2–3-inch (5–7.5-cm) daisies with ragged, blue rays and fuzzy, white centers, set off by a collar of green leaves. The flowers can often be 4 inches (10 cm) across.

Height and spread Height 1–2 feet (30–60 cm); spread 2 feet (60 cm).

Flower color and season Blue flowers bloom in summer.

Best climate and site Zones 5–9. Grow in all-purpose container mix. Prefers full sun to light shade. Established plants tolerate dry conditions, but prefer moisture.

Growing guidelines Plants can grow undisturbed for many years. Divide in spring or fall as necessary. Sow seed outdoors in fall or indoors in winter after stratification. To stratify, mix seed with moist peat moss or seed-starting medium in a plastic bag. Close the bag with a twist-tie and place it in the refrigerator for 4–6 weeks. Then sow the mixture as you would normal seed.

Possible problems No serious problems.

Comments Combine with verbenas (*Verbena* spp.), phlox, columbines (*Aquilegia* spp.), and ornamental grasses.

Tiarella cordifolia
SAXIFRAGACEAE

ALLEGHENY FOAMFLOWER

A large pot of Allegheny foamflower, fringed bleeding heart (Dicentra eximia), hostas, and ferns looks fabulous in a shady position.

Description This evergreen native of eastern North American forests forms clumps of heart-shaped, lobed and toothed, green leaves. The leaves are up to 4 inches (10 cm) wide and turn bronze to burgundy in fall; they are evergreen in the South. The plant has feathery, bottlebrush-like spikes of tiny white flowers.
Height and spread Height of foliage to 6 inches (15 cm); spread to 2 feet (60 cm). Flower stems 9–12 inches (22.5–30 cm) tall.
Flower color and season White flowers bloom in midspring.
Best climate and site Zones 3–8. Light shade. Grow in a large container in all-purpose container mix.
Growing guidelines Set plants 1 foot (30 cm) apart in spring. Removing spent flower spikes may extend the blooming season. Propagate by division in spring or fall or sow seed in spring.
Possible problems No serious problems.
Cultivars 'George Shenk Pink' has foamy, pink flowers in spring. 'Oakleaf' has deeply lobed leaves and airy, deep pink blooms that last for several weeks.
Comments Allegheny foamflower is an ideal container plant for shady positions.

Tradescantia x andersoniana
COMMELINACEAE

COMMON SPIDERWORT

Each flower of common spiderwort lasts only a day, but the clumps produce so many buds that you'll enjoy up to 2 months of blooms.

Description Spiderworts have 1–1½-inch (2.5–3.5-cm), satiny flowers that open in the morning and fade in the afternoon. Rounded flowers are borne in clusters at the tips of the stems. The thick, succulent stems bear grass-like, light green foliage. Plants grow from thick, spidery roots.
Height and spread Height 1–2 feet (30–60 cm); spread 2 feet (60 cm).
Flower color and season Spring and early summer bloom for the blue, purple, or white flowers.
Best climate and site Zones 3–9. Full sun or partial shade. Plant in all-purpose container mix.
Growing guidelines After flowering, plants tend to look shabby; cut them to the ground to encourage new growth. Plants in dry containers go dormant in summer. Divide in fall to renew overgrown clumps or to propagate cultivars. Self-sown seedlings often appear.
Possible problems No serious problems.
Other common names Spiderwort, tradescantia.
Comments Combine common spiderwort with bellflowers (*Campanula* spp.), columbines (*Aquilegia* spp.), hostas, ferns, tulips, and spring-blooming perennials.

Uvularia grandiflora
CONVALLARIACEAE

GREAT MERRYBELLS

The nodding flowers of great merrybells look wonderful in a large container with other spring wildflowers and bulbs.

Description Great merrybells is a graceful wildflower with nodding, bell-shaped, yellow flowers. Each flower has three petals and three petal-like sepals that twist in the middle. The main stalk pierces the blade of the gray-green leaves.
Height and spread Height 1–1½ feet (30–45 cm); spread 1–2 feet (30–60 cm).
Flower color and season The lemon-yellow flowers bloom in spring.
Best climate and site Zones 3–8. Partial to full shade. Spring sun is important for bloom, but summer shade is mandatory. Plant in an all-purpose container mix.
Growing guidelines Great merrybells spreads to form attractive clumps. When flowers fade, the gray-green foliage expands to form a leafy groundcover. Divide plants in early spring or fall.
Possible problems No serious problems.
Other common names Large-flowered bellwort.
Other species *U. sessilifolia*, wild oats, is a slender, delicate plant with straw-colored flowers and narrow leaves. Zones 4–8.
Comments Combine great merrybells with wildflowers such as wild bleeding heart (*Dicentra eximia*). Ferns and hostas are also good companions.

Verbascum chaixii
SCROPHULARIACEAE

NETTLE-LEAVED MULLEIN

Nettle-leaved mullein produces clumps of crinkled green leaves and tall stems topped with spikes of yellow flowers.

Description Nettle-leaved mullein has thick flower spikes and stout stems clothed in broadly oval, pointed leaves. The small, five-petaled flowers are tightly packed into dense clusters. Plants form tight rosettes from fibrous-rooted crowns that overwinter and form next year's bloom stalk.
Height and spread Height 2–3 feet (60–90 cm); spread 1–2 feet (30–60 cm).
Flower color and season Yellow flowers bloom in summer; the foliage is attractive in spring and summer.
Best climate and site Zones 4–8. Full sun or light shade. Plant in a large container in well-drained, all-purpose container mix.
Growing guidelines Established plants spread slowly and seldom need division. For propagation, take root cuttings in early spring or dig and move young self-sown seedlings to desired position.
Possible problems No serious problems.
Cultivars The variety 'Album' has white flowers with purple centers.
Other species *V. olympicum*, olympic mullein, has broadly oval, pointed, silver-gray, hairy leaves and yellow flowers. Zones 6–8.
Comments Combine nettle-leaved mullein with fine-textured perennials such as cranesbills (*Geranium* spp.).

Veronica spicata
SCROPHULARIACEAE

SPIKE SPEEDWELL

Spike speedwell grows slowly to form neat clumps. It is an excellent companion for ornamental grasses and a wide variety of summer-blooming perennials.

Description Spike speedwell has pointed flower clusters atop leafy stems. The small, two-lipped flowers are tightly packed into erect spikes. The opposite leaves are oval to oblong and clothed in soft hairs. Plants grow from fibrous-rooted crowns.
Height and spread Height 1–3 feet (30–90 cm); spread 1½–2½ feet (45–75 cm).
Flower color and season Summer bloom for the pink, blue, or white flowers; the foliage is attractive all season.
Best climate and site Zones 3–8. Full sun or light shade. Plant in a large container in an all-purpose container mix.
Growing guidelines To encourage continued bloom or control rangy growth, cut stems back after flowering; plants will produce fresh growth. Divide overgrown plants in spring or fall. Propagate by division, or take stem cuttings in late spring or early summer; remove the flower buds.
Possible problems No serious problems.
Cultivars 'Blaufuchs' has bright lavender-blue flowers. 'Blue Peter' has dark blue flowers in very compact spikes. 'Red Fox' has crimson flowers.
Comments Combine with other summer-blooming perennials such as yarrows (*Achillea* spp.), catmints (*Nepeta* spp.), and sundrops (*Oenothera* spp.).

Viola odorata
VIOLACEAE

SWEET VIOLET

Sweet violets are beloved for their delicate, fragrant, early-season flowers. They produce rosettes of heart-shaped leaves from creeping, fibrous-rooted rhizomes.

Description For the size of this little perennial, the flowers are relatively large, being up to 1 inch (2.5 cm) across. The deep purple or blue flowers have five petals. Two point upward and three point outward and down. The two outfacing petals have fuzzy beards. Their perfume is sweet and quite strong.
Height and spread Height 2–8 inches (5–20 cm); spread 4–8 inches (10–20 cm).
Flower color and season The purple flowers bloom in spring.
Best climate and site Zones 6–9. Sun or shade. Grow in all-purpose container mix.
Growing guidelines Violets are prolific spreaders and can fill large containers. Divide plants after flowering or in fall.
Possible problems No serious problems.
Cultivars 'Deloris' has deep purple flowers. 'White Queen' has small white flowers.
Other species *V. sororia*, woolly blue violet, is similar but has hairier foliage. 'Freckles' has pale blue flowers flecked with purple. 'Priceana', the confederate violet, has white flowers with purple-blue centers. Zones 3–9.
Comments Plant violets in a container underneath a deciduous small tree such as a Japanese maple (*Acer palmatum*).

Ageratum houstonianum
ASTERACEAE

AGERATUM

This Mexican native combines rare blue colors with a neat, compact, edging habit. The name "ageratum" is from the Greek for "not growing old," a testament to its staying power.

Description Ageratum forms 3–6-inch (7.5–15-cm) tall mounds, bearing soft, green, hairy leaves. Fuzzy, tassel-like, ½-inch (12-mm) flowers bloom above the leaves.
Height and spread Height 6–12 inches (15–30 cm); spread 6–8 inches (15–20 cm).
Flower color and season Flowers in lavender, blue, pink, and white bloom from early summer until frost.
Best climate and site Zones 5–10. Full or half-day of sun; protect from hot midday sun. Plant in an all-purpose container mix. Keep the container mix evenly moist.
Growing guidelines Set plants 6–8 inches (15–20 cm) apart. Regularly pinch off spent blossoms. Start from seed sown indoors 6–8 weeks before the last frost. Grow in separate pots to prevent root disturbance at transplant time. Take cuttings of young growth anytime.
Possible problems Plants can look ragged by midsummer. Shear them to 2 inches (5 cm) tall to promote new growth, or replace them with new plants.
Other common names Floss flower.
Comments Try ageratum with dwarf yellow marigolds, pink petunias, white lobelia, English ivy, wax begonias, sweet alyssum, chives, and eggplant.

Amaranthus caudatus
AMARANTHACEAE

LOVE-LIES-BLEEDING

Love-lies-bleeding is lovely in fresh or dried arrangements. To preserve the flowers, stand the cut stems in a heavy bucket so the tassels hang naturally as they dry.

Description This tender annual produces thick, sturdy, branched stems with large, oval, pale green leaves. Long clusters of tightly packed, deep crimson flowers dangle from the stem tips. The ropy, tassel-like clusters can grow to 1½ feet (45 cm) long.
Height and spread Height 3–5 feet (90–150 cm); spread to 2 feet (60 cm).
Flower color and season Crimson flowers bloom from midsummer until frost.
Best climate and site Zones 6–10. Full sun. Grow in a very large container, such as a half-barrel, in all-purpose container mix.
Growing guidelines Sow seed indoors, ⅛ inch (3 mm) deep, 4–6 weeks before last frost date. Use one or or two plants only per pot; plant out 2–3 weeks after the last frost date. Seed germinates quickly in warm soil, so you could sow it directly into the container in late spring.
Possible problems No serious problems.
Other common names Tassel flower.
Cultivars 'Pygmy Torch' has upright, crimson clusters above purplish leaves on 1½–2-foot (45–60-cm) tall stems. 'Viridis' is similar but has green flower clusters.
Comments Grow love-lies-bleeding in a large container with eggplant, white cosmos, petunias, and begonias.

Antirrhinum majus
SCROPHULARIACEAE

SNAPDRAGON

A large container filled with snapdragons makes an eye-catching accent. Pinch the stem tips of dwarf types once after transplanting to promote branching.

Description Snapdragons are usually grown as hardy or half-hardy annuals. The slender stems are topped with spikes of 1½-inch (35-mm), tubular flowers that resemble puckered lips.
Height and spread Height ranges from 1 foot (30 cm) for dwarf types up to 4 feet (120 cm) for tall types; spread ranges from 8–18 inches (20–45 cm).
Flower color and season Flowers bloom in a huge variety of colors (except true blue). Flowers bloom in late summer to fall.
Best climate and site Zones 6–10. Full sun to light shade (especially in hot-summer areas). Plant in an all-purpose container mix. Keep mix evenly moist.
Growing guidelines Buy transplants in spring, or start your own by planting seed indoors 6–8 weeks before your last frost date. Sow seedlings directly into container after the last frost date. Pinch or cut off spent flower spikes, especially early in the season, to promote more flowers.
Possible problems Snapdragons are prone to rust. The best prevention is to pull the plants out in fall.
Comments Snapdragons are excellent container companions for rounded flowers, such as daisies.

Begonia Semperflorens-Cultorum hybrids
BEGONIACEAE

WAX BEGONIA

Wax begonias are among the most popular and dependable bedding plants. In containers, these rugged, heat-resistant annuals flower nonstop from late spring until frost.

Description Wax begonias produce small, mounded, fibrous-rooted plants that normally grow 6–9 inches (15–22.5 cm) tall. Their rounded, shiny leaves may be green, reddish, bronze, or variegated.
Height and spread Height 6–8 inches (15–20 cm); spread 6–8 inches (15–20 cm).
Flower color and season Small flowers in white, pink, or red bloom among the leaves from late spring to fall.
Best climate and site Zones 5–10. A half-day of sun is best, with shade during the hottest hours, in the middle of the day. Grow in all-purpose container mix. Keep the mix evenly moist, especially if the plants are growing in sun.
Growing guidelines Set plants 6–8 inches (15–20 cm) apart. Start the fine seed indoors 8–12 weeks before the last frost; leave the seed uncovered. Take cuttings of young growth anytime.
Possible problems No serious problems.
Other common names Bedding begonias.
Comments Grow wax begonias with ageratum, large periwinkle (*Vinca major*), or clematis. Begonias make good winter houseplants if you bring them indoors before frost.

Begonia Tuberhybrida hybrids
BEGONIACEAE

HYBRID TUBEROUS BEGONIAS

Hybrid tuberous begonias produce their spectacular large flowers from summer until frost. Both the upright and pendulous types make a sensational show in containers.

Description These showy plants grow from frost-tender tubers to produce lush, bushy plants. The succulent stems may be upright or trailing, with green or bronze leaves.
Height and spread Height 1–1½ feet (30–45 cm); spread is variable, depending on whether it's upright or trailing.
Flower color and season Flowers come in all colors except blue, and bloom from summer until frost.
Best climate and site Zones 6–10. A half-day of sun or filtered sun; tolerates shade. Grow the plants in an all-purpose container mix.
Growing guidelines Plant two or three tubers per 8–10-inch (20–25-cm) pot. To keep tubers over winter, reduce watering in fall and bring the pot indoors before or just after the first frost. Cut back remaining top growth; store the pot in a frost-free place. Replant the tubers in fresh container mix the following spring.
Possible problems If powdery mildew is a problem, spray affected leaves with sulfur or a baking soda solution (1 teaspoon of baking soda in 1 quart [1 l] of water).
Comments Try growing hybrid tuberous begonias with coleus or large periwinkle (*Vinca major*).

Bellis perennis
ASTERACEAE

ENGLISH DAISY

Pinch off the spent flower stems of English daisies at the base to prolong bloom and prevent reseeding. Pull out plants after bloom and start new ones for next year.

Description These easy-to-grow, short-lived perennials are usually grown as hardy annuals or biennials. Plants form rosettes of oval, green leaves. Short, thick stems are topped with 1–2-inch (2.5–5-cm) daisies or pompon-like blooms.
Height and spread Height to 6 inches (15 cm); spread 6–8 inches (15–20 cm).
Flower color and season White, pink, or red flowers bloom from April to June.
Best climate and site Zones 3–9. Full sun to partial shade. Grow in an all-purpose container mix.
Growing guidelines In cool-summer areas, start seed indoors in midwinter and set plants out in midspring for bloom the same year. In hot-summer areas, or for earliest spring bloom elsewhere, grow English daisies as biennials. Sow seed in pots indoors or outdoors in June or July. Grow seedlings in pots or in a nursery bed until fall, then transplant to containers. Space plants 6 inches (15 cm) apart.
Possible problems No serious problems.
Other common names Common daisy.
Comments For extra excitement, grow English daisies with forget-me-nots (*Myosotis sylvatica*) as well as spring-flowering bulbs.

Brachyscome iberidifolia
ASTERACEAE

SWAN RIVER DAISY

In full sun and cool temperatures, this Australian native blooms freely for months and produces a sweet scent as a bonus. It is an excellent annual for hanging baskets.

Description Swan River daisy has finely divided, 3-inch (7.5-cm) leaves on many-branched mounds. The plant bears masses of exquisite 1-inch (2.5-cm) wide daisies.
Height and spread Branched mounds grow to a height of 1 foot (30 cm) and can trail to 1½ feet (45 cm) wide.
Flower color and season Blue, white, or rose-colored flowers bloom from spring through summer.
Best climate and site Zones 6–10. Full sun. Plant in an all-purpose container mix.
Growing guidelines Set plants 6 inches (15 cm) apart. Stick some short, twiggy prunings into the pot to support the floppy stems. Sow seed indoors 6–8 weeks before the last frost, or plant directly into the container in late spring.
Possible problems Swan River daisy tends to stop blooming in hot weather. Shearing the plants back by half and watering them well can encourage new growth and a second flush of bloom.
Other common names Brachycome.
Comments Swan River daisy is a good companion to zonal geraniums (*Pelargonium* spp.) or sweet alyssum.

Bracteantha bracteata
ASTERACEAE

STRAWFLOWER

Cutting strawflowers for fresh arrangements or drying will promote branching and prolong the bloom season. The flowers dry quickly when hung upside down in a dark, airy place.

Description This half-hardy annual is grown for its colorful, long-lasting blooms. The bushy plants have long, narrow, green leaves and the colorful heads are stiff and papery. Fully open flower heads are 1–2 inches (2.5–5 cm) wide and have yellow centers.
Height and spread Height 2–4 feet (60–120 cm); spread to 1 foot (30 cm).
Flower color and season The flower heads bloom from midsummer until frost in white, pink, rose, red, orange, or yellow.
Best climate and site Zones 5–10. Full sun. Grow in a well-drained container mix.
Growing guidelines For earliest blooms, buy transplants or start your own by sowing seed indoors 6–8 weeks before your last frost date. Just press the seed lightly into the surface and enclose the pot in a plastic bag until seedlings appear. Set plants out 2 weeks after the last frost date. Or sow seed directly into the container after the last frost date. Set transplants or thin seedlings to stand 10–12 inches (25–30 cm) apart.
Possible problems No serious problems.
Other common names Everlasting daisy.
Comments Strawflowers are ideal for drying. Harvest flowers when they are about one-quarter open.

Brassica oleracea
BRASSICACEAE

ORNAMENTAL CABBAGE

Ornamental cabbages add a showy accent to late-season container gardens. They withstand frost and can look good until late fall or even early spring.

Description This biennial is grown as an annual for its rosettes of colorful fall foliage. As temperatures get cooler in fall, the leaves in the center of the rosette become much more colorful, to the point where they are only green around the edge.
Height and spread Height 1–1½ feet (30–45 cm); spread to 1½ feet (45 cm).
Flower color and season The smooth, glossy, blue-green leaves are marked with pink, purple, cream, or white in fall.
Best climate and site Zones 6–9. Full sun to light shade. Grow in an all-purpose container mix.
Growing guidelines In hot-summer areas, sow seed indoors; elsewhere, sow outdoors in pots or a nursery bed. Plant seed ¼ inch (6 mm) deep in midsummer. Move plants to containers in fall. Set them in holes 1 foot (30 cm) apart and deep enough to cover the stem up to the lowest set of leaves.
Possible problems If caterpillars damage the leaves, pick them off by hand or spray with BT.
Other common names Flowering cabbage.
Comments Ornamental cabbage looks attractive in large window boxes. Transplants are sold in fall.

Browallia speciosa
SOLANACEAE

BROWALLIA

Browallia adds a cool, blue accent to window boxes and baskets in partial shade. Before first frost, cut plants back and bring them indoors to enjoy in winter.

Description This easy annual has a graceful, sprawling habit. Five-petaled flowers to 2 inches (5 cm) wide bloom just above the emerald green foliage in white or many shades of blue or lilac.

Height and spread Height 14 inches (35 cm); spread 15 inches (37.5 cm).

Flower color and season White, blue, or lilac flowers bloom from summer until frost.

Best climate and site Zones 6–9. A half-day of sun is best. Plants tolerate full to filtered sunlight, although flower color may fade in too much sun. Grow browallia in all-purpose container mix. Water often to keep the mix evenly moist.

Growing guidelines Space plants 10 inches (25 cm) apart. Pinch off the stem tips of young plants once or twice to promote branching. Sow seed indoors 8–10 weeks before the last frost; leave it uncovered. Take cuttings anytime during the season.

Possible problems Plants may look tired by midsummer; cut them back by half in midsummer to promote new growth and more flowers.

Other common names Amethyst flower.

Comments Plant browallia with marigolds, sweet alyssum, dahlias, petunias, and large periwinkle (*Vinca major*).

Calendula officinalis
ASTERACEAE

POT MARIGOLD

After the first flush of blooms, shear off spent pot marigold flowers to promote later rebloom, or deadhead individual flowers regularly.

Description This is an easy-to-grow, hardy annual. The clumps of lance-shaped, aromatic leaves are topped with single or double, 2–4-inch (5–10-cm) wide daisies. The flowers tend to close during cloudy weather and at night.

Height and spread Height usually 1–2 feet (30–60 cm); spread to 1 foot (30 cm).

Flower color and season The orange and yellow flowers bloom from summer to fall in most areas.

Best climate and site Zones 4–9. Full sun. Grow in an all-purpose container mix.

Growing guidelines For summer and fall bloom, sow seed indoors 6–8 weeks before your last frost date or outdoors in early to late spring. Set plants out around the last frost date. In hot-summer areas, sow seed directly into containers in midfall for late-winter bloom. Plant seed ¼ inch (6 mm) deep. Space plants or thin seedlings to stand 8–12 inches (20–30 cm) apart. Pot marigolds may self-sow if you let some seeds form at the end of the season.

Possible problems No serious problems.

Other common names Calendula, English marigold.

Comments Pot marigolds are sunny accents for containers. The strong-stemmed blooms are excellent as cut flowers.

Callistephus chinensis
ASTERACEAE

CHINA ASTER

China asters bloom in white, cream, pink, red, purple, or blue. To minimize disease problems, plant them in a different container and new mix each year.

Description China aster's stems carry broadly oval, toothed leaves and are topped with puffy, many-petaled flowers up to 5 inches (12.5 cm) wide.

Height and spread Height 1–2 feet (30–60 cm); spread 1–1½ feet (30–45 cm).

Flower color and season White, cream, pink, red, purple, or blue flowers bloom from late summer to frost.

Best climate and site Zones 4–9. Full sun. Grow in an all-purpose container mix.

Growing guidelines For late-summer bloom, buy transplants in spring or sow seed indoors, ⅛ inch (3 mm) deep, 6 weeks before last frost date. Set plants out 12 weeks after the last frost date, when weather is warm. For fall bloom, sow seed directly into container after the last frost date. Space plants or thin seedlings of most types to stand 10–12 inches (25–30 cm) apart. Pinch off stem tips once in early summer to promote branching.

Possible problems Control aphids with soap sprays to prevent the spread of aster yellows, which causes yellowed, stunted growth. Destroy infected plants. Aster wilt is a soilborne disease that causes plants to droop. Destroy infected plants.

Comments Plant with pot marigolds and ornamental grasses.

Catharanthus roseus
APOCYNACEAE

MADAGASCAR PERIWINKLE

In most areas, Madagascar periwinkle blooms from early summer until frost; it can flower nearly anytime of the year in frost-free climates.

Description Madagascar periwinkle forms compact, bushy clumps of glossy, dark green leaves with white central veins. Stems are topped with flat, five-petaled flowers up to 2 inches (5 cm) wide.
Height and spread Height and spread usually 1–1½ feet (30–45 cm); larger in frost-free areas.
Flower color and season White, rose, or pink flowers bloom almost throughout the year, but mainly in spring and summer.
Best climate and site Zones 5–10. Full sun. Grow in an all-purpose container mix. Tolerates heat, pollution, and drought.
Growing guidelines For best results, buy transplants in spring. Sow seed indoors, ¼ inch (6 mm) deep, 10–12 weeks before last frost date. Keep pots in a warm place (75–80°F [24–27°C]) until seedlings appear; then move pots to regular room temperature. Set transplants out 12 weeks after last frost date, when the soil is warm. Space plants 6–12 inches (15–30 cm) apart. Pinch off stem tips in early summer to promote compact growth and more flowers.
Possible problems No serious problems.
Other common names Rosy periwinkle, vinca, pink periwinkle.
Comments Looks pretty in a large container with an airy ornamental grass.

Celosia cristata
AMARANTHACEAE

CELOSIA

Plumed celosia has feathery flower spikes. Pinching off the stem tips in early summer will promote branching and more, but smaller, flower plumes.

Description These tender perennials are grown as tender annuals. Their sturdy stems carry oval to narrow, pointed leaves that are green or tinted with bronze. Compact types are best for pots.
Height and spread Height 1–2 feet (30–60 cm); spread to 1 foot (30 cm).
Flower color and season The flowers can bloom all summer until frost in shades of fiery red, pink, orange, or yellow.
Best climate and site Zones 5–10. Full sun. Grow in an all-purpose container mix.
Growing guidelines Celosias can be tricky to get started but are easy once established. If plants are disturbed during transplanting, later growth may be slow and stunted. For best results, sow seed directly into container after last frost date, or buy small transplants. Sow seed indoors about 4 weeks before last frost date. Plant seed ⅛ inch (3 mm) deep in individual pots. Set transplants out 12 weeks after last frost date. Space plants 6–8 inches (15–20 cm) apart.
Possible problems No serious problems.
Other common names Cockscomb, plumed celosia.
Comments Combine with silver-leaved plants such as dusty miller (*Senecio cineraria*), lamb's-ears (*Stachys byzantina*), and snow-in-summer (*Cerastium tomentosum*).

Centaurea cyanus
ASTERACEAE

CORNFLOWER

Stick brushy prunings into the container mix around young cornflower plants to support the stems as they grow. Pinching off spent blooms can prolong the flowering season.

Description Cornflower plants have narrow, lance-shaped, silvery green leaves and thin stems topped with 1–2-inch (2.5–5-cm), fluffy flower heads.
Height and spread Height 1–2½ feet (30–75 cm); spread to 1 foot (30 cm).
Flower color and season White, blue, pink, purple, or red flowers bloom throughout summer.
Best climate and site Zones 5–9. Full sun. Grow in an all-purpose container mix.
Growing guidelines Grows easily from seed sown directly into container in early fall (in mild-winter areas) or early spring. Plant seed ⅛ inch (3 mm) deep. To extend flowering season from an early-spring planting, sow again every 2–4 weeks until midsummer. Other ways to establish cornflowers include buying transplants in spring or starting the seed indoors about 8 weeks before your last frost date. Set plants outdoors about 2 weeks before last frost date. Space or thin plants to stand 8–12 inches (20–30 cm) apart.
Possible problems No serious problems.
Other common names Bachelor's buttons, blue bottle.
Comments Pot marigolds and cornflowers make a bright container mix.

Cleome hasslerana
CAPPARIDACEAE

CLEOME

Cleome is a must for butterfly gardens; it's also popular with bees. Plant it in a large container to show off the spidery white, pink, or lavender flowers.

Description Cleome has tall, sturdy stems and palm-like leaves that have a musky (some say skunk-like) odor. Long stamens protrude from the four-petaled flowers, giving them a spidery look. The blooms are followed by long, narrow seedpods.

Height and spread Height 3–4 feet (90–120 cm); spread 1½ feet (45 cm).

Flower color and season White, pink, or lavender flowers bloom from midsummer to midfall.

Best climate and site Zones 4–10. Full sun to light shade. Grow in a large container in an all-purpose container mix.

Growing guidelines Easy to grow from seed sown directly in the container in mid- to late spring. For earlier bloom, buy transplants or start your own by sowing seed indoors about 4 weeks before last frost date. Set plants out around the last frost date. Space transplants or thin seedlings to stand 1 foot (30 cm) apart. Cleome usually self-sows prolifically. Pinching off the seedpods regularly can reduce or eliminate self-sown seedlings.

Possible problems No serious problems.

Other common names Spider flower, spider plant.

Comments Combine in a large pot with a tall ornamental grass for a striking display.

Consolida ambigua
RANUNCULACEAE

ROCKET LARKSPUR

Tall cultivars of rocket larkspur may need support to stay upright. Push pieces of twiggy brush into the container around young plants to hold them up as they grow.

Description This hardy annual is grown for its showy flowers. The plants produce tall stems with finely divided, bright green leaves. There is a curving spur on the back of each flower. Rocket larkspur is also listed in seed catalogs as *C. ajacis*, *Delphinium ajacis*, and *D. consolida*.

Height and spread Height 1–4 feet (30–120 cm); spread to 1 foot (30 cm).

Flower color and season Spikes of purple-blue, rose, pink, or white flowers bloom atop the stems from late spring through summer.

Best climate and site Zones 4–9. Full sun. Grow in an all-purpose container mix.

Growing guidelines Grows best from seed sown directly into the container. Plant seed ¼ inch (6 mm) deep in fall or early spring. If you choose to start seedlings indoors, sow seed in individual peat pots 6–8 weeks before your last frost date. Set seedlings out in mid- to late spring. Thin or space plants to stand 8–12 inches (20–30 cm) apart.

Possible problems No serious problems.

Other common names Larkspur.

Comments The spiky flowers mix well with cornflowers and also make great cut flowers.

Convolvulus tricolor
CONVOLVULACEAE

DWARF MORNING GLORY

This easy annual looks much like the common vining morning glory, but it is a clumper rather than a climber. Another difference is that dwarf morning glory flowers stay open all day.

Description Dwarf morning glory produces bushy plants with small, narrow, green leaves. Funnel-shaped, 2-inch (5-cm) flowers appear during summer.

Height and spread Height 1 foot (30 cm); spread 2 feet (60 cm).

Flower color and season Blue flowers with a yellow throat and white central band bloom all summer. Rainbow mixes are now available.

Best climate and site Zones 5–10. Full sun. Grow in a well-drained, all-purpose container mix; allow to dry out a little between waterings.

Growing guidelines Space plants 1 foot (30 cm) apart. Pinch off spent flowers. Sow seed indoors in large containers 6 weeks before the last frost. You can also sow directly into the planter after the last frost date. Either way, nick the tough seed coat with a knife or nail file before planting.

Possible problems Plants may grow slowly or even die if the roots are damaged during transplanting.

Other common names Bush morning glory.

Comments Dwarf morning glory is a super hanging basket plant. It's also wonderful for edging pots and planters. The seeds are poisonous if eaten.

Coreopsis tinctoria
ASTERACEAE

COREOPSIS

Coreopsis grows easily from direct-sown seed and needs little fussing. Shearing the plants back by one-third in mid- to late summer can prolong the bloom season.

Description Coreopsis is a colorful, fast-growing, hardy annual. Its wiry stems carry narrow, green leaves and 1–2-inch (2.5–5-cm) wide, single or double daisies.
Height and spread Height 2–3 feet (30–90 cm), depending on the cultivar; spread to 1 foot (30 cm).
Flower color and season Golden yellow flowers with maroon centers, plain yellow, or orange flowers bloom from midsummer until frost.
Best climate and site Zones 6–10. Full sun. Grow in an all-purpose container mix.
Growing guidelines Grows quickly from seed sown directly into the container in early to midspring. You can also sow seed ⅛ inch (3 mm) deep indoors about 6 weeks before your last frost date. Set plants out around the last frost date. Space transplants or thin seedlings to stand about 8 inches (20 cm) apart. Push twiggy brush into the mix around young plants of tall-growing cultivars to support the stems as they grow.
Possible problems No serious problems.
Other common names Tickseed, plains coreopsis, calliopsis.
Comments Plant in a large container with pink cosmos and a tall ornamental grass.

Cosmos bipinnatus
ASTERACEAE

COSMOS

Use fast-growing cosmos to fill empty containers left by early-blooming annuals and perennials. Pinch off spent flowers to encourage more blooms.

Description These popular, half-hardy annuals are grown for their colorful blooms. The bushy plants bear many finely cut leaves. The single or semidouble daisies are up to 4 inches (10 cm) across.
Height and spread Height 3–4 feet (90–120 cm); spread to 1½ feet (45 cm).
Flower color and season White, pink, or rosy red flowers bloom from late summer through fall.
Best climate and site Zones 4–10. Full sun is best, although plants can take partial shade. Grow in all-purpose container mix.
Growing guidelines For earliest blooms, buy transplants in spring or start seed indoors 3–4 weeks before last frost date. Plant seed ¼ inch (6 mm) deep. Set plants out 12 weeks after last frost date. You can also sow seed directly into the container around the last frost date. Space transplants or thin seedlings to stand 6–12 inches (15–30 cm) apart. Young plants may need support. Or just let the plants sprawl; they'll send up more flowering stems.
Possible problems No serious problems.
Other common names Common cosmos, Mexican aster.
Comments Planted alone in a container or mixed with a tall ornamental grass, cosmos makes an arresting display.

Cosmos sulphureus
ASTERACEAE

YELLOW COSMOS

Yellow cosmos is generally trouble-free through the season. The colorful blooms lend a cheerful touch to fresh arrangements.

Description Yellow cosmos is a half-hardy annual that forms bushy mounds of deeply lobed, dark green leaves. The thin stems carry showy, single or semidouble daisies which are 1–2 inches (2.5–5 cm) wide.
Height and spread Height 2–3 feet (60–90 cm); spread to 1½ feet (45 cm).
Flower color and season Yellow, orange, or red flowers bloom from late summer until frost.
Best climate and site Zones 4–10. Full sun. Grow in an all-purpose container mix.
Growing guidelines For the earliest flowers, start seed indoors 4–6 weeks before your last frost date. Plant seed ¼ inch (6 mm) deep. Set plants out after the last frost date. Also grows easily from seed sown directly into the container around the last frost date. Set plants or thin seedlings to about 1 foot (30 cm) apart. Pinching off spent flowers can prolong the bloom season. If you leave a few flowers to mature at the end of the season, you can collect seed for the following spring.
Possible problems No serious problems.
Other common names Klondike cosmos.
Comments Combine with deep blue delphiniums for a bright display.

Dianthus barbatus
CARYOPHYLLACEAE

SWEET WILLIAM

Sweet Williams may rebloom the following year if you shear them back after flowering, but you'll generally get a better show by starting new plants each year.

Description This short-lived perennial is grown as a hardy biennial or annual. An old-fashioned favorite, Sweet William forms clumps of narrow, lance-shaped, green leaves. The stems are topped with dense, slightly rounded clusters of five-petaled flowers. Each fragrant bloom is ¼–½ inch (6–12 mm) wide.
Height and spread Height 1–1½ feet (30–45 cm); spread 8–12 inches (20–30 cm).
Flower color and season Red, pink, or white flowers bloom from early to midsummer; some flowers have eyes, or zones, of contrasting colors.
Best climate and site Zones 6–9. Full sun to partial shade. Grow in an all-purpose container mix.
Growing guidelines For earliest bloom, grow as a biennial: Sow seed in pots or in a nursery bed in summer, then move plants to container in fall. For bloom the same year, sow seed indoors (just barely cover it) about 8 weeks before last frost date. Set plants out 2–3 weeks before last frost date. Space transplants 8–10 inches (20–25 cm) apart.
Possible problems No serious problems.
Comments Sweet William looks pretty in a pot with cornflowers, sedums, and a gray-leaved ornamental grass.

Dianthus chinensis
CARYOPHYLLACEAE

CHINA PINK

China pinks look lovely in container plantings. Place the containers near the front door or alongside a path where the perfumed flowers may be appreciated.

Description This biennial or short-lived perennial is usually grown as an annual. Plants form tufts of narrow, green leaves. The upright stems bear 1-inch (2.5-cm) wide, flat flowers with broad petals that are fringed at the tips.
Height and spread Height 8–12 inches (20–30 cm); similar spread.
Flower color and season The white, pink, or red flowers bloom through summer.
Best climate and site Zones 6–9. Full sun (afternoon shade in hot-summer areas). Grow in a well-drained, all-purpose container mix.
Growing guidelines Buy plants in spring, or start seed indoors (just barely cover it) 6–8 weeks before last frost date. Sow seed directly into container 2–3 weeks before last frost date. Thin seedlings or set transplants to stand 6–8 inches (15–20 cm) apart.
Possible problems China pinks are susceptible to rust. Thin clumps to promote air circulation, and dust affected plants with sulfur.
Other common names Rainbow pink, Chinese pink, Indian pink.
Comments Combine in a container with thyme and silver-leaved lamb's-ears (*Stachys byzantina*).

Erysimum cheiri
BRASSICACEAE

WALLFLOWER

The fragrant blooms of wallflowers are normally orange or yellow, but they also bloom in shades of red, pink, or creamy white. The flowers are ideal for spring arrangements.

Description This perennial is commonly grown as a half-hardy annual or biennial for spring color. The bushy clumps of slender, green leaves are topped with clusters of 1-inch (2.5-cm) wide, four-petaled flowers.
Height and spread Height 1–2 feet (30–60 cm); spread to 1 foot (30 cm).
Flower color and season Red, pink, or creamy white flowers bloom from midspring to early summer.
Best climate and site Zones 6–9. Full sun to partial shade. Grow in an all-purpose container mix.
Growing guidelines To grow as annuals, sow outdoors in early spring or indoors about 8 weeks before last frost date. Plant seed ¼ inch (6 mm) deep. Set plants out 8–12 inches (20–30 cm) apart around last frost date. In frost-free areas, grow wallflowers as biennials. Sow seed in pots or in a nursery bed in early summer; move plants to their flowering position in early fall. Water during dry spells to keep the mix evenly moist. Pull out plants when they have finished blooming.
Possible problems No serious problems.
Comments Underplant wallflowers with blue forget-me-nots (*Myosotis sylvatica*).

Eschscholzia californica
PAPAVERACEAE

CALIFORNIA POPPY

The cup-shaped flowers of California poppy open during sunny days but close in cloudy weather and at night. Pinch off developing seedpods to prolong the bloom season.

Description California poppies form loose clumps of deeply cut, blue-green leaves. The thin stems are topped with pointed buds that unfurl into single, semidouble, or double flowers up to 3 inches (7.5 cm) across with silky-looking petals.
Height and spread Height 1–1½ feet (30–45 cm); spread 6–12 inches (15–30 cm).
Flower color and season The orange, yellow, white, pink, or red flowers bloom from early summer through fall.
Best climate and site Zones 6–10. Full sun. Grow in a well-drained, all-purpose container mix.
Growing guidelines California poppy transplants poorly, so it's usually not worth starting seed indoors. Plants will grow quickly from seed sown directly into the container in very early spring (or even in fall in frost-free areas). Scatter the seed over the soil surface and rake it in lightly. Thin seedlings to stand 6 inches (15 cm) apart. If blooms are sparse by midsummer, cut plants back by about one-third to encourage a new flush of flowers. Plants usually self-sow in mild-winter areas.
Possible problems No serious problems.
Comments Plant Californian poppy with sedums, yuccas, and ornamental grasses.

Euphorbia marginata
EUPHORBIACEAE

SNOW-ON-THE-MOUNTAIN

Snow-on-the-mountain forms showy clumps of white-marked leaves by late summer. Use this old-fashioned favorite as a filler or accent plant in containers.

Description Snow-on-the-mountain is grown for its showy foliage. Young plants produce oblong to pointed, green leaves. In mid- to late summer, the plant produces leaves edged with white. At the branch tips, clusters of tiny flowers are surrounded by petal-like bracts.
Height and spread Height 2–4 feet (60–120 cm); spread 1–1½ feet (30–45 cm).
Flower color and season Tiny flowers surrounded by white, petal-like bracts appear in summer.
Best climate and site Zones 6–9. Full sun. Grow in an all-purpose container mix.
Growing guidelines For earliest color, start seed ½ inch (12 mm) deep indoors 4–6 weeks before your last frost date. Set plants out after the last frost date. Or sow seed directly into the container around the last frost date. Thin seedlings or space transplants to stand 1 foot (30 cm) apart. Plants may lean or flop by late summer; prevent this by staking plants in early to midsummer, while they're still young. Plants often self-sow.
Possible problems No serious problems.
Other common names Ghostweed.
Comments Handle cut stems carefully, since they will leak a milky sap that can irritate your skin, eyes, and mouth.

Eustoma grandiflorum
GENTIANACEAE

PRAIRIE GENTIAN

Prairie gentian looks lovely planted alone in a container or in a large container underneath a Japanese maple (Acer palmatum).

Description Prairie gentian's slender, upright stems carry oblong, gray-green leaves and are topped with pointed buds. The buds unfurl to produce long-lasting, 2–3-inch (5–7.5-cm), single or double flowers that resemble poppies or roses.
Height and spread Height usually 2–4 feet (60–120 cm); spread to 1 foot (30 cm).
Flower color and season White, cream, pink, rose, and purple-blue flowers bloom in summer.
Best climate and site Zones 6–9. Full sun to partial shade. Grow in an all-purpose container mix.
Growing guidelines You'll get the quickest results by buying transplants in spring. If you want to try raising your own, sow them indoors in January. Set the transplants out 12 weeks after your last frost date. Space them about 6 inches (15 cm) apart in clumps of three or more plants. Pinching off stem tips once or twice in early summer will promote branching and more blooms. Remove spent blooms to prolong flowering.
Possible problems No serious problems.
Other common names Texas bluebell, lisianthus.
Comments Plant prairie gentian in small containers outdoors and bring them indoors when they are in bloom.

Gaillardia pulchella
ASTERACEAE

BLANKET FLOWER

Blanket flower blooms are often orange-red with yellow tips, but they may also be red, yellow, or orange around a reddish purple center.

Description These plants produce clumps of narrow, hairy, gray-green leaves. They are highlighted all summer by single or double daisies which may be up to 3 inches (7.5 cm) wide, with toothed petals that give them a fringed appearance.

Height and spread Height 1–2 feet (30–60 cm); similar spread.

Flower color and season Red, yellow, or orange flowers bloom in summer.

Best climate and site Zones 5–9. Full sun. Grow in an average, well-drained, all-purpose container mix. Blanket flowers are heat- and drought-tolerant.

Growing guidelines You'll get best results by sowing seed directly into the container. Plant seed ⅛ inch (3 mm) deep in spring around last frost date (or even in fall in mild-winter areas). If your summers are short and cool, sow seed indoors 4–6 weeks before last frost date. Space transplants or thin seedlings to stand 1 foot (30 cm) apart. Support young plant stems. Pinch off spent flowers to prolong bloom season. Plants self-sow if you allow a few flowers to set seed.

Possible problems No serious problems.

Comments Combine blanket flowers in a large container with other drought-tolerant perennials such as coreopsis (*Coreopsis* spp.), yarrows (*Achillea* spp.), or yuccas.

Gazania rigens
ASTERACEAE

TREASURE FLOWER

Pinch off the spent flowers of treasure flowers to prolong the bloom season. Bring the containers indoors before frost, for winter bloom.

Description This eye-catching, tender perennial is grown as a half-hardy annual. Plants form low mats of narrow-lobed, green leaves that are silvery underneath. Plants are topped with brilliantly colored daisies which are 3 inches (7.5 cm) across. The petals may have a contrasting center stripe and usually have a dark brown or green spot at the base.

Height and spread Height 8–12 inches (20–30 cm); spread to 1 foot (30 cm).

Flower color and season Mainly red, orange, or yellow flowers bloom from midsummer until frost.

Best climate and site Zones 6–10. Full sun. Grow in a well-drained, all-purpose container mix.

Growing guidelines For earliest bloom, buy transplants or start seed indoors 6–8 weeks before last frost date. Plant seed ⅛ inch (3 mm) deep. Set transplants out after last frost date. Or sow seed directly into the container 12 weeks after the last frost date for late-summer bloom. Thin seedlings or set transplants to stand 8 inches (20 cm) apart.

Possible problems No serious problems.

Comments Combine with coreopsis (*Coreopsis* spp.), yuccas, or blue oat grass (*Helictotrichon sempervirens*).

Gomphrena globosa
AMARANTHACEAE

GLOBE AMARANTH

Globe amaranth is generally trouble-free. The flowers are pretty in fresh or dried arrangements; the compact cultivars are best suited to containers.

Description Globe amaranth is grown for its long-lasting flower heads. The oblong to elliptical, green leaves grow in pairs along the sturdy stems. Tiny flowers peek out from between layers of colorful, papery bracts that make up the clover-like, 1-inch (2.5-cm) wide flower heads.

Height and spread Height 8–18 inches (20–45 cm); spread 8–12 inches (20–30 cm).

Flower color and season Magenta, pink, or creamy white flowers bloom from midsummer until frost.

Best climate and site Zones 6–10. Full sun. Grow in an average, well-drained all-purpose container mix.

Growing guidelines Buy transplants in spring, or start your own by sowing seed indoors 4–6 weeks before your last frost date. Plant the seed ⅛–¼ inch (3–6 mm) deep. Set transplants out 2–3 weeks after the last frost date. If your area has a long, warm growing season, you can also sow seed directly into the container after the last frost date. Space transplants or thin seedlings to stand 8–10 inches (20–25 cm) apart.

Possible problems No serious problems.

Other common names Bachelor's buttons.

Comments Plant globe amaranth with blanket flower (*Gaillardia* spp.) and coreopsis (*Coreopsis* spp.).

Helichrysum petiolare
ASTERACEAE

LICORICE PLANT

Licorice plant has soft, silvery leaves that complement both pale pastels and bold, bright hues. It's a perfect choice for cascading over the edges of pots, planters, hanging baskets, and window boxes.

Description Licorice plant has a shrubby form that's partly upright and partly trailing. The woody stems carry oval, felted, white-green-gray foliage.

Height and spread Height 1 foot (30 cm); spread 2 feet (60 cm).

Flower color and season Yellow-white flowers bloom in spring.

Best climate and site Zones 6–10. Full sun. Grow in a well-drained, all-purpose container mix; allow the mix to dry somewhat between waterings.

Growing guidelines Use one plant per pot. Pinch off the shoot tips every few weeks to encourage bushy growth. Bring the plant indoors to a cool sunroom or greenhouse for overwintering, or start a new plant the following spring. Sow seed indoors or outdoors in late spring or early summer. Take cuttings anytime during the growing season.

Possible problems The stems can get leggy if you don't pinch them regularly.

Comments Licorice plant is good with dark-leaved plants, such as 'Purple Ruffles' basil, 'Palace Purple' heuchera (*Heuchera micrantha* var. *diversifolia*), or purple-leaved bush beans.

Iberis umbellata
BRASSICACEAE

ANNUAL CANDYTUFT

Annual candytuft is a hardy, spring-flowering annual. In hot-summer areas, pull out plants after bloom and replace them with summer- to fall-blooming annuals.

Description Annual candytuft forms mounds of narrow, green leaves on many-branched stems. The rounded flower clusters are approximately 2 inches (5 cm) across. Each cluster contains many ¼–½-inch (6–12-mm) wide, four-petaled blooms.

Height and spread Height 8–12 inches (20–30 cm); spread 8–10 inches (20–25 cm).

Flower color and season White, pink, pinkish-purple, rose, or red flowers bloom from late spring through midsummer.

Best climate and site Zones 5–9. Full sun to partial shade. Grow in a well-drained, all-purpose container mix.

Growing guidelines Sow seed indoors 6–8 weeks before last frost date. Set plants out around the last frost date. Or sow seed directly into the container. Make the first sowing in early to midspring. Sowing again every 3–4 weeks until early summer can extend the bloom season until fall if your summer temperatures don't get much above 90°F (32°C). Space plants to stand 6–8 inches (15–20 cm) apart.

Possible problems No serious problems.

Other common names Globe candytuft.

Comments Plant with columbines (*Aquilegia* spp.) and basket of gold (*Aurina saxatilis*).

Impatiens balsamina
BALSAMINACEAE

GARDEN BALSAM

The bright flowers of garden balsam bloom near the tops of the stems, among the lance-shaped, green leaves. This old-fashioned favorite can grow in sun if the container mix is moist.

Description This tender annual has a bushy, upright habit. It has 1–2-inch (2.5–5-cm) wide, single or double flowers and lance-shaped, bright green leaves.

Height and spread Height 2–2½ feet (60–75 cm); spread to 1½ feet (45 cm).

Flower color and season White, pink, purple, rose, or red flowers bloom from midsummer until frost.

Best climate and site Zones 5–10. Full sun to partial shade. Grow in an all-purpose container mix.

Growing guidelines Garden balsam is sometimes sold as transplants, but it is also easy to start from seed. To grow your own transplants, sow seed indoors 6–8 weeks before the last frost date. Set plants out 12 weeks after the last frost date. You can also sow seed directly into the container after the last frost date. Plant seed ⅛ inch (3 mm) deep and keep the soil moist until seedlings appear. Thin seedlings or space transplants 12–16 inches (30–40 cm) apart. Water during dry spells. Plants often self-sow freely.

Possible problems No serious problems.

Comments Good container plants for shady areas. Combine with ferns and hostas.

Lathyrus odoratus
FABACEAE

SWEET PEA

Dozens of sweet pea cultivars are available in a range of heights and colors. Many modern cultivars aren't very fragrant; check catalog descriptions.

Description Sweet pea plants produce leafy vines that climb by tendrils. Dainty, pea-like flowers to 2 inches (5 cm) long bloom on long, slender flower stems. The flowers often have crimped or ruffled petals.
Height and spread Height 4–6 feet (120–180 cm); spread 6–12 inches (15–30 cm).
Flower color and season Flowers in white, pink, red, or purple bloom from midspring into summer.
Best climate and site Zones 6–10. Full sun (or afternoon shade in hot-summer areas). Grow in an all-purpose container mix.
Growing guidelines Start seed indoors 6–8 weeks before last frost date. Soak seed in warm water for 4 hours, then plant ½ inch (12 mm) deep in peat pots. Set plants out in midspring, after danger of frost has passed. Or sow seed directly into container in early spring. Set transplants or thin seedlings to stand 4–6 inches (10–15 cm) apart. Mulch plants to keep the roots cool and moist. Water during dry spells. Pull out the vines when they stop blooming in summer.
Possible problems Do not overwater seed while germinating.
Comments Make a tepee in a container to grow sweet peas, or let them trail from a hanging basket.

Limonium sinuatum
PLUMBAGINACEAE

ANNUAL STATICE

Annual statice is a natural for fresh or dried arrangements. To dry it, pick stems when the clusters are about three-quarters open; hang them in a dark, airy place.

Description Annual statice plants form low rosettes of wavy-edged, green leaves that send up sturdy, winged stems in summer. The loosely branched stems are topped with flattened clusters of ¼-inch (6-mm) wide, white flowers, each surrounded by a papery, tubular calyx— the colorful part of the flower head.
Height and spread Height 1–2 feet (30–60 cm); width to 1 foot (30 cm).
Flower color and season Flowers in white, pink, peach, red, orange, yellow, purple, and blue bloom in summer and early fall.
Best climate and site Zones 6–10. Full sun. Grow in an all-purpose container mix.
Growing guidelines Buy transplants in spring, or start your own by sowing seed indoors 6–8 weeks before last frost date. Plant seed ¼ inch (6 mm) deep. Move seedlings to individual pots when they have two or three sets of leaves. Plant them in the container around the last frost date, or sow seed directly into the container after the last frost date. Thin seedlings to stand 8–10 inches (20–25 cm) apart.
Possible problems No serious problems.
Other common names Sea lavender.
Comments Plant with blanket flower (*Gaillardia* spp.) for a bright summer display.

Lobelia erinus
LOBELIACEAE

EDGING LOBELIA

The tiny blue flowers of edging lobelia add sparkle to spring and early-summer containers. Use them to fill in until summer-blooming plants start to flower.

Description Edging lobelia has a bushy or trailing habit. The ¾-inch (18-mm), tubular flowers bloom in a variety of colors.
Height and spread Height 6–8 inches (15–20 cm); spread 6–10 inches (15–25 cm).
Flower color and season Flowers in blue, violet, pink, or white, with a yellow or white throat, bloom in summer.
Best climate and site Zones 5–10. Partial to full sun. Partial shade is best in hot weather. Grow in an all-purpose container mix. Keep the mix evenly moist.
Growing guidelines Sow seed indoors 6 weeks before the last frost. Space plants 4–6 inches (10–15 cm) apart.
Possible problems Edging lobelia tends to look ragged by midsummer; shear the plants back by half to promote rebloom.
Other common names Lobelia.
Comments An effective way to display edging lobelia is in strawberry-jar planters, with two or three plants tucked into each hole. For season-long container bloom, combine with plants such as dusty miller (*Senecio cineraria*), pansies, petunias, and clematis. For a blue-and-yellow planting, try it with torenia (*Torenia fournieri*) and golden creeping Jenny (*Lysimachia nummularia* 'Aurea'). It also looks good with peppers, parsley, or rosemary.

Lobularia maritima
BRASSICACEAE

SWEET ALYSSUM

Sweet alyssum is one of the best edging plants for containers. Its tiny blooms release a light but noticeable, fresh, honey-like fragrance that's especially delightful near porches, patios, and decks.

Description Sweet alyssum produces branched or trailing plants with slender stems carrying 1-inch (2.5-cm) long, narrow leaves, and clusters of tiny flowers.
Height and spread Height 4–8 inches (10–20 cm); spread 10–12 inches (25–30 cm).
Flower color and season White, pink, or purple flowers bloom from summer to fall.
Best climate and site Zones 5–9. Full sun is best, although plants can survive with a half-day of sun. Grow sweet alyssum in a well-drained, all-purpose container mix. Keep the mix evenly moist.
Growing guidelines Set plants 6 inches (15 cm) apart. Sow seed indoors 6–8 weeks before the last frost date, or plant it directly into the container in mid- to late spring.
Possible problems Plants tend to look ragged by midsummer. To encourage more flowering, shear plants back by half 4 weeks after the first bloom.
Other common names Sweet Alice.
Comments Don't plant sweet alyssum by itself, since eventually it will need to be cut back. Good partners include petunias, bulbs, roses, ageratum, salvias (*Salvia* spp.), clematis, flowering tobacco (*Nicotiana* spp.), and eggplant.

Lunaria annua
BRASSICACEAE

HONESTY

Honesty is a hardy biennial grown for its pretty flowers and showy, dried seedpods. Leave a few plants in the container to self-sow; harvest the rest for arrangements.

Description Honesty's loosely branched stems are topped with elongated clusters of ½-inch (12-mm) wide, four-petaled flowers. The lightly fragrant blooms are followed by flat, circular seedpods with papery outer skins and a satiny, white central disk.
Height and spread Height 1½–3 feet (45–90 cm); spread to 1 foot (30 cm).
Flower color and season Purple-pink flowers bloom in spring and early summer, followed by silvery, circular seedpods.
Best climate and site Zones 7–10. Partial shade. Grow in all-purpose container mix.
Growing guidelines Buy and set out nursery-grown plants in early spring for bloom the same year, or start your own from seed for bloom next year. Sow seed directly into container, ⅛–¼ inch (3–6 mm) deep, in spring or late summer. Set transplants to stand about 1 foot (30 cm) apart.
Possible problems No serious problems.
Other common names Money plant, silver dollar.
Comments When the seedpods turn beige, cut the stems off at ground level and bring them indoors. Once seedpods feel dry, gently peel off the outer skins to reveal the silvery center membrane.

Malcomia maritima
BRASSICACEAE

VIRGINIA STOCK

Virginia stock can bloom in as little as 4 weeks from the time seed is sown directly into a garden container. Sow every 3 to 4 weeks through midsummer to have flowers from summer until frost.

Description The upright, branching stems of this fast-growing, hardy annual carry small, pointed, grayish-green leaves. Flat, four-petaled, lightly fragrant flowers bloom in loose clusters atop the stems, and are popular with bees.
Height and spread Height 6–8 inches (15–20 cm); spread to 4 inches (10 cm).
Flower color and season The purple, pink, or white flowers bloom from midsummer until frost.
Best climate and site Zones 6–10. Full sun to partial shade (in hot-summer areas). Grow in an all-purpose container mix.
Growing guidelines Grows best from seed sown directly into the container. For the longest bloom season, sow at 3–4-week intervals from early spring through midsummer. (In mild-winter areas, you can sow in fall for even earlier spring bloom.) Cover the seed lightly, then keep the mix moist until seedlings appear. Thin seedlings to stand 3–4 inches (7.5–10 cm) apart. Plants may self-sow freely.
Possible problems No serious problems.
Other common names Virginian stock.
Comments Grow the fragrant flowers of Virginia stock in window boxes or in pots for courtyards and patios.

Matthiola incana
BRASSICACEAE

COMMON STOCK

The fragrant, single or double flowers of common stock bloom in a variety of colors, from white through shades of pink, yellow, and purple.

Description This biennial or short-lived perennial is usually grown as a hardy annual. The fast-growing, bushy plants have upright stems and lance-shaped, grayish leaves. The stems are topped with spikes of four-petaled, 1-inch (2.5-cm) wide flowers.
Height and spread Height 1–2 feet (30–60 cm); spread to 1 foot (30 cm).
Flower color and season White, pink, red, yellow, or purple flowers bloom in summer.
Best climate and site Zones 6–9. Full sun. Grow in an all-purpose container mix.
Growing guidelines Grows easily from seed sown directly into the container. Make the first sowing about 1 month before last frost date. To extend bloom season, make another sowing in late spring or early summer. (In mild-winter areas, you can also sow in late summer for winter and early-spring bloom.) Thin seedlings to stand 6–8 inches (15–20 cm) apart. Mulch plants to keep the roots cool and moist. Water during dry spells.
Possible problems No serious problems.
Other common names Gillyflower.
Comments Plant in a container in an outdoor sitting area, where you can enjoy the fragrance.

Mimulus x hybridus
SCROPHULARIACEAE

MONKEY FLOWER

You can overwinter monkey flowers by bringing containers indoors; grow them in a cool, sunny room. You may also take stem cuttings in late summer.

Description Monkey flower plants form clumps of green to reddish stems with oval, light green leaves with toothed edges. Velvety, tubular flowers with flat faces bloom atop the plants through summer.
Height and spread Height 6–12 inches (15–30 cm); similar spread.
Flower color and season Flowers in orange, yellow, or red bloom in summer.
Best climate and site Zones 5–9. Partial shade. Grow in an all-purpose container mix. Plants can take full sun if the mix is kept evenly moist.
Growing guidelines Start seed indoors 8–10 weeks before your last frost date. Scatter the dust-like seed over the soil surface, but don't cover it. Just press the seed lightly into the soil and enclose the pot in a plastic bag until seedlings appear. Set transplants out 6 inches (15 cm) apart after the last frost date. Water during dry spells. If plants stop blooming in hot weather, cutting them back halfway and watering thoroughly may promote rebloom.
Possible problems No serious problems.
Other common names Musk flower.
Comments Grow in a container with large-leaved hostas.

Mirabilis jalapa
NYCTAGINACEAE

FOUR-O'CLOCK

Four-o'clocks have fragrant flowers that open in the late afternoon. They tend to close the next morning, unless the weather is cloudy.

Description These bushy, fast-growing plants have branching stems and oval to lance-shaped, deep green leaves. The 1-inch (2.5-cm) wide flowers are fragrant and trumpet-shaped.
Height and spread Height 2–3 feet (60–90 cm); spread to 2 feet (60 cm).
Flower color and season Flowers in white or shades of pink, magenta, red, and yellow bloom from midsummer until frost; sometimes different colors appear on the same plant.
Best climate and site Zones 6–10. Full sun to partial shade. Grow in an all-purpose container mix.
Growing guidelines For earliest bloom, start indoors 4–6 weeks before last frost date. Soak seed in warm water overnight, then plant it ¼–½ inch (6–12 mm) deep in peat pots. Transplant seedlings to the container about 2 weeks after the last frost date. You can also sow seed directly into the container after the last frost date. Space transplants to stand 1–1½ feet (30–45 cm) apart. Plants may self-sow in mild areas.
Possible problems No serious problems.
Other common names Marvel-of-Peru.
Comments Grow four-o'clocks in an outdoor area, where you can sit and enjoy the flowers and fragrance after a long day.

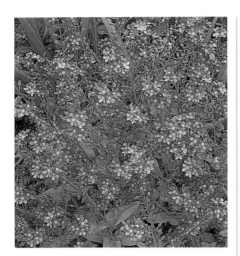

Myosotis sylvatica
BORAGINACEAE

FORGET-ME-NOT

The dainty, blue flowers of forget-me-not are traditional spring favorites. Combine in a container with bulbs for a touch of early-season color.

Description Forget-me-nots have narrow, hairy, green leaves. They usually grow as biennials, producing leaves the first year and flowering stems the second, but they can bloom the first year if started early indoors.
Height and spread Height 6–12 inches (15–30 cm); spread 6–9 inches (15–22.5 cm).
Flower color and season The tiny, blue or pink, white-centered flowers are borne in small clusters from May to June.
Best climate and site Zones 5–9. Partial shade to a half-day of sun. Grow in an all-purpose container mix. Keep mix moist.
Growing guidelines Plant 6–9 inches (15–22.5 cm) apart. Sow outdoors in late summer to fall for bloom next spring or sow seed indoors in late winter for bloom the same year.
Possible problems If spider mites cause yellow stippling on leaves, spray the leaves with cold water or superior oil. If mildew is a problem, pinch off affected leaves and move the pot to an airier spot.
Other common names Garden forget-me-not.
Comments Forget-me-nots look great with many other early-blooming plants, including tulips, pansies, hostas, torenia (*Torenia fournieri*), nasturtium (*Tropaeolum majus*), and periwinkles (*Vinca* spp.).

Nemophila menziesii
HYDROPHYLLACEAE

BABY-BLUE-EYES

Sow baby-blue-eyes among the emerging shoots of spring bulbs to form a colorful, fast-growing carpet that will cover the ripening bulb foliage after bloom.

Description Baby-blue-eyes is a hardy annual that forms sprawling mounds of slender, trailing stems and small, finely cut, green leaves. The 1-inch (2.5-cm) wide flowers are bowl-shaped.
Height and spread Height 6–8 inches (15–20 cm); spread to 1 foot (30 cm).
Flower color and season Sky-blue flowers with a white center bloom in summer.
Best climate and site Zones 5–9. Full sun to partial shade (morning sun and afternoon shade is ideal). Grow in an all-purpose container mix.
Growing guidelines For an extra-early start, sow seed indoors 4–6 weeks before your last frost date. Plant seed ⅛ inch (3 mm) deep. Set plants out 12 weeks before the last frost date. Or sow seed directly into the container. Make the first sowing in early spring (or even in fall in mild-winter areas). Sow seed again every 2–3 weeks from spring through early summer to extend bloom season through summer. Set plants or thin seedlings to stand 6 inches (15 cm) apart. If plants stop blooming in midsummer, shear them back halfway and water thoroughly to promote rebloom. Plants often self-sow.
Possible problems No serious problems.
Comments Baby-blue-eyes looks super trailing out of pots and planters.

Nicotiana spp.
SOLANACEAE

FLOWERING TOBACCO

One of the most fragrant garden plants, flowering tobacco forms a tall, stately accent for containers. The original species are mostly white, but the hybrids come in a range of sizes and colors.

Description These shrubby, upright plants have large, soft, slightly sticky leaves and branched stems. The stems are topped with small, petunia-like flowers. Evening-blooming *N. alata* normally grows to 3 feet (90 cm) and usually has a good scent. Night-flowering *N. sylvestris* is tall, with downward-facing, very fragrant, tubular blooms.
Height and spread Height 1½–3 feet (45–90 cm); spread 1 foot (30 cm).
Flower color and season White, pink, or red flowers bloom from summer until frost.
Best climate and site Zones 6–10. Partial shade to full sun. Grow in a large container in all-purpose container mix. Keep the mix evenly moist.
Growing guidelines Space plants 10 inches (25 cm) apart. Pinch off faded flowers. Sow seed indoors 4–6 weeks before the last frost date; leave uncovered.
Possible problems Mealybugs and aphids may feed on plants. Knock the pests off with a strong spray of water, or spray with insecticidal soap.
Comments Try flowering tobacco with sweet alyssum, ferns, and petunias. Place pots near windows or doors so the fragrance may be appreciated.

Nigella damascena
RANUNCULACEAE

LOVE-IN-A-MIST

Sowing every 3 to 4 weeks from early spring to early summer can extend the bloom season of love-in-a-mist through the summer and possibly into fall.

Description Love-in-a-mist is a fast-growing, hardy annual that forms bushy mounds of slender stems and has thread-like, bright green leaves. Single or double, 1–2-inch (2.5–5-cm) wide flowers are nestled into the leaves at the tops of the stems. The flowers are followed by swollen, striped seedpods with short, pointed horns.
Height and spread Height 1½–2 feet (45–60 cm); spread 6–8 inches (15–20 cm).
Flower color and season Blue, pink, or white flowers bloom in summer.
Best climate and site Zones 5–9. Full sun to partial shade. Grow in an all-purpose container mix.
Growing guidelines For the earliest flowers, start seed indoors 6–8 weeks before last frost date. Sow seed in peat pots. Move plants to the garden after the last frost date. Usually, though, you'll get better results by sowing directly into container, starting in early spring. Thin seedlings to stand 6 inches (15 cm) apart. Established plants are care-free. Plants may self-sow.
Possible problems No serious problems.
Other common names Fennel flower, devil-in-the-bush.
Comments Use some of the flowers in fresh arrangements; leave the rest to mature into the puffy seedpods.

Papaver nudicaule
PAPAVERACEAE

ICELAND POPPY

Removing spent flower stems can prolong Iceland poppy's bloom season. As summer approaches and new growth slows, leave a few flowers to mature so plants can self-sow.

Description This short-lived perennial is usually grown as a hardy biennial or annual. Plants form compact rosettes of hairy, deeply cut, gray-green leaves. Long, slender, leafless stems are topped with plump, hairy, nodding buds that open to bowl-shaped, four-petaled flowers. The 2–4-inch (5–10-cm) wide, lightly fragrant flowers have crinkled petals.
Height and spread Height 1–1½ feet (30–45 cm); spread 4–6 inches (10–15 cm).
Flower color and season White, pink, red, orange, or yellow flowers bloom in early to midsummer.
Best climate and site Zones 2–10. Full sun. Grow in an average, well-drained, all-purpose container mix.
Growing guidelines Easiest to grow from seed sown directly into the container. Plant in late fall or very early spring for summer bloom. Scatter the fine seed over the soil and rake it in lightly. Thin seedlings to stand about 6 inches (15 cm) apart.
Possible problems No serious problems.
Comments Grow Iceland poppies for fresh cut flowers. Harvest stems in the morning, when buds are facing upright but not yet open. Singe the stem ends in a gas flame or dip in boiling water to prolong vase life.

Papaver rhoeas
PAPAVERACEAE

CORN POPPY

Corn poppy is a hardy annual grown for its summer flowers. Remove spent blooms at the base of the stem to extend the flowering season through most of the summer.

Description Corn poppies form clumps of ferny, blue-green leaves. Bowl-shaped flowers with silky, crinkled petals open from plump, hairy buds atop thin, hairy stems.
Height and spread Height 2–3 feet (60–90 cm); spread 6–8 inches (15–20 cm).
Flower color and season Scarlet, red, white, pink, and bicolor flowers bloom during summer.
Best climate and site Zones 4–9. Full sun. Grow in an all-purpose container mix.
Growing guidelines Corn poppy is rewardingly easy to grow from seed sown directly into the container in late fall or early spring. A second sowing in midspring can help extend the bloom season. Scatter the fine seed over the soil surface, then rake it in lightly. Thin seedlings to stand 6–8 inches (15–20 cm) apart. Leave a few flowers at the end of the season and plants will self-sow.
Possible problems No serious problems.
Other common names Flanders poppy, Shirley poppy, field poppy.
Comments Corn poppies are nice in arrangements. Pick them just as the buds are starting to open, then sear the ends of cut stems in a gas flame or dip them in boiling water to prolong their vase life.

Petunia x hybrida
Solanaceae

PETUNIA

Petunias are tender perennials usually grown as half-hardy annuals. They may self-sow, but the seedlings seldom resemble the parent plants.

Description Petunia plants form clumps of upright or trailing stems with oval, green leaves; both the leaves and stems are hairy and somewhat sticky. Funnel-shaped, single or double flowers bloom from early summer until frost in nearly every color of the rainbow; some have stripes, streaks, or bands of contrasting colors. Petunias are usually divided into groups, based on their flower forms. Grandifloras have the largest flowers (up to 4–5 inches [10–12.5 cm] across). They are very showy but tend to be damaged easily by heavy rain. Multifloras have smaller flowers (usually 2 inches [5 cm] across) but produce many durable blooms on each plant. Floribundas are an intermediate type, with 3-inch (7.5-cm) wide flowers on fast-growing plants.

Height and spread Height 6–10 inches (15–25 cm); spread to 1 foot (30 cm).

Flower color and season Red, salmon, pink, deep purple, lavender, blue, yellow, orange, cream, or white flowers bloom from early summer until frost.

Best climate and site Zones 6–10. Full sun is best; tolerates half-day sun. Grow petunias in well-drained, all-purpose container mix. Keep the mix evenly moist.

Growing guidelines Space plants 8 inches (20 cm) apart. Fertilize monthly. About

2 weeks after planting, pinch seedlings back by half to promote bushy growth. Remove faded blooms, along with the seedpod that develops at the base of each flower. Near the end of summer, cut plants back by half to encourage rebloom. Start seed indoors 6–8 weeks before the last frost date; leave uncovered.

Possible problems Botrytis blight is common on large-flowered (grandiflora) petunias. Pinch off affected parts.

Cultivars 'Blue Daddy' has large, purple-blue flowers with deep purple veining. 'Celebrity Mixed' is a long-flowering floribunda type that grows quickly from seed and blooms in a range of colors. 'Fluffy Ruffles Mixed' has large, grandiflora-type flowers with wavy, crinkled edges. Plants in the 'Resisto' series of petunias are multifloras with masses of single flowers on compact, bushy plants. 'Summer Sun' has small, yellow flowers.

Comments Grandiflora types look great spilling out of containers, hanging baskets, and window boxes. The stems tend to drop their bottom leaves by late summer, so combine them with other bushy plants that will cover their bare ankles. Petunias combine well with many plants, including dusty miller (*Senecio cineraria*), geraniums, dahlias, parsley, ageratum, zinnias, periwinkle (*Vinca* spp.), edging lobelia (*Lobelia erinus*), and boxwood (*Buxus* spp.).

Phlox drummondii
POLEMONIACEAE

ANNUAL PHLOX

Annual phlox is a hardy annual grown for its colorful flowers. If plants stop blooming, cut them back by half and water thoroughly; they should resprout and rebloom in fall.

Description Plants form bushy clumps of narrow, lance-shaped, green leaves. The leafy stems are topped with clusters of flat, five-petaled flowers.

Height and spread Height 6–18 inches (15–45 cm); spread 6–8 inches (15–20 cm).

Flower color and season The flowers bloom from midsummer to fall in a wide range of colors, including white, pink, red, pale yellow, blue, and purple; some have a contrasting eye.

Best climate and site Zones 6–10. Full sun. Grow in well-drained, all-purpose container mix.

Growing guidelines For the earliest flowers, buy transplants in spring, or grow your own by starting seed indoors 6–8 weeks before last frost date. Sow seed ⅛ inch (3 mm) deep in individual pots. Set plants out around last frost date. You can also sow seed directly into container around the last frost date. Thin seedlings to stand 6 inches (15 cm) apart. Pinching off spent flowers and watering during dry spells can prolong the bloom season.

Possible problems No serious problems.

Comments Combine with ornamental grasses, blanket flower (*Gaillardia* spp.) and dusty miller (*Senecio cineraria*).

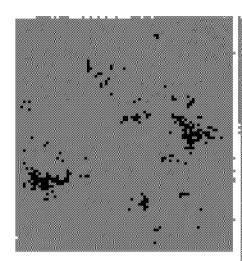

Portulaca grandiflora
PORTULACEAE

ROSE MOSS

Rose moss really shines in hot, dry spots, with small, rose-like flowers in neon colors over narrow, green leaves. If you tend to forget about watering and fertilizing, this is the container plant for you!

Description Rose moss is an annual with trailing stems with succulent, needle-like leaves. The single or double, 2-inch (5-cm) wide flowers come in a range of colors.

Height and spread Height to 6 inches (15 cm); spread 6–8 inches (15–20 cm).

Flower color and season White, pink, red, orange, yellow, and magenta flowers bloom from summer through fall.

Best climate and site Zones 6–10. Full sun. Rose moss grows well in shallow containers of loose, free-draining, sand-based container mix. Allow the mix to dry between waterings.

Growing guidelines Space plants 6 inches (15 cm) apart. Do not fertilize. Pinch off faded flowers. Sow seed indoors 6–8 weeks before last frost date, or plant directly into the container outdoors after last frost. Do not cover the seed; it needs light to sprout.

Possible problems Rose moss tends to rot if overwatered.

Other common names Sun plant, portulaca.

Comments Rose moss is a suitable container plant for dry, hot conditions where nothing else grows. Its flowers only open when the sun is out, closing in late afternoon and in cloudy weather.

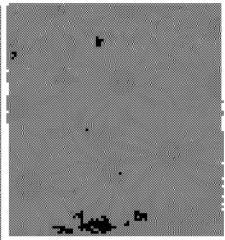

Rudbeckia hirta
ASTERACEAE

BLACK-EYED SUSAN

The big blooms of black-eyed Susans have golden-yellow, outer petals and a purple-brown or black, raised center. They make excellent cut flowers.

Description This short-lived perennial or biennial is usually grown as a hardy annual. Plants form clumps of long, hairy leaves that taper to a point. Stiff, hairy stems are topped with 2–3-inch (5–7.5-cm) wide flowers.

Height and spread Height 2–3 feet (60–90 cm); spread to 1 foot (30 cm).

Flower color and season Golden-yellow flowers bloom from summer into fall.

Best climate and site Zones 3–10. Full sun (can take light shade). Grow in well-drained, all-purpose container mix.

Growing guidelines For earliest bloom, sow seed indoors 8–10 weeks before your last frost date. Just barely cover the seed. You can also sow seed directly into the container after the last frost date, although those plants probably won't bloom until the following year. Space plants or thin seedlings to stand 1 foot (30 cm) apart. Plants often self-sow; if this is a problem, remove spent flowers before they set seed.

Possible problems No serious problems.

Other common names Gloriosa daisy.

Comments Combine with sedums, phlox, and ornamental grasses.

Salvia farinacea
LAMIACEAE

MEALY-CUP SAGE

Mealy-cup sage is fairly drought-tolerant but appreciates watering during extended dry spells. The plants sometimes live through mild winters; they may also self-sow.

Description Mealy-cup sage plants produce bushy clumps of narrow, lance-shaped, green leaves with slightly toothed edges. Stiff, purple-blue stem tips are topped with long spikes of dusty blue buds.

Height and spread Height 1½–2 feet (45–60 cm); spread 1 foot (30 cm).

Flower color and season Purple-blue flowers bloom from midsummer until frost.

Best climate and site Zones 6–9. Full sun. Grow in a well-drained, all-purpose container mix.

Growing guidelines Buy transplants in spring, or grow your own by starting seed indoors 8–10 weeks before last frost date. Soaking the seed overnight before planting can promote quicker sprouting. Don't cover the sown seed; just press it lightly into the soil and enclose the pot in a plastic bag until seedlings appear. Set plants out after the last frost date; space them 1 foot (30 cm) apart.

Possible problems Too much shade will lead to spindly growth and poor flowers.

Other common names Blue salvia.

Comments Combine the spiky blooms of mealy-cup sage with petunias, phlox, sedums, and gray-leaved lamb's-ears (*Stachys byzantina*) for a pretty summer display.

Salvia splendens
LAMIACEAE

SCARLET SAGE

Scarlet sage's fire-engine-red color adds an unmistakable accent to summer containers. It can easily eclipse more subdued companions. Tall types bloom longer than dwarf cultivars.

Description These bushy annuals have shiny, dark green leaves. The plants are topped with tall, long-lasting stems of tubular flowers.

Height and spread Height 1–2 feet (30–60 cm); spread to 1 foot (30 cm).

Flower color and season The mostly red flowers bloom from early summer until frost. Besides hot reds, they also come in pink, purple, salmon, and white.

Best climate and site Zones 6–10. Full sun; tolerates partial shade. Grow in an all-purpose container mix; keep mix moist.

Growing guidelines Space plants 1 foot (30 cm) apart (slightly closer for dwarf types). Deadhead each flower stalk when it fades, reaching back into the plant so the cut end is hidden by the foliage. Sow seed indoors 8 weeks before the last frost date; leave it uncovered.

Possible problems Too much shade will lead to spindly growth and poor bloom.

Comments Plant scarlet sage by itself, or combine it with gray-leaved plants, such as dusty miller (*Senecio cineraria*) or lamb's-ears (*Stachys byzantina*). It also looks lovely with white flowers, such as 'Pretty in White' vinca (*Catharanthus roseus* 'Pretty in White').

Sanvitalia procumbens
ASTERACEAE

CREEPING ZINNIA

Creeping zinnia's trailing stems look wonderful cascading from hanging baskets and over container rims. This easy, heat- and drought-tolerant annual blooms from July until frost.

Description Creeping zinnia's creeping stems carry small leaves and 1-inch (2.5-cm) wide, single- or double-flowered blooms in yellow or bright orange, with purple-brown centers.

Height and spread Height to 6 inches (15 cm); spread to 1½ feet (45 cm).

Flower color and season Yellow or orange flowers bloom from midsummer until frost.

Best climate and site Zones 5–10. Full sun. Grow creeping zinnia in light, fast-draining mix. Allow the mix to dry between waterings.

Growing guidelines Space the plants 5–6 inches (12.5–15 cm) apart. Do not fertilize. Established plants need virtually no care. Creeping zinnia doesn't transplant well, so plant seed directly into container in late spring; leave the seed uncovered.

Possible problems Overhead watering can promote disease; try to avoid wetting the foliage when you water.

Comments Try creeping zinnia as an underplanting for Japanese maple (*Acer palmatum*), euonymus (*Euonymus* spp.), or yuccas. The yellow types look good with dwarf morning glory (*Convolvulus tricolor*).

Solenostemon scutellarioides
LAMIACEAE

COLEUS

Coleus is unsurpassed for foliage interest in shady spots. Pinch off stem tips often to remove dull-looking flower spikes and promote bushy new growth.

Description Coleus has been bred for over a century to create laced, fringed, oak-leaved, and filigreed foliage shapes in a huge range of colors and variegations.

Height and spread Height 6–24 inches (15–60 cm); spread 8–12 inches (20–30 cm).

Flower color and season Pale blue flower spikes bloom in late spring to early summer but coleus is grown for its attractive foliage with zones, edges, or splashes in shades of red, pink, orange, yellow, and cream.

Best climate and site Zones 8–10. High, indirect light is preferable, although coleus can take quite a bit of shade. Plant coleus in loose, average to rich, well-drained mix. Keep the mix evenly moist.

Growing guidelines Space plants 6–9 inches (15–22.5 cm) apart. Fertilize every 2–3 weeks with fish emulsion. Sow seed indoors 8–10 weeks before last frost. Take cuttings in spring.

Possible problems Leaf colors fade in low light. Too much light promotes flower spikes instead of leaves.

Other common names Painted leaves, flame nettle, painted nettle.

Comments Grow coleus by itself, with green ferns, or with single-colored flowers, such as tuberous begonias. Dwarf types are best for window boxes.

Tagetes spp.
ASTERACEAE

MARIGOLDS

These sturdy, dependable sun-lovers may be clichéd to some, but they've earned a place in the "Annuals Hall of Fame." Pinching off spent flowers once a week can prolong the bloom season.

Description Marigolds produce branching to semi-trailing plants with ferny, strongly scented foliage and single or double flowers. Signet marigold (*T. tenuifolia*) has small but profuse blooms on 8-inch (20-cm) plants. It has a trailing habit, perfect for hanging baskets and window boxes. Other compact marigolds include the French types (*T. patula*), which grow 6–18 inches (15–45 cm) tall.
Height and spread Height 6–36 inches (15–90 cm); spread 6–18 inches (15–45 cm).
Flower color and season Yellow, orange, gold, cream, brown, or maroon flowers bloom in summer.
Best climate and site Zones 5–10. Full sun to a half-day of sun. Grow in all-purpose container mix. Keep mix moist.
Growing guidelines Space 6–9 inches (15–22.5 cm) apart; leave 1 foot (30 cm) between larger types. Sow seed indoors 4–6 weeks before last frost date, or plant directly into containers after last frost date.
Possible problems Overhead watering may cause flowers to rot; pinch off affected blooms and water more carefully.
Comments Marigolds look great with eggplants, peppers, parsley, basil, tomatoes, lettuce, or blue salvia (*Salvia farinacea*).

Tanacetum parthenium
ASTERACEAE

FEVERFEW

Feverfew is pretty but can become a pest by dropping lots of seed. Cutting off bloom stalks after the flowers fade will prevent this problem and promote new leafy growth.

Description This short-lived perennial or biennial is often grown as a hardy annual. The plants form ferny mounds of deeply cut, aromatic, green leaves. The leafy stems are topped with 1-inch (2.5-cm) wide, single or double flowers.
Height and spread Height 1–2½ feet (30–75 cm); spread 1–1½ feet (30–45 cm).
Flower color and season White or yellow flowers bloom in early to midsummer.
Best climate and site Zones 4–9. Full sun to partial shade. Grow in an all-purpose container mix.
Growing guidelines Starts easily from seed sown directly into container in mid- to late spring. You can also start seed indoors 6–8 weeks before your last frost date. Plant the fine seed in a pot, press it lightly into the mix, and enclose the pot in a plastic bag until seedlings appear. Move young plants outdoors after the last frost date. Space plants or thin seedlings to stand 8–12 inches (20–30 cm) apart.
Possible problems No serious problems.
Comments The sprays of small flowers are lovely in fresh arrangements. Combine feverfew in a container with cornflowers and pot marigolds.

Tithonia rotundifolia
ASTERACEAE

MEXICAN SUNFLOWER

Mexican sunflowers are popular with bees and butterflies, and they make good cut flowers. Pinch off spent blooms to extend the flowering season.

Description Mexican sunflower is a half-hardy annual with colorful blooms. Plants produce tall, sturdy, hairy stems with velvety, lobed or broadly oval, pointed, dark green leaves. During summer, the shrubby clumps are accented with many 3-inch (7.5-cm) wide daisies.
Height and spread Height 4–6 feet (120–180 cm); spread 1½–2 feet (45–60 cm).
Flower color and season Glowing orange flowers bloom in summer.
Best climate and site Zones 5–10. Full sun. Grow in a large container in an all-purpose container mix.
Growing guidelines For earliest flowers, start seed indoors 6–8 weeks before your last frost date. Sow seed ¼ inch (6 mm) deep in individual pots (two or three seeds per pot); thin to leave one seedling per pot. Set plants out after the last frost date. Mexican sunflowers also grow quickly and easily from seed sown directly into the container about 2 weeks after the last frost date. Set plants or thin seedlings to stand 1½ feet (45 cm) apart. Water during dry spells.
Possible problems No serious problems.
Other common names Torch flower.
Comments Combine with blue salvia (*Salvia farinacea*), petunias, sedums, and ornamental grasses.

Torenia fournieri
SCROPHULARIACEAE

WISHBONE FLOWER

Look into the yellow throat of the little sky-blue flowers, and you'll find the tiny, wishbone-shaped stamens. This rugged annual makes a fine container plant for partial shade.

Description These bushy, compact plants have small, bronzy green leaves. Their fascinatingly marked flowers are light and deep blue, with yellow or white throats.

Height and spread Height to 1 foot (30 cm); spread 6–8 inches (15–20 cm).

Flower color and season Purplish-blue flowers with a yellow throat bloom from summer to fall.

Best climate and site Zones 6–9. Partial shade. Wishbone flower grows well in all-purpose container mix. Water abundantly to keep the mix evenly moist.

Growing guidelines Set plants 6–8 inches (15–20 cm) apart. In fall, you can bring the pots indoors and enjoy wishbone flower as a winter-blooming houseplant. Discard plants at the end of the winter. Sow seed indoors 8–10 weeks before the last frost date, or plant it directly into the container outdoors after the last frost date.

Possible problems Plants may sulk if the soil is cold.

Other common names Bluewings.

Comments Wishbone flower looks particularly good with hostas, sweet alyssum, edging lobelia (*Lobelia erinus*), forget-me-not (*Myosotis sylvatica*), and periwinkles (*Vinca* spp.).

Tropaeolum majus
TROPAEOLACEAE

NASTURTIUM

Nasturtiums form lush clumps of bold, round, bright green leaves topped with neon-bright, spurred flowers. These colorful, mounding or trailing annuals are easy to grow and look pretty in containers.

Description Plants grow either as a climbing or trailing vine or as a bushy mound. Each rounded, light green leaf grows from a leaf stalk that emerges from the center of the leaf. The plants bear showy, fragrant, five-petaled blooms to 2 inches (5 cm) wide. Each flower has a prominent spur in back.

Height and spread Height of vining types to about 8 feet (2.4 m), bush types to about 1 foot (30 cm); spread 6–12 inches (15–30 cm).

Flower color and season Nasturtiums bloom in a range of colors, including cream, rose, red, orange, and yellow, from early summer through fall.

Best climate and site Zones 5–9. Full sun is best; tolerates a half-day of sun. Grow nasturtiums in a light, well-drained container mix. Allow the mix to dry between waterings. Nasturtiums prefer cool weather and tend to grow poorly in hot-summer areas.

Growing guidelines Space dwarf types of nasturtiums 6 inches (15 cm) apart; plant other kinds 8–12 inches (20–30 cm) apart. Nasturtiums prefer poor soil, so do not fertilize. A common axiom for success is, "Be nasty to nasturtiums." Sow the seed

indoors 6–8 weeks before the last frost. Use large containers to minimize root disturbance at transplanting time, or sow directly into outdoor pots in early spring.

Possible problems Aphids are a common pest, causing yellowed or distorted growth; spray plants with pyrethrin. Lush foliage but sparse blooms can indicate overwatering and/or overfertilizing. Plants may bloom poorly in hot weather.

Cultivars 'Alaska Mixed' grows 8–12 inches (20–30 cm) tall and has bright flowers over green leaves that are marbled and striped with cream. 'Climbing Mixed' and 'Fordhook Favorites Mixed' produce plants that can climb or trail to 6 feet (180 cm); the single flowers bloom in a range of colors. 'Gleam Mixed' is a semi-trailing type, with stems that can reach 3 feet (90 cm) long; it has semidouble or double flowers in a mix of colors. 'Peach Melba' has peachy orange, single flowers on 1-foot (30-cm) tall plants. 'Strawberries and Cream' grows to 8 inches (20 cm) and has semidouble flowers that are creamy yellow with red blotches. 'Whirlybird Mixed' has upward-facing, semidouble flowers in a range of colors on compact, 1-foot (30-cm) plants.

Comments Use nasturtiums to cover the fading foliage of spring bulbs. Nasturtiums also look good with forget-me-nots (*Myosotis sylvatica*) and dwarf morning glory (*Convolvulus tricolor*).

Vinca major
APOCYNACEAE

LARGE PERIWINKLE

Large periwinkle's trailing habit makes it a must for hanging baskets and window boxes. It is beautiful, easy to grow, and resistant to heat and humidity.

Description Large periwinkle spreads by trailing, rooting stems to form mounds. The plants have 1–3-inch (2.5–7.5-cm) long, oval, glossy green leaves, accented by 1–2-inch (2.5–5-cm) blooms.
Height and spread Height 6–12 inches (15–30 cm); spread to 6 feet (180 cm).
Flower color and season The brilliant violet flowers bloom in spring.
Best climate and site Zones 5–9. Light shade is best; plants will tolerate full sun if well watered. Large periwinkle grows fine in all-purpose container mix, as long as it's not cold. Keep the mix evenly moist, especially if plants are in full sun.
Growing guidelines If the plants start to look stringy, shear them back to the ground to promote fresh new growth. Take cuttings anytime.
Possible problems No serious problems.
Other common names Greater periwinkle, vinca.
Comments Large periwinkle is often confused with annual vinca (*Catharanthus roseus*), which has white or pink blooms. Try large periwinkle with petunias, impatiens, coleus, dahlias, dusty miller (*Senecio cineraria*), or browallia.

Viola x wittrockiana
VIOLACEAE

PANSY

The fresh "faces" of pansies are a cheerful addition to spring containers. They are among the first of all bedding plants to flower.

Description Pansies produce branching stems and oval leaves. The 2–4-inch (5–10-cm) flowers come in a variety of colors; they may be solid, bicolored, striped, or blotched.
Height and spread Height 6–8 inches (15–20 cm); spread 8–12 inches (20–30 cm).
Flower color and season White, pink, red, orange, yellow, purple, blue, and near-black flowers bloom in spring and fall.
Best climate and site Zones 5–9. Part shade is usually best, although plants can take full sun if protected from midday heat. Grow in a well-drained container mix. Keep the mix evenly moist.
Growing guidelines Space plants 4–6 inches (10–15 cm) apart. Sow seed indoors 10–12 weeks before the last frost, or sow outdoors in mid-July to mid-August for next year's bloom.
Possible problems Pansies tend to sulk in hot weather. If they stop blooming, shear the plants back by half, or simply remove them and replace them with summer-blooming flowers.
Other common names Viola.
Comments Try pansies with dwarf snapdragons, edging lobelia (*Lobelia erinus*), forget-me-not (*Myosotis sylvatica*), parsley, daylilies, and spring-flowering bulbs.

Zinnia spp.
ASTERACEAE

ZINNIA

Zinnias are colorful annuals for sunny containers. To keep common zinnias looking their best, fertilize monthly and pinch off faded blooms.

Description Zinnias come in two forms: common zinnia (*Z. elegans*) and narrow-leaved zinnia (*Z. angustifolia*, also listed as *Z. linearis*). Common zinnias have single or double flowers that appear all summer in a wide range of colors. Narrow-leaved zinnia forms trailing mounds of small, thin leaves topped with single, daisy-like flowers.
Height and spread Height 6–36 inches (15–90 cm); spread 1–2 feet (30–60 cm).
Flower color and season Zinnias come in nearly every color except true blue, and bloom from midsummer to frost.
Best climate and site Zones 5–10. Full sun. Grow in an all-purpose container mix. For narrow-leaved zinnia, let the soil dry out somewhat between waterings.
Growing guidelines Space plants 6–12 inches (15–30 cm) apart. Sow seed indoors 6 weeks before the last frost date. Sow directly into containers in May to June.
Possible problems Common zinnia is prone to powdery mildew. Try pinching off the affected leaves and moving the pot to an airier spot.
Comments Try zinnias with petunias, lettuce, tomatoes, flowering tobacco (*Nicotiana* spp.), or boxwoods (*Buxus* spp.).

Allium christophii
LILIACEAE

STAR OF PERSIA

Star of Persia produces strap-like, blue-green leaves that arch outward from the bulbs. Starry flowers radiate from stout stalks.

Description Star of Persia has broad, 1½-foot (45-cm) long leaves that are green and shiny on top and white underneath. Flowers are carried in 10-inch (25-cm) globose heads, atop the sturdy, 1–1½-foot (30–45-cm) stems. The individual flowers turn black as the seeds ripen.
Height and spread Height 1–1½ feet (30–45 cm); spread 1 foot (30 cm).
Flower color and season Metallic, lilac-pink flowers bloom early to midsummer.
Best climate and site Zones 4–8. Full sun. Grow in a well-drained, all-purpose container mix.
Growing guidelines New bulbs planted in fall multiply slowly to form spectacular flowering clumps. Plants go dormant after flowering. Divide in mid- to late summer as plants go dormant. Sow ripe seed outdoors in summer or fall. Mulch with organic matter to keep the mix evenly moist.
Possible problems No serious problems.
Other species *A. sphaerocephalum*, drumstick chives, has slender 1½–3-foot (45–90-cm) stems crowned by tight heads of small, red-violet flowers. Zones 4–9.
Comments Looks striking in a container with tall ornamental grasses and sedums.

Anemone blanda
RANUNCULACEAE

GRECIAN WINDFLOWER

Grecian windflowers bloom in mid- to late spring in most areas. In warm Southern gardens, they may appear in late winter or early spring.

Description Grecian windflowers grow from knobbly tubers to produce carpets of deeply lobed, toothed, green leaves. Daisy-like flowers to 2 inches (5 cm) across bloom just above the ferny leaves.
Height and spread Height of leaves and flowers to 6 inches (15 cm); spread 4–6 inches (10–15 cm).
Flower color and season Blue, pink, or white flowers bloom in mid- to late spring.
Best climate and site Zones 5–8. Full sun to partial shade. Grow in an all-purpose container mix.
Growing guidelines Buy and plant the tubers in late spring through early fall. Soak them overnight before planting, and set them in containers 2 inches (5 cm) deep. It can be hard to tell which side is up. If you can see a shallow depression on one side, plant with that side up; otherwise, plant the tubers on their sides or just drop them into the hole. Space the tubers 4–6 inches (10–15 cm) apart. Grecian windflowers propagate themselves by spreading and self-sowing.
Possible problems No serious problems.
Comments Grecian windflowers combine well with daffodils. They look good in window boxes.

Arum italicum
ARACEAE

ITALIAN ARUM

By late summer, the spring flowers of Italian arum mature into columns of reddish-orange berries. These colorful spikes add interest until the new leaves appear in fall.

Description Italian arum has a greenish-white, hood-like spathe sheltering a narrow column known as the spadix. These unusual flowers are interesting, but the plant is mainly grown for its arrowhead-shaped, semi-glossy, dark green leaves that are marked with creamy white. The leaves emerge in fall and last through the winter, finally dying in summer.
Height and spread Height 1–1½ feet (30–45 cm); spread to 1 foot (30 cm).
Flower color and season The greenish-yellow flowers bloom in mid- to late spring.
Best climate and site Zones 6–10. Partial shade. Grow in all-purpose container mix.
Growing guidelines Plant in late summer or early fall. Set the tubers into individual holes or larger planting areas dug 2–3 inches (5–7.5 cm) deep. Space tubers 8–12 inches (20–30 cm) apart. Keep the mix moist during leaf growth and flowering. For propagation, divide in early fall; otherwise, allow plants to form handsome clumps.
Possible problems No serious problems.
Comments Combine Italian arum with hellebores (*Helleborus* spp.) and snowdrops (*Galanthus nivalis*) for an extra-pretty picture in late winter through early spring.

Colchicum speciosum
COLCHICACEAE

SHOWY AUTUMN CROCUS

Showy autumn crocus grows from large, plump corms. Once established, each corm will produce showy clumps of rosy pink, goblet-shaped flowers, the size of small tulips.

Description Wide, flat, glossy, green leaves emerge in late fall or early spring. They elongate through spring, then turn yellow and die to the ground in early summer. Rosy pink, 4-inch (10-cm) wide, stemless flowers rise directly from the ground in late summer to early fall.
Height and spread Height of leaves to about 8 inches (20 cm); flowers 4–6 inches (10–15 cm). Spread to 6 inches (15 cm).
Flower color and season Pink flowers bloom in late summer to early fall.
Best climate and site Zones 4–9. Full sun to partial shade. Grow in a well-drained, all-purpose container mix.
Growing guidelines Plant corms in summer, as soon as they are available; they may bloom before you plant them if you delay. Set them individually or in groups about 4 inches (10 cm) deep. Space bulbs 6 inches (15 cm) apart. Divide just after the leaves die down if needed for propagation.
Possible problems No serious problems.
Other common names Autumn crocus.
Comments Combine in a large container with hellebores (*Helleborus* spp.) and Italian arum (*Arum italicum*) for pretty fall and winter effect.

Crocosmia x crocosmiiflora
IRIDACEAE

CROCOSMIA

Crocosmia is a brightly colored perennial with vivid red or orange, summer flowers and fans of sword-like leaves resembling gladiolus. They grow from button-like corms.

Description The flowers of crocosmia are tubular, orange or red, and are carried on erect, sparsely branched, zigzag stems.
Height and spread Height 2–3 feet (60–90 cm); spread 1–2 feet (30–60 cm).
Flower color and season Red or orange flowers bloom in summer and early fall; season varies with individual cultivars.
Best climate and site Zones 6–9. Full sun. Grow in an all-purpose container mix.
Growing guidelines Crocosmias spread to form broad clumps of tightly packed foliage fans. Remove spent stalks after flowering. Divide overgrown clumps or remove outside corms in spring. In colder zones, lift corms in fall and store in a cool, dry place. If you store corms over winter, replant them when temperatures are moderate.
Possible problems Spider mites and thrips cause white or brown stippling or streaks on the leaves. Spray with insecticidal soap or with a botanical insecticide such as pyrethrin. Cut badly damaged plants to the ground and destroy the infested portions.
Comments Plant with summer perennials such as phlox, daylilies, and poppies.

Cyclamen hederifolium
PRIMULACEAE

HARDY CYCLAMEN

Hardy cyclamen grows well in containers placed under shrubs and trees and are attractive through most of the year.

Description Hardy cyclamen grow from smooth tubers. Heart-shaped, silver-marked, green leaves emerge shortly after the blooms finish. The leaves die back by midsummer but return by midfall.
Height and spread Height 4–6 inches (10–15 cm); similar spread.
Flower color and season Pink or white flowers bloom in early fall.
Best climate and site Zones 5–9. Partial shade. Grow in a well-drained, all-purpose container mix.
Growing guidelines Buy nursery-propagated tubers or start your own from seed. Soak the seed overnight, then sow it ¼ inch (6 mm) deep. Set the pot in a plastic bag in a dark place. Check monthly for sprouting, which may take up to a few years. Set plants into the container in spring or summer, or plant dormant tubers shallowly in summer, smooth-side down. Space plants 6 inches (15 cm) apart.
Possible problems Spray the plant with insecticidal soap to control spider mites and cyclamen mites.
Other common names Cyclamen.
Comments Hardy cyclamen provide fall color when combined in containers with ferns and hellebores (*Helleborus* spp.).

Dahlia hybrids
ASTERACEAE

DAHLIAS

Dahlias come in two types: tall, border selections and dwarf, bedding types. The dwarf types are usually best for container gardening.

Description Dahlias grow from frost-tender, tuberous roots. They produce single or branched stems.
Height and spread Height 1–5 feet (30–150 cm); spread 1–4 feet (30–120 cm).
Flower color and season Red, orange, pink, purple, white, and yellow flowers bloom from midsummer through fall.
Best climate and site Zones 9–10. Partial to full sun. Grow in a well-drained, peat moss-and-sand-based mix. Keep evenly moist after growth begins.
Growing guidelines If you're growing full-sized types, plant one tuber per 10-inch (25-cm) pot. If you're using dwarf plants, space them about 10 inches (25 cm) apart. North of Zone 9, bring the roots indoors for winter storage in dry peat moss in a cool, dry spot. Divide the root clumps in fall or spring, keeping one eye (bud) on each. You can grow bedding types from seed; sow indoors 6–8 weeks before the last frost.
Possible problems Scraggly growth means not enough light. Too much fertilizer encourages leaves instead of flowers.
Comments Try dahlias with large periwinkle (*Vinca major*), coleus, petunias, zonal geraniums (*Pelargonium* spp.), impatiens, or boxwood (*Buxus* spp.).

Fritillaria imperalis
LILIACEAE

CROWN IMPERIAL

Crown imperials may take a few seasons to get established and bloom well; mature clumps can live for many years. All parts of the plant have a musky (some say skunk-like) odor.

Description Crown imperial grows from a large, fleshy bulb. Sturdy shoots of green stems and glossy, green leaves emerge in early spring and elongate for several weeks. By mid- to late spring, the tall stems are topped with a tuft of green leaves, which die back to the ground by midsummer.
Height and spread Height 2–4 feet (60–120 cm); spread to 1 foot (30 cm).
Flower color and season Yellow, orange, or red, hanging, bell-shaped, flowers bloom in mid- to late spring.
Best climate and site Zones 5–9. Full spring sun. Grow in a well-drained, all-purpose container mix.
Growing guidelines Plant the bulbs in late summer or early fall about 8 inches (20 cm) deep. When you set the bulb in the hole, tilt it slightly to one side to discourage water from collecting in the depression at the top of the bulb. Space bulbs 1 foot (30 cm) apart. Lift and divide bulbs in summer only if needed for propagation.
Possible problems No serious problems.
Comments Good companions include honesty (*Lunaria annua*), forget-me-nots (*Myosotis* spp.), and daffodils. Follow them with later-blooming annuals.

Fritillaria meleagris
LILIACEAE

CHECKERED LILY

The nodding flowers of checkered lilies add a charming touch to spring containers. Combine them with daffodils for a pretty feature.

Description Checkered lily grows from small bulbs. Slender, arching stems with narrow, gray-green leaves rise in early spring. By midspring, broad, nodding, bell-like blooms dangle from the ends of the nodding stems. The 1–2-inch (2.5–5-cm) long flowers range in color from white to deep purple; many are marked with a checkered pattern. Checkered lilies die back to the ground by midsummer.
Height and spread Height to 1 foot (30 cm); spread 2–4 inches (5–10 cm).
Flower color and season Flowers from white to deep purple bloom in spring.
Best climate and site Zones 3–8. Partial shade. Grow in a well-drained, all-purpose container mix.
Growing guidelines Plant in early fall, as soon as the bulbs are available. Dig the holes 2–3 inches (5–7.5 cm) deep. Space bulbs 4–6 inches (10–15 cm) apart.
Possible problems No serious problems.
Other common names Guinea-hen flower, snake's-head lily, bloody warrior, leopard lily.
Cultivars 'Alba' has white flowers.
Comments These small bulbs combine beautifully with ferns and hellebores (*Helleborus* spp.).

Galanthus nivalis
AMARYLLIDACEAE

COMMON SNOWDROP

Common snowdrops are among the earliest flowers to bloom in spring containers. Established bulbs are trouble-free; grow them under a Japanese maple (Acer palmatum).

Description Common snowdrops grow from small bulbs. Each bulb produces two or three flat, narrow, bluish-green leaves and an upright to arching green flower stem in midwinter through early spring. Dainty, nodding flowers to 1 inch (2.5 cm) long bloom at the tips of the stems. The single or double flowers are white; each of the shorter, inner petals has a green tip. Plants die back to the ground by early summer.
Height and spread Height 6 inches (15 cm); spread 2–3 inches (5–7.5 cm).
Flower color and season White flowers bloom in late winter or early spring.
Best climate and site Zones 3–9. Full sun to partial shade. Grow in an all-purpose container mix.
Growing guidelines Plant bulbs in fall. Set them in individual holes or larger planting areas dug 3–4 inches (7.5–10 cm) deep. Space bulbs 3–4 inches (7.5–10 cm) apart.
Possible problems No serious problems.
Comments Combine with daffodils, jonquils, and forget-me-nots (*Myosotis* spp.) for spring color. Can also be grown with hellebores (*Helleborus* spp.)

Hyacinthoides hispanica
HYACINTHACEAE

SPANISH BLUEBELLS

Spanish bluebells are one of the easiest of all spring bulbs to grow in containers. Try them combined with tulips, for a beautiful display.

Description Spanish bluebells grow from small bulbs. In spring, the plants form clumps of sprawling, strap-like, green leaves. Upright, leafless flower stems topped with spikes of many bell-shaped blooms appear in late spring. The ¾-inch (18-mm) wide flowers bloom in a variety of colors. Plants go dormant by midsummer.
Height and spread Height of flowers 1–1½ feet (30–45 cm); leaves usually to 8 inches (20 cm) tall. Spread 4–6 inches (10–15 cm).
Flower color and season White, pink, and purple-blue flowers bloom in spring.
Best climate and site Zones 4–8. Full sun to partial shade. Grow in an all-purpose container mix.
Growing guidelines Plant bulbs in fall. Set them in individual holes or larger planting areas dug 3–4 inches (7.5–10 cm) deep. Space bulbs 4–6 inches (10–15 cm) apart.
Possible problems No serious problems.
Other common names Bluebells.
Cultivars 'Azalea' has many shorter spikes of pink-lilac flowers.
Comments Grow Spanish bluebells with daffodils and snowdrops (*Galanthus nivalis*), or under a shrub or Japanese maple (*Acer palmatum*).

Hyacinthus orientalis
HYACINTHACEAE

HYACINTH

After the first year, hyacinth bloom spikes tend to be smaller. Sometimes, they may not flower at all. Plant new bulbs every year or two to ensure a good display.

Description Hyacinths have sturdy shoots with wide, strap-like leaves and upright flower stalks that emerge in early spring. Hyacinths go dormant in early summer.
Height and spread Height 8–12 inches (20–30 cm); spread to 4 inches (10 cm).
Flower color and season White, pink, red, orange, yellow, blue, and purple flowers bloom in spring.
Best climate and site Zones 4–8. Full sun. Grow in an all-purpose container mix.
Growing guidelines Plant bulbs in midfall. Set them in containers 5–6 inches (12.5–15 cm) deep. Space the bulbs 6–10 inches (15–25 cm) apart. Remove the spent flower stalks. For propagation, dig up and divide crowded clumps as the leaves yellow.
Possible problems No serious problems.
Cultivars 'Carnegie' has white flowers. 'City of Haarlem' has a strong spike of creamy yellow flowers, which bloom late in the season. 'Delft Blue' produces pale blue blooms. 'Lady Derby' has soft, pale pink flowers.
Comments Combine hyacinths with primroses and pansies for extra excitement. They are suitable for winter forcing indoors.

Iris reticulata
IRIDACEAE

RETICULATED IRIS

Reticulated irises return year after year to grace your containers with their delicate spring flowers. Grow them with daffodils or in small containers, which may be brought indoors while in bloom.

Description Reticulated irises grow from small bulbs. The dainty flowers have three upright petals (known as standards) and three outward-arching petals (known as falls). The falls have gold and/or white markings. The grass-like, dark green leaves are short at bloom time but elongate after the flowers fade; they ripen and die back to the ground by early summer.

Height and spread Height of leaves to about 1 foot (30 cm); flowers to 4–6 inches (10–15 cm); spread to 2 inches (5 cm).

Flower color and season Blue, purple, or white flowers bloom in early spring.

Best climate and site Zones 5–9. Full sun. Grow in an all-purpose container mix.

Growing guidelines Plant the bulbs in fall. Set them in individual holes or larger planting areas dug 3–4 inches (7.5–10 cm) deep. For propagation, lift and divide clumps after the leaves turn yellow.

Possible problems No serious problems.

Other common names Netted iris.

Comments For extra color, combine them with Grecian windflowers (*Anemone blanda*). Reticulated irises are also suitable for winter forcing indoors.

Iris sibirica
IRIDICEAE

SIBERIAN IRIS

Siberian irises produce graceful flowers in a wide range of colors. Plants form tight fans of narrow, sword-like leaves from slow-creeping rhizomes.

Description Siberian iris flowers have three falls ringing the outside of the flowers, with three slender standards in the center. Three flat columns decline over the falls.

Height and spread Height 1–3 feet (30–90 cm); spread 1–2 feet (30–60 cm).

Flower color and season Summer flowers range from pure white to purple.

Best climate and site Zones 3–9. Full sun to partial shade. Grow in an all-purpose container mix. Heat- and cold-tolerant.

Growing guidelines Plant in spring, summer, and fall. Divide and replant in late summer.

Possible problems Susceptible to iris borer. Good culture is the best preventive; cut off affected portions of the rhizome. Remove dead foliage in spring and fall.

Other common names Siberian flag iris.

Cultivars 'Caesar', 'Dewful', 'Ego', 'My Love', 'Orville Fay', and 'Sky Wings' have blue flowers of varying shades.

Comments Plant with perennials such as peonies, baptisia (*Baptisia* spp.), cranesbills (*Geranium* spp.), ornamental grasses, as well as ferns.

Leucojum aestivum
AMARYLLIDACEAE

SUMMER SNOWFLAKE

Despite their name, summer snowflakes actually bloom in spring. Plant the small bulbs in groups; over time, they'll form large clumps.

Description Clumps of strap-like, green leaves emerge in early spring. In mid- to late spring, plants produce slender, green, flowering stems tipped with loose clusters of nodding, bell-shaped, ¾-inch (18-mm) wide flowers. The white flowers have a green spot near the tip of each petal. After bloom, the leaves turn yellow and die back to the ground by midsummer.

Height and spread Height of foliage and flowers to 1½ feet (45 cm); spread to 6 inches (15 cm).

Flower color and season White flowers bloom in mid- to late spring.

Best climate and site Zones 4–9. Full sun to partial shade. Grow in an all-purpose container mix.

Growing guidelines In early fall, set bulbs in individual holes or larger planting areas dug 4 inches (10 cm) deep. Space them about 6 inches (15 cm) apart. For propagation, divide in early fall.

Possible problems No serious problems.

Other common names Giant snowflake.

Comments Grow summer snowflake with tulips and daffodils. Interplant with summer- and fall-blooming annuals that will fill in when the bulbs go dormant.

Lilium hybrids
LILIACEAE

LILIES

Lilies are excellent as cut flowers; pick them when the first one or two buds open. You may want to remove the orange anthers to keep them from dropping pollen on furniture, as it can stain.

Description Lilies grow from scaly bulbs. They produce upright, unbranched stems with narrow to lance-shaped, green leaves in spring through early summer. By early to late summer (depending on the hybrid), the long, plump flower buds open to showy, flat or funnel-shaped flowers. After bloom, the leaves and stems usually stay green until late summer or early fall.

Height and spread Height 2–5 feet (60–150 cm), depending on the hybrid; spread usually 6–12 inches (15–30 cm).

Flower color and season Lilies bloom in early summer in a huge variety of colors including shades of white, yellow, red, pink, and orange. Some flowers may be spotted or striped.

Best climate and site Zones 4–8. Full sun to partial shade. Grow in an all-purpose container mix.

Growing guidelines Handle the scaly bulbs gently, planting them in fall or early spring, as soon as they are available. Plant some in small containers, which may be brought indoors while in flower. Plant 4 inches (10 cm) deep in a container which is at least 1 foot (30 cm) deep. After carefully filling in around the bulbs, water to settle the mix. Keep pot evenly moist

always. Pinch off spent flowers where they join the stem. Cut stems to the ground when the leaves turn yellow; divide clumps at the same time only if needed for propagation.

Possible problems Protect new growth from snails.

Hybrids Asiatic hybrids bloom in early summer in a range of bright and pastel colors. The 4–6-inch (10–15-cm) wide flowers usually face upward but can also be outward facing or nodding. They bloom on sturdy stems that are usually 2–3 feet (60–90 cm) tall.

Aurelian hybrids bloom in midsummer and have large, trumpet-shaped, bowl-shaped, nodding, or starry flowers on 4–6-foot (120–180-cm) stems. The 6–8-inch (15–20-cm) wide flowers come in a wide range of colors and are usually fragrant.

Oriental hybrids bloom in late summer and have large flowers in crimson-red, pink, white, or white with yellow stripes; many blooms are spotted with pink or red. The richly fragrant flowers grow to 10 inches (25 cm) long and may be bowl-shaped or flat-faced; some have petals with recurved tips.

Comments Combine lilies with mounding annuals, perennials, or groundcovers that can shade the mix and keep the bulbs cool. Dwarf hybrids are best for smaller pots.

Muscari armeniacum
HYACINTHACEAE

GRAPE HYACINTH

Grape hyacinths bloom for only a short time, but their early spring color is definitely a welcome sight to winter-weary gardeners. They often self-sow and increase rapidly.

Description Grape hyacinths grow from small, plump bulbs. The bulbs send up 4–8-inch (10–20-cm) tall, grassy leaves in fall or late winter.

Height and spread Height 6–8 inches (15–20 cm); spread 3–4 inches (7.5–10 cm).

Flower color and season Purple-blue, white-rimmed flowers bloom in early spring.

Best climate and site Zones 3–10. Full sun to light shade. Grow in an all-purpose container mix. Keep the mix evenly moist from fall through spring; provide little or no summer water.

Growing guidelines In the fall, set the bulbs 2 inches (5 cm) deep and 3 inches (7.5 cm) apart. Allow the foliage to turn yellow before storing the pot, dry, over summer. Replant the bulbs into fresh container mix the following fall.

Possible problems Generally trouble-free. Bulbs can rot if overwatered in summer.

Comments Try grape hyacinths with nasturtiums (*Tropaeolum majus*), rose moss (*Portulaca grandiflora*), lantana (*Lantana camara*), dwarf morning glory (*Convolvulus tricolor*), and creeping zinnia (*Sanvitalia procumbens*). Also try grape hyacinths with small tulips, daffodils, and pansies.

Narcissus hybrids
AMARYLLIDACEAE

DAFFODILS

It's hard to imagine a garden without daffodils for spring color. Grow them in containers and window boxes with pansies, bluebells, and snowdrops.

Description Daffodils grow from large, pointed bulbs. Clumps of flat, strap-like, green leaves emerge in early spring, along with leafless flower stalks. Depending on the cultivar, the sometimes-fragrant flowers appear in early, mid-, or late spring. Each flower has a cup or trumpet (technically known as a corona) and an outer ring of petals (known as the perianth). The single or double blooms are most commonly white or yellow but may also have pink, green, or orange parts or markings. The leaves usually remain green until midsummer, at which time they turn yellow and die back to the ground.

Height and spread Height 6–20 inches (15–50 cm), depending on the cultivar; spread 4–8 inches (10–20 cm).

Flower color and season The mostly yellow or white flowers bloom in spring.

Best climate and site Zones 4–8. Full sun to partial shade. Grow in a well-drained, all-purpose container mix.

Growing guidelines For the best display, plan to grow daffodils in a pot for a single season only. That way, you don't have to worry about leaving space between them. You can cram as many bulbs together as will fill the pot. Fill the pot three-quarters full with container mix, level off, then

place the bulbs on top. They can touch each other, but leave a little space between the bulbs and the sides of the pot. Cover the bulbs with more container mix so that they are about 1 inch (2.5 cm) below the surface. Tap the bottom of the pot on the ground to settle the container mix, then water in well. You may need to add a little more mix. Place the pot in a shady, cool place until shoots appear, then move into full sun. When flowers have finished, let the leaves die down naturally and allow the pot to go dry. Next fall, plant those bulbs in the garden and buy new bulbs for your pot. For propagation, divide clumps after the leaves die back.

Possible problems No serious problems.

Cultivars In catalogs, daffodils are often listed under different divisions, based on their flower forms. Check the photographs and plant descriptions to find the colors, shapes, and sizes you like best.

Comments Create unforgettable combinations by grouping daffodils with other early bloomers, including pansies, crocus, Siberian squill (*Scilla sibirica*), grape hyacinths (*Muscari* spp.), and Grecian windflower (*Anemone blanda*).

Scilla sibirica
HYACINTHACEAE

SIBERIAN SQUILL

The deep blue blooms of Siberian squill look marvelous in containers. They also combine beautifully with other spring-flowering bulbs, annuals, and perennials.

Description Siberian squills grow from small bulbs. They produce narrow, strap-like, green leaves and leafless flower stems starting in late winter. By early to midspring, the flower stems are topped with clusters of nodding, starry, or bell-shaped blue flowers to ½ inch (12 mm) across. By early summer, the leaves gradually turn yellow and die back to the ground.

Height and spread Height to 6 inches (15 cm); spread 2–3 inches (5–7.5 cm).

Flower color and season The deep blue flowers bloom in spring.

Best climate and site Zones 3–8. Full sun to partial shade. Grow in a well-drained, all-purpose container mix.

Growing guidelines Plant bulbs in early to midfall, as soon as they are available. Set them in individual holes or larger planting areas dug 3–4 inches (7.5–10 cm) deep. For propagation, divide bulbs after the leaves turn yellow; otherwise, leave them undisturbed to spread into large clumps.

Possible problems Bad drainage will rot the bulbs. Established bulbs are trouble-free.

Comments Take containers of Siberian squill indoors for winter forcing. Combine with pansies as well as other spring-flowering bulbs.

Tulipa hybrids
LILIACEAE

TULIPS

Hybrid tulips often bloom poorly after the first year. For a great show each year, pull them out after bloom and replace them with summer annuals; plant new tulips in fall.

Description Tulips grow from plump, pointed bulbs. They produce broad, dusty-green leaves that are sometimes striped with maroon in early to midspring. The slender, upright, usually unbranched flower stems are topped with showy single or double flowers up to 4 inches (10 cm) across. By midsummer, leaves gradually turn yellow and die back to the ground.

Height and spread Height 6–30 inches (15–75 cm), depending on the cultivar; spread 6–10 inches (15–25 cm).

Flower color and season Flowers in orange, pink, purple, red, white, green, and yellow bloom in spring.

Best climate and site Usually best in Zones 3–8; in Zones 9 and 10, treat hybrid tulips as annuals and plant precooled bulbs each year in late fall or early winter. Full sun to partial shade. Grow in an all-purpose container mix.

Growing guidelines Fill container with free-draining container mix, leaving enough space at the top for the bulbs plus another 2 inches (5 cm). Level off, then put bulbs on top. Tulips have big, wide leaves, so you'll have to leave a 2-inch (5-cm) space between each bulb. Cover bulbs with more mix and tap pot on the ground to settle.

(The bulbs only have to be covered by an inch or two of mix.) Water in, and keep moist. Place pot in a cool spot until shoots appear, then move into sun. When flowers are finished, discard the bulbs.

Possible problems Bad drainage will cause the bulbs to rot. Watch for aphids in early spring. Spray with insecticidal soap.

Cultivars 'Angelique' has ruffled, petal-packed, double, pale pink flowers on 16-inch (40-cm) tall stems. 'Apricot Beauty' has beautiful, peach-colored blooms on 14-inch (35-cm) tall stems. 'Ballade' grows to 2 feet (60 cm) tall and has reddish-purple, white-edged, pointed petals that arch outward. 'Maureen' reaches 3 feet (90 cm) tall and has white flowers. 'Mrs J. T. Scheepers' has sunny yellow blooms on 3-foot (90-cm) tall stems. 'Negrita' grows to 16 inches (40 cm) tall and has purple flowers. 'Queen of the Night' has dark maroon-black blooms on 2-foot (60-cm) tall stems. 'Red Emperor' grows to 1½ feet (45 cm) tall and has large, scarlet flowers. 'Red Riding Hood' has black-centered, red flowers and purple-striped leaves on 8-inch (20-cm) tall stems.

Comments Grow hybrid tulips with daffodils, pansies, primroses, bleeding hearts (*Dicentra* spp.), grape hyacinths (*Muscari* spp.), and forget-me-nots (*Myosotis* spp.). Tulips are also charming as cut flowers; pick them when the flowers are fully colored but still in bud. Tulips are also suitable for forcing for winter bloom indoors.

Tulipa kaufmanniana
LILIACEAE

KAUFMANNIANA TULIP

Kaufmanniana tulips come in a range of colors, including pink, yellow, red, and white; most also have deep-colored blazes on the outside of the petals.

Description Kaufmanniana tulips have starry flowers composed of three petals and three petal-like sepals. The leaves are broad, with wavy margins and pointed tips, and are colored sea-green with dark brown stripes. Plants grow from true bulbs.

Height and spread Height 4–8 inches (10–20 cm); spread 4–6 inches (10–15 cm), although established clumps may be up to 1 foot (30 cm) across.

Flower color and season The pink, yellow, red, and white flowers bloom in early spring.

Best climate and site Zones 4–8. Full sun or light shade. Plant in all-purpose container mix. Plants go dormant after flowering and can withstand considerable drought and shade.

Growing guidelines Plant bulbs 2 inches (5 cm) deep and 1 inch (2.5 cm) apart. Keep cool and moist until shoots appear, then move pot into sun. After flowering, discard the bulbs.

Possible problems No serious problems.

Other common names Waterlily tulip.

Comments Combine Kaufmanniana tulips with primroses, lungworts (*Pulmonaria* spp.), sweet woodruff (*Galium odoratum*), and ferns.

Arabis caucasica
BRASSICACEAE

WALL ROCK CRESS

The spreading, evergreen mounds of wall rock cress are accented with masses of sweetly scented, white flowers in spring.

Description Wall rock cress forms spreading mounds of grayish-green, 1-inch (2.5-cm), toothed leaves. In spring, the mounds are smothered in clusters of small, fragrant, white, four-petaled flowers.
Height and spread Height 4–6 inches (10–15 cm); spread to 1½ feet (45 cm). Flower height to 1 foot (30 cm).
Flower color and season White flowers bloom in spring.
Best climate and site Zones 3–7. Full sun. Grow in an all-purpose container mix.
Growing guidelines Set plants 1 foot (30 cm) apart. Cut plants back by half after bloom to remove the spent flowers and to promote compact new growth. Propagate by division in fall, by seed in spring, or by cuttings in early summer.
Possible problems No serious problems.
Cultivars 'Compinkie' has rosy-pink flowers on 6–8-inch (15–20-cm) stems in spring. 'Flore Pleno', with double flowers, stays in bloom longer than the species.
Other species A. procurrens grows in sun or light shade. Clusters of tiny, white flowers in spring rise 1 foot (30 cm) above mats of shiny, green leaves. Zones 5–7.
Comments The white flowers are a good complement to spring-flowering bulbs.

Arenaria montana
CARYOPHYLLACEAE

MOUNTAIN SANDWORT

Mountain sandwort is a dense, mat-forming groundcover with tiny, needle-like leaves and flat, white, five-petaled flowers.

Description These easy-to-grow, creeping plants form dense mats of grass-like, shiny, gray-green foliage. Many five-petaled, 1-inch (2.5-cm) wide flowers bloom just above the foliage.
Height and spread Height 2–4 inches (5–10 cm); 1 foot (30 cm) when in flower; spread 10–12 inches (25–30 cm); larger with age.
Flower color and season White flowers with a yellow eye bloom in spring and early summer.
Best climate and site Zones 4–8. Full sun. Grow in a well-drained container mix.
Growing guidelines Mountain sandwort is shallow-rooted, so keep moist during dry spells. Divide in spring or fall. Sow seed outdoors in fall or inside in early spring.
Possible problems No serious problems.
Other common names Sandwort.
Other species A. balearica is a miniature species with white flowers. Zones 7–9. A. verna, moss sandwort, grows 1–2 inches (2.5–5 cm) tall and spreads rapidly. It has star-like flowers in spring and mossy, evergreen leaves.
Comments Mountain sandwort is perfect for trough culture.

Cerastium tomentosum
CARYOPHYLLACEAE

SNOW-IN-SUMMER

Snow-in-summer is a low-mounding plant with small, woolly leaves and clusters of white flowers on wiry stems. Plants grow from a dense tangle of fibrous roots.

Description This fast-growing evergreen with light gray, woolly foliage forms large mats with its creeping stems. The abundant, snow-white, 1-inch (2.5-cm) flowers have five deeply notched petals that give the impression of a 10-petaled flower. They are borne in open clusters held well above the foliage.
Height and spread Height 6–10 inches (15–25 cm); spread 1 foot (30 cm).
Flower color and season White flowers bloom in spring and early summer.
Best climate and site Zones 2–7. Full sun. Grow in a well-drained container mix. Extremely cold-tolerant.
Growing guidelines Shear plants to the ground after flowering to promote fresh, compact growth. Clumps spread easily and may overgrow their container. Divide in spring or fall and replant vigorous portions. Take tip cuttings in early summer.
Possible problems May suffer from fungal rots that blacken the leaves and stems. Remove and destroy infected foliage. Well-drained soil and cool summer temperatures are the best preventive.
Comments The profusion of white flowers complements late spring bulbs. Snow-in-summer also looks good in a hanging basket.

Delosperma cooperi
AIZOACEAE

HARDY ICEPLANT

Long-blooming hardy iceplant offers a colorful show of purple flowers throughout summer. It looks wonderful cascading out of hanging baskets or urns.

Description This low-growing South African succulent is becoming increasingly popular for its pretty, small, daisy-like flowers, which bloom over mats of narrow, curving leaves.

Height and spread Height 4 inches (10 cm); spread to 1 foot (30 cm).

Flower color and season Rosy purple flowers bloom from summer until frost.

Best climate and site Zones 7–9. Full sun. Grow in a well-drained container mix with added sand.

Growing guidelines Set plants 1 foot (30 cm) apart in spring. They like dry container mix in winter and do best when temperatures don't go below 50°F (10°C). In warm climates, the plants bloom all year but grow mostly in the summer. Established plants need little care. Propagate by seed or cuttings in spring or summer.

Possible problems No serious problems.

Other species *D. nubigenum* grows to 2 inches (5 cm) tall and 8–10 inches (20–25 cm) wide. This fast-growing, tough plant has bright yellow flowers in late spring and yellow-green leaves that turn red in winter. Zones 5–9.

Comments Hardy iceplant is ideal for hot, sunny spots. Combine in a container with a tall ornamental grass.

Helianthemum nummularium
CISTACEAE

SUN ROSE

Sun rose is a low-growing shrub with small green or gray-green leaves. It blooms for many weeks, although each flower only lasts one day.

Description This low-maintenance, woody shrub forms spreading mounds of narrow, hairy, evergreen leaves. Clusters of flowers bloom just above the foliage.

Height and spread Height 8–18 inches (20–45 cm); spread to 3 feet (90 cm).

Flower color and season Yellow, pink, or white flowers bloom in late spring and early summer.

Best climate and site Zones 6–8. Full sun. Grow in a well-drained, sandy, all-purpose container mix.

Growing guidelines Set plants 2 feet (60 cm) apart in spring or fall. Prune back by one-third to one-half to stimulate a second bloom. Protect plants with a light winter mulch in the coldest parts of their range. You may also need to trim them back in early spring to remove winter-damaged tips. Propagate by cuttings in summer.

Possible problems No serious problems.

Other common names Rock rose.

Cultivars 'Dazzler' has dazzling magenta flowers. 'Goldilocks' is covered with golden yellow blooms. 'Wisley Pink' has delicate, pink blooms over silvery foliage.

Comments Combine with other low-maintenance plants such as purple cone-flower (*Echinacea purpurea*), gaillardia, and ornamental grasses.

Lamium galeobdolon
LAMIACEAE

YELLOW ARCHANGEL

Yellow archangel is fast-spreading with long surface runners that take root as they creep over the container mix. It is ideal for large containers in shady areas where few other plants grow.

Description The silvery green, heart-shaped or oval, toothed, 3-inch (7.5-cm) long leaves produce a strong odor when bruised. Dense clusters of small, yellow, hooded flowers bloom in whorls along the stems. The foliage is evergreen in warm climates but deciduous in cold climates. This species looks similar to dead nettles (*Lamiastrum* spp.) and is sometimes sold as *Lamiastrum galeobdolon*.

Height and spread Height 1–1½ feet (30–45 cm); spread 3 feet (90 cm).

Flower color and season Yellow flowers bloom in late spring.

Best climate and site Zones 4–9. Partial to full shade. Grow in all-purpose container mix.

Growing guidelines Set plants 14 inches (35 cm) apart in spring. Because yellow archangel spreads so rapidly and can quickly overpower other plants, plant in a large container by itself. Propagate by division in spring or fall or by stem cuttings in summer.

Possible problems No serious problems.

Comments Yellow archangel is an ideal container plant for shady areas. May also be grown in a hanging basket.

Lamium maculatum
LAMIACEAE

SPOTTED LAMIUM

Spotted lamium is a vigorous groundcover for shady containers. It also looks pretty trailing out of a hanging basket.

Description This plant quickly forms a dense cover of dark green, oval or heart-shaped leaves with a silvery white mid-rib. Lavender-pink, hooded, 1-inch (2.5-cm) flowers bloom in clusters. Spotted lamium is less invasive than yellow archangel (*Lamium galeobdolon*).
Height and spread Height 12–14 inches (30–35 cm); spread to 2 feet (60 cm).
Flower color and season Lavender-pink flowers bloom throughout summer.
Best climate and site Zones 3–8. Partial to deep shade. Prefers an all-purpose container mix.
Growing guidelines Set plants about 12–14 inches (30–35 cm) apart in spring or fall. Cut back by half in midsummer to promote new growth. Plants often self-sow. Propagate by division in spring or fall or by cuttings in summer.
Possible problems No serious problems.
Other common names Spotted dead nettle.
Cultivars 'Shell Pink' has silvery striped leaves and clear pink flowers. 'White Nancy' has silver leaves with green margins and white flowers.
Comments Perfect for low-maintenance containers or under a potted Japanese maple (*Acer palmatum*).

Lysimachia nummularia
PRIMULACEAE

CREEPING JENNY

Creeping Jenny is an attractive, low-maintenance groundcover. It is ideal planted in a large container under a Japanese maple (Acer palmatum).

Description This creeping perennial has shiny, round, ¾-inch (18-mm) leaves that resemble coins. The trailing stems bear bright, 1-inch (2.5-cm) flowers. The stems root rapidly as they creep over the soil.
Height and spread Height 4–8 inches (10–20 cm); spread to 3 feet (90 cm).
Flower color and season Yellow flowers bloom throughout summer.
Best climate and site Zones 3–8. Full sun (in cool climates) to full shade (in warm climates). Grow in an all-purpose container mix.
Growing guidelines Set plants 8 inches (20 cm) apart in spring or fall. Creeping Jenny can rapidly engulf the container. Propagate by division in spring or fall.
Possible problems No serious problems.
Other common names Moneywort.
Cultivars 'Aurea', golden creeping Jenny, grows 2 inches (5 cm) tall with golden-yellow spring foliage that turns lime-green in summer. It is a vigorous mat-forming creeper but not as invasive as the species. Zones 4–8.
Comments Grow creeping Jenny in window boxes or hanging baskets for year-round interest.

Mazus reptans
SCROPHULARIACEAE

MAZUS

Mazus forms ground-hugging mats of small leaves topped with tubular, lipped flowers in spring and early summer.

Description This creeping plant from the Himalayas sends out roots along its stems to form a carpet of bronze-green, toothed, 1-inch (2.5-cm) leaves. Light blue-violet, ¾-inch (18-mm) flowers have a lower lip spotted in white, greenish-yellow, and purple. Mazus plants are evergreen only in warm climates.
Height and spread Height 1–2 inches (2.5–5 cm); spread 15–18 inches (37.5–45 cm).
Flower color and season Light blue-violet flowers bloom in spring and early summer.
Best climate and site Zones 5–8. Full sun to partial shade. Grow in an all-purpose container mix.
Growing guidelines Set plants 1 foot (30 cm) apart in spring. It can be invasive so care must be taken that it does not overtake other plants in the container. Propagate by division in spring or fall or by cuttings in summer.
Possible problems No serious problems.
Cultivars 'Alba' has white flowers.
Other species *M. radicans*, swamp musk, has bluish-pink to purple summer flowers.
Comments Grow mazus with creeping thyme and similar low-growing plants in a shallow container or trough.

Omphalodes verna
BORAGINACEAE

BLUE-EYED MARY

Blue-eyed Mary is a charming little groundcover whose blue, spring flowers closely resemble those of forget-me-nots. It looks pretty with yellow daffodils.

Description Blue-eyed Mary has loose clusters of lavender-blue, ½-inch (12-mm) flowers. The oval, dark green, textured leaves are evergreen in warm climates. The plant spreads quickly by runners.
Height and spread Height to 8 inches (20 cm); spread to 2 feet (60 cm).
Flower color and season Lavender-blue flowers bloom in spring.
Best climate and site Zones 5–8. Partial shade. Grow in all-purpose container mix.
Growing guidelines Set these easy-to-grow plants 1 foot (30 cm) apart in spring or fall. Mulch in hot climates to lengthen the bloom period. Propagate by division in spring or by seed in summer.
Possible problems No serious problems.
Other common names Creeping forget-me-not.
Comments Grow blue-eyed Mary in a container with spring-flowering bulbs such as dwarf daffodils.

Phlox stolonifera
POLEMONIACEAE

CREEPING PHLOX

Creeping phlox is available in many colors, making it a versatile plant for mixing in containers with other spring-flowering bulbs and perennials.

Description Creeping phlox, a native of eastern North America, is grown for its masses of delicate, 1-inch (2.5-cm) wide flowers. Strawberry-like runners clad in small, oval, evergreen leaves root to form solid mats.
Height and spread Height of foliage 3–5 inches (7.5–12.5 cm); spread to 1½ feet (45 cm). Flower height 6–12 inches (15–30 cm).
Flower color and season Lavender, pink, blue, or white flowers bloom in late spring.
Best climate and site Zones 2–8. Prefers partial to full shade; will grow in sun. Grow in an all-purpose container mix.
Growing guidelines Set plants 1–2 feet (30–60 cm) apart in spring. For more compact growth, trim back flowering shoots after blooming. Propagate by division after flowering or by cuttings in late spring to early summer.
Possible problems Powdery mildew may be a problem. It causes white patches on leaves. Spray with sulfur to keep the disease from spreading.
Comments Combine purple cultivars with bright yellow primroses or pink-fringed bleeding heart (*Dicentra eximia*).

Pulmonaria saccharata
BORAGINACEAE

BETHLEHEM SAGE

Bethlehem sage is a lovely, spring-blooming foliage plant with hairy leaves variously spotted and blotched with silver. Plants grow from crowns with thick, fibrous roots.

Description Bethlehem sage has wide, oval, hairy leaves. The nodding, five-petaled flowers are held in tight clusters on short-lived stems. Plants grow from crowns with thick, fibrous roots.
Height and spread Height 9–18 inches (22.5–45 cm); spread 1–2 feet (30–60 cm).
Flower color and season Pink to medium blue flowers bloom in spring. Some buds open pink and change to blue.
Best climate and site Zones 3–8. Partial to full shade. Grow in an all-purpose container mix.
Growing guidelines The foliage remains attractive all season unless mix remains dry for an extended period. If necessary, divide in spring (after bloom) or fall.
Possible problems Watch out for slugs.
Other common names Lungwort.
Cultivars 'Janet Fisk' has densely spotted white leaves and lavender-pink flowers. 'Mrs Moon' has spotted leaves and pink flowers. 'Sissinghurst White' is a hybrid with white flowers.
Comments Plant Bethlehem sage in a large container with spring bulbs, primroses, bleeding hearts (*Dicentra* spp.), foamflowers (*Tiarella* spp.), wildflowers, and ferns.

Saponaria ocymoides
CARYOPHYLLACEAE

ROCK SOAPWORT

Rock soapwort produces many bright pink flowers in summer. Cut the stems back by half after flowering to keep plants compact and to promote rebloom.

Description Rock soapwort is a trailing, mat-forming plant with semi-evergreen leaves less than 1 inch (2.5 cm) long. Its star feature is the clusters of phlox-like, five-petaled, ½-inch (12-mm) flowers.

Height and spread Height 5–8 inches (12.5–20 cm); spread to 2 feet (60 cm).

Flower color and season Bright pink flowers bloom in early to midsummer.

Best climate and site Zones 4–10. Full sun. Grow in a well-drained, all-purpose container mix.

Growing guidelines Set plants about 20 inches (50 cm) apart in spring. Propagate by seed in spring, by division in spring or fall, or by cuttings in early summer.

Possible problems No serious problems.

Cultivars 'Alba' has white flowers that are somewhat smaller than the species. 'Rubra Compacta' forms compact mounds of deep pink to red flowers. 'Splendens' has rose-pink flowers.

Comments Combine with ornamental grasses, gaillardia, and coneflowers (*Echinacea* spp.). May also be grown in a hanging basket.

Sedum spurium
CRASSULACEAE

TWO-ROW STONECROP

Two-row stonecrop is a tough, durable spreader for dry containers. Its mats of fleshy green leaves are topped with clusters of pink flowers in midsummer.

Description This semi-evergreen, creeping succulent quickly forms a carpeting groundcover with a shallow root system. Dark green, 1-inch (2.5-cm) long leaves turn reddish in late fall.

Height and spread Height of foliage to 6 inches (15 cm); spread to 2 feet (60 cm). Flower height to 10 inches (25 cm).

Flower color and season Flat, pink, 2-inch (5-cm) clusters of flowers appear in midsummer.

Best climate and site Zones 3–8. Light to partial shade. Grow in a well-drained, all-purpose container mix with added sand.

Growing guidelines Set plants 10 inches (25 cm) apart in spring. Remove spent blooms. Propagate by seed or division in early spring or by cuttings in early summer.

Possible problems Plants can rot if the container mix is too wet.

Cultivars 'Album Superbum' is a vigorous, white-flowered cultivar; Zones 6–10. 'Dragon's Blood' has bronze foliage and deep red blooms. 'Fuldaglut' has reddish-pink blooms and bronze foliage; Zones 5–9. 'Red Carpet' is only 4 inches (10 cm) tall.

Comments Grow two-row stonecrop in hanging baskets or in shallow pots with hens-and-chickens (*Sempervivum tectorum*) and other succulents.

Sempervivum tectorum
CRASSULACEAE

HENS-AND-CHICKENS

The round, fleshy rosettes of hens-and-chickens make eye-catching, low-maintenance container plants. They are available in a range of sizes and colors.

Description This evergreen succulent has pointed leaves in flat, open rosettes that are 3–4 inches (7.5–10 cm) wide. New plants form in dense masses around the base of old plants.

Height and spread Height of foliage to 6 inches (15 cm); spread to 8 inches (20 cm) or more. Flower stalks 8–18 inches (20–45 cm).

Flower color and season Small, purple-red, aster-like flowers to 1 inch (2.5 cm) wide bloom in summer.

Best climate and site Zones 5–9; grows well down to Zone 3 if there is good snow cover in winter. Full sun. Grow in a well-drained, all-purpose container mix with added sand. Will thrive in hot, dry spots.

Growing guidelines Set plants 1½ feet (45 cm) or more apart anytime during the growing season. Propagate by splitting off offsets or by sowing seed in spring.

Possible problems Crown rot and rust sometimes affect them. Dust with sulfur if rust becomes a problem. Plants can rot if overwatered or inadequately drained.

Other common names Houseleek, roof houseleek.

Comments In medieval times, hens-and-chickens were planted on the roofs of homes, to ward off lightning.

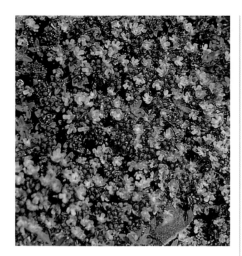

Thymus serpyllum
LAMIACEAE

MOTHER-OF-THYME

Mother-of-thyme looks pretty growing in shallow containers. Combine with small bulbs, such as miniature daffodils for spring interest.

Description Mother-of-thyme is an aromatic, creeping, mat-forming evergreen with tiny, green, ¼-inch (6-mm) leaves. Small, ½-inch (12-mm) flowers bloom in clusters atop 4-inch (10-cm) stems.

Height and spread Height of foliage to 2 inches (5 cm); spread unlimited. Flower height 3–4 inches (7.5–10 cm).

Flower color and season Rose-purple flowers bloom in summer.

Best climate and site Zones 4–7; grows well in Zone 3 with snow cover. Full sun. Grow in a well-drained, all-purpose container mix.

Growing guidelines Set plants about 8 inches (20 cm) apart in spring. Propagate by division or seed in spring or by cuttings in early summer.

Possible problems As long as they grow in full sun, they are remarkably free of pests and diseases.

Cultivars 'Album' has white flowers in early summer. 'Coccineum' has reddish-purple flowers in early summer over dense mats of green leaves that turn bronze in fall. Zones 3–9.

Comments Grow with the culinary common thyme (*T. vulgaris*) or combine in shallow containers with succulents. The flowers attract bees to the garden.

Veronica prostrata
SCROPHULARIACEAE

ROCK SPEEDWELL

The spreading foliage mats of rock speedwell are accented by spikes of blue flowers in late spring. Rock speedwell is a perfect choice for containers in sunny courtyards.

Description Deep blue flower spikes bloom on upright stems above creeping foliage mats of 1½-inch (3.7-cm) green leaves.

Height and spread Height 8–10 inches (20–25 cm); spread to 1½ feet (45 cm).

Flower color and season Deep blue flowers bloom in late spring.

Best climate and site Zones 4–8. Prefers full sun; tolerates partial shade. Grow in a well-drained, all-purpose container mix.

Growing guidelines Set plants 2 feet (60 cm) apart in spring or fall. Propagate by division in spring or fall, by stem cuttings in summer, or by seed in spring.

Possible problems No serious problems.

Other common names Hungarian speedwell, harebell speedwell.

Cultivars 'Alba' has white flowers that bloom over a long season. 'Mrs Holt' has rose-pink flowers.

Comments Grow rock speedwell in large containers with yarrow (*Achillea* spp.), catmint (*Nepeta* spp.), as well as ornamental grasses.

Waldsteinia fragarioides
ROSACEAE

BARREN STRAWBERRY

Barren strawberry has shiny, evergreen leaves that take on a purplish color in cold weather. It grows well in partial shade but will take sun if the mix is kept moist.

Description This evergreen plant is native to eastern North America. It spreads by creeping roots to form a thick, flat carpet of shiny, strawberry-like foliage that turns purplish in fall. Clusters of five-petaled, ½-inch (12-mm) wide flowers appear on 6–8-inch (15–20-cm) stems in late spring, followed by inedible, dry, hairy fruits.

Height and spread Height to 6 inches (15 cm); spread unlimited.

Flower color and season Yellow flowers bloom in late spring.

Best climate and site Zones 5–8. Prefers partial shade; will tolerate sunny spots if kept moist. Grow in a well-drained, all-purpose container mix.

Growing guidelines Set plants about 2 feet (60 cm) apart in spring. Keep watered in dry periods and divide when overcrowded. Propagate by division in early spring or fall or by seed in spring.

Possible problems No serious problems.

Other species *W. ternata* grows 6–8 inches (15–20 cm) tall with glossy, green, evergreen leaves and clusters of yellow, strawberry-like flowers in spring. Zones 4–9.

Comments Grow barren strawberry in hanging baskets.

Andropogon glomeratus
POACEAE

BUSHY BLUESTEM

Grow bushy bluestem for its showy flower plumes and purplish fall color. Keep the mix evenly moist for the best growth, especially in hot, sunny sites.

Description Bushy bluestem is a warm-season, perennial grass with clumps of attractive green foliage.
Height and spread Height 1–2 feet (30–60 cm); similar spread. Flowering stems grow 2–3 feet (60–90 cm) tall.
Flower color and season Produces dense clusters of fluffy, cotton-like flowers in late summer. In late fall the seed heads become orange, and the leaves turn purplish.
Best climate and site Zones 5–10. Prefers full sun; tolerates light shade. Grow in an all-purpose container mix. Keep the mix evenly moist.
Growing guidelines One plant per 2–2½-foot (60–75-cm) wide container. Plant in spring. Cut them back to about 6 inches (15 cm) by late winter. Propagate by seed or division in spring.
Possible problems No serious problems.
Other species *A. scoparius*, little bluestem, grows 1½–2 feet (45–60 cm) tall and has orange-toned foliage. This drought-resistant grass is excellent for containers in dry sites. Zones 4–9.
Comments Use the flowers or seed heads of bushy bluestem in arrangements. Be aware that the plant reseeds readily in moist areas and can become invasive under those conditions.

Bouteloua curtipendula
POACEAE

SIDE OATS GRAMMAGRASS

Side oats grammagrass takes its name from the arrangement of delicate, individual flowers on one side of the stem. It looks great in large containers.

Description This warm-season, perennial grass forms clumps of fine, gray-green leaves. Numerous delicate, wiry stems terminate in finger-like, purplish-brown flowers, which sit on one side of the flowering stem.
Height and spread Height to 2 feet (60 cm); similar spread.
Flower color and season Purple or reddish flowers bloom in early summer and eventually dry to a tan color in winter.
Best climate and site Zones 4–9. Full sun. Grow in an all-purpose container mix.
Growing guidelines Set plants 2 feet (60 cm) apart in spring or fall. They will tolerate drought and the dead leaves may be cut back in late fall. Propagate either by seed or division in spring.
Possible problems No serious problems.
Other common names Grama grass.
Other species *B. gracilis*, blue grammagrass or mosquito grass, is an upright grower to 2 feet (60 cm) tall. Its odd flowers resemble mosquito larvae. It is sometimes mixed with buffalo grass in a mowed lawn in the Southeast. Blue grammagrass adapts well to dry containers. Zones 3–9.

Carex elata 'Bowles Golden'
CYPERACEAE

'BOWLES GOLDEN' SEDGE

Grow containers of 'Bowles Golden' sedge as accent plants near ponds and water gardens. Pots may be placed in shallow water.

Description This outstanding clump-forming foliage plant has bright golden, semi-evergreen leaves with green edges.
Height and spread Height to 2 feet (60 cm); spread 2–5 feet (60–150 cm).
Flower color and season Brownish flowers appear in late spring.
Best climate and site Zones 5–9. Half a day of sun or light, all-day shade. Grow in an all-purpose container mix with some added compost.
Growing guidelines One plant per 2–3-foot (60–90-cm) wide container. Plant in spring. Pots may be placed in shallow water up to 4 inches (10 cm) deep. Plants prefer acid soil. Remove brown leaves as needed. Propagate by division in spring.
Possible problems Soil must be kept moist at all times or leaves will die.
Other species *C. glauca*, blue sedge, is a blue-toned groundcover that forms a low-growing, 6-inch (15-cm) tall mat. Zones 5–9. *C. morrowii* 'Variegata', silver-variegated Japanese sedge, grows well in shade. Height 1 foot (30 cm). Zones 5–9.
Comments Containers of 'Bowles Golden' sedge add a touch of light to the garden. Place them on the edge of ponds.

Chasmanthium latifolium
POACEAE

NORTHERN SEA OATS

Northern sea oats adapt to either sunny or shady containers. The flattened seed heads dangle from the stem tips.

Description The stems of this native American, warm-season, clumping grass are covered with bamboo-like, light green foliage that becomes coppery in fall and brown in winter. The plant is usually grown for its unusual seed heads, which can be used as dried decorations.
Height and spread Height 2–3 feet (60–90 cm) in leaf and flower; clumps expand quickly to 2 feet (60 cm) and then spread slowly.
Flower color and season Green flower spikes bloom in summer. The seed heads turn copper in fall and last into winter.
Best climate and site Zones 5–9. Full sun; prefers partial shade in warm climates. Grow in an all-purpose container mix. Salt-tolerant.
Growing guidelines Place one plant per 2-foot (60-cm) wide container. Plant in spring. Cut back dead foliage in early spring or fall to prevent self-sown seedlings, which can be prolific. Propagate by transplanting self-sown seedlings, or by division in spring.
Possible problems No serious problems.
Other common names Spike grass, wild oats.
Comments Northern sea oats are excellent in fresh or dried arrangements.

Coix lacryma-jobi
POACEAE

JOB'S TEARS

Job's tears is grown for its hard, bead-like seeds. It is perennial in very warm climates, but it will grow as an annual in the rest of the United States. It is suitable for very large containers.

Description Job's tears is probably one of the first grasses ever grown as an ornamental. Its hard seeds were once used as beads in necklaces and rosaries. Coarse, shiny, upright leaves to 1 foot (30 cm) long surround the stems. The ¼-inch (6-mm) seeds drop when ripe.
Height and spread Height to 6 feet (180 cm); spread to about 2 feet (60 cm).
Flower color and season Short, tassel-like, gray flowers bloom in midsummer. The light green seeds turn white or black when ripe.
Best climate and site Zones 9–10; grows as an annual in colder climates. Full sun. Grow in an all-purpose container mix.
Growing guidelines Plant seed indoors in late winter or outdoors in late spring after soaking for 24 hours for better sprouting. Job's tears is extremely sensitive to cold, so wait until after the last frost date to set out seedlings 1 foot (30 cm) apart. Water during dry spells to keep the mix evenly moist.
Possible problems Soil must be kept moist to prevent leaves from dying.
Comments Large containers of Job's tears make a good living screen in warm climates.

Festuca glauca
POACEAE

BLUE FESCUE

The leaf color of blue fescue can range from dark green to bright blue, depending on the cultivar. Most plants will produce spiky clumps of blue-gray foliage, which look fabulous in containers.

Description This cool-season, clumping grass is noted for its rounded mounds of silver-blue, spiky, evergreen foliage.
Height and spread Height 8–12 inches (20–30 cm); spread to 2 feet (60 cm).
Flower color and season Insignificant gray-green flowers bloom in summer.
Best climate and site Zones 4–9. Full sun; light shade in hot climates. Use a well-drained, all-purpose container mix. Plants are drought-resistant.
Growing guidelines One plant per 1–2-foot (30–60-cm) wide container. Plant in spring or fall. Cut back in early spring or fall to promote tidy, new growth. Individual plants are short-lived; divide and replant every 2–3 years. Blue fescue may self-sow readily, and the seedlings may range in color from blue to green. Start species plants from seed or division and cultivars by division in early spring.
Possible problems Plants dislike humidity.
Comments The showy foliage color and interesting texture make blue fescues attractive accent plants for containers. They thrive near the seaside. Grow them with gaillardia and sedums.

Hystrix patula
POACEAE

BOTTLEBRUSH GRASS

Bottlebrush grass is a charming grass for shady containers. Enjoy the flowers in summer, or pick them before they open for arrangements.

Description Bottlebrush grass is grown for its brushy spikes of greenish flowers that rise above hummocks of dark green foliage. The seed heads turn brown and break apart in early fall.
Height and spread Height 1–2 feet (30–60 cm); spread to 1 foot (30 cm). Flowering stems 2–4 feet (60–120 cm).
Flower color and season Greenish flowers bloom throughout summer.
Best climate and site Zones 5–9. Full sun (with moisture) to light shade. Grow in a well-drained, all-purpose container mix.
Growing guidelines Bottlebrush grass grows poorly in dry, sunny locations, so set plants in moist mix 1–2 feet (30–60 cm) apart. It self-sows easily. Cut back in fall or early spring. Propagate by seed or division in spring or fall.
Possible problems Dry container mix will result in poor growth.
Comments Bottlebrush grass is a clumping grass that looks superb when its bottlebrush-like flowers appear. Combine with the showy leaved Queen-of-the-prairie (*Filipendula rubra*).

Imperata cylindrica 'Red Baron'
POACEAE

'RED BARON' BLOOD GRASS

If possible, site containers of 'Red Baron' blood grass where the morning or late afternoon sun can shine through the leaves; backlighting can really make the red color glow.

Description 'Red Baron' blood grass is a warm-season, slow-spreading grass. Unlike the species, the cultivar 'Red Baron' does not flower, so it does not set seed and is not invasive.
Height and spread Height 1–1½ feet (30–45 cm); spread to 2 feet (60 cm).
Flower color and season The grass does not flower, but is grown for its spectacular green, red-tipped foliage in spring. The grass becomes more red and, toward the end of summer, it is a deep blood-red color.
Best climate and site Zones 6–9. Full sun; partial shade in hot climates. Grow in a well-drained container mix.
Growing guidelines Set plants 1–2 feet (30–60 cm) apart in spring or early fall. Red color is best in full sun, except in hot climates, where plants need partial shade during the heat of the day. Blood grass tolerates drought, but watering during dry spells will prevent leaf tips from turning brown. Propagate in spring by division.
Possible problems No serious problems.
Other common names Japanese blood grass.
Comments Blood grass is dramatic as a mass planting in a large container. Combine it with blue delphiniums.

Koeleria glauca
POACEAE

LARGE BLUE HAIRGRASS

Large blue hairgrass is a short-lived, perennial grass that tends to die out in the center as it ages. Divide and repot clumps every 2 or 3 years to keep them looking vigorous.

Description The narrow, flat, blue-green leaves of this cool-season grass grow upright in tight clumps.
Height and spread Height 6–12 inches (15–30 cm) for leaves; similar spread. Flowering stems to 1½ feet (45 cm).
Flower color and season Striking blue-green flower clusters rise above the foliage in late spring; the flowers later change to a buff color.
Best climate and site Zones 6–9; can survive in colder areas with dependable winter snow cover. Full sun. Use a well-drained, somewhat alkaline container mix.
Growing guidelines Set plants 1 foot (30 cm) apart in spring or early fall. Cut back leaves and flower stems in midsummer to encourage new growth. Propagate by seed in spring or division in spring or fall.
Possible problems No serious problems.
Other common names Hair grass.
Other species *K. macrantha*, June grass, grows to 1½ feet (45 cm). It has blue-green foliage with glossy, green flowers in early summer. It goes dormant early. Zones 4–9.
Comments The flowers are beautiful in arrangements. Combine with cottage pinks (*Dianthus plumaris*), coreopsis, coneflowers (*Rudbeckia* spp.), and daylilies.

Luzula nivea
JUNCACEAE

SNOWY WOODRUSH

Grow snowy woodrush with ferns for an easy-care container planting. It also makes a wonderful companion for spring bulbs.

Description Among the best of the woodrushes, snowy woodrush has gray-green, grass-like, usually evergreen leaves covered with soft, white hairs. In spring, creamy white flowers stand in rounded clusters above the foliage clump; they dry later to brownish-tan.

Height and spread Height 9–12 inches (22–30 cm); spread to 1 foot (30 cm). Flowering stems to 2 feet (60 cm) tall

Flower color and season Creamy white flowers bloom in spring.

Best climate and site Zones 4–9. Tolerates full sun in cool climates; needs light shade in warm regions. Grow in an all-purpose container mix.

Growing guidelines Set plants 1 foot (30 cm) apart in spring or late summer. Cut back leaves in winter if they turn brown. Propagate by division in spring.

Possible problems No serious problems.

Cultivars 'Schattenkind' is lower growing with fluffier flower heads. 'Schneehaschen' is taller with pure white flower heads.

Comments Looks pretty in a container with spring bulbs, forget-me-nots (*Myosotis* spp.), and columbines (*Aquilegia* spp.).

Pennisetum alopecuroides
POACEAE

FOUNTAIN GRASS

Fountain grass is one of the most beautiful and adaptable of all ornamental grasses. The showy seed heads cascade like a fountain over mounds of glossy green leaves.

Description Fountain grass is a warm-season, clumping grass. It has flowers in 4–10-inch (10–25-cm) long clusters shaped like little foxtails.

Height and spread Height of foliage to 3 feet (90 cm); similar spread. Flowering stems grow to 4 feet (120 cm) tall.

Flower color and season Creamy white to pinkish flowers bloom in midsummer. The seed heads later turn reddish-brown and remain until fall.

Best climate and site Zones 5–9. Full sun; tolerates light shade. Grow in an all-purpose container mix.

Growing guidelines Set plants 1–2 feet (30–60 cm) apart in spring. Keep them watered in dry weather for best growth. Cut off seed heads in fall to keep them from spreading throughout the garden. Cut back dead leaves by early spring. Propagate the species by division or seed and cultivars by spring division only.

Possible problems No serious problems.

Cultivars 'Hameln' is a compact form that grows 2–3 feet (60–90 cm) tall. Zones 6–8.

Comments Fountain grasses are a good choice for coastal containers, since they tolerate wind. Combine in large containers with gaillardia.

Phalaris arundinacea var. *picta*
POACEAE

WHITE-STRIPED RIBBON GRASS

White-striped ribbon grass can be invasive in the garden so it is ideal for containers. Its variegated green and white leaves add a touch of light to container gardens.

Description This clump-forming perennial grass is easy to grow. White-striped ribbon grass has striped foliage that gives it the amusing common name "gardener's garters."

Height and spread Height 2–3 feet (60–90 cm); spread unlimited. Flowering stems grow to 4 feet (120 cm) tall.

Flower color and season Pretty white flower spikes bloom in early summer. In fall, leaves turn buff-colored.

Best climate and site Zones 4–9. Light shade. Grow in all-purpose container mix.

Growing guidelines Place one plant per pot as this grass spreads rapidly by rhizomes. Leaves may turn brown in hot sun. Cut back sprawling plants in summer to stimulate dense, new growth. Weed out all-green shoots. Propagate by division in spring.

Possible problems Move to a shadier position if the leaves turn brown.

Other common names Gardener's garters, reedy grass.

Cultivars 'Feesey's Form' has handsome, white-striped foliage touched with pink.

Comments Plant in a bright blue container to brighten up a shady corner.

Abelia x grandiflora
CAPRIFOLIACEAE

GLOSSY ABELIA

Glossy abelia is a dense, semi-evergreen shrub with dark green, opposite leaves that turn bronze or purple in fall. The delicate flowers are lightly fragrant.

Description Glossy abelia has arching, reddish-brown canes and small, glossy, dark green leaves that turn a purplish-bronze color. Small, tubular flowers are borne in loose, terminal clusters. The calyces remain after the flowers fall.
Height and spread Height to 6 feet (180 cm); similar spread.
Flower color and season Pinkish-purple or white flowers bloom in late spring to early summer.
Best climate and site Zones 6–10. Place container in a protected site in the colder portion of its range. Full sun. Plant in an all-purpose container mix.
Growing guidelines Plant in spring or winter. Prune in late winter or early spring to remove old or winter-damaged wood. Take softwood cuttings in early summer, hardwood cuttings in fall.
Possible problems No serious problems.
Cultivars 'Compacta' is a low-growing form only 3 feet (90 cm) tall, which is ideal for containers. 'Francis Mason' has yellow-edged leaves.
Comments Glossy abelia can be clipped to form a compact shape to suit larger containers at the expense of some flowers.

Acer palmatum
ACERACEAE

JAPANESE MAPLE

No other container tree can claim Japanese maple's exquisite combination of graceful form, delicate leaf texture, and blazing fall color. It can live in the same pot for years.

Description Japanese maple's deciduous, green or red branches carry 2–4-inch (5–10-cm) long, deeply cut leaves that are reddish in spring, green in summer, and scarlet, orange, or gold in fall.
Height and spread Height 2–5 feet (60–150 cm); similar spread.
Flower color and season Insignificant flowers—grown for its colorful foliage.
Best climate and site Zones 2–9. Filtered light or morning sun position. Use top grade, all-purpose container mix.
Growing guidelines Provide plenty of water, but allow the mix to dry somewhat between waterings. Tap water may stress container plants; use rainwater if possible. Prune as needed in fall to midwinter. Grow species from seed.
Possible problems Hot, dry wind can cause brown patches on leaves. Leach container often with rainwater to prevent salt buildup, which can turn leaf edges brown.
Cultivars Plants in the Dissectum group make easy-care pot specimens.
Comments Underplant Japanese maple with rose moss (*Portulaca grandiflora*), creeping zinnia (*Sanvitalia procumbens*), thymes, or spring bulbs such as grape hyacinths (*Muscari* spp.).

Aucuba japonica
CORNACEAE

JAPANESE AUCUBA

Brighten a shady corner of the terrace with a pot of Japanese aucuba. For a real accent, choose a cultivar with yellow-speckled foliage.

Description While the species has glossy, dark green, evergreen foliage, the leaves of some cultivars are highlighted with yellow markings. If you have both male and female plants, you can also enjoy bright red berries in fall and winter.
Height and spread Height 4–12 feet (1.2–3.6 m); spread 6 feet (180 cm).
Flower color and season Insignificant flowers—grown for foliage effect.
Best climate and site Zones 7–10. Grows best and produces the brightest leaves when protected from sun, wind, and heat. Tolerates dense shade. Use good quality, moisture-retentive container mix.
Growing guidelines Water when the mix begins to dry out. Remove individual long branches to shape; shearing will disfigure the large leaves.
Possible problems Prevent pests by keeping the plant growing vigorously. Treat scale and mites with neem oil; spray mealybugs with insecticidal soap.
Other common names Spotted laurel.
Comments The foliage looks good with gold flowers; try violas in yellow tones at the base of the plant. If the container is in a damp, shady situation combine with plants with light green foliage and contrasting texture, such as low-growing ferns.

Buxus sempervirens
BUXACEAE

BOXWOOD

Boxwood is invaluable for adding year-round interest to container plantings. It grows slowly, and it's easy to clip into a variety of shapes, including geometric and animal forms.

Description Boxwood is a dense, branching, woody shrub with shiny, dark green, oval leaves.
Height and spread Height and spread 10–15 feet (3–4.5 m), but easily kept smaller in containers.
Flower color and season Tiny, pale green blooms appear in early spring.
Best climate and site Zones 6–10. Full sun to part shade. Use a well-drained, slightly acid container mix; keep the mix evenly moist.
Growing guidelines Grow boxwood in a deep container in a sheltered spot. Shear as needed to maintain desired shape.
Possible problems Knock mites off with a strong spray of water; rub scale off stems with your fingernail or a brush. If leafminers cause browned, blistered foliage, pinch off affected leaves. Alkaline container mix can lead to poor growth or even death. Take cuttings in summer.
Other common names Box, English or European boxwood, common box.
Cultivars 'Suffruticosa' has a naturally compact habit to 3 feet (90 cm).
Comments Combine with dwarf mondo grass or allow foliage to develop at soil level.

Calluna vulgaris
ERICACEAE

HEATHER

Heather thrives in full sun and infertile, acid container mix. In cold climates, protect plants from freezing winter winds by moving containers into a protected area.

Description The evergreen mounds of this shrub have tiny, scale-like, overlapping leaves covering the branches. Some plants turn red in fall.
Height and spread Height to 2 feet (60 cm) but varies according to cultivar; spread 2–4 feet (60–120 cm).
Flower color and season Tiny, pinkish, bell-shaped flowers bloom along the shoot tips from late summer to fall.
Best climate and site Zones 5–7. Full sun necessary to produce flowers, though it will grow in partial shade. Grow in an acid, well-drained, unenriched container mix.
Growing guidelines For a good display, arrange three plants in a 2-foot (60-cm) wide container in spring or early fall. Prune off shoots of the previous season in early spring to encourage tight, compact growth. Propagate by seed anytime, by cuttings in early summer, or, if pot is sufficiently large, by layering in spring.
Possible problems Plants can rot in warm, humid conditions. Does not grow well in fertile or alkaline conditions.
Other common names Ling.
Comments If container is large enough, plant different cultivars together. Heather is excellent for dried arrangements.

Camellia japonica
THEACEAE

CAMELLIA

In cold climates, you'll need to bring potted camellias indoors for the winter. You'll enjoy their large flowers from early winter through to spring and their polished, dark green leaves year-round.

Description Camellias are woody shrubs with leathery, oval leaves, and single, semidouble, or double winter blooms to 5 inches (12.5 cm) across.
Height and spread Height to 10 feet (3 m); spread 3–6 feet (90–180 cm).
Flower color and season White, pink, or red flowers bloom in winter.
Best climate and site Zones 8–10. Partial shade. Grow in a lime-free, well-drained container mix; allow it to dry slightly between waterings.
Growing guidelines Plant in wooden tubs and mulch with a 2-inch (5-cm) layer of wood chips. Repot, prune, and thin the stems after blooming. Take cuttings during late summer.
Possible problems Yellowed leaves with green veins usually indicate iron deficiency. Brown or dropping leaves may indicate overfertilizing. Leach container with rainwater to remove excess fertilizer. Brown or dropping flowers are a sign of petal blight; destroy fading blooms and replace mulch. Flower buds may drop if the mix is too dry.
Comments Underplant camellias with English ivy or low-growing summer annuals such as dwarf marigolds.

Camellia sasanqua
THEACEAE

SASANQUA CAMELLIA

Add fall or early winter interest to a warm-climate courtyard with a pot of sasanqua camellia. The showy flowers bloom in a range of colors over the evergreen foliage.

Description Of Japanese origin, this small-leaved species is a particularly versatile camellia. Sasanqua camellias have evergreen, small, shiny, dark green leaves and lightly fragrant flowers, which can be single or semidouble.
Height and spread Height 4–6 feet (120–180 cm), but can grow to 15 feet (4.5 m); spread 3–6 feet (90–180 cm).
Flower color and season Large pink, red, white, or lavender flowers bloom in fall.
Best climate and site Zones 7–9, but the flowers are best in the warmer areas of Zones 8 and 9. Protected site with full sun is best. In hot areas, provide afternoon shade. For protection from early fall frosts, plant near a warm wall. Use a rich, moist, well-drained, acid container mix. Add a little organic matter or buy specially formulated camellia container mix.
Growing guidelines Mulch around the base of the plant with compost each spring. Prune after flowering.
Possible problems If scale is a problem, treat with neem oil.
Comments Depending on the cultivar, sasanqua camellias can be used in many situations from hanging baskets to large tubs in full sun.

Caryopteris x *clandonensis*
VERBENACEAE

HYBRID BLUEBEARD

Bluebeard is a deciduous subshrub of hybrid origin with blue flowers and dull green leaves. In the colder areas of its range it dies back to the roots each winter.

Description This pretty plant develops long canes along which the flowers develop. Tip pruning in early spring will produce a dense framework when container grown.
Height and spread Height to 4 feet (120 cm); similar spread.
Flower color and season Purple-blue flowers bloom in mid- to late summer.
Best climate and site Zones 5–9. Full sun. In colder zones, place in a sheltered position, such as near a sunny wall. Grow in a moist, well-drained container mix.
Growing guidelines Plant in late winter or spring. Cut back nearly to the base in late winter, since flowers grow on new wood. Take cuttings in early summer. Divide and repot in spring.
Possible problems No serious problems.
Other common names Blue-mist shrub.
Cultivars 'Dark Knight' is a compact cultivar with darker foliage and deep blue flowers. 'Ferndown' has dark blue flowers. 'Heavenly Blue' has light blue flowers. 'Kew Blue' has darker green leaves and dark blue flowers.
Comments While the species are attractive, the newer cultivars are more rewarding for container gardening.

Chamaecyparis spp.
CUPRESSACEAE

FALSE CYPRESS

Compact forms of false cypress come in a variety of growth habits and colors. Their evergreen foliage provides year-long interest.

Description These evergreens are available in a wide range of shapes and sizes. Hinoki false cypress (C. *obtusa*) cultivars make good container specimens, while the many cultivars of the Sawara cypress (C. *pisifera*) tend to have a more open habit.
Height and spread Height 8 inches–15 feet (20 cm–4 m); spread 8 inches–12 feet (20 cm–3 m).
Flower color and season Plants are grown for foliage interest only.
Best climate and site Zones 5–8. Full sun. Plant in well-drained, light, soil-based container mix. Allow to dry slightly between waterings.
Growing guidelines Place the container in a protected spot for winter, wrapping the plant in burlap if shoot tips turn brown. Take cuttings in fall.
Possible problems Knock off spider mites with a strong spray of water. Remove and destroy bagworms. Overwatering may lead to root rot. Dead foliage in the center of the plant indicates too much shade.
Other common names Hinoki cypress, sawara false cypress.
Comments Underplant with grape hyacinths (*Muscari* spp.) for spring interest; add creeping zinnia (*Sanvitalia procumbens*) for summer color.

Cotinus coggygria
ANACARDIACEAE

SMOKE TREE

Smoke tree is a rounded, bushy, deciduous tree or shrub with glossy, green or purplish leaves that turn yellow or red in fall. Showy plumes appear in summer.

Description Smoke tree is grown for its lovely fall color and profusion of large, feathery flower stalks, which eventually turn a smoky-gray. They look rather like puffs of smoke.
Height and spread Height to 12 feet (3.6 m); spread slightly wider; smaller when grown in containers.
Flower color and season Pink, purple, or gray plumes bloom from midsummer to fall.
Best climate and site Zones 5–9. Full sun. Grow in a moist, well-drained container mix.
Growing guidelines Plant in spring. Water frequently until plants are established. Do not overfeed since excessive nutrients produce vegetative growth at the expense of flowers. Sow seed in fall. Take cuttings in summer.
Possible problems Heavy pruning tends to force long, thin shoots. A light trim after flowering is best as it will produce more compact growth.
Other common names Venetian sumach, smokebush.
Comments When grown in containers, it is possible to hard-prune smoke tree to produce water shoots. These, combined with fertilizing, can produce large leaves on sappy canes, but at the expense of flowers.

Daphne cneorum
THYMELEACEAE

ROSE DAPHNE

Rose daphne is a low-growing, evergreen shrub with narrow, deep green leaves and exceptionally fragrant spring flowers. It is native to central and eastern Europe.

Description Rose daphne is a popular plant on account of its fragrant, rose-pink flowers, which are borne in dense, terminal clusters on prostrate branches.
Height and spread Height to 1 foot (30 cm); spread 3 feet (90 cm).
Flower color and season Pink flowers bloom in late spring, and sometimes in fall.
Best climate and site Zones 4–9. Full sun with protection from winter winds. Grow in a moist, well-drained container mix.
Growing guidelines Transplant container-grown plants in early fall or early spring. Take cuttings in late summer.
Possible problems Rose daphne does not like strong fertilizers. A leafy mulch applied in early spring will supply adequate nutrients. Plants are often slow to establish.
Other common names Garland flower.
Cultivars 'Alba' has white flowers. 'Eximia' is larger in leaf and flower.
Comments Daphnes resent root disturbance so when grown as container plants do not underplant with annuals. Feed with mulches or slow-release fertilizers rather than risk losing plant through repotting. Keep container raised on feet to ensure perfect drainage.

Deutzia gracilis
SAXIFRAGACEAE

SLENDER DEUTZIA

Slender deutzia is a graceful, mounding shrub from Japan with wide-spreading branches. Grow slender deutzia in a spot where you need a spreading, shrubby display.

Description The arching stems of slender deutzia are clad in bright green, oblong to lance-shaped, deciduous leaves and covered with clusters of ¾-inch (18-mm), white flowers.
Height and spread Height 3–5 feet (90–150 cm); spread to 3 feet (90 cm).
Flower color and season White flowers bloom in late spring or early summer.
Best climate and site Zones 5–9. Full sun. Use a well-drained, all-purpose container mix.
Growing guidelines Pot in spring in most places (slender deutzias can take fall planting in Zones 8–9). After flowering, an established bush can be thinned out by cutting some of the oldest shoots at the base. Plants benefit from winter mulch in the coolest parts of their range. Propagate by cuttings anytime during the growing season.
Possible problems No serious problems.
Cultivars 'Nikko' is a dwarf selection; it grows only 12–15 inches (30–37.5 cm) tall and has double, white flowers in late spring. The foliage turns burgundy in fall. Zones 6–9.
Comments These plants prefer a moist, semi-shaded site away from drying winds.

Enkianthus campanulatus
ERICACEAE

REDVEIN ENKIANTHUS

Native to Japan, redvein enkianthus is a tall, deciduous shrub with oval, whorled leaves clustered at the ends of the branchlets. The leaves turn brilliant scarlet in fall.

Description Redvein enkianthus has a profusion of drooping clusters of bell-shaped flowers, up to ½ inch (12 mm) long. The elliptical leaves, which are 3 inches (7.5 cm) long, with bristly, toothed margins, appear before the flowers open.
Height and spread Height to 12 feet (3.6 m), but much smaller in containers; spread slightly less.
Flower color and season Creamy yellow flowers, lightly tinged with red, bloom in late spring.
Best climate and site Zones 4–8. Full sun to dense shade. Use a humus-rich, well-drained, acid container mix.
Growing guidelines Plant in spring. Expose to western sun for best fall color. No pruning necessary. Take cuttings in late spring. Sow seed in early spring.
Possible problems Will not flourish in dry or alkaline container mixes. Mulch with compost to keep the mix evenly moist.
Other species *E. perulatus* has a bushy habit, making it a good tub specimen.
Comments Belonging to the erica family of plants, redvein enkianthus likes a slightly acid container mix, so a mix suitable for camellias or rhododendrons would be ideal.

Euonymus fortunei
CELASTRACEAE

WINTERCREEPER

This tough, tolerant evergreen can climb or cascade, making it a good choice for less-than-ideal conditions in the garden.

Description Wintercreeper grows as an evergreen vine or shrub with scallop-edged leaves to 2 inches (5 cm) long.
Height and spread Height 2–3 feet (60–90 cm); as a vine, it can eventually spread to 20 feet (6 m) by clinging stems.
Flower color and season Inconspicuous flowers—grown for foliage effect.
Best climate and site Zones 5–9. Full sun to full shade. Prefers a sandy mix, but it can adapt to an all-purpose container mix as long as it has good drainage. Allow pot to dry between waterings.
Growing guidelines Prune as needed in late spring. Take cuttings anytime in late summer from mature wood. Sow seed outdoors in fall.
Possible problems Wintercreeper is particularly prone to scale; spray plants with superior oil. Anthracnose can cause blackened leaves and shoots or brown spots on leaves; prune off and destroy affected parts. Leaves turn yellow and brown if exposed to harsh cold; move the container to a sheltered spot for the winter.
Cultivars Many variegated forms exist, including 'Emerald 'n' Gold'—its bushy habit making it ideal for containers.
Comments Variegated, trailing types are easy-care plants for use in containers.

Fuchsia x hybrida
ONAGRACEAE

FUCHSIA

Fuchsias make splendid hanging basket plants for shady, cool spots; protect them from midday sun. The dramatic blooms always attract attention (and they may attract hummingbirds, too).

Description Fuchsias are shrubby plants with an upright or trailing habit. They bloom all summer, with pendant, single or double flowers up to 3 inches (7.5 cm) long.
Height and spread Upright forms can grow to 6 feet (180 cm); similar spread.
Flower color and season White, red, or pink with violet, purple, or red flowers bloom during summer.
Best climate and site Hardy to Zone 7. Filtered light is best. Plant in a moist, well-drained container mix.
Growing guidelines Feed every 10 days or so. Pinch off the shoots to keep the plants bushy, or train a single stem upward to produce a standard form. Remove spent flowers. In cold areas, cut the plants back by half, repot and move indoors before frost. Take tip cuttings anytime.
Possible problems Direct sun can produce tan patches on leaves. The plant may wither if you let the soil dry out. Flowering may stop in hot weather.
Other common names Lady's eardrops.
Cultivars 'Baby Blue Eyes' has red and purple-pink flowers. It is ideal for pots.
Comments These showy specimens are best planted alone in hanging baskets in a protected position away from drying winds.

Gardenia augusta
RUBIACEAE

COMMON GARDENIA

Native to China, common gardenia is an evergreen shrub with very glossy, thick leaves. Its creamy white, waxy flowers are intensely fragrant.

Description Gardenias are cherished for their perfume, their white perfection, and their long flowering period. The solitary flowers stand clear of the top-most leaves and open from bright green buds in a spiral of overlapping petals.

Height and spread Height to 6 feet (180 cm); similar spread. Annual pruning keeps it smaller.

Flower color and season Very fragrant single, semidouble, or double white flowers bloom in early to midsummer.

Best climate and site Zones 8–10. Partial shade; protect from hot afternoon sun. Grow in a rich, moisture-retentive, acid container mix. Protect from frost.

Growing guidelines Cut untidy plants back in early spring. Take cuttings in summer; repotting can be done in fall.

Possible problems Avoid damaging plants with gardening tools; these wounds are common entry points for pests and diseases. If mealybugs, aphids, or whiteflies attack, spray with insecticidal soap. Common gardenias are sensitive to pots drying out; mulch to help retain moisture.

Other common names Cape jasmine.

Comments Gardenia repays regular fertilizing in spring with abundant blooms.

Hebe speciosa
SCROPHULARIACEAE

VERONICA

Veronica is a compact shrub often used in troughs. Its purplish flower spikes are bottlebrush-shaped. The dark green leaves are glossy and decorative.

Description This evergreen New Zealand native produces flowers over a long period. The leaves are glossy and purple underneath so veronica looks attractive even when not in flower.

Height and spread Height 5 feet (150 cm); spread 3 feet (90 cm). Can be kept smaller.

Flower color and season Deep magenta flower spikes bloom during summer.

Best climate and site Zones 7–10. Full sun or light shade. Use a fertile, well-drained container mix.

Growing guidelines A light prune after each flush of flowers promotes more flowers. Can be pruned to a formal shape. Very tolerant of seaside conditions.

Possible problems No serious problems.

Cultivars 'Waireka' reaches a height of 3 feet (90 cm), has light purple flowers with leaves margined and overlaid with cream.

Other species *H. diosmifolia*, white hebe, grows to 5 feet (150 cm) and has dense clusters of lavender-white flowers. *H. salicifolia*, koromiko, has spikes of white-tinged, lilac flowers. The cultivar 'Rosea' has pink flowers and 'Variegata' has leaves broadly margined with cream.

Comments Regular tip pruning, once the flowers have faded, will result in more bushy, compact shrubs.

Hibiscus syriacus
MALVACEAE

ROSE-OF-SHARON

Rose-of-Sharon is a late-blooming, deciduous shrub with upright branches and a bushy habit. The showy hibiscus-like, single or double flowers bloom in a range of colors.

Description A hardy, deciduous shrub, rose-of-Sharon is valued for its large, trumpet-shaped flowers, which vary greatly in color.

Height and spread Height to 15 feet (4.5 m); spread 10 feet (3 m); much smaller when container grown.

Flower color and season Flowers in white, pink, red, lavender, or purple bloom in late summer to early fall.

Best climate and site Zones 5–9. Full sun. Grow in a moist, good-quality container mix.

Growing guidelines Prune in winter to ensure large blooms. Remove at least two-thirds of the previous season's growth. Take cuttings during summer.

Possible problems If aphids or whiteflies attack, spray with insecticidal soap. Knock any Japanese beetles into soapy water. Young plants can be winter-killed if not protected in cold winter areas. Shelter from wind and do not fertilize after midsummer.

Other common names Syrian hibiscus, mallow.

Comments The hybrids *Hibiscus* 'Dixie Belle' and 'Southern Belle' can be grown as annuals.

Hydrangea macrophylla
HYDRANGEACEAE

BIG-LEAVED HYDRANGEA

Big-leaved hydrangea has blue or pink flowers, depending on the pH of the container mix. The white-flowering cultivars do not seem to be color-affected by pH.

Description Big-leaved hydrangea, which is of Japanese origin, has broad, thick leaves and flowers that are borne in large, flat clusters up to 10 inches (25 cm) across.
Height and spread Height to 10 feet (3 m); similar spread. Much smaller when grown in a container.
Flower color and season Big-leaved hydrangeas have blue flowers in acid container mixes or pink in alkaline. They bloom in midsummer.
Best climate and site Zones 6–9. Partial shade; protect from hot afternoon sun. Grow in a moist, humus-enriched, well-drained container mix.
Growing guidelines Keep well-watered during summer. Cut back by half after flowering; take cuttings anytime during the growing season. Mulch pots with organic matter. Prune big-leaved hydrangeas in summer after bloom.
Possible problems Buds or stems may be damaged in cold-winter areas. Plants will usually resprout from the roots but will not flower until the following year. In warm climates, sun may scorch leaves and flowers.
Cultivars 'Geoffrey Chadbund' has bright red flowers. 'Nikko Blue' flowers are a rich blue retained over a wide pH range.

'Mariesii' bears flowers that are nearly always pink. 'Shower' produces hot pink blooms. 'Veitchii' has flowers that open white but turn a soft pink with age.
Other species
H. arborescens, hills-of-snow, forms a 2–5-foot (60–150-cm) spreading mound. Flat or rounded, white flower clusters bloom from spring into summer. Zones 4–8. 'Annabelle' has large blooms.

H. paniculata, panicle hydrangea, has elliptical, dark green leaves and white flowers that turn rose-purple as they age. 'Grandiflora' (peegee hydrangea) has huge inflorescences of creamy white flowers that turn purple with age. 'Praecox' has smaller flowers than 'Grandiflora', but blooms 6 weeks earlier. 'Tardiva' is a fall-flowering cultivar. Zones 4–9.

H. quercifolia, oak-leaved hydrangea, has large, scalloped leaves that turn rich red in fall. It produces white flowers that eventually fade to pink and purple. 'Snowflake' is a double-flowered cultivar. 'Snow Queen' is notable for the number and size of its flower clusters and its rich, deep red-purple fall color. Zones 5–8.
Comments Hydrangea flowers take on interesting hues as they age and can be cut and used for dried indoor arrangements through winter. Flowers may be left on the bush to dry naturally.

Juniperus communis
CUPRESSACEAE

COMMON JUNIPER

Junipers are tough and drought-tolerant, placing them among the best evergreens for container planting. There are many dwarf cultivars.

Description While common juniper can grow into tall trees, the dwarf types are the best choice for container gardens.
Height and spread Dwarf species height 30 inches (75 cm); spread 1½ feet (45 cm).
Flower color and season Inconspicuous green or yellow spring flowers, followed by small, blue fruit on the female plants.
Best climate and site Zones 2–9. Full sun is best. Plant in well-drained, all-purpose container mix and allow it to dry out between waterings.
Growing guidelines Do not prune. Take cuttings in late summer. Sow seed in fall.
Possible problems Control spider mites with superior oil. Prune off damaged tips if affected by fungal blight or twig borers.
Cultivars 'Compressa' grows 2 inches (5 cm) per year in a perfect, tight, upright column to around 30 inches (75 cm), but does not have berries.
Other species *J. conferta* 'Emerald Sea', grows to about 3 feet (90 cm) tall. It has blue-green foliage and a trailing habit. *J. horizontalis* 'Blue Mat', grows to 6 inches (15 cm) tall and spreads to 2 feet (60 cm).
Comments Junipers are best given a pot of their own as foliage competition can cause irreparable damage.

Kalmia latifolia
ERICACEAE

MOUNTAIN LAUREL

Mountain laurel thrives in cool climates in containers kept evenly moist and well drained. It flowers best in sun, but it can also be beautiful in a shady corner of the terrace.

Description Mountain laurel has saucer-shaped flowers, crinkled at the edges, which bloom in white or pink with darker rose markings. Some cultivars have flower buds with contrasting colors.
Height and spread Height in containers to 5 feet (150 cm); similar spread.
Flower color and season The white, pink, or rose flowers bloom from late spring to early summer.
Best climate and site Zones 4–7. Flowers best in full sun if the roots are cool; tolerates medium shade. Grow in a moist, well-drained, acid container mix.
Growing guidelines Keep container moist, especially during prolonged dry summer weather. Thin out older branches to encourage growth and flowers. Or preserve the older branches and underprune to give the shrub an open, sculpted look. Deadhead after flowering. Mulch top of container with compost every spring.
Possible problems No serious problems.
Other common names Calico bush.
Cultivars 'Carousel' has white flowers, striped purple. 'Ostybo Red' produces red buds that open to pink blooms.
Comments This is one of the most valued evergreen shrubs for a cold-climate garden.

Lantana camara
VERBENACEAE

LANTANA

This fast-growing shrub is rugged enough to withstand heat and drought but not cold winters. You can train it to grow upright into a standard (tree) form.

Description Lantana is a coarse, upright shrub. It has stiff branches and dark green foliage that is aromatic when crushed. Lantana can survive winters outdoors in milder climates; elsewhere, grow it as an annual or bring it inside for the winter.
Height and spread Height 3 feet (90 cm); spread 3 feet (90 cm).
Flower color and season Yellow, orange, red, or bi-colored flowers bloom in summer. The flowers are followed by black berries.
Best climate and site Zones 7–10. Full sun. Grow in an all-purpose container mix, allowing it to dry between waterings.
Growing guidelines Set plants 1 foot (30 cm) apart. Prune by one-half to two-thirds in spring. Sow seed indoors in midwinter; it may take 8 weeks to germinate. Take cuttings of young growth in late summer.
Possible problems Mildew may produce gray patches on the leaves if there is insufficient light and air circulation. Pinch off severely infected leaves; spray the rest with a solution of 1 teaspoon of baking soda in 1 quart (1 l) of water.
Other common names Yellow sage, shrub verbena.
Comments Try lantana in a hanging basket.

Magnolia spp.
MAGNOLIACEAE

MAGNOLIA

Magnolias are popular for their dramatic spring flowers, beautiful summer foliage, showy seeds, and attractive bark. For container culture, choose the small, more compact cultivars.

Description Magnolias are evergreen or deciduous single- or multiple-trunked trees or shrubs. They have oval, smooth-edged leaves and large, fragrant flowers. The exquisite flowers vary in shape from narrow and goblet-shaped to saucer-shaped.
Height and spread Height to 25 feet (4.5 m), spread to 10 feet (3 m); smaller when cultivated in a container.
Flower color and season Creamy-white, pink, or purple flowers bloom from late spring to midsummer.
Best climate and site Zones 7–10. Partial shade. Grow in a moist, well-drained container mix.
Growing guidelines Pot up balled-and-burlapped or container-grown plants in spring. Prune after flowering if necessary. Sow seed in fall. Take cuttings in mid- to late summer.
Possible problems If scale attack, prune out infested growth; spray the remaining stems with horticultural oil.
Other species M. *stellata* is a good plant for containers. M. *kobus*, M. x *soulangiana*, and M. *virginiana* are suitable for larger tubs.
Comments Flowers are followed by cone-like or strawberry-like fruit.

Nandina domestica
BERBERIDACEAE

HEAVENLY BAMBOO

Heavenly bamboo is an evergreen shrub with glossy, green, compound leaves that turn rich red in fall. Young foliage is often tinged with pink or bronze when unfurling.

Description Heavenly bamboo is not a true bamboo; it is a graceful, evergreen shrub. The white midsummer flowers are followed by persistent clusters of red fruit in the fall.

Height and spread Height to 10 feet (3 m); spread 6 feet (180 cm); can be kept smaller by pruning.

Flower color and season White flowers bloom in midsummer.

Best climate and site Zones 6–10. Full sun to dappled shade. Use a deep, moisture-retentive, well-drained container mix.

Growing guidelines Repot container-grown plants in late winter or spring. Take cuttings in summer. Remove seed from its fleshy covering and sow in fall.

Possible problems No serious problems. Plants may be damaged by low winter temperatures, especially in the colder parts of their range.

Other common names Sacred bamboo.

Cultivars 'Harbor Dwarf' only grows 1½–2 feet (45–60 cm) high. 'Nana' is a rounded, dwarf form about 1½ feet (45 cm) tall. It becomes red-toned during fall.

Comments An easy-care container plant that will repay with better growth if given regular fertilizing.

Pelargonium peltatum
GERANIACEAE

IVY GERANIUM

Ivy geranium is an excellent choice for hanging baskets and window boxes. It offers bright green, ivy-like leaves, cascading stems, and delicately marked blooms.

Description Ivy geraniums are shrubby plants with trailing stems and ivy-shaped, glossy, green leaves.

Height and spread Height 1 foot (30 cm); spread 2–4 feet (60–120 cm). The long trailing stems can be trained to climb.

Flower color and season Clusters of single or double white, pink, red, or lavender flowers appear all summer.

Best climate and site Zones 9–10. Cooler zones if treated as annuals. Full sun to light shade. Grow in a free-draining, peat moss-based container mix, allowing it to dry somewhat between waterings.

Growing guidelines Set two or three plants in each basket. Deadhead faded flowers. Pinch back growing tips to encourage branching. To keep plants in frost-prone areas, bring them indoors for the winter. Take cuttings from overwintered plants in spring or from outdoor plants in late summer to early fall. Start seed indoors 10 weeks before the last frost date.

Possible problems Lack of water can cause wilting and leaf drop. Fertilize to encourage blooms.

Comments Combine with petunias, dusty miller (*Senecio cineraria*), clematis, and edging lobelia (*Lobelia erinus*).

Pelargonium Zonal Hybrids
GERANIACEAE

ZONAL GERANIUM

Zonal geraniums are a mainstay for window boxes and other containers. They bloom cheerily from early spring until cut by frost in the fall.

Description These tender perennials are usually grown for their attractive leaves and colorful flowers. They bear 3–5-inch (7.5–12.5-cm), velvety, scallop-edged leaves. The foliage is usually green, often marked by various rings (zones) of green, brown, red, white, or gold. Zonal geraniums are perennial in frost-free climates; elsewhere, grow as annuals or bring indoors for the winter.

Height and spread Height 1–2 feet (30–60 cm); spread 1–1½ feet (30–45 cm).

Flower color and season The single or double flowers bloom from late spring until frost in white or shades of pink, rose, red, salmon, white, and bi-colors.

Best climate and site Zones 5–10. Full sun to light shade. Zonal geraniums thrive in a fast-draining, non-alkaline, peat moss-based container mix. Allow to dry out between waterings.

Growing guidelines Space plants about 1 foot (30 cm) apart. Zonal geraniums need little or no feeding. Take cuttings of overwintered plants in spring. Sow seed indoors 10 weeks before the last frost date, after nicking the seed with a knife or nail file or soaking it in water for 24 hours.

Possible problems Old plants tend to get woody; take cuttings from the stem tips

Potentilla fruticosa
ROSACEAE

Rhododendron spp.
ERICACEAE

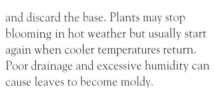

and discard the base. Plants may stop blooming in hot weather but usually start again when cooler temperatures return. Poor drainage and excessive humidity can cause leaves to become moldy.

Other common names Bedding geranium, common geranium, zonal pelargonium.

Cultivars Many cultivars are available in a wide range of heights and colors. Plants in the 'Elite' series have large flower heads in a mix of white, pinks, and reds on compact, 8–10-inch (20–25-cm) plants. 'Ben Franklin' has white-edged leaves and semidouble, magenta-pink blooms; it is raised from cuttings. 'Big Red' has large, scarlet flower clusters on 14-inch (35-cm) tall stems. Plants in the seed-raised 'Orbit' series have zoned leaves on well-branched, 1–1½-foot (30–45-cm) tall stems; they bloom in white and shades of red, pink, and orange. 'Apple Blossom Orbit' is a selection with light and dark pink blooms.

Other species *P. graveolens*, rose geranium, is grown for its scented, lobed leaves. *P. tomentosum*, peppermint geranium, has broad, fuzzy, mint-scented leaves; it prefers partial shade.

Comments For mixed plantings, try zonal geraniums with petunias, dusty miller (*Senecio cineraria*), dahlias, alyssum, edging lobelia (*Lobelia erinus*), or large periwinkle (*Vinca major*). Or arrange a traditional one-color display as a window-box decoration.

SHRUBBY CINQUEFOIL

Shrubby cinquefoil is a compact, deciduous shrub with compound leaves. The flowers are usually yellow, but cultivars with red, pink, orange, or white flowers are also available.

Description Usually a rounded bush, this deciduous shrub is hardy and has flowers like small, single roses that are displayed over a long season. Its erect stems bear hairy, green to gray leaves divided into five to seven leaflets.

Height and spread Height to 4 feet (120 cm); similar spread.

Flower color and season Yellow, five-petaled flowers bloom in early summer to early fall.

Best climate and site Zones 2–8. Full sun to very light shade. Plant in a good quality, free-draining container mix.

Growing guidelines Plant in container in spring. In winter, cut all stems back by one-third or remove a few of the oldest stems at base. Take cuttings in summer. Sow seed in fall.

Possible problems Will not thrive in dense shade.

Other common names Bush cinquefoil.

Cultivars 'Mount Everest' has large, white flowers. 'Tangerine' has orange flowers when grown in light shade.

Comments The color of the cultivar flowers will be more intense if grown in a position where they are protected from the heat of the afternoon sun.

RHODODENDRONS AND AZALEAS

Low-growing rhododendrons and azaleas can make excellent container plants for shady decks and patios. Use a container with drainage holes.

Description Rhododendrons and azaleas are closely related and share the same growth needs. Azaleas have small leaves. Rhododendrons generally have larger leaves and are evergreen.

Height and spread Range from ground-hugging plants to 50-foot (15-m) tall shrubs; spread 15 inches to 5 feet (37.5–150 cm).

Flower color and season White, yellow, pink, orange, or red blooms appear over the colder months.

Best climate and site Zones 4–9. Filtered shade. Plant in fast-draining, acid container mix, keeping it evenly moist.

Growing guidelines Mulch with wood chips. Use acid fertilizer before and after flowering. Prune shoots after bloom. Take cuttings in midsummer. Layer in summer if container is of a sufficient size.

Possible problems Yellow leaves and green veins indicate chlorosis; add iron.

Cultivars 'Carmen' is a 1-foot (30-cm), red-flowered cultivar. 'White Nymph' is low-growing with heavy, midseason bloom. 'William Van Orange' has a cascading habit that's perfect for hanging baskets.

Comments Don't disturb the roots by planting annual companions, as *Rhododendron* spp. are shallow-rooted.

Rosa Large-flowered
ROSACEAE

ROSE

Roses are popular container plants. Choose a highly perfumed performer for a container and place it where the scent, as well as its color, can be enjoyed.

Description Large-flowered roses have either single blooms, or up to three or four blooms on long stems.
Height and spread Height to 6 feet (180 cm); spread 3–4 feet (90–120 cm).
Flower color and season White, pink, orange, yellow, red, lavender, or multi-colored single or double flowers, bloom from late spring to late summer.
Best climate and site Zones 4–10, varying with cultivar. Full sun. Use a moist, well-drained, humus-rich container mix.
Growing guidelines Pot up bareroot plants in fall or winter or container-grown plants in fall or spring. Fertilize regularly in spring and summer. Prune in early spring in cold areas or in late winter in milder climates. Take softwood cuttings in summer, hardwood cuttings in winter.
Possible problems Avoid wetting foliage to reduce black spot. Spray aphids or spider mites with insecticidal soap. Knock Japanese beetles into soapy water.
Cultivars Thousands of hybrid cultivars are available. 'Angel Face' has fragrant, lavender flowers. 'Michelle Meilland' has light pink-and-cream fragrant flowers. 'Mister Lincoln' has deep red, fragrant flowers.
Comments Choose a site with full sun and good air circulation.

Rosa Miniature hybrids
ROSACEAE

MINIATURE ROSES

The everblooming miniature roses have taken the container gardening world by storm. More than 200 types are now available.

Description These diminutive, shallow-rooted roses have ½–2-inch (12–50-mm) wide flowers.
Height and spread Height 4–18 inches (10–45 cm); spread to 20 inches (50 cm).
Flower color and season Miniature roses come in all colors except green and blue; blooms often display multi-colored shading. Some may flower year-round.
Best climate and site Zones 4–9. At least 6 hours of full sun. Use a blend of two parts well-drained, all-purpose container mix to one part compost; keep container moist.
Growing guidelines Prune in early spring. In cold-winter regions, sink the pot into the ground for the winter. Take cuttings in summer. Layer in spring or fall.
Possible problems Knock aphids off with a strong spray of water, or apply insecticidal soap or neem. Avoid getting oil on the flowers. Knock Japanese beetles into soapy water. Pick off any spotted leaves and move the pot to an airier spot.
Other common names Patio roses.
Cultivars 'Gold Coin' is yellow. 'Little Opal' has pale pink blooms. 'Little Tiger' has striped blooms in red, yellow, and white.
Comments Plant alyssum at the base to keep the soil moist, or clematis as a twining backdrop.

Rosa rugosa
ROSACEAE

RUGOSA ROSE

Rugosa rose is an upright grower with many arching canes often covered with pliable, green prickles and glossy, crinkly, green foliage.

Description This popular shrub rose blooms throughout the summer with either single or semidouble flowers, which are very fragrant. The flowers are followed by large, bright red hips, which are rich in vitamin C and can be used to make jelly or tea. The green leaves turn orange in fall.
Height and spread Height to 6 feet (180 cm); spread unlimited.
Flower color and season Pink, red, or white flowers bloom in summer.
Best climate and site Zones 2–9. Full sun. Plant in a well-drained container mix with a neutral pH.
Growing guidelines Plant one or two roses per pot in spring or fall. Prune old stems to the ground in late winter. Propagate by transplanting rooted suckers or by hardwood cuttings in early spring or softwood cuttings in early summer.
Possible problems No serious problems.
Other common names Salspray or Ramanuas rose.
Cultivars 'Alba Plena' has double, fragrant, white flowers; it does not produce fruits. 'Belle Poitevine' is rose-pink. 'Chaplain' is bright red. 'F. J. Grootendorst' is red. 'Sir Thomas Lipton' is white.
Comments Rugosa rose is tolerant of salty air in seaside conditions.

Santolina chamaecyparissus
ASTERACEAE

LAVENDER COTTON

Lavender cotton is an aromatic evergreen shrub, native to the Mediterranean. The dried leaves and stems were once used indoors to repel moths.

Description Lavender cotton forms bushy clumps of many branches with fine, needle-like, aromatic, silvery gray leaves. The plant has a profusion of ¼-inch (18-mm) flowers. Lavender cotton tolerates both dry heat and drought.
Height and spread Height 1½–2 feet (45–60 cm); spread to 3 feet (90 cm).
Flower color and season Bright gold flowers bloom in profusion in midsummer.
Best climate and site Zones 5–9. Full sun. Grow in a dry, poor, well-drained container mix, which could include a little sand and gravel.
Growing guidelines Cut stems back by half after blooming each year (or before blooming, if you don't like the flowers) to encourage compact growth. Propagate by cuttings in early summer or by division in early spring.
Possible problems Care-free in the right conditions; plants do not like humidity.
Cultivars 'Nana' is a dwarf form.
Other species *S. virens*, green lavender cotton, has dark green, fine, needle-like leaves and light yellow flowers in summer. Height to 1½ feet (45 cm); spread to 30 inches (75 cm). Zones 7–8.
Comments The gray shade combines well with lavender and ornamental grasses.

Stephanandra incisa
ROSACEAE

LACE SHRUB

Lace shrub is native to Japan and Korea. Its leaves are small and very finely cut, and turn purple or red in fall. It tends to spread by suckering, but this will not be a problem when grown in a container.

Description Lace shrub has graceful, arching stems and small, finely cut leaves that give a lacy appearance. Clusters of tiny, greenish-white flowers appear in late spring. The leaves turn orange-red in fall.
Height and spread Height 4–7 feet (1.2–2.1 m); spread to 3 feet (90 cm).
Flower color and season Greenish-white flowers bloom in spring.
Best climate and site Zones 5–9. Full sun. Grow in a well-drained, good-quality container mix.
Growing guidelines Pot up in spring. If needed, trim in early spring. Stems may become winter-damaged, but spring growth will cover any blemishes. Propagate by transplanting rooted stem tips, by division in spring, or by cuttings in summer.
Possible problems No serious problems.
Other common names Cut-leaved stephanandra.
Cultivars 'Crispa' grows 1½–3 feet (45–90 cm) tall. It needs little pruning.
Comments Choose a site with full sun and good air circulation while in growth. Move to a less conspicuous site when dormant.

Yucca filamentosa
AGAVACEAE

YUCCA

Few plants make as dramatic an architectural statement as yuccas. The spiky clumps are crowned by spectacular flower spikes in early summer.

Description Yucca produces bold rosettes of evergreen, sword-shaped, light green leaves with sharp points. Tall spires of 2–3-inch (50–75-mm) flowers bloom above the rosettes in summer.
Height and spread Height 3 feet (90 cm); spread 5 feet (150 cm).
Flower color and season White flowers bloom in late spring and early summer.
Best climate and site Zones 5–9. Full sun. Grow in a large container of well-drained, all-purpose container mix; added sand is a plus. Allow the mix to dry between waterings.
Growing guidelines Cut down faded flower stems in fall. Sow seed outdoors in fall, or remove rooted offsets from the base of the parent plant.
Possible problems Overwatering can lead to wilting and root rot.
Other common names Adam's needle.
Other species *Y. glauca* is a smaller, clump-growing species not inclined to form a trunk and has blue-gray foliage.
Comments Since the leaves have sharp points, do not place near walkways or children's areas. Plant alone with a decorative mulch of fine pebbles, or offset it with creeping zinnia (*Sanvitalia procumbens*) or rose moss (*Portulaca grandiflora*).

Clematis x jackmanii
RANUNCULACEAE

JACKMAN CLEMATIS

These slender, perennial vines have large, starry, rich purple blooms. They flower mainly in June and July but may repeat in fall. Add a trellis to their pot so they can climb.

Description Jackman clematis is a deciduous vine with dark green leaves and twisting, curling leaf stalks. The flowers are 4–5 inches (10–12.5 cm) wide.
Height and spread The vine can climb to 10 feet (3 m) in a season; spread around 3 feet (90 cm) when grown in pots.
Flower color and season Deep violet-purple flowers bloom in mid- to late summer and fall.
Best climate and site Zones 5–9. Full sun. The general rule for success is to plant clematis with its "head in the sun and feet in the shade." Grow in a 3–5-gallon (13.5–22.5-l) tub of loose, quick-draining, peat-based container mix that contains added lime.
Growing guidelines Mulch or set lower-growing plants around the base. Fertilize monthly from spring to late summer. Prune the vines to just above the lowest pair of strong buds in late winter or early spring. Take cuttings in spring or early summer.
Possible problems Clematis borers cause wilting or broken stems; prune out damaged parts and seal the cuts with paraffin.
Cultivars 'Rubra' has plum-red flowers. 'Superba' has violet blooms.
Hybrids Many hundreds of hybrids exist,

varying in vigor, color, and flowering period. A few of the most popular are: 'General Sikorski', with lavender-blue flowers in early summer and again in fall; 'Henryi', with white flowers in early summer and again in early fall; and 'Nelly Moser', with soft pink flowers marked with red, which bloom in early summer.
Other species
C. florida is a native of Japan and China, and is best planted against a warm wall, for protection from the elements. It is particularly suited to container growing. It has a long flowering period from late spring through summer. Flowers are greenish-white, later turning to purple.

C. integrifolia, is unlike other clematis species as it is an erect perennial or subshrub, and forms a bushy mound, arising from a clump of stems, growing to 2–3 feet (60–90 cm). The lavender-blue flowers bloom for a long period in midsummer. The flowers are followed by charming, silvery seed heads.

C. maximowicziana, sweet autumn clematis, is a vigorous plant, with compound leaves of three to five leaflets.

C. montana, anemone clematis, has three leaflets to each leaf. 'Grandiflora' has white flowers that are 3–4 inches (7.5–10 cm) in width.
Comments Grow Jackman clematis with roses, impatiens, wax begonias, petunias, or edging lobelia (*Lobelia erinus*).

Clerodendrum thomsoniae
VERBENACEAE

BLEEDING GLORYBOWER

Eyecatching bleeding glorybower, native to West Africa, is a twining, delicate, evergreen vine with 5-inch (12.5-cm) leaves and striking flowers.

Description The flower of bleeding glorybower is a crimson tube encased in a large, white calyx with long, white stamens.
Height and spread Height to 10 feet (3 m) with support, but can be kept much less rampant in containers; spread variable, depending on constraints of support.
Flower color and season Red and white flowers hang in forking clusters from summer to fall.
Best climate and site Zones 9–10. Partial shade. Grow in a rich, moisture-retentive container mix.
Growing guidelines Plant in spring. Prune lightly after flowering, if needed to control vigorous growth. Never allow mix to dry out. Sow seed in spring. Take cuttings in spring and summer.
Possible problems Avoid overwatering during winter when plant is not growing as quickly. Mulch with organic matter to keep mix evenly moist during spring and summer.
Other common names Bleeding heart vine, bag flower.
Other species *C. splendens* is a species that can be grown in conservatories or glass houses in colder areas. It has clusters of scarlet flowers.
Comments Bleeding glorybower makes an excellent hanging basket plant.

Cobaea scandens
POLEMONIACEAE

CUP-AND-SAUCER VINE

The bell-shaped flowers of cup-and-saucer vine open light green and age to purple or white. Mature flowers have a sweet, honey-like fragrance.

Description Cup-and-saucer vine has compound leaves and tendrils that help the stems climb. The flowers are 2 inches (5 cm) long and bell-shaped.

Height and spread Vines can grow to 10 feet (3 m) or more; spread to 3 feet (90 cm) if constrained by support.

Flower color and season Flowers begin as yellow-green and mature to purple or white. They bloom from late summer until frost.

Best climate and site Zones 5–10. Full sun. Grow in well-drained container mix.

Growing guidelines Provide a sturdy support to climb on. Train on a tepee of fine bamboo stakes, or up a trellis positioned in or next to container. Sow seed indoors eight to 10 weeks before your last frost date. Soak seeds in warm water overnight, then plant them on their edge, ¼ inch (6 mm) deep, in peat pots. As the weather warms place into larger container.

Possible problems Generally disease-free if grown outdoors. However, aphids and two-spotted mite can be a problem when grown under glass.

Other common names Cathedral bells, Mexican ivy.

Comments Cup-and-saucer vine can be very fast growing and somewhat rampant in warmer areas of its range.

Hedera helix
ARALIACEAE

ENGLISH IVY

This hardy garden classic comes in many colors and sizes. Let it trail to soften the edge of a pot, or train it to grow upward on a support or wire topiary form.

Description English ivy is an evergreen, woody vine that produces clinging stems. The thick, green leaves have lobed, ruffled, or curled edges and may be marked with yellow, gray, or white.

Height and spread Height 30–40 feet (9–12 m) with support; spread unlimited. Small-leaved cultivars are less rampant.

Flower color and season Insignificant cream flowers bloom on mature plants in fall, followed by black berries.

Best climate and site Zones 5–10. Full sun to full shade. Grow ivy in well-drained, peat-based container mix; allow to dry between waterings. Established plants are drought-tolerant.

Growing guidelines Once established, ivy grows easily. Fertilize with fish emulsion in early spring and again in high summer. Trim stems as needed. Take cuttings anytime.

Possible problems Pick slugs and snails off plants at night, or place the pot on a table. Wet leaves can lead to bacterial leaf spot; remove and destroy infected leaves; water early in the day.

Other common names Common ivy.

Comments English ivy looks great with petunias, zonal geraniums (*Pelargonium* spp.), or it can be grown alone in a hanging basket.

Ipomoea lobata
CONVOLVULACEAE

CRIMSON STARGLORY

Crimson starglory is a vigorous, twining, herbaceous vine usually grown as an annual in cooler climates. The plant is also still known as Mina lobata *and* Quamoclit lobata.

Description An evergreen in warmer climates, crimson starglory has bright green leaves that are deeply cut, or three-lobed.

Height and spread Height to 20 feet (6 m) with support, but much more restrained in a container; spread to 3 feet (90 cm) if constrained by support.

Flower color and season Clusters of reddish flower buds fade to orange and yellow as the flowers open giving an arresting tri-color display all summer.

Best climate and site Zones 8–10; in colder regions, treat as an annual. Full sun to light shade. Grow in a light, well-drained container mix.

Growing guidelines Plant in spring. Mulch with organic matter and ensure container mix is kept evenly moist. Start seed indoors in pots about five weeks before planting outside.

Possible problems Will not thrive in poorly drained soil or in dense shade.

Other common names Spanish flag.

Comments An easy-care plant ideal for a sunny patio container collection, be it weeping over the edges of a hanging basket, or in a container with fine bamboo canes to provide support.

Ipomoea purpurea
CONVOLVULACEAE

COMMON MORNING GLORY

Common morning glory is a twining vine that is grown mostly for its colorful flowers. Although perennial in the warmest zones, it is most commonly planted as an annual in cooler areas.

Description A vigorous twining vine, morning glory has broadly ovate leaves, and large, open flowers that bloom in profusion during summer.
Height and spread Height to 15 feet (4.5 m) with support; spread is determined by dimensions of support.
Flower color and season Purple, white, pink, red, blue, or variegated flowers, varying with the species and cultivar, bloom from summer to early fall.
Best climate and site Zone 10; grow it as an annual in colder regions. Full sun. Grow in all-purpose container mix.
Growing guidelines Plant in spring. Water freely during spring and summer; less at other times. Thin out or cut back congested growth. Sow seed in spring. Take cuttings in summer. Provide support such as a trellis against a wall, or a tepee of bamboo stakes.
Possible problems Avoid overfeeding, which promotes succulent growth that is attractive to pests. Seedlings slow to develop. Excessive fertility and moisture can promote vegetative growth at the expense of flowers.
Comments Early morning sun position is ideal for best possible display of these short-lived blooms.

Ipomoea tricolor
CONVOLVULACEAE

MORNING GLORY

Morning glory grows slowly at first, then really takes off when the weather heats up in midsummer. Established vines are generally problem-free; they often self-sow freely.

Description Morning glory is a tender perennial vine grown as a tender annual. This fast-growing climber has twining stems and heart-shaped, green leaves. The early morning flowers are showy and trumpet-shaped, and up to 5 inches (12.5 cm) across.
Height and spread Height to 8 feet (2.4 m) or more; ultimate height and spread depend on the size of the support.
Flower color and season Purple flowers bloom in summer.
Best climate and site Zones 4–10. Full sun. Grow in an average, well-drained container mix.
Growing guidelines Morning glory needs a sturdy support to climb on. For earliest flowers, sow seed indoors four weeks before last frost date. Soak seed in warm water overnight, then sow it ½ inch (12 mm) deep in peat pots. Transfer plants to permanent containers two weeks after last frost date. Alternatively, sow seed directly into permanent containers after the last frost. Set plants or thin seedlings to stand 8–12 inches (20–30 cm) apart.
Possible problems Can be very rampant in warm areas.
Comments Don't overfeed plants with a nitrogen-rich fertilizer.

Mandevilla laxa
APOCYNACEAE

CHILEAN JASMINE

Chilean jasmine is a fast-growing, semi-evergreen vine with narrow, heart-shaped leaves. Clusters of fragrant, white flowers grace the plant in summer.

Description A vigorous grower in warm climates, Chilean jasmine prefers the shelter of surrounding foliage in cooler climates. The intensely fragrant flowers are funnel-shaped and grow in sprays, mostly at the tops of the long, arching, slender branches.
Height and spread Height to 20 feet (6 m) with support, but much more restrained in a container; spread depends on constraints of support.
Flower color and season White flowers bloom in late spring to midsummer.
Best climate and site Zones 9–10. Full sun to light shade. Use any well-drained, good-quality container mix.
Growing guidelines Plant in spring. Water freely when in full growth; sparingly at other times. Thin out and prune to shape in early spring. Take cuttings or sow seed in spring. Can be trained around a stake, or given a slender trellis support when grown in a container.
Possible problems No serious problems when grown outdoors. As a greenhouse plant, whiteflies and spider mites may cause trouble. Spray with insecticidal soap to deter pests. Very sensitive to frost.
Comments Makes an excellent hanging basket plant. Previously known as *Mandevilla suaveolens.*

Stephanotis floribunda
ASCLEPIADACEAE

STEPHANOTIS

The delightful fragrance of this beautiful, trumpet-shaped flower has made it a highly prized bloom for floral arrangements, especially wedding bouquets.

Description Stephanotis is a twining vine with large, glossy, green leaves. Its flowers are narrowly tubular and highly fragrant.
Height and spread Height to 12 feet (3.6 m) with support; spread 3–5 feet (90–150 cm), depending on the width of the support.
Flower color and season Clusters of white flowers bloom from midspring to fall.
Best climate and site Zone 10. Full sun to light shade. Grow in a good-quality, moisture-retentive container mix.
Growing guidelines Plant in spring. Cut back long or crowded stems in fall, or twist and tie into support to make a densely clothed tripod. Take cuttings in summer. Can be intertwined around a tepee or through lattice to produce dense foliage coverage and maximize blooms, rather than prune to a given size.
Possible problems Ensure adequate air circulation. Subject to scale and mealybugs when grown as a greenhouse plant. Treat plants with insecticidal soap.
Other common names Wax flower, bridal wreath, Madagascar jasmine.
Comments The leaves are attractive when the plant is well grown so it can be left in a permanent position, in suitable climates.

Thunbergia alata
ACANTHACEAE

BLACK-EYED SUSAN VINE

Black-eyed Susan vine is a perennial climber that is commonly grown as an annual. The triangular, bright green leaves are accented by the colorful, summer flowers.

Description This well-known, twining vine has toothed, triangular leaves on little, winged stems. The slender stems and light appearance are deceptive. It can grow very vigorously.
Height and spread Height to 6 feet (180 cm) with support, spread to 6 feet (180 cm), depending on the width of the support.
Flower color and season White, yellow, or orange blooms, often with purple-black centers, bloom in midsummer.
Best climate and site Zone 10; in colder regions, treat as an annual. Full sun to partial shade. Grow in a moist, well-drained container mix. Do not allow the mix to dry out.
Growing guidelines Plant in spring. Thin crowded stems in early spring. Water during periods of drought. Sow seed in spring. Take cuttings in summer. Can be trained on a tepee of fine bamboo stakes to provide a pyramid of color.
Possible problems Very sensitive to frost; protect with mulch.
Other common names Clock vine.
Comments Black-eyed Susan vine looks lovely cascading from a hanging basket.

Trachelospermum jasminoides
APOCYNACEAE

STAR JASMINE

Star jasmine is a rapidly growing, evergreen, twining vine with glossy, green leaves up to 4 inches (10 cm) long. It has very fragrant, white flowers.

Description Star jasmine's wiry stems with their milky sap will develop into a sturdy trunk after many years. The perfumed, 1-inch (2.5-cm), star-shaped flowers bloom in profusion.
Height and spread Height to 20 feet (6 m); spread to 6 feet (180 cm), but depends on width of support.
Flower color and season White flowers bloom in late spring to early summer.
Best climate and site Zones 8–10. Sun to partial shade. Grow in a moisture-retentive, humus-rich container mix.
Growing guidelines Plant in spring; mulch to keep the roots cool. Take cuttings in late summer or fall. Star jasmine can be contained in a tripod shape with support. Train on a tepee of fine bamboo stakes. Prune after flowering to control the vigorous growth habit.
Possible problems Take care not to damage plant when pruning; these wounds are common entry points for pests and diseases. Tends to grow beyond desired bounds. Prune back annually.
Other common names Chinese jasmine, Confederate jasmine.
Comments Star jasmine is a care-free plant with a very heady perfume. It can be overpowering in a semi-enclosed area.

Allium cepa
LILIACEAE

ONION

Onions are an indispensable ingredient in many dishes. Pick the young greens for scallions, or wait for the tops to turn brown to harvest the bulbs.

Description Onions have long, grass-like leaves. The edible bulb develops under the ground.

Height and spread Height 15 inches (38 cm); spread 2–4 inches (5–10 cm).

Best climate and site All Zones for scallions; Zone 3 and warmer for bulbs. Full sun. Use a fertile, light container mix.

Growing guidelines In colder areas, plant long-day onions in spring. In warmer areas, grow short-day onions during fall and winter. Space sets or transplants 2 inches (5 cm) deep and 4–6 inches (10–15 cm) apart. After planting, mulch with compost. Water if the pot begins to dry out.

Possible problems If onion fly is a problem in your area, keep the crop covered with floating row covers.

Other species *A. cepa* (Cepa group), red onion, also called Italian onion, is a red-skinned cultivar. *A. cepa* (Cepa group), Spanish onion, is a large bulb with a mild flavor, usually yellow- or white-skinned. *A. fistulosum*, scallion, does not form a bulb, but rather a slender, white stalk.

Comments The bulb often appears through surface of container mix to let you know the onions are nearly ready to harvest. Green onions (sometimes called scallions) are immature bulbs, pulled before bulbs form.

Beta vulgaris subsp. *cicla*
CHENOPODIACEAE

SWISS CHARD

Vigorous and easy to grow, a single container of Swiss chard can provide a full season of fresh greens. Use it like spinach.

Description Swiss chard has large, deep green, crinkly leaves on, traditionally, white stalks, but it is now available with rich yellow or red stalks.

Height and spread height Height 2 feet (60 cm); spread 1 foot (30 cm).

Best climate and site Zone 5 and warmer; grow as a winter vegetable in mild areas. Full sun or, in warm areas, partial shade. Plant in rich, well-drained container mix.

Growing guidelines Sow one to two weeks before last spring frost. Plant ½ inch (12 mm) deep. Thin to stand 8–12 inches (20–30 cm) apart, using thinnings in salads or transplant them to new pots. Water regularly. Pick large, outer leaves by pulling stems from the base with a slight twist; leave the center to sprout new leaves. Leaves can be cooked separately from the wide inner rib, which is often steamed and eaten like asparagus. You can freeze leaves as you would spinach.

Possible problems Non-woven covers will deter flea beetles. Swiss chard is fairly drought-tolerant, but water stress causes tough stems.

Other common names Leaf beet, silverbeet.

Comments The colored-stemmed cultivars taste the same as traditional Swiss chard.

Brassica oleracea, Acephala Group
BRASSICACEAE

KALE

Hardy and nutritious, as well as ornamental, kale provides tasty greens late into the season, even under a blanket of snow.

Description Kale is a kind of cabbage that has either curly or flat leaves, and doesn't form a tightly packed head.

Height and spread Height 12–15 inches (30–45 cm); similar spread.

Best climate and site All Zones; may overwinter in areas as cool as Zone 6. Full sun. Grow in a well-drained container mix, with adequate calcium; pH 6.5–6.8.

Growing guidelines Direct-seed 4–6 weeks before last spring frost, about ½ inch (12 mm) deep. Thin to 12–15 inches (30–38 cm) apart. Plant fall crop 6–8 weeks before first frost, or later to overwinter. Give fish emulsion or compost tea liberally once a month. Plants take 55–65 days to mature. Young plants will take light frost; mature ones, severe frost.

Possible problems Use row covers to protect from flea beetles and cabbageworms, or use BT to control cabbageworms. Rotate kale and other cabbage-family plants to avoid soilborne diseases.

Other common names Borecole, colewort.

Cultivars 'Red Russian' is a non-curly cultivar with purplish stems and leaves.

Comments Keep plant well picked. Sweeter after frost.

Capsicum annuum
SOLANACEAE

PEPPER

Peppers make excellent container plants, especially when they are covered with their colorful fruits. Fertilize once or twice a month, particularly just before and during fruit set.

Description These bushy plants have oval, green leaves and small, white flowers. The flowers are followed by edible green, yellow, red, purple, or even chocolate-colored fruits from summer until frost.

Height and spread Height 2 feet (60 cm); spread 2 feet (60 cm).

Best climate and site Zones 4–10. Full sun is generally best, with midday shade. Grow in well-drained container mix with added dolomitic limestone. Keep the container evenly moist.

Growing guidelines Sow seed indoors 8–10 weeks before the last frost date. Set plants out a week or two after last frost date, 10–15 inches (25–38 cm) apart. In early to midsummer, cover the surface of the container with a dark-colored mulch. Pick green peppers for use, but leave some fruit on the plant to mature. The fully ripe pepper's color will depend on the cultivar. Pick mature peppers when 50–75 percent colored to ripen at room temperature. Fresh peppers will keep for two weeks or more if stored at around 55°F (13°C), or freeze them for winter cooking. Freeze or pickle thick-fleshed hot peppers such as jalapeño and hot cherry; dry thin-fleshed ones such as cayenne.

Possible problems Knock aphids and whiteflies off plants with a strong spray of water, or spray with insecticidal soap. If plants are too hot or too cold, they may stop growing and be vulnerable to disease and insects. Blossom end rot results from uneven watering or a nutrient imbalance.

Other species

C. annuum (Grossum group), sweet (bell) pepper, is blocky in shape and thick-fleshed. Most cultivars turn yellow or red once ripe. Purple and "chocolate" peppers are colored at their immature stage and turn red when fully ripe.

C. annuum (Grossum group), sweet pepper, is also called frying pepper, Italian pepper, ramshorn, Cubanelle, or banana pepper. It has elongated fruit up to 1 foot (30 cm) long. They are generally thinner-fleshed than bell peppers.

C. annuum (Longum group), hot pepper or chili pepper, comes in a wide variety of shapes, sizes, and degrees of "heat." Milder cultivars include 'Ancho' or 'Poblano'. Medium-hot peppers include jalapeño and Hungarian wax. Fiery peppers include cayenne and Thai, or bird's eye, pepper.

Comments Good pepper partners include lettuce, sage, marigolds, and zinnias.

x *Citrofortunella microcarpa*
RUTACEAE

CALAMONDIN

Calamondins grow as bushes or small trees. The fruits are small, round, and reddish-orange. The sweet, edible rind easily peels away from the segmented flesh, which is juicy and tart.

Description Calamondin is a hybrid between cumquats (*Fortunella margarita*) and mandarins (*Citrus reticulata*). It is a mostly ornamental shrub, although the small, bright orange fruits are edible. They are easy to grow in containers.

Height and spread Height 6–24 feet (1.8–7.2 m); spread 3–12 feet (90–360 cm); smaller in a container.

Best climate and site Zones 9–10 for outdoor culture. Full sun. Grow in a slightly acid, well-drained container mix.

Growing guidelines Repot container-grown plants anytime. Space them 1–3 feet (30–90 cm) apart in a tub for use as a hedge, or in individual pots. Calamondins are self-fertilizing, so you only need one plant. Water container regularly to keep the mix evenly moist, especially during bloom. Prune if you want to keep plant small. Plants can be sheared as hedges.

Possible problems Keep an eye out for scale, mealybugs, mites, and whiteflies.

Other common names Panama orange.

Comments Store harvested fruit in a refrigerator crisper. The fruit is too tart to just pop into your mouth, but you can use it to flavor drinks, or use whole fruit to make marmalade.

Cucurbita spp.
CUCURBITACEAE

WINTER SQUASH

Winter squash are so called because of the harvesting season rather than their growing requirements. Many cultivars are available with compact growth habit, making them ideal container plants.

Description Winter squash are annual vines with large, slightly hairy, green leaves and edible, yellow flowers that can be harvested at the expense of the fruit.

Height and spread Height 10 inches (25 cm); spread 8 feet (2.4 m).

Best climate and site Zones 4–10. Full sun. Grow in a good-quality, well-drained container mix.

Growing guidelines Sow one to two weeks after the last spring frost, three plants to a 2-foot (60-cm) wide container. In short-season areas, start indoors in individual pots two to three weeks before planting. Harvest when the shell cannot be dented with a fingernail. Harvest all fruit as soon as light frost has killed the vines. Wipe skin with a cloth dipped in a weak bleach solution.

Possible problems Straw mulch will help deter insects, as will underplantings of radishes or basil. At first sign of mildew, spray foliage with a baking-soda solution (1 teaspoon per quart (1 l) of water).

Other common names Pumpkins.

Comments The smaller, trailing types, such as 'Sweet Dumpling' squash (*C. pepo*) and vegetable marrow squash (*C. pepo* var. *pepo*) are especially good for container growing. Give them a trellis for support.

Daucus carota var. *sativus*
APIACEAE

CARROT

If you water containers regularly to keep the container mix evenly moist, they can provide perfect growing conditions for these tasty root crops. Try the short-rooted kinds in standard-sized pots.

Description Aboveground, carrots produce fern-like, green foliage that grows from a thick, juicy, orange, vitamin-rich taproot.

Height and spread Height 9 inches (22.5 cm); spread of upper growth governed by size of root, which can vary from rounded to slender.

Best climate and site All Zones. Full sun. Grow in large containers in a loose, sandy container mix, keeping mix evenly moist.

Growing guidelines Seed may take 3 weeks to germinate. Sow directly into container outdoors in early spring. When seedlings are 2 inches (5 cm) tall, thin them to 1 inch (2.5 cm) apart. Avoid high-nitrogen fertilizers. Harvest at 45–70 days. Pull and sample a few to see if they are ready.

Possible problems If you let the mix get too dry and then too wet, the roots may split; try to keep the pots evenly moist.

Cultivars 'Minicor' grows to 4 inches (10 cm) tall and has slender, finger-like roots. 'Thumbelina' and 'Planet' have small, rounded roots; they can grow in window boxes. Other short-rooted types include 'Nantes', 'Chantenay', and 'Lady Finger'.

Comments Grow carrots with tomatoes, chives, or lettuce and other greens.

Eruca sativa
BRASSICACEAE

ARUGULA

The tender leaves of this low-growing, European salad vegetable add a nutty, peppery bite to salads and sandwiches.

Description Arugula forms a rosette of deeply lobed leaves. White flowers are borne in terminal racemes.

Height and spread Height 2 feet (60 cm); spread of a rosette of leaves to 20 inches (50 cm).

Best climate and site Zones 7–10. Full sun, half-day of sun or partial shade. Avoid hot, dry positions. In mild climates, grow as a winter vegetable in a moist container mix.

Growing guidelines Direct-seed in spring, placing three or five seeds to each large pot. Light frost will not harm the seedlings. In cold climates, sow seed indoors and set outside in containers as soon as likelihood of frost is over. A fall crop will stand longer without bolting if direct-seeded or set out as seedlings one to two months before the first fall frost. The plant matures in around 40 days. Younger leaves have a better flavor. Use fresh; do not freeze.

Possible problems Cover with a spun-bonded row cover to deter flea beetles. Sown too late, spring-planted arugula will bolt in warm weather before reaching harvestable size.

Other common names Rocket, roquette, rucola, rugula.

Comments You can also add the flowers to salads.

Fortunella spp.
RUTACEAE

KUMQUAT

Kumquat fruit looks like a miniature orange and is either round or elongated. The skin is edible and sweet, but the juicy flesh is tart.

Description Kumquats are compact, small shrubs with white, fragrant flowers that bloom in spring or summer. The edible orange fruits appear from summer to fall.
Height and spread Height 8–15 feet (2.4–4.5 m); spread 6–12 feet (1.8–3.6 m). Much smaller in containers.
Best climate and site Zones 9–10. Full sun. Grow in a well-drained, slightly acid container mix. Kumquat tolerates winter weather as cold as 18 °F (–7.7 °C), but without sufficient heat in summer, the fruits are few and of poor quality.
Growing guidelines Plant container-grown stock anytime, making sure not to cover graft union. Provide a sheltered, sunny position. Kumquats are usually grafted onto trifoliate orange (*Poncirus trifoliata*), sour orange (*Citrus aurantium*), or grapefruit rootstock. Harvest the fruits when they are fully colored.
Possible problems Look out for scale, mealybugs, mites, and whiteflies.
Other common names Cumquat.
Other species The *Citrus limon*, Seville orange, cultivar 'Meyer' makes an ideal container plant.
Comments Prune kumquat to shape the plant and thin out crowded branches.

Fragaria spp.
ROSACEAE

STRAWBERRIES

With their sprawling habit, pretty foliage, and prolific, sweet, red berries, strawberries are beautiful and rewarding container plants for small gardens.

Description Strawberries produce long runners. White flowers are followed by juicy, red berries. June-bearers produce one large crop in early summer. Ever-bearing types yield a moderate main crop in early summer and a scattering of berries through the rest of the season.
Height and spread Height 6–8 inches (15–20 cm); spread up to 1 foot (30 cm).
Best climate and site Zones 3–9. Full sun to partial shade. Grow in a well-drained mix; water frequently and deeply.
Growing guidelines Space plants 14–18 inches (35–45 cm) apart in large containers. Make sure the crown is at or just above the soil surface. Mulch. Fertilize with high-phosphorus fertilizer twice yearly—when growth starts and then after the first crop. Detach and plant offsets from runners.
Possible problems Prevent damage by snails and slugs by setting the pots up on a table, or grow in hanging baskets or bags.
Other species *F. vesca* 'Semperflorens', alpine strawberry, produces pointed fruits on low, clump-forming plants.
Comments Strawberries grow best when planted alone

Lactuca sativa
ASTERACEAE

LETTUCE

Crisp lettuce grows best when temperatures are cool. In warm climates, a fall sowing can give you an early spring harvest; elsewhere, plant in early spring and midsummer.

Description Hybridization has provided lettuces with a wonderful array of leaf shapes, colors, and textures to add interest to both salad and container growing. Traditionally, lettuces form a heart and the complete plant is picked. However, nowadays, you can grow lettuce that can be picked a leaf at a time.
Height and spread Height 1–1½ feet (30–45 cm); spread 1 foot (30 cm).
Best climate and site All Zones. Grows best in cool temperatures and full sun; light shade in hot temperatures. Use a fertile, moist (but not wet) container mix.
Growing guidelines Scatter the seeds thinly over the top of the container mix and cover with a fine seed-raising mix. Starting in early spring, plant seeds or seedlings every two weeks during cool, mild weather. Thin plants to stand 8–10 inches (20–25 cm) apart. You can use the thinnings in salads. Fertilize with fish emulsion every two weeks, if needed, to keep the plants growing quickly, or mulch with compost. Water if the container mix begins to dry, out even during the heat of the day. Pick individual leaves or harvest an entire plant. Cut off the rosettes of leafy types or the heads of heading types when

Lactuca sativa continued

Lycopersicon esculentum
SOLANACEAE

TOMATO

You don't need a big space to grow this popular vegetable. Tomatoes now come in dwarf types that can produce tasty fruit even in small containers.

they get full but before they send up a flowering stalk and become bitter.

Possible problems To avoid rot or mold diseases, plant in well-drained container mix, and thin overcrowded plants. Rotate planting containers or discard container mix and begin anew.

Other species
L. sativa, Bibb lettuce, also called Boston, butterhead, or cabbage lettuce, forms loose heads of soft, folded leaves.

L. sativa, iceberg lettuce, also called crisphead or cabbage lettuce, forms a tight head of crisp-textured leaves.

L. sativa, leaf lettuce, also called cutting lettuce, forms loose leaves that may be harvested while quite small.

L. sativa, Romaine lettuce, also called Cos lettuce, forms an upright, elongated head of crisp, ribbed leaves.

Comments If you have a short cool season, grow cultivars such as 'Lollo Rossa', 'Red Sails', and 'Summertime' that tolerate heat. Red or frilly-leaved types can double as ornamentals.

Description Tomatoes are bushy or vining plants with a main, thick trunk and many branches. Indeterminate types produce fruit over a long season. Determinate tomatoes grow to a certain height, then flower and set fruit. Small, yellow blossoms develop into red, gold, or pink fruits.

Height and spread Indeterminate types climb to 6 feet (180 cm) or more, with a spread of up to 5 feet (150 cm); dwarf types may be as small as 6 inches (15 cm) tall, with a spread of 6–12 inches (15–30cm).

Best climate and site All Zones. Full sun. Plant tomatoes in a well-drained container mix; keep the mix moist.

Growing guidelines Sow seed indoors eight weeks before the last frost. Set out transplants after the last frost date, and cover to protect them through a light early frost. Smallest types can fit in a 1-gallon (4.5-l) container. Give dwarfs a 3–5-gallon (13.5–22.5-l) container and standards a 30-gallon (135-l) planter or half-barrel. Plant tomatoes by burying the stem horizontally; new roots will emerge from the buried stem. Pruning is not necessary. Water tomatoes regularly and fertilize only when the plant is in full blossom. Then give weak compost tea or fish emulsion. Avoid giving plant too much nitrogen. Do not mulch

tomatoes until the weather warms. Harvest all fruit when severe frost threatens. Completely green tomatoes will not ripen; pickle them or make into chutney.

Possible problems Uneven watering and nutrient imbalances can produce blossom end rot; keep the mix evenly moist and add dolomitic limestone. Fruit may not set if temperatures are over 90°F (32°C). Protect young plants from cutworms with cardboard or metal collars. Handpick tomato hornworms or control them with BT.

Other common names Love apple.

Cultivars Patio tomato: bred for growing in containers. Cultivars include 'Better Bush' and 'Patio'. Cherry tomato: prolific bearers of fruit borne in grape-like clusters. Cultivars include 'Gold Nugget' (yellow-orange, determinate), and 'Sweet 100' (red, indeterminate). Slicing tomato: grown primarily for fresh use. Cultivars include 'Big Boy' (large red fruit) and 'Early Girl' (small red fruit, early-ripening). Low-acid tomato: reduced acidity means milder flavor. Try 'Jetstar' (red skin, determinate) or 'Lemon Boy' (yellow skin, indeterminate).

Other species L. pimpinellifolium, currant tomato, has tiny, currant-sized, red or yellow fruit.

Comments Try tomatoes with mint, parsley, basil, marigolds, or lettuce growing at the base of the pot.

Nasturtium officinale
BRASSICACEAE

WATERCRESS

At its best in fall and early spring, watercress is a tasty, peppery-flavored, healthy addition to salads and sandwiches.

Description Watercress is a low-growing, semi-aquatic plant with a creeping habit and heart-shaped leaves held on long stalks.
Height and spread Height 6 inches (15 cm); spread determined by size of container as stalks will root where nodes touch moist container mix.
Best climate and site Zones 3–10; grow as a winter vegetable in warmer areas or indoors in pots almost anywhere. Full sun or partial shade. Grow in moist container mix with a little lime.
Growing guidelines Start indoors four to eight weeks before the last spring frost. Or, sprinkle seeds as thinly as possible over the surface of container, pressing them into the mix, about a month before the last frost. Set pots in pans of water and change the water daily. Harvest leaves as needed, midfall through early spring, including winter where climate permits. Flavor deteriorates during flowering.
Possible problems No serious problems.
Other species *N. microphyllum* is very similar to the common watercress but with slightly larger flowers.
Comments In short-season areas, a newly established watercress container may not produce sufficient leaves to harvest during the first year.

Phaseolus spp.
FABACEAE

BEANS

Container gardens can support many kinds of beans, from the dwarf types of edible bush beans to the beautiful, climbing vines of scarlet runner beans.

Description Bean plants may be bushy or vining, with heart-shaped leaves. The flowers are followed by edible, green, yellow, or purple pods about 60 days after sowing.
Height and spread Height 12–60 inches (30–150 cm) tall, with a similar spread. Spread in containers is governed by support.
Best climate and site Zones 3–10. Full sun. Grow in a large container in all-purpose container mix. Keep the mix evenly moist and with a nearly neutral pH.
Growing guidelines Erect support for climbing types of beans. Sow seed directly a week after the last frost date. Fertilize once growth starts, then again when pods are forming.
Possible problems Knock whiteflies and aphids off with a spray of water, or spray with insecticidal soap. If powdery mildew occurs, pinch off affected parts and move to an airier spot.
Other species *P. coccineus*, scarlet runner bean, is a climber with brilliant red, edible flowers. *P. lunatus*, pole lima bean, is a climber that requires plenty of warm weather and a sturdy support. *P. vulgaris*, pole or runner bean, requires support for its long vines.
Comments Pick beans any size, but before seeds swell noticeably.

Raphanus sativus
BRASSICACEAE

RADISH

One of the easiest vegetables to grow in a container, fast-growing radish adds a crisp, colorful touch to spring salads. Harvest radishes while they are still young and tender.

Description The edible portion of the radish grows underground with either tapered or rounded roots with a tuft of slightly prickly, green foliage—young leaves can be used in salads.
Height and spread Height 6 inches (15 cm); spread 4 inches (10 cm).
Best climate and site All Zones; grow as a winter vegetable in mild areas. Grow in a loose, moisture-retentive container mix.
Growing guidelines Sow spring radishes 3–5 weeks before last spring frost, ½ inch (12 mm) deep. Sow crops every two weeks until a month after frost. Sow fall crops starting eight weeks before fall frost and continuing until frost. Thin spring radishes to 1–2 inches (2.5–5 cm) apart, or seed sparingly. Sow winter radishes 8–10 weeks before fall frost and thin to 4–6 inches (10–15 cm) apart. Mulch pots and keep moist in hot weather. Pull crops when large enough for use. Store in damp sand or sawdust in a cool place, or pickle.
Possible problems Rotate radishes to reduce damage from root maggots. Spring crops are more vulnerable than fall crops and become woody and bitter when overmature.
Comments Interplant spring radishes with slower-growing crops.

Rumex acetosa
POLYGONACEAE

GARDEN SORREL

In the spring, use sorrel's tender, new leaves to make a delicate soup or add them to salads. The plant produces abundantly during spring and fall.

Description This edible, hardy perennial forms large, leafy clumps. It has wavy, lemon-flavored, green leaves and, in midsummer, greenish-yellow to red flowers.
Height and spread Height 30–36 inches (75–90 cm); spread 1½ feet (45 cm).
Best climate and site Zones 3–9. Full sun. Use a moderately fertile, moist container mix.
Growing guidelines Sow seed shallowly outdoors in late spring, thinning and using the leaves as they begin to grow. Thin to stand 6–8 inches (15–20 cm) apart. Divide older plants in early spring or fall and repot using newer plants. Harvest the outside leaves regularly to promote new growth. The plant is less productive in hot weather.
Possible problems No serious problems.
Other common names Sour dock.
Other species *R. scutatus*, French sorrel, is a lower-growing perennial with triangular, gray-green, more bitter leaves. It is more drought-tolerant than garden sorrel and has a more definite lemony flavor.
Comments Freeze garden sorrel leaves for use in soups and sauces.

Solanum melongena
SOLANACEAE

EGGPLANT

Eggplant is easy to overlook in the garden, but it makes a handsome addition to a container planting. Enjoy its bushy habit, pretty, lavender flowers, and glossy fruits.

Description Eggplants are bushes with large, felt-like leaves that often have a purple tinge. The starry, purple flowers are followed by oval or cylindrical fruits, which range from white to deep purple-black.
Height and spread Height 2–3 feet (60–90 cm); spread 2 feet (60 cm).
Best climate and site Zones 5–10. Full sun. Grow in a well-drained, all-purpose container mix. Allow to dry slightly between waterings.
Growing guidelines Grow one plant in each 16-inch (40-cm) wide container. Fertilize when the first flowers appear, then twice a month until the weather turns cold. Sow seed indoors 10–12 weeks before the last frost date. Set transplants out when the soil is warm.
Possible problems Knock aphids and whiteflies off with a strong spray of water, or spray with insecticidal soap.
Other common names Aubergine, mad apple.
Cultivars 'Long Purple', or 'Listada de Gandia' is an Italian heirloom variety with white skin streaked with purple.
Comments Grow eggplant in a container with lettuce, sweet alyssum, ageratum, or marigolds.

Solanum tuberosum
SOLANACEAE

POTATO

Potatoes produce the best crops in light, loose container mix. Alternatively, you can plant tubers in the base of a deep container and add composted material as they grow upward.

Description Potatoes have brittle stems, compound green leaves, and white or pale lilac flowers. The edible tubers grow underground. Tubers are ready to be harvested when the foliage turns yellow and begins to die back.
Height and spread Height 30 inches (75 cm); spread 1½ feet (45 cm).
Best climate and site Zones 3–10. Full sun. Grow in a deep, light, fertile good-quality container mix.
Growing guidelines Grow potatoes from pieces of "seed potatoes." Cut so each piece has at least one "eye," cure in a warm place; or plant whole seed potatoes without curing. Set them about 5 inches (12.5 cm) deep and 1 foot (30 cm) apart. Add compost or decaying straw as they grow. Unearth new potatoes when the vines flower. Dig mature potatoes once the vines die back. Cure the tubers for 3 weeks in total darkness, 55°F (13°C), and high humidity.
Possible problems Plant certified, disease-free tubers. Destroy any rotten tubers or vines. Use pyrethrin powder on Colorado potato beetles.
Comments Potatoes with gold, purple, red, or brown flesh add interest to meals.

Spinacia oleracea
CHENOPODIACEAE

SPINACH

Spinach needs cool, moist conditions for best growth. In warm temperatures, maneuver the container of spinach into the shade of taller plants, or protect plants with shade cloth.

Description Spinach has bright green leaf blades that grow from a central base with a long tap root.

Height and spread Height 20–30 inches (50–70 cm); spread 1–1½ feet (30–45 cm).

Best climate and site All Zones during the cool growing seasons. Full sun. Grow in a rich, moist container mix. In warm weather, light shade can delay bolting.

Growing guidelines Plant seed ½ inch (12 mm) deep and 2 inches (5 cm) apart in a couple of containers (two weeks apart) in spring or fall—winter in the warmer states. Mulch seedlings with compost, thin to stand 4–6 inches (10–15 cm) apart. Fertilize with fish emulsion and keep the container moist. Pick individual outer leaves or cut off the entire plant when it forms a full rosette but before it sends up a flowering stalk.

Possible problems Thin plants for good air circulation. Keep pests off plants with floating row covers.

Other common names English spinach.

Comments Spinach freezes well for use as a cooked vegetable.

Vaccinium spp.
ERICACEAE

BLUEBERRIES

Blueberry bushes bear luscious, sweet berries, and the plants are attractive, too. Hardy dwarf types are excellent for containers, with three-season interest.

Description These shrubby plants produce small leaves that are bronze in spring, green in summer, and scarlet or gold in fall. Clusters of tiny, whitish-pink, bell-shaped blooms appear in spring, followed by the attractive and edible fruits.

Height and spread Height from 1 foot (30 cm) to 6 feet (180 cm); similar spread.

Best climate and site Zones 3–9, although the range can vary depending on the species. Full sun is best. Plants tolerate some shade but tend to be leggier. Grow in a well-drained, acid container mix that's been amended with plenty of compost, peat moss, ground bark chips, and sand; keep the mix evenly moist.

Growing guidelines Set one dormant plant in a large tub. Mulch the top of the pot. For abundant crops, remove flowers for the first couple of years.

Possible problems Protect the ripening fruit from birds.

Cultivars 'Elliott' grows to 1–1½ feet (30–45 cm) tall and is self-pollinated.

Comments Most blueberries produce better crops if cross-pollinated. Grow at least two different cultivars, or choose a cultivar that is self-pollinating.

Valerianella locusta
VALERIANACEAE

CORN SALAD

Small, tender, green corn salad can be planted in fall to grace spring's earliest salads. It's expensive to buy, but easy to grow.

Description This winter lettuce substitute has somewhat succulent leaves that grow in a rosette. Flowers are white, rose, or blue.

Height and spread Height to 15 inches (37.5 cm); spread to 1 foot (30 cm).

Best climate and site Zones 2–9. Overwinters in Zones 5 and warmer; grow as a winter vegetable in mild areas. Full sun or partial shade. Will withstand light frost. Prefers moisture-retentive container mix; pH 6.0–7.0.

Growing guidelines Sow in early spring, two to four weeks before last frost. Plant thickly; just cover with mix and firm with the palm of hand; keep moist. Thin to 2 inches (5 cm) apart; use thinnings in salads. Avoid plantings that will mature in hot weather. Plant in fall near first frost date; mulch lightly after hard freeze. Remove mulch in early spring. Harvest entire rosettes. Some cultivars remain sweet even when in flower; taste to check.

Possible problems In colder areas, mulch more heavily to avoid heaving of plants over winter or move container into more sheltered position.

Other common names Fetticus, lamb's lettuce, mache.

Comments Plants grown in warmer weather tend to bolt to seed.

Agastache foeniculum
LAMIACEAE

ANISE HYSSOP

Anise hyssop has the appearance of a mint with square stems and attractive lavender blossoms, but the leaves have a distinctive licorice scent and flavor.

Description Anise hyssop is an erect perennial herb. The veined, oval leaves have a downy and whitish underside and pointed tip.

Height and spread Height to 3 feet (90 cm); spread 5 feet (150 cm).

Flower color and season Spikes of lavender flowers bloom from midsummer to fall.

Best climate and site Zones 6–10. Prefers full sun but will tolerate partial shade. Use a good-quality container mix in a large, well-drained container and keep moist.

Growing guidelines Sow seed shallowly in spring indoors or outdoors, thinning to 1 foot (30 cm). Anise hyssop transplants very well. The tall plants occasionally require staking. Harvest fresh leaves as necessary throughout the summer. The best time to collect foliage is just before blooming; hang bunches to dry them. Alternatively, cut whole plants after blooming, hanging them to dry both foliage and flowers.

Possible problems No serious problems.

Other common names Fennel giant hyssop.

Cultivars 'Alabaster' is a white-flowering form of anise hyssop.

Comments Anise hyssop is an excellent herb to attract bees to the garden.

Allium sativum
LILIACEAE

GARLIC

Garlic is one of the most familiar herbs, used to flavor dishes from almost every ethnic group. It dies back in winter, then re-shoots in warmer months.

Description This clump-forming herb has narrow, strap-like foliage and white to pinkish blooms atop a tall, central stalk.

Height and spread Height 1–2 feet (30–60 cm); spread 1 foot (30 cm).

Flower color and season White to pinkish flowers bloom in early summer.

Best climate and site Zones 6–10. Full sun. Grow in a well-drained container mix.

Growing guidelines Separate individual cloves from the bulb immediately before planting. Plant in October for harvesting the following summer; space 6 inches (15 cm) apart and 2 inches (5 cm) deep. For largest bulbs, prune away flowering stems that shoot up in early summer. Side-dress with compost in early spring; avoid planting after heavy applications of fresh manure. Dig bulbs after the tops have died down, and before bulb skins begin to decay underground. Place them in a single layer in a shaded spot to dry, then cut away tops leaving a 2-inch (5-cm) stem; or plait the tops together. Hang in nets from the ceiling in a cool, dark place.

Possible problems Avoid wet soil to prevent bulb diseases.

Comments Check with local gardeners for home-grown bulbs that will be most suitable for your area.

Allium schoenoprasum
LILIACEAE

CHIVES

Chives grow in grass-like tufts of slender leaves and stems adorned by lavender-pink, pompon flowers in spring. Both the leaves and the flowers have a mild onion flavor.

Description Chives grow in clumps of hollow, grassy leaves with small, underground rhizomes with bulb clusters.

Height and spread Height 8–12 inches (20–30 cm); spread 2 inches (5 cm).

Flower color and season Pink, pompon-like flowers bloom in spring.

Best climate and site Zones 3–10. Full sun to light shade. Chives thrive in regular, all-purpose mix. Add a mulch of compost to the surface each spring.

Growing guidelines Divide and repot clumps after bloom every 3–4 years if they get crowded. Keep the soil evenly moist. Sow seed indoors in late winter; it germinates slowly. Snip leaves as needed.

Possible problems Chives are generally trouble-free. If the clumps look ragged, cut them to 2 inches (5 cm) tall in midsummer to promote a flush of new growth.

Other species *Allium tuberosum*, garlic chives, have flat, narrow leaves, white flowers, and a garlicky aroma and flavor.

Comments Good partners include carrots, tomatoes, and marigolds. Chive flowers add a colorful touch to salads.

Aloe vera
ALOEACEAE

ALOE

The long, tapering leaves of Aloe vera *contain a medicinal, as well as cosmetic, gel. This plant was previously known as* Aloe barbadensis.

Description This clump-forming herb is a stemless rosette of spiny, tapered leaves. The flowers are drooping and tubular and appear atop a leafless stalk.
Height and spread Height to 1 foot (30 cm); spread unlimited.
Flower color and season Yellow flowers appear during summer. Rarely flowers in cool climates.
Best climate and site Zones 9–10, or greenhouse not below 41°F (5°C). Prefers full sun but tolerates light shade. Grow in a well-drained, regular container mix.
Growing guidelines Separate new shoots from established plants. In cool climates move pots indoors in winter. Aloes thrive with little attention. Indoors, avoid excess water around roots and mix coarse sand with potting soil to facilitate good drainage. Cut leaves for gel as needed; remove outer leaves first.
Possible problems Spray with insecticidal soap to control mealybugs, or purchase biological controls.
Other common names First-aid herb, healing herb, medicine plant.
Comments Grow as an ornamental pot plant on sunny windowsills in the kitchen and bathroom. Unsafe to use internally.

Aloysia triphylla
VERBENACEAE

LEMON VERBENA

Grown for its strongly lemon-scented leaves used in teas, cosmetics, or in potpourri, lemon verbena is well worth the extra care required.

Description This deciduous, woody shrub has leaves in whorls of threes. Dried leaves retain their scent for a number of years.
Height and spread Height 5–10 feet (1.5–3 m); similar spread.
Flower color and season White to pale mauve flowers bloom in late summer and early fall.
Best climate and site Zones 9–10. Grow in a frost-free greenhouse in cooler areas. Plant in a well-drained container mix.
Growing guidelines In cold climates, grow in pots placed outdoors in summer and indoors in winter. Keep the mix moist, but never soggy; feed with compost and water regularly. Pinch tips to encourage bushy growth. In fall, prune away long branches before bringing pots indoors; overwinter in a greenhouse kept at 45°F (7°C). Snip sprigs of leaves or cut foliage back halfway in midsummer and again in fall. Dry foliage in a shady spot; store in an airtight container.
Possible problems Wash mites from foliage with a spray of water. For stubborn infestations, wipe infected areas with cotton soaked in alcohol, or spray with citrus oil, pyrethrin, or derris powder.
Comments Lemon verbena will train as a mop-headed standard.

Anethum graveolens
APIACEAE

DILL

Dill's tall, graceful habit makes it an attractive plant for containers. Unripe seeds are used to flavor vinegar, sauerkraut, and pickled cucumbers.

Description This hardy annual with its fine, lacy foliage somewhat resembles fennel.
Height and spread Height 2–3 feet (60–90 cm); spread 1 foot (30 cm).
Flower color and season Flattened umbels of yellow flowers bloom in summer.
Best climate and site Zones 6–10. Full sun. Grow in a good-quality container mix and keep well watered.
Growing guidelines Dill dislikes disturbance once established. Sow seed shallowly in containers outdoors in early spring after danger of frost; thin to 8–10 inches (20–25 cm). Keep seedlings moist and weed diligently until plants shade the soil. Clip fresh leaves at the stem as needed. Freeze whole leaves, or chop first. Alternatively, foliage can be dried on non-metallic screens. Collect flower heads before the seeds mature and fall; hang in paper bags or dry on paper. Store the dried foliage and seeds in an airtight container. The fresh leaves can be refrigerated for up to one week.
Possible problems No serious problems.
Comments Sow seeds at 2- or 3-week intervals for a continuous leaf harvest through to fall.

Anthriscus cerefolium
APIACEAE

CHERVIL

Chervil grows best when temperatures are cool, in spring and fall. Grow this lacy, delicate-looking plant for medicinal, culinary, and craft uses.

Description This annual herb has fern-like leaves and flowers in small, umbrella-like clusters.
Height and spread Height 1–2 feet (30–60 cm); spread 10 inches (25 cm). Habit similar to parsley.
Flower color and season White flowers bloom in summer.
Best climate and site Zones 6–10. Full sun or shade. Grow in a moist, well-drained container mix.
Growing guidelines Chervil transplants poorly. Sow fresh seed shallowly in containers in early spring or fall; thin to 9–12 inches (23–30 cm); keep seedlings moist. Sow again at 2-week intervals until mid-July for continuous harvest. Mulch to protect fall-sown seeds. Chervil can seed itself each year if flowers are left to mature in the container. Snip leaves continuously after 6–8 weeks; best used fresh.
Possible problems No serious problems.
Other common names Garden chervil.
Other species *Anthriscus sylvestris* is the pretty meadow plant, Queen Anne's lace.
Comments Chervil loses flavor quickly when heated, so add to recipes at the end.

Artemisia absinthium
ASTERACEAE

COMMON WORMWOOD

Common wormwood is a stout, shrubby perennial with stems that become woody with age. Dried leaves can be used in potpourri as well as in moth-repellent sachets.

Description Common wormwood is a subshrub that spreads by rhizomes. It has inconspicuous flowers that are borne in loose, terminal clusters. Soft hair on the deeply lobed, aromatic foliage gives the plant a muted, gray-green tone.
Height and spread Height 2–3 feet (60–90 cm); spread 2 feet (60 cm).
Flower color and season Yellow flowers bloom in late summer and fall.
Best climate and site Zones 3–9. Full sun. Grow in an all-purpose container mix and occasionally feed.
Growing guidelines Encourage compact growth by pruning back untidy plants by at least half. Grow from stem cuttings taken in late summer or spring. Dust the cut surfaces with a rooting hormone to speed production of new roots.
Possible problems No serious problems.
Cultivars 'Lambrook Silver' has beautiful, silver-gray foliage. It has a tidy habit and is a good foil for brightly colored flowers.
Comments Plant in a large container with yarrows (*Achillea* spp.) and other drought-tolerant perennials.

Artemisia dracunculus var. *sativa*
ASTERACEAE

FRENCH TARRAGON

Tarragon has a heavy licorice flavor that holds well in cooking, making it an extremely useful herb in the kitchen.

Description This hardy perennial herb has long, branched, green stems, narrow mid-green leaves and inconspicuous blossoms.
Height and spread Height to 2–3 feet (60–90 cm); spread 1 foot (30 cm).
Flower color and season Yellowish-green flowers bloom in late summer.
Best climate and site Zones 6–9. Full sun to partial shade. Grow in an all-purpose, well-drained container mix.
Growing guidelines Take basal cuttings of new growth in spring or fall. Divide older plants every 3 years in late winter; space 1–2 feet (30–60 cm) apart. Prune away flower stems each year. To grow indoors in winter, pot young plants in summer, cutting foliage to just above the soil. Seal pot in a plastic bag, and then refrigerate. In fall, unwrap and place in a sunny window for winter harvests. Remove blossoms to encourage growth of foliage. Clip foliage as needed outdoors all summer, or indoors in winter. Foliage may be harvested entirely twice each summer. Keep fresh foliage in the refrigerator, wrapped in paper towels, placed in a plastic bag. Bunch and hang to dry away from sunlight.
Possible problems No serious problems.
Comments Tarragon is one of the most important herbs in French cuisine.

Borago officinalis
BORAGINACEAE

BORAGE

This green, robust, and bristly plant contrasts nicely with dark greens in the garden. The drooping clusters of blossoms attract honeybees, and the leaves have a cucumber flavor.

Description This annual herb has broad, hairy leaves arising from a central stalk. It has star-shaped circles of flowers in a variety of colors, with black centers.

Height and spread Height 1½–2 feet (45–60 cm); spread up to 1½ feet (45 cm).

Flower color and season Pink, purple, lavender, or blue flowers bloom continuously from midsummer until frost.

Best climate and site Zones 6–10. Full sun to partial shade. Plant in well-drained container mix; keep evenly moist.

Growing guidelines Sow seed 10 mm deep outdoors after danger of hard frost. Indoors, plant directly into pots to avoid disturbing the sensitive taproot when transplanting. To promote blooming, go easy on the nitrogen. Tall plants may need support. Harvest foliage anytime and use it for cooking, raw, steamed, or sautéed. Snip blossoms just after they open and then candy, toss fresh in a salad, or dry with silica gel for flower arrangements.

Possible problems Mulch with light materials, such as straw, to keep foliage off mix and prevent rotting.

Comments Some sources suggest that borage is toxic when consumed in large quantities over long periods of time.

Brassica spp.
BRASSICACEAE

MUSTARD

Most mustards are annuals or biennials. Some are "winter annuals" that remain green even when buried under snow.

Description Mustards are hardy herbs. *B. nigra*, black mustard, is a tall, much-branched annual that is cultivated as the main source of pungent table mustard. *B. hirta*, white mustard, is an annual cultivated for greens and mustard- and oil-producing seeds.

Height and spread *B. nigra* grows to a height of 6 feet (180 cm) or more; *B. hirta* grows to a height of 4 feet (120 cm); spread about 1 foot (30 cm).

Flower color and season Yellow flowers bloom in early summer.

Best climate and site Zones 6–10. Full sun. Plant in well-drained container mix.

Growing guidelines Easily grows from seed sown shallowly outdoors from early spring until fall; thin the seedlings to 9 inches (23 cm). Collect and dry seeds when ripe.

Possible problems Can attract the same pests as its close relatives in the cabbage family, but usually trouble-free.

Other species *Brassica juncea*, brown mustard, is cultivated for its pungent seeds. There are various Chinese mustard greens.

Comments Seedlings in the seed-leaf stage can be added to salads.

Carum carvi
APIACEAE

CARAWAY

The seeds of this annual or biennial have been used for 5,000 years for flavoring and for their carminative effect. The seeds are also aromatic and can be used in potpourris.

Description Caraway has glossy, fine, dissected foliage that somewhat resembles the carrot plant. Flowers are carried in umbels on stalks.

Height and spread Height 1–2 feet (30–60 cm); spread 1 foot (30 cm).

Flower color and season White or pink flowers bloom in summer of the second year if fall sown; late summer if spring sown.

Best climate and site Zones 6–10. Ideally grown in full sun. Use an all-purpose container mix.

Growing guidelines Sow seed shallowly outdoors in spring, or indoors in pots. Thin seedlings to 6–12 inches (15–30 cm); don't allow them to dry out. A long taproot makes transplanting difficult. Snip tender leaves in spring and use fresh in salads, soups, and stews. Cut plants after blooming, when seeds are brown and almost loose, then hang them upside down in paper bags to dry. Collect seeds and dry for a few more days in the sun, then store in a tightly sealed container.

Possible problems Watch for pests in dried, stored seeds.

Comments Excessive pruning during the first year weakens the plant.

Chamaemelum nobile
ASTERACEAE

ROMAN CHAMOMILE

Roman chamomile is a delightful, low-growing herb with feathery, green leaves that have a sweet, apple-like scent. The white daisies can be used to make a soothing tea.

Description Small, white daisies with yellow centers appear over the spreading mat of feathery, green foliage.
Height and spread Height to about 1 foot (30 cm); spread to 3 feet (90 cm). Flower stems 6–12 inches (15–30 cm) tall.
Flower color and season White flowers bloom in mid- to late summer.
Best climate and site Zones 3–8. Full sun; tolerates partial shade. Grow in a well-drained, all-purpose container mix.
Growing guidelines Set plants 6 inches (15 cm) apart in spring. New plants need regular watering to keep the mix evenly moist; established, vigorous plants survive without much care. They drop seeds readily, so remove spent flowers to prevent invasive reseeding. Propagate by division or seed in spring or by cuttings in summer.
Possible problems No serious problems.
Other common names Perennial chamomile, Russian chamomile.
Comments Chamomile is a poor competitor, so ensure that the container is weeded often.

Coriandum sativum
APIACEAE

CORIANDER

Coriander seeds become more fragrant with age, and are popular ingredients in the kitchen as well as in potpourri. The whole of the plant, including the roots, is used in Thai cooking.

Description Coriander is an annual herb with graceful, glossy, finely dissected foliage that resembles Queen Anne's lace. Tiny, white flowers are carried in umbels.
Height and spread Height 1–3 feet (30–90 cm); spread 8 inches (20 cm).
Flower color and season The white flowers bloom in early to late summer, depending on when sown.
Best climate and site Zones 6–10. Ideally placed in full sun but some shade tolerated. Grow in a well-drained container mix.
Growing guidelines Sow seed 10 mm deep outdoors in containers after danger of frost, or in fall. Thin seedlings to 4 inches (10 cm). Coriander can self-sow. Weed diligently to protect delicate seedlings. Harvest foliage before seeds form and use fresh. Harvest the ripe seeds before they shatter, dry them and store in air-tight containers in the refrigerator. Dried foliage is of lesser quality and it freezes poorly.
Possible problems No serious problems.
Other common names Cilantro, Chinese parsley.
Comments Sow every 2–3 weeks for a continuous supply of fresh leaves.

Echinacea purpurea
ASTERACEAE

PURPLE CONEFLOWER

Purple coneflowers are showy, summer daisies with purplish or pink flowers with broad, drooping rays, surrounding raised, bristly cones.

Description Purple coneflower has 6-inch (15-cm) oval, broad, lance-shaped leaves on stout, hairy stems. Plants grow from thick, deep taproots.
Height and spread Height 2–4 feet (60–120 cm); spread 1–2 feet (30–60 cm).
Flower color and season Reddish-purple to rose-pink flowers bloom from mid- to late summer.
Best climate and site Zones 3–8. Full sun. Drought-tolerant once established; extremely heat-tolerant. Grow in a well-drained, all-purpose container mix.
Growing guidelines Plants increase from basal buds to form broad, long-lived clumps. Division is seldom necessary and not recommended. Sow seed outdoors in fall or indoors after stratification. To stratify, mix seed with moist peat moss or seed-starting medium in a plastic bag. Close the bag with a twist-tie and place it in the refrigerator for 4–6 weeks. Sow the mixture as you would normal seed. Take root cuttings in fall.
Possible problems No serious problems.
Other common names Echinacea.
Comments The flowers combine well with most perennials and ornamental grasses. The dried, edible roots are used in herbal medicine to increase the body's resistance to infection.

Foeniculum vulgare
APIACEAE

FENNEL

Grow licorice-scented fennel as an ornamental in a container, and for its culinary properties in the kitchen. Both leaves and seeds are used.

Description Fennel is a semi-hardy perennial herb that is usually grown as an annual. The leaves are a feathery, blue-green color, and the small flowers are carried in umbels.

Height and spread Height to 4 feet (120 cm); spread 1 ½ feet (45 cm).

Flower color and season Yellow flowers bloom from July to October.

Best climate and site Zones 6–9. Full sun. Grow in a well-drained container mix with added compost.

Growing guidelines Sow seed shallowly outdoors in spring or fall and keep moist; thin to 6 inches (15 cm). Transplants poorly. Snip leaves before blooming for fresh use or for freezing. Collect the seeds when dry but before they shatter, and dry them on paper.

Possible problems No serious problems.

Cultivars 'Purpurascens' is a bronze-leaved variety of fennel.

Other species *F. vulgare* var. *azoricum*, Florence fennel, has a crisp, bulb-like base that is eaten as a vegetable.

Comments Fennel's delicate flavor is destroyed by heat, so add at the end of cooking time. Try the bronze-colored variety for foliage contrast outdoors, and on the dinner plate as a garnish.

Galium odoratum
RUBIACEAE

SWEET WOODRUFF

Delicate-looking sweet woodruff is a fast-spreading groundcover, that forms a carpet. It is ideal for containers in shady spots.

Description Sweet woodruff has 1-inch (2.5-cm) leaves in whorls on square stems. The leaves have a sweet fragrance when dried. In early spring, loose clusters of small, star-shaped flowers appear just above the leaves. Sweet woodruff was formerly known as *Asperula odorata*.

Height and spread Height 6–12 inches (15–30 cm); spread to 2 feet (60 cm).

Flower color and season White flowers bloom in late spring.

Best climate and site Zones 3–8. Partial to full shade. Grow in a well-drained but moist container mix.

Growing guidelines Set plants 8 inches (20 cm) apart in spring. Trim back established plants in spring to prevent leggy growth, but always leave the foliage closest to the soil surface intact. Propagate by division in spring or fall.

Possible problems No serious problems.

Other common names Bedstraw.

Comments The dried leaves are used in sachets, and smell like vanilla. May be toxic when taken internally.

Hypericum calycinum
CLUSIACEAE

ST. JOHN'S WORT

One of the easiest groundcovers to grow, St. John's wort needs little care. Its bright yellow flowers bloom throughout summer over the blue-green leaves.

Description St. John's wort is a vigorous, fast-spreading, shrubby perennial. Its trailing stems are clad in shiny, 4-inch (10-cm), blue-green leaves that are evergreen in warm climates. Bright yellow, 2–3-inch (5–7.5-cm) wide flowers bloom throughout the summer. The stems root as they rest on the soil.

Height and spread Height 1–1½ feet (30–45 cm); spread to 2 feet (60 cm).

Flower color and season Yellow flowers with showy stamens bloom in summer.

Best climate and site Zones 6–8. Sun to partial shade. Prefers moist, well-drained container mix.

Growing guidelines Set plants about 2 feet (60 cm) apart in spring or fall. Prune stems back in early spring to within a few inches of the soil surface to keep plants compact. Propagate by cuttings after flowering or by seed or division in spring or fall.

Other common names Aaron's Rod, Aaron's beard.

Cultivars 'Hidcote' has large, golden flowers in early summer. Height 3–4 feet (90–120 cm); spread 4–5 feet (120–150 cm).

Comments You can place a container of St. John's wort under the shade of a tree. However, it flowers more profusely if it is in sunshine.

Hyssopus officinalis
LAMIACEAE

HYSSOP

The blossoms of this evergreen, shrubby plant attract honeybees and butterflies. The leaves add a minty aroma and flavor to salads and soups.

Description Hyssop is a bushy perennial with narrow, pointed, dark green leaves and spikes of small, violet-blue flowers in whorls along the stem tops.
Height and spread Height 1–2 feet (30–60 cm); spread to 3 feet (90 cm).
Flower color and season Blue or violet-blue flowers bloom from June to August.
Best climate and site Zones 6–9. Prefers full sun. Grow in a light, well-drained container mix.
Growing guidelines Sow seed ¼ inch (6 mm) deep in early spring, thinning to 1 foot (30 cm). Take cuttings or divide and repot mature plants in spring or fall. Prune to 6 inches (15 cm) in spring and lightly mulch with compost. Replace every 4–5 years. For medicinal use, harvest only green material and cut stems just before flowers open and hang bunches to dry; store in an airtight container.
Possible problems No serious problems.
Cultivars 'Albus' has white flowers; 'Rosea' has pink flowers.
Comments Do not take hyssop if pregnant.

Laurus nobilis
LAURACEAE

BAY

This handsome, glossy, evergreen shrub does double duty. You can enjoy the beauty of the plant all year and use the leaves to flavor your dinner.

Description Bay is an upright, woody shrub with dark green, 2–4-inch (5–10-cm) leaves that are leathery and aromatic. The inconspicuous flowers are followed by ½-inch (12-mm), black berries.
Height and spread Height to 7 feet (2.1 m); spread to 3 feet (90 cm) or more.
Flower color and season Yellow flowers bloom in late spring.
Best climate and site Zones 7–9. Plant in a well-drained container mix. Full sun or filtered shade. North of Zone 8, bring the container indoors in winter.
Growing guidelines Bay responds well to pruning, so you can trim it as needed into formal or informal shapes. You can even train it to grow as a standard—on a single stem with a rounded, tree-like top. Allow the mix to dry between watering. Lightly mulch with compost or shredded leaves. Bay can be difficult to propagate; cuttings can take six months to root and seed must stay at 75°F (24°C) for a month to sprout.
Other common names Grecian laurel, sweet bay, bay laurel.
Comments Set off bay's dark green leaves against silver-foliaged plants, such as dusty miller (*Senecio cineraria*). Or, for a more colorful container, underplant bay with creeping zinnia (*Sanvitalia procumbens*).

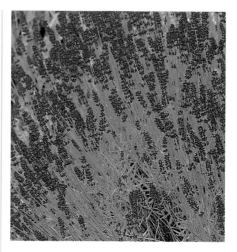

Lavandula angustifolia
LAMIACEAE

ENGLISH LAVENDER

Most herb growers can never have enough lavender, since this aromatic garden ornamental is also useful for crafts and cosmetics. Lavender also makes a good potted topiary plant.

Description The beautiful, lavender-blue spikes of this shrub, which are carried in tight, narrow clusters, attract bees to the garden. The slender, gray-green leaves have a similar scent to the flowers.
Height and spread Height 2–3 feet (60–90 cm); similar spread.
Flower color and season Lavender-blue flowers bloom from June to July.
Best climate and site Zones 6–9. Full sun. Extremely drought-tolerant. Grow in an all-purpose, well-drained container mix with lime content.
Growing guidelines As seeds do not always produce plants identical to the original, the best way to propagate is by cuttings 2–3 inches (5–7 cm) long taken from sideshoots in spring or fall; space 1 foot (30 cm) apart. Pinch away flowers on first-year plants to encourage vigorous growth. Provide shelter from winter winds; hardiness varies with species. Some growers find that plants weaken with age and require replacement every 5 years. Remove old plants in spring, and replace mix with new container mix that has been enriched with compost before planting new, young plants. Harvest foliage after the first year; pick flower spikes in the early blossom

Levisticum officinale
APIACEAE

LOVAGE

If you are unsuccessful growing celery, try this easy and flavorful substitute. The tiny flowers are followed by slightly ribbed, aromatic seeds.

Description Lovage is a perennial with hollow, ribbed stems and glossy, dark green, celery-like leaves.

Height and spread Height 6 feet (180 cm) or more; spread 3 feet (90 cm).

Flower color and season Greenish-yellow flowers bloom from June to July.

Best climate and site Zones 6–9. Prefers full sun but tolerates partial shade. Grow in an all-purpose container mix and keep evenly moist, especially during hot weather.

Growing guidelines Sow ripe seed shallowly in late summer or early fall. Prune away flowers to encourage vegetative growth. Each spring, mulch with compost or well-rotted manure. Replace plants every 4–5 years. Once established, harvest leaves as needed for fresh use. In fall, bunch foliage and stems and hang to dry. Alternatively, blanch small bunches before freezing for winter use. Seeds are ripe and ready to harvest when the fruits begin to split open. Dig roots in late fall, wash, slice, and dry before storing.

Possible problems No serious problems.

Comments The tender, young leaves of lovage are used in salads. The roots and shoots are used as a vegetable and the seeds for flavoring.

Melissa officinalis
LAMIACEAE

LEMON BALM

Fresh-smelling lemon balm forms attractive clumps in potted herb gardens. Place containers along paths so you can brush by or pick the foliage.

Description Lemon balm is a fragrant, perennial herb grown for its lemon-scented foliage. The broad, oval leaves are bright, glossy green. The loosely branched plants grow from fibrous roots. Small, white flowers are produced among the leaves at the tops of the stems.

Height and spread Height 1–2 feet (45–60 cm); spread 2 feet (60 cm).

Flower color and season White flowers bloom in late summer and fall. There is season-long interest from the foliage.

Best climate and site Zones 4–9. Full sun to partial shade. Plant in average to rich, well-drained container mix.

Growing guidelines Plants have an open, often rangy appearance, especially in shade. If plants flop, cut them back by two-thirds to encourage fresh growth. Propagate by dividing plants in spring or fall; or take cuttings in early summer. Fresh leaves are used in a calming herbal tea.

Other common names Balm.

Cultivars 'All Gold' has yellow foliage that turns greenish during summer.

Comments Combine lemon balm with shasta daisies (*Leucanthemum* x *superbum*), artemisias, ornamental onions (*Allium* spp.), other herbs, and ornamental grasses.

stage during dry weather. Hang lavender in bunches away from sunlight.

Possible problems No serious problems.

Cultivars 'Dwarf Blue' has dark blue flowers on 1-foot (30-cm) plants. 'Hidcote' grows 1½ feet (45 cm) tall with purple-blue flowers. 'Jean Davis' has pale pink flowers. 'Munstead' has lavender-blue flowers on 1½-foot (45-cm) plants.

Other species *L. latifolia*, Italian or Spanish lavender, produces more oil, but of a lesser quality, than English lavender. Oil from Italian lavender is sometimes mixed with higher-quality lavender oil. *L. stoechus*, French lavender has dark purple, spring flowers and is less hardy than English lavender.

Comments Place pots of lavender in a spot where the fragrance can be appreciated. Combine with yarrows (*Achillea* spp.) and sundrops (*Oenothera* spp.).

Mentha spp.
LAMIACEAE

MINT

The fresh scent of mint adds an extra-special touch to a container garden. Make sure you place the plants where you can easily pick the leaves or brush by them to release the fragrance.

Description Mints are herbaceous perennials that thrive in most locations. Fresh and dried foliage provide flavor for both sweet and savory dishes. Mints are prized for their small, scented leaves, which grow on creeping or upright stems. The tiny blossoms are carried in whorled spikes. There are a number of species and cultivars, most of which adapt well to containers.
Height and spread Height to 30 inches (75 cm) or more; spread 3 feet (90 cm), or more with invasive species.
Flower color and season Tiny, pink or purple flowers bloom from July to August.
Best climate and site Zones 5–9. Full sun or partial shade. Grow in an all-purpose container mix with some added compost. Keep the soil evenly moist, especially during hot weather.
Growing guidelines Add bonemeal in spring. Harvest the leaves and stems as needed. Pinch off flowers as they appear. After 3 years, plants may be worn out and need replacing. Propagate by division in spring or fall; or take cuttings during the growing season. Harvest the fresh leaves as needed. Just before blooming, cut the stalks and hang them in bunches to dry; store in airtight containers.

Possible problems No serious problems.
Other species M. *arvensis* var. *piperescens*, Japanese mint, has large, green leaves with hairy stems and a strong peppermint flavor. It is a major source of menthol in Japan.
   M. x *gentilis*, golden ginger mint, grows to 2 feet (60 cm), with rounded, yellow-marked, green leaves.
   M. *piperita*, peppermint, grows to 2 feet (60 cm), with pungent, pointed, green leaves.
   M. *pulegium*, pennyroyal, is reported to deter ants and fleas. It likes some shade and will attractively spill over the sides of a container.
   M. *requienii*, Corsican mint, is a rapid-growing, ½-inch (12-mm) tall, mossy creeper that needs extra moisture. It has tiny, bright green leaves with a strong, peppermint flavor.
   M. *spicata*, spearmint, has lance-shaped, serrated leaves with a spearmint flavor.
   M. *suaveolens*, apple mint, is apple-scented and has broad, hairy leaves; a variegated cultivar is sometimes called pineapple mint.
Comments Low-growing mints can be used in just about any container to fill space. Try them with tomatoes or marigolds.

Monarda didyma
LAMIACEAE

BEE BALM

The flowers of bee balm add brilliant color to the summer garden and are favored by hummingbirds. The leaves have a citrus-like aroma.

Description Bee balm is a perennial with dark green, slightly toothed leaves on sturdy stems that grow from fast-creeping runners. Tight heads of flowers are surrounded by a whorl of colored, leafy bracts.
Height and spread Height 2–4 feet (60–120 cm); spread 2–3 feet (60–90 cm).
Flower color and season Red, tubular flowers bloom in summer; the foliage is attractive in spring and early summer.
Best climate and site Zones 4–8. Full sun or partial shade. Plant bee balm in evenly moist container mix. If plants dry out, the lower leaves will drop off.
Growing guidelines Divide plants every 2–3 years to avoid overcrowding. Lift clumps in spring before new growth begins, or in fall, and discard the less vigorous portions. Propagate by division or take tip cuttings in late spring or early summer.
Possible problems Powdery mildew causes white blotches on the foliage; thin the stems to allow good air circulation.
Other common names Bergamot, Oswego tea.
Comments Combine bee balm with summer flowers such as garden phlox (*Phlox paniculata*), yarrows (*Achillea* spp.), and purple coneflower (*Echinacea purpurea*).

Myrrhis odorata
APIACEAE

SWEET CICELY

Sweet cicely has a scent like lovage and a sweet licorice taste. The numerous, fragrant, white flowers are carried in flatttened umbels, and are followed by ribbed, shiny, brown seeds.

Description Sweet cicely is an ornamental and hardy perennial. The leaves are fern-like and finely divided.
Height and spread Height to 3 feet (90 cm); similar spread.
Flower color and season White flowers bloom from May to June.
Best climate and site Zones 5–9. Partial shade. Grow in a well-drained container mix that has been enriched with compost.
Growing guidelines Sow seed shallowly outdoors in late spring, thinning to 2 feet (60 cm); germination is slow. Sweet cicely self-sows. Divide older plants in spring or fall, leaving each new piece with a bud. Replant strong, healthy divisions into new containers in good-quality container mix. Mulch each spring with compost or well-rotted manure. Use fresh leaves as needed all summer in salads and cooking. Collect seed heads and dry on paper in a shady spot; store in airtight containers. Use the seeds in cakes and desserts. Dig roots after the first year, scrub them, and dry until brittle or use them fresh like parsnips.
Possible problems No serious problems.
Other common names Myrrh, anise, sweet chervil.

Nepeta cataria
LAMIACEAE

CATMINT

Catmint is closely related to mint and is similarly hardy. Look for it growing wild among the weeds near homes, in gardens, or in fields.

Description Catmint produces new stems each season from a perennial root. The grayish-green leaves are heart-shaped and toothed, and the flowers are carried in branching spikes.
Height and spread Height 1–3 feet (30–90 cm); similar spread.
Flower color and season The white, purple-dotted flowers bloom from summer to early fall.
Best climate and site Zones 4–9. Full sun to partial shade. Grow in a light, well-drained, all-purpose container mix.
Growing guidelines Sow seed outdoors when ripe or in early spring; thin to 1½ feet (45 cm). Take cuttings in early summer. In summer, strip topmost leaves from stems and spread them to dry on a screen in the shade, or hang bunches upside down. Store in tightly sealed containers. You can make a tea from the dried leaves to use as a carminative, tonic, and mild sedative. Use the fresh leaves in salads.
Possible problems No serious problems.
Other common names Catnip.
Other species *Nepeta* x *faassenii* has grayish-green leaves and grows indoors.
Comments Grow enough to share with your cat, since the bruised foliage releases a scent that turns cats into playful kittens.

Ocimum basilicum
LAMIACEAE

BASIL

Green or purple, smooth or ruffled, basil looks as beautiful in containers as it is tasty in salads and sauces. Pinch off flower stems as they appear, to encourage leafy growth.

Description This annual herb has branching stems. The aromatic foliage is usually bright green, but purple-leaved types are also available. Spikes of small flowers rise above the leaves in summer.
Height and spread Height 1½ feet (45 cm); similar spread.
Flower color and season White flowers bloom continuously from midsummer.
Best climate and site Zones 6–10, but needs a sheltered site in the colder areas. Thrives on heat and full sun. Grow in an all-purpose container mix kept evenly moist, especially during hot weather.
Growing guidelines Space plants 10 inches (25 cm) apart. Liquid feed monthly during the summer. Sow seed indoors in early spring. To have a continuous supply, sow again every 2 weeks until early summer.
Possible problems If you set basil plants out too early, their growth may be stunted, or they may die. Wait until after the last frost date, when the weather is settled and the container soil is warm. Lack of water causes wilting. Plant away from mint to prevent damage from plant bugs.
Other common names Sweet basil, St. Josephwort.
Cultivars The many different cultivars

Ocimum basilicum continued

Origanum majorana
LAMIACEAE

SWEET MARJORAM

Some herb growers find this bushy, highly aromatic plant with lush foliage an easy-to-grow substitute for oregano.

Origanum vulgare subsp. hirtum
LAMIACEAE

GREEK OREGANO

This low-growing mint relative makes a handsome, dark green "groundcover" for container plantings. It was previously known as Origanum heracleoticum.

range widely in foliage size, color, aroma, and plant habit. 'Anise', anise basil, grows to 4 feet (120 cm). The leaves have a sweet, licorice scent and the seed heads are a medium purple-red. This cultivar is easy to grow. 'Citriodorum', lemon basil, has flowers and foliage with a strong lemony fragrance. The plant and leaves are smaller and more compact than sweet basil. 'Minimum', bush basil, is a dwarf, bushy, compact, globe-like form with white flowers and small, green leaves. It grows well in pots. 'Purple Ruffles', purple ruffles basil, is a low-growing, delicate seedling. Plant early indoors in pots to minimize disturbance; do not overwater seedlings. Best preserved in salad vinegars. Several types offer a range of color and leaf texture. 'Purpurascens', dark opal basil, has lavender blossoms and deep purple, shiny foliage.

Comments Green basil looks great with marigolds and sage. The purple-leaved types are effective with silver or white leaves or flowers; try dusty miller (*Senecio cineraria*), sweet alyssum, or licorice plant (*Helichrysum petiolare*). Plant near tomatoes and peppers to enhance their growth. Some gardeners plant a second crop to ensure a plentiful supply when older plants become woody.

Description Sweet marjoram is a bushy perennial with spicy, small, softly hairy, gray-green leaves. The flowers open from tiny, green knots.
Height and spread Height to 2 feet (60 cm); spread 1½ feet (45 cm) or more.
Flower color and season White or pink flowers bloom from August to September.
Best climate and site Zones 6–9. Full sun. Grow sweet marjoram in an all-purpose, well-drained container mix.
Growing guidelines Sow seed shallowly indoors in spring; they germinate slowly. Set plants out after danger of frost, spacing plants 6–12 inches (15–30 cm) apart. Cut back by half just before blooming to maintain vegetative growth. In fall, divide roots and bring indoors in pots or place in a frost-free greenhouse. Best raised annually from seed. Cut fresh leaves as needed for cooking. Hang small bunches to dry, then store in air-tight containers.
Possible problems No serious problems.
Other common names Knotted marjoram.
Comments The dried leaves retain their flavor very well and are said to aid digestion. Sweet marjoram was one of the fragrant strewing herbs used during the Middle Ages.

Description Greek oregano has a semishrubby habit, with thin stems and small, oval, dark green, aromatic foliage.
Height and spread Height 1 foot (30 cm); spread to 1½ feet (45 cm) or more.
Flower color and season Clusters of small, pink or white flowers appear from August to September.
Best climate and site Zones 5–10. Full sun. Grow Greek oregano in well-drained, all-purpose container mix.
Growing guidelines Pinch off flowers to promote leaf production. Plants tend to get woody with age, so replant every 3 years in fresh container mix. Allow the soil to dry out between waterings. Take cuttings in fall and divide clumps in spring.
Possible problems No serious problems.
Other species *Origanum vulgare*, common oregano or wild marjoram, grows to 1–2½ feet (30–75 cm). Zones 5–9.
Comments Greek oregano is lower-growing, less invasive, and has more flavor than common oregano. Pair Greek oregano in a large container with other herbs, such as sage, rosemary, and thyme. Alternatively, use it as a green foreground for colorful flowers, including marigolds, creeping zinnia (*Sanvitalia procumbens*), and dwarf morning glory (*Convolvulus tricolor*).

Pelargonium spp.
GERANIACEAE

SCENTED GERANIUM

Add the fragrant leaves of scented geraniums to potpourri. The many cultivars offer a variety of flavors and scents and all make excellent container plants.

Description The foliage and growth habit of scented geraniums varies with species or cultivar. The leaves can be frilly, variegated, ruffled, velvety, or smooth.

Height and spread The dimensions vary considerably with the species. The height is usually no more than 3 feet (90 cm); similar spread.

Flower color and season Rose, rosy-white, or white flowers are produced in small clusters from spring to summer.

Best climate and site Zones 9–10 or cool greenhouse in cooler areas. Full sun. Grow scented geraniums in an all-purpose, well-drained container mix.

Growing guidelines Cuttings root quickly and easily from new growth in spring or late summer. Apply a liquid plant-food, such as fish emulsion or compost tea, but hold back on the nitrogen for the best fragrance. Plants more than one year old tend to get over-large; take new cuttings and discard the old plants. Remove dead foliage regularly. Pick leaves throughout the summer and dry them, storing in an airtight container, to use in winter potpourris. Use fresh leaves in jellies and tea, or as an aromatic garnish.

Possible problems Vacuum whiteflies from foliage, or control with weekly sprays of insecticidal soap or a botanical insecticide. You can purchase parasitic wasps from suppliers of biological controls to control whiteflies indoors. Avoid overwatering.

Cultivars 'Mabel Grey' has deeply lobed, lemon-scented leaves. The leaves of 'Old Spice' have a strong, spicy aroma.

Other species

P. crispum, lemon-scented geranium, is a woody, lemon-scented plant with small, three-lobed leaves with crinkled margins. Flowers are rose or rosy-white.

P. graveolens, rose-scented geranium, is woody with leaves that are softly hairy, five- to seven-lobed, and toothed. The small flowers are rose-colored.

P. odoratissimum, apple-scented geranium, is apple-scented with frilly, heart-shaped leaves and white flowers.

P. tomentosum, the refreshing peppermint geranium, has attractive, velvety, heart-shaped leaves.

Comments *Pelargonium graveolens* is grown commercially for geranium oil used in the perfume industry.

Petroselinum crispum
APIACEAE

PARSLEY

Parsley has such an attractive form that you may forget it's also useful as a flavoring. Curly-leaved types are especially ornamental.

Description Parsley produces compact clumps of bright green, frilly foliage. It produces its flavorful leaves the first year and then flowers and sets seed the second year.

Height and spread Height 30 inches (75 cm); spread 2 feet (60 cm).

Flower color and season Tiny, greenish-yellow umbels flower in early spring of the second year.

Best climate and site Zones 5–9. Partial shade to full sun. Grow parsley in an all-purpose container mix. Keep the mix moist, but not waterlogged.

Growing guidelines Soak seed 24 hours before sowing directly into outdoor containers in early spring. The seed may take 6 weeks to germinate. Cut leaf stalks at the base for fresh foliage all summer. Freeze or hang in bunches to dry in shade.

Possible problems Parsley may grow poorly in hot weather.

Cultivars 'Afro' has tightly curled leaves.

Other species *P. crispum* var. *neapolitanum*, flat-leaved or Italian parsley, has a stronger flavor and is often the preferred parsley in Italian cooking.

Comments Parsley looks great in large pots combined with pansies, lettuce, marigolds, edging lobelia (*Lobelia erinus*), impatiens, petunias, and tomatoes.

Pimpinella anisum
APIACEAE

ANISE

Use anise's licorice-scented leaves and seeds in salads, especially when combined with apples. The crushed, aromatic seeds enhance the fragrance of homemade potpourris.

Description Anise is an annual herb with bright green, lacy foliage and dainty, white blossoms carried in umbels.
Height and spread Height up to 2 feet (60 cm); similar spread.
Flower color and season White flowers bloom in summer.
Best climate and site Zones 6–10. Full sun. Grow in a light, all-purpose container mix in a deep container.
Growing guidelines Sow seed outdoors in containers in spring, or indoors in pots several months before the last frost, in a warm (70°F/21°C) room. Transplants poorly. Stake or grow in clumps to prevent sprawling. Seeds are ready to harvest when they fall easily from the head. Dry seeds on paper for several sunny days outdoors, then pasteurize in an oven at 100°F (38°C) for 15 minutes and store in airtight containers. Snip foliage as needed.
Possible problems Anise oil is said to have insect-repellent properties; few pests bother this plant.
Comments Anise enhances the growth of coriander. Anise was once used as bait in mousetraps. It is also the base of some alcoholic drinks.

Rosmarinus officinalis
LAMIACEAE

ROSEMARY

This beautiful Mediterranean shrub thrives in hot sun and dry spots. It has aromatic leaves on strong, woody stems. Trailing types are excellent for softening the edge of containers.

Description Rosemary is a shrubby herb with narrow, thick, glossy, green leaves that are grayish underneath.
Height and spread Height 2–6 feet (60–180 cm); similar spread.
Flower color and season Clusters of blue flowers appear in spring and sometimes in fall. Plants also bloom in winter when grown indoors or in warm areas.
Best climate and site This herb may survive the winter outdoors in Zones 7–10; in Zones 7 and north, bring the pot inside in the fall. Full sun. Plant in well-drained, nutrient-poor, all-purpose mix. Don't feed.
Growing guidelines Pinch shoot tips back, and occasionally thin out crowded stems. Allow mix to dry between waterings. Take cuttings anytime. Rosemary will grow from seed, but germination and growth are slow.
Possible problems Lanky growth indicates either overfertilizing or overwatering.
Cultivars The ground-covering 'Prostratus' has deep blue flowers. It is particularly good for hanging baskets.
Comments Grow rosemary with other herbs, such as sage, thyme, and oregano, or with colorful, drought-tolerant flowers, such as creeping zinnia (*Sanvitalia procumbens*).

Salvia officinalis
LAMIACEAE

SAGE

Sage's low, shrubby habit and aromatic leaves are a lovely complement to other herbs and colorful flowers. Try it in a pot near a bench or path, where you can easily brush past and pick the leaves.

Description Sage is a shrubby herb that develops a woody base over time. It forms upright or sprawling clumps. The elliptical, gray-green, aromatic leaves are up to 3 inches (8 cm) long.
Height and spread Height 1–2 feet (30–60 cm); spread 3 feet (90 cm).
Flower color and season Spikes of purple-lavender flowers appear in early summer.
Best climate and site Zones 4–8. Full sun. Plant in well-drained container mix with added lime. Do not fertilize.
Growing guidelines Shear off the flower stems after bloom. Divide plants every 3–4 years. Allow the container mix to dry between waterings; sage tolerates drought. Take cuttings in early summer. You can grow sage from seed, but it is very slow to mature. Leaves can be dried for use during winter months.
Possible problems No serious problems.
Other common names Garden sage, culinary sage.
Comments The youngest, unflowered growth has the highest-quality leaves. Combine sage with rosemary, basil, thyme, oregano, lettuce, or rose moss (*Portulaca grandiflora*). Avoid planting with cucumber, which it inhibits.

Symphytum officinale
BORAGINACEAE

COMFREY

Comfrey is an attractive plant with large, broad, lance-shaped, deep green leaves and nodding clusters of tubular flowers.

Description Comfrey is a clump-forming perennial. New leaves sprout each spring from a perennial root. Flowers are held in terminal clusters.
Height and spread Height 2–4 feet (60–120 cm); similar spread.
Flower color and season Purple-pink, white, or cream flowers bloom in early to late summer.
Best climate and site Zones 6–9. Full sun to partial shade. Grow in an all-purpose container mix.
Growing guidelines Propagate by seed, division, or cuttings; space new plants 3 feet (90 cm) apart. Divide every few years to prevent crowding. Replant strong, healthy divisions into fresh container mix. Pick leaves and use fresh or dry. Leaves for drying are best picked in spring. Dig up roots when the plant has died down in fall and dry; store leaves and roots in airtight containers. Use roots and leaves to treat external bruises, wounds, and sores.
Possible problems No serious problems.
Other common names Knitbone, slippery root, healing herb.
Comments Suspected carcinogen; do not take internally. Shaded plants will be smaller, with few blossoms.

Tanacetum vulgare
ASTERACEAE

TANSY

This easy-to-grow, aromatic, and attractive perennial has brilliant green foliage and yellow, button-like flowers.

Description Tansy has erect, branched stems with fern-like, strongly aromatic leaves. The button-like, yellow blossoms are held in terminal clusters.
Height and spread Height 3–4 feet (90–120 cm); unlimited spread.
Flower color and season Yellow flowers bloom from July to September.
Best climate and site Zones 6–9. Full sun to partial shade. Grow in a well-drained container mix.
Growing guidelines Sow seed shallowly in late winter indoors; transplant outdoors in containers after danger of frost, 4 feet (120 cm) apart. Divide established plants in spring or fall. Spreads easily. Prune vigorously in midsummer for lush growth in late fall. Plants may need support. Collect foliage anytime during summer and hang in bunches to dry. Flowers dry well but lose their bright yellow color. Use leaves and flowers to make green-gold dye. Use flowers in dried-flower arrangements.
Possible problems Aphids may be a problem in some Northern locations; to control, dislodge them with a spray of water.
Other common names Golden buttons.
Comments May be toxic when taken internally. Do not use during pregnancy. Tansy is said to repel pests.

Thymus vulgaris
LAMIACEAE

THYME

Thyme is great for carpeting the soil in containers. Its spreading stems and silvery or gray-green leaves complement taller, more colorful plants.

Description Thyme is a small, shrubby herb with ¼-inch (6-mm), oval, gray-green leaves and tiny, lavender flowers.
Height and spread Height 1 foot (30 cm); spread 16 inches (40 cm).
Flower color and season Lavender blooms appear from May to October.
Best climate and site Zones 5–9. Full sun to light shade. Plant in well-drained container mix.
Growing guidelines Set plants 6–12 inches (15–30 cm) apart. Fertilize with fish emulsion in early summer. Harvest shoots as needed; pick before bloom for the most intense flavor. Allow mix to dry between watering. Take stem cuttings anytime. Divide clumps in spring. Thyme grows slowly from seed; sow indoors in late winter.
Possible problems Thyme rots if kept too wet; avoid overwatering.
Other common names Common thyme.
Other species *T.* x *citriodorus*, lemon thyme, is a 4–12-inch (10–30-cm) spreader that's great in pots and hanging baskets.
Comments Common thyme is the most flavorful, with the most fragrant flowers as well. It looks good in pots with other herbs, as well as with marigolds, dusty miller (*Senecio cineraria*), and grape hyacinths (*Muscari* spp.).

USDA Plant Hardiness Zone Map

These maps of the United States, Canada, and Europe are divided into ten zones. Each zone is based on a 10°F (5.6°C) difference in average annual minimum temperature. Some areas are considered too high in elevation for plant cultivation and so are not assigned to any zone. There are also island zones that are warmer or cooler than surrounding areas because of differences in elevation; they have been given a zone different from the surrounding areas. Many large urban areas, for example, are in a warmer zone than the surrounding land. Plants grow best within an optimum range of temperatures. The range may be wide for some species and narrow for others. Plants also differ in their ability to survive frost and in their sun or shade requirements.

The zone ratings indicate conditions where designated plants will grow well and not merely survive. Many plants may survive in zones warmer or colder than their recommended zone range. Remember that other factors, including wind, soil type, soil moisture, humidity, snow, and winter sunshine may have a great effect on growth.

Some nursery plants have been grown in greenhouses and they might not survive in your garden, so it's a waste of money, and a cause of heartache, to buy plants that aren't right for your climate zone.

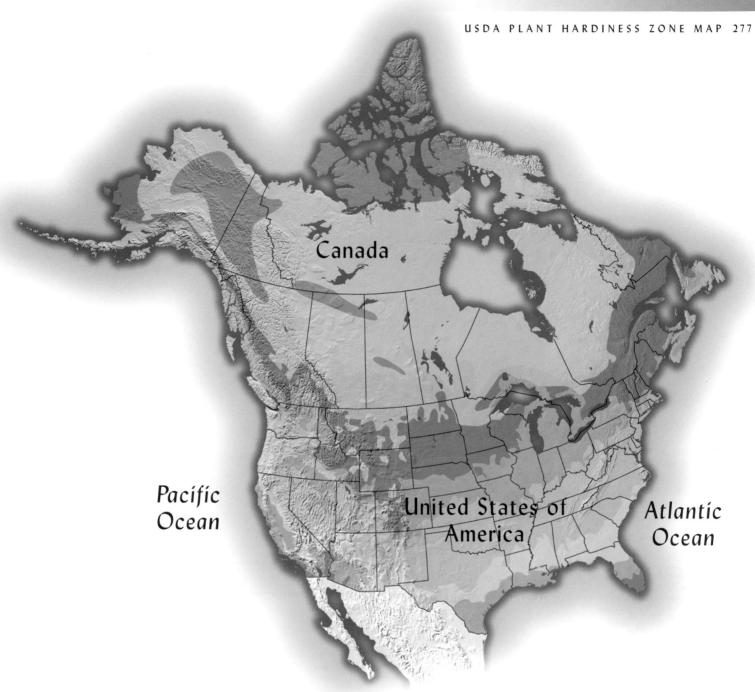

Canada

Pacific
Ocean

United States of
America

Atlantic
Ocean

Average annual minimum temperature °F (°C)

Zone 1		Below -50°F (Below -45°C)	**Zone 6**		-10° to 0°F (-23° to -18°C)
Zone 2		-50° to -40°F (-45° to -40°C)	**Zone 7**		0° to 10°F (-18° to -12°C)
Zone 3		-40° to -30°F (-40° to -34°C)	**Zone 8**		10° to 20°F (-12° to -7°C)
Zone 4		-30° to -20°F (-34° to -29°C)	**Zone 9**		20° to 30°F (-7° to -1°C)
Zone 5		-20° to -10°F (-29° to -23°C)	**Zone 10**		30° to 40°F (-1° to 4°C)

Index

Page references in *italics* indicate photos and illustrations

A

Abelia x grandiflora 104, 126, *238*
   'Compacta' 238
   'Francis Mason' 238
Abutilon hybrids 34, 68, *134*
Acalypha hispida 68, *134*
Acer palmatum 16, 29, *100*, 126, 238
   Dissectum group 238
Achillea tomentosa 81, 114, *166*
Aconite *166*
Aconitum
   x bicolor 114, *166*
   carmichaelii 114, *166*
Actaea alba 114, *167*
Adam's needle 249
Adiantum spp. 55, *154*
   bulbiferum 154
   hispidulum 154
Aechmea fasciata 149
Aeschynanthus hybrids 68
African violets 26, 35, *44*, 45, 46, 58, 69, *144*
Agastache foeniculum 129, *262*
   'Alabaster' 129, *262*
Agave spp. *19*, 70, *146*
Ageratum houstonianum 76, 89, 105, 119, *198*
Aglaeonema spp. 38, 70, *146*
   'Silver Queen' *38*
Agrimony 92
Air layering 46
Air plants *149*
Ajuga reptans 114, *167*
Alchemilla mollis 27, 81, 114, *167*
Alkanet 169
Allegheny foamflower 118, *196*
Allegheny pachysandra 117, *188*
Allegheny spurge *188*
Allium spp. 88, 89
   cepa 128, *254*
   christophii *123*, 220
   fistulosum 254
   giganteum 82
   sativum 129, *262*
   schoenoprasum 61, 89, 130, *262*
   tuberosum 262
Aloe spp. 70, *146*
   vera 47, 130, *263*
Aloysia triphylla 130, *263*
Alpine strawberry 257
Alstroemeria aurea 114, *168*
Aluminum plant *159*

Amaranthus caudatus 80, 104, 119, 198
   'Pygmy Torch' 198
   'Viridis' 198
Amaryllis 59, 69, *139*
Amethyst flower *201*
Amethyst sea holly 116, *180*
Amsonia tabernaemontana 114, *168*
Ananas comosus 149
Anaphalis triplinervis 114, *168*
Anchusa azurea 114, *169*
Andropogon
   glomeratus 125, *234*
   scoparius 234
Anemone
   blanda *123*, 220
   tomentosa 'Robustissima' 81, 114, *169*
Anethum graveolens 61, 61, 92, 130, *263*
Angel geraniums 143
Angelica 92
Angelwing begonias 135
Anise 131, *271*, *274*
Anise hyssop 129, *262*
Annual candytuft 121, *208*
Annual phlox 122, *214*
Annual statice 121, *209*
Annuals 16, 17, 18, 74, 76, 78, 79–80, 84
Anthriscus
   cerefolium 61, 61, 92, 130, *264*
   sylvestris 264
Anthurium spp. 68, *134*
Antirrhinum majus 119, *198*
Aphelandra squarrosa 70, *147*, 156

Aphids 48, *49*, 91
Aporocactus flagelliformis 150
Apple mint 270
Aquilegia x hybrida 114, *169*
Arabis caucasica 124, *228*
   'Compinkie' 228
Aralia 27, 70, *153*
Araucaria heterophylla 70, *147*
Arenaria montana 124, *228*
Argyranthemum frutescens 114, *170*
Armeria maritima 81, 114, *170*
   'Alba' 170
   'Dusseldorf' 170
   'Robusta' 170
Artemisia
   absinthium 92, 130, *264*
    'Lambrook Silver' 130, *264*
   dracunculus var. sativa 92, 130, 264
Artillary plant *159*
Arugula 129, *256*
Arum italicum 77, *220*
Asclepias
   speciosa 170
   tuberosa 78, 81, 115, *170*
Asparagus densiflorus 47, 70, *147*
Asparagus fern 47, 70, *147*
Aspidistra elatior 70, *148*
Asplenium nidus 38, *154*
Aster
   x frikartii 115, *171*
   lateriflorus 171
   novae-angliae 78, 81, *171*
   'Purple Dome' 171
Astilbe
   arendsii 78, 115, *171*
   chinensis var. pumila 115, *172*
Astrantia major 115, *172*
Astrophytum myriostigma 67, *149*
Aubergine 260
Aubrieta deltoidea 115, *172*
   'Aurea Variegata' 172
   'Carnival' 172
   'Royal Blue' 172
Aucuba japonica 28, 29, 85, 126, 238
Aurinia saxatilis 105, 115, *173*
   'Apricot' 173
   'Citrinum' 173
   'Compactum' 173
   'Sunny Border' 173
Australian maidenhair 154
Australian umbrella tree 148
Autumn crocus *221*
Azure monkshood 114, *166*

B

Baby jade *151*
Baby-blue-eyes 76, 121, *212*
Baby's breath 31, 116, *182*
Baby's tears 71, *162*
Bachelor's buttons *202*, *207*
Bag flower 250
Balcony gardens 102, *102*, 103, 104–5
Balloon flower 81, 118, *191*
Balm 269
Baptisia
   alba 173
   australis 78, 81, 115, *173*
Barbershop plant *148*
Bark 22, 86
Barrel cacti 149
Barren strawberry 125, *233*
Basil 15, 61, 61, 92, 131, *271*
Basket-of-gold 115, *173*
Bathtub (as container) 20
Bay 92, 130, 268
Beans 85, 88, 89, 129, 259
Bedding begonias 199
Bedding geranium 246–7
Bedstraw 267
Bee balm 131, 270
Beetles 91
Beetroot 89
Begonia spp. 63, 68, 70, 119, *148*
   x cheimantha
    'Gloire de Lorraine' 135
   Lorraine hybrids 135
   rex 148
   Semperflorens-Cultorum hybrids 30, 63, 80, 119, *199*
   sutherlandii 135
   Tuberhybrida hybrids 27, 99, 119, 135, *199*
Bell pepper 128
Bellis perennis 82, 119, *199*
Bergamot 92, 270
Bergenia cordifolia 77, 80, 115, *173*
   'Purpurea,' *173*
Beta vulgaris subsp. cicla 128, *254*
Bethlehem sage 125, *231*
Betony 92
Bibb lettuce 258
Bicolor monkshood 114, *166*
Biennials 17
Big-leaved hydrangea 127, *244*
Bigroot cranesbill 181
Bird's eye 255

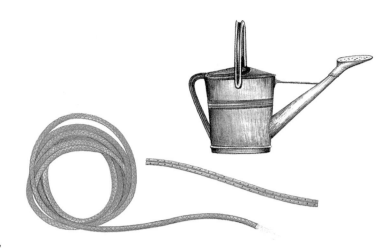

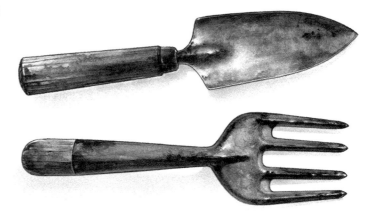

Credits and Acknowledgments

l=left, r=right, c=center, t=top, b=bottom, f=far
APL=Australian Picture Library; BC=Bruce Coleman; CN=Clive Nichols; DW=David Wallace; HS=Harry Smith Collection; HSI=Holt Studios International; GW=Gerry Whitmont; JP=Jerry Pavia; LC=Leigh Clapp; PH=Photos Horticultural; SO=S & O Matthews; TE=Thomas Eltzroth.

1l PH; c Leigh Clapp; r SO 2c Leigh Clapp 4c Leigh Clapp 6c Leigh Clapp 10–11c GW 12tr APL/Corbis/Lee Snider; b Lorna Rose 13t CN; b APL/Premium Houses 14b GW; tr, cr CN 15b PhotoDisc; t Leigh Clapp 16t, bl Corbis; br CN 17tr APL/GW 18t Denise Greig; b Artville 19tl CN; tr Denise Greig; b Leigh Clapp 20t, b GW; 21r CN 22t PhotoDisc 23tl, tc Artville; tr Joanne Pavia; br Weldon Owen; bl CN 24–25c GW 26br Lorna Rose; tr Ad-Libitum/S. Bowey 27c PhotoDisc; tl Leigh Clapp; br GW 28bl Ad-libitum/S. Bowey; tr APL/Steven Mangold/West Light; bc, br Ad-Libitum/S. Bowey; 29c PhotoDisc; t G. R. "Dick" Roberts; br SO; cr Ad-Libitum/S. Bowey 30t, b GW; c PhotoDisc 31t G.R. "Dick" Roberts; l Leigh Clapp; b, c, cr, br PhotoDisc 32–33c JP 34t APL/Corbis 35b Garden Picture Library/Lynne Brotchie 36b Leigh Clapp 37t Leigh Clapp; b PhotoDisc 38t PH 39b Garden Picture Library/Mayer/Le Scanff 40t Lorna Rose; b Leigh Clapp 41cr PH 43tr PH; b Ad-Libitum/S. Bowey 44t HSI/John Adams 45b Garden Picture Library/Michael Howes; t Ad-Libitum/S. Bowey 46t Ad-Libitum/S. Bowey 47b Leigh Clapp; t Ad-Libitum/S. Bowey 48tr Garden Picture Library/Lynne Brotchie; c Ad-Libitum/S. Bowey 49bl, bc PH 52–53c Leigh Clapp 54t Lorna Rose 55br Lorna Rose; bl Garden Picture Library/Lamontagne 56t Garden Picture Library/Zara McCalmont; b Andrew Lawson 57tl Garden Picture Library/Linda Burgess; tr Corel; c Ad-Libitum/S. Bowey; c Ad-Libitum/S. Bowey 58bl APL/Corbis; r PhotoDisc 59tl PH 61tl APL/Corbis; tr, c, br Artville 62t Leigh Clapp; b APL/GW 63tr CN; b JP 64t Lorna Rose 65tl APL/Michael Cook; tr Leigh Clapp 66bl PhotoDisc; br GW 67t PH; b Leigh

Clapp 68tl PhotoDisc 70tl PhotoDisc 72–73c GW 74b JP 75t, b Leigh Clapp 76t Graham Strong 77b G. R. "Dick" Roberts 78t SO 79b Graham Strong 80t PhotoDisc 81l GW 82t, b CN 83t, b Leigh Clapp 84l, b Leigh Clapp 85t APL/Premium Houses; b CN 86b CN 87t CN 88t JP; b APL/GW 89bl GW; t Joanne Pavia 90b Leigh Clapp; t TE 92t Leigh Clapp; b Ad-Libitum/S. Bowey; 93tr Photo-Disc; b Gerry Whitmont 94–95c Leigh Clapp 96b Ad-Libitum/S. Bowey; t GW 97t CN; b PH 98t CN; b APL/GW 99b GW 101b GW; t Andrew Lawson 102t Denise Greig; b GW 103t Denise Grieg; bc Garden Picture Library/Lynn Brotchie; br Artville 104t Leigh Clapp 105t GW; b Photo-Disc 106–107c GW 108tl PhotoDisc 109bl CN 110t Garden Picture Library/John Legate; b GW 111b Garden Picture Library/Lamontagne 112t CN; b GW 114tl Power Photos 119l Power Photos 123tl Power Photos 124tl PhotoDisc 125tl Photo-Disc 126tl PhotoDisc 128tl, bl Photo-Disc 129bl PhotoDisc 132c Lorna Rose 134tr TE; tc PH 135tl, tc TE; tr HS 136tl HS; tc A–Z Botanical Collection/Anthony Cooper; tr Thomas Eltzroth 137tl HSI/Inga Spence; tc Gillian Beckett; tr A–Z Botanical Collection/K. Jayaram/The Picture Store 138tr Photodisc; tl Garden Picture Library/Lynne Brotchie; tc HS 139tl, tr Gillian Beckett; tc TE 140tl Garden Picture Library/Brian Carter; tc HSs ; tr Corel 141tl Stirling Macoboy; tc CN; tr Corel 142tl Corel; tc Stirling Macoboy; tr HS 143tl TE; tc CN; tr Corbis 144tl, tc Corel; tr Gillian Beckett 145tl HSI/Nigel Cattlin; tc TE; tr Gillian Beckett 146tl Gillian Beckett; tc, tr TE 147tl, tr Gillian Beckett; tc PH 148tl HS; tc Gillian Beckett; tr HSI 149tl JP; tc Gillian Beckett; tr Corbis 150tl TE; tc, tr HS 151tl Gillian Beckett; tc TE; tr HS 152tl TE; tc Corel; tr Gillian Beckett 153tc APL/Corbis; tl HS; tr HSI/Nigel Cattlin 154tl HS; tc Denise Greig; tr HSI/Nigel Cattlin 155tl, tr HS; tc Denise Greig 156tl, tc HS; tr TE 157tl Gillian Beckett; tc, tr HS 158tl HS; tc Denise Greig; tr HSI/Bob Gibbons 159tl, tr Gillian Beckett; tc JP; 160tl Corel; tc HS; tr TE 161tl PH; tc HS; tr Gillian Beckett 162tl,

tr Gillian Beckett; tc TE; 163tl Gillian Beckett; tc HS; tr PH 166tl TE; tr Tony Rodd 167tl PH; tc, tr TE 168tl TE; tc, tr PH 169tl, tr TE; tc HS 170tl JP; tc Gillian Beckett; tr HS 171tl, tr TE; tc Allan Armitage 172tl HS; tc CN; tr TE 173tl John Callanan; tc HS; tr JP 174tl JP; tc, tr HS 175tl PH; tc, tr HS 176tl HS; tc Anna Sabarese; tr Gillian Beckett 177tl DW; tc Derek Fell; tr HS 178tl JP; tc John Callanan; tr PH 179tl SO; tc Allan Armitage; tr TE 180tl JP; tc, tr PH 181tl, tc HS; tr PH 182tc TE; tr JP; tl PH 183tl SO; tc HS; tr DW 184tl, tr TE; tc SO 185tl Gillian Beckett; tc, tr TE 186tl BC Limited/John Shaw; tc, tr TE 187tl TE; tc A–Z Botanical Collection/Malcolm Richards; tr Gillian Beckett 188tl TE; tc Derek Fell; tr HS 189tl JP; tc Garden Picture Library/Marijke Heuff; tr Holt Studios/Rosemary Mayer 190tl HS; tc, tr, tl, tc TE; tr SO 192tl CN; tc TE; tr Gillian Beckett 193tl PH; tc JP; tr HS 194tl HS; tc TE; tr PH 195tl SO; tc CN; tr TE 196tl Gillian Beckett; tc TE; tr SO 197tl Gillian Beckett; tc, tr TE 198tl, tc, tr TE 199tl HS; tc Gillian Beckett; tr TE 200tl HS; tr SO; tc Gillian Beckett 201tl, tr TE; tc SO 202tl, tc, tr TE 203tl JP; tc TE; tr HS 204tl, tc, tr TE 205tl TE; tc JP; tr Garden Picture Library/Lamontagne 206tl, tc, tr TE 207tl TE; tc Gillian Beckett; tr TE 208tl, tc JP; tr TE 209tl SO; tc Garden Picture Library/Lynne Brotchie; tr JP 210tl HSI; tc, tr HS 211tl TE; tc Gillian Beckett; tr HS 212tl HS; tc TE; tr Stirling Macoboy 213tl Garden Picture Library/John Glover; tc TE; tr HSI/Nigel Cattlin 214tl HSI; tc, tr TE 215tl Gillian Beckett; tc TE; tr JP 216tl HS; tc TE; tr PH 217tl, tr HS; tc CN 218tl, tc, tr TE 219tl TE; tc Gillian Beckett; tr Stirling Macoboy 220tl PH; tc SO; tr Garden Picture Library/Lamontagne 221tl CN; tc TE; tr Gillian Beckett 222tl HS; tc CN; tr TE 223tl CN; tc SO; tr JP 224tl CN; tc, tr TE 225tl SO; tc JP; tr HS 226tl JP; tc SO; tr PH 227tl JP; tc SO; tr Gillian Beckett 228tl Gillian Beckett; tc, tr TE 229tl, tr Gillian Beckett; tc TE 230tl Gillian Beckett; tc HSI; tr A–Z Botanical Collection/Malcom Richards 231tl, tc HS; tr PH 232tl TE; tc HS; tr HSI/Primrose Peacock 233tl, tc HS; tr Gillian Beckett

234tl BC Limited/Sullivan and Rogers; tc PH; tr HS 235tl, tc TE; tr Gillian Beckett 236tl Bluemount Nurseries/Richard Simon; tc HS; tr PH 237tl Derek Fell; tc TE; tr Joanne Pavia 238tl HS 238tc, tr HS 239tl PH; tc Gillian Beckett; tr HS 240tl TE; tc PH; tr HS 241tl TE; tc PH; tr HS 242tl Susan Roth; tc JP; tr TE 243tl Tony Rodd; tc Stirling Macoby; tr TE 244tl CN; tr HS; tc Photo Essentials 245tl Garden Picture Library/John Glover; tc TE; tr Weldon Owen 246tl Weldon Owen; tc HS; tr TE 247tl Corel; tc Tony Rodd; tr CN 248tl Corel; tc HS; tr HS 249tl HS; tc A–Z Botanical Collection/Derek Gould; tr HS 250tl, tc HS; tr TE 251tc The Garden Picture Library/Lamontagne; tl TE; tr PH 252tl PH; tc TE; tr Tony Rodd 253tl, tc, tr TE 254tl PH; tc, tr DW 255tc Gillian Beckett; tr SO ; tl Weldon Russell/John Callanan 256tl Derek Fell; tc TE; tr DW 257tl TE; tc HS; tr DW 258tc HSI; tl Cheryl Maddocks; tr TE 259tl DW; tr Stirling Macoby 260tl BC/Eric Crichton; tc HSI; tr DW 261tl TE; tc HS; tr DW 262tl Joanne Pavia; tc Rodale Stock Images; tr Gillian Beckett 263tc, tr DW; tl G.R. "Dick" Roberts 264tl, tr DW; tc TE 265tl Tony Rodd; tc, tr DW 266tl HS; tc DW; tr TE 267tl Tony Rodd; tc, tr TE 268tl HS; tc TE; tr CN 269tl Rodale Stock Images; tc HS; tr DW 270tl HS; tc Tony Rodd; tr SO 271tl BC/Eric Crichton; tc DW; tr PH 272tl Patrick S. Michalak; tc DW; tr Stirling Macoby 273tl Tony Rodd; tc DW; tr HS 274tl A–Z Botanical Collection; tc BC; tr HS 275tl DW; tc DW; tr Weldon Owen/Kylie Mulquin.

All illustrations by Barbara Rodanska except the following:

Tony Britt-Lewis 104. Stuart McVicar 276, 277. Nicola Oram 78. Edwina Riddell 7br, 39tl, 39tr, 39tr, 42b, 42tr, 44bl, 46, 54b, 60t, 64, 66, 99, 100b, 111, 113

With special thanks to Kate Brady, Kathy Ehmann, Megan Wardle (editorial assistance); Bronwyn Sweeney, Debbie Duncan, Moira Elliott, Diana Grivas, Helen Bateman (proofreading); Elegant Outdoors, Turramurra, Sydney (props); Caroline Colton & Associates (indexing).